T0141827

Integrated Series in Information Systems

Volume 38

Series editors

Ramesh Sharda
Oklahoma State University, Stillwater, OK, USA

Stefan Voß
University of Hamburg, Hamburg, Germany

More information about this series at http://www.springer.com/series/6157

Lazar Rusu · Gianluigi Viscusi
Editors

Information Technology Governance in Public Organizations

Theory and Practice

 Springer

Editors
Lazar Rusu
Department of Computer and Systems
   Sciences
Stockholm University
Kista, Stockholm
Sweden

Gianluigi Viscusi
EPFL CDM MTEI CSI
École Polytechnique Fédérale de Lausanne
Lausanne
Switzerland

ISSN 1571-0270   ISSN 2197-7968   (electronic)
Integrated Series in Information Systems
ISBN 978-3-319-86522-5   ISBN 978-3-319-58978-7   (eBook)
DOI 10.1007/978-3-319-58978-7

This Springer imprint is published by Springer Nature
The registered company is Springer International Publishing AG
The registered company address is: Gewerbestrasse 11, 6330 Cham, Switzerland

Foreword

Nowadays, information technology (IT) is crucial in the support, sustainability and growth of many organizations. Given this pervasive role of IT in organizations, its governance has become an important subject of study over the past two decades.

Building on our own research, we defined IT governance as the organizational capacity that addresses the definition and implementation of processes, structures and relational mechanism that enable both business and IT people to execute their responsibilities in support of business/IT alignment and the creation of value from IT-enabled business investments.

Our research showed that organizations can and are deploying IT governance by using a holistic mixture of various structures, processes and relational mechanisms. IT governance structures include organizational units and roles responsible for making IT decisions and for enabling contacts between business and IT management decision-making functions (e.g. IT steering committee). This can be seen as a kind of blueprint of how the governance framework will be structurally organized. IT governance processes refer to the formalization and institutionalization of strategic IT decision-making and IT monitoring procedures, to ensure that daily behaviours are consistent with policies and provide input back to decisions (e.g. portfolio and service management). The relational mechanisms finally are about the active participation of, and collaborative relationship among, corporate executives, IT management and business management and include announcements, advocates, channels and education efforts.

In the many case organizations we visited we saw that most organizations are indeed leveraging a mix of IT governance structures, processes and mechanisms. Of course, it should be noted that a "silver bullet approach" does not exist in this matter. Each organization has to select its own set of IT governance practices, suitable for their sector, size, culture, etc.

This excellent book contributes to this latter challenge. More specifically, this book takes a contingency perspective on IT governance and aims to contribute to better understanding how IT governance can be designed in the context of public sector organizations. By offering conceptual models and many case examples, managers from public sector organizations are now better equipped to analyse and benchmark their own IT governance models, and, by extension, to extract recommendations for further improving their current approaches.

As such, we think this book is a must-read for public sector managers who want to implement and manage a modern enterprise governance of IT model.

Steven De Haes
Wim Van Grembergen
Antwerp Management School,
University of Antwerp
Antwerp, Belgium

Preface

Information technology (IT) plays a key role in private organizations and is part of the business strategy, asking for IT leaders capable to effectively plan and manage IT resources of an organization that are including technology infrastructure, human resources and business/IT relationships (Brown et al. 2012). Furthermore, IT has also a pervasive role in society and public sphere, thus having a lot to offer to public organizations as well, which should be able to capture and govern the opportunities for internal change and new services offering. In fact, public organizations can benefit the most by using IT to achieve organization's strategies and improve their services. According to Campbell et al. (2009, p.7), "public sector organizations are a collection of a nation's administrative and economic institutions that provide services and goods for and on behalf of the government", and these types of organizations are dependent on governmental budget funding. In opinion of Hoch and Payan (2008), IT governance is a critical capability for the leaders in the public sector that are looking to create IT value. Furthermore, public organizations are now very committed to make more steps towards digitalization and transform their services. Therefore, this requires from organization's management to focus on having an effective IT governance in their organization that as result will enable business/IT alignment and will create business value from IT investments. For this purpose, organization's management has given a special attention to IT governance that has grown in importance. IT governance or enterprise governance of IT is defined as "an integral part of enterprise governance exercised by the board and address the definition and implementation of processes, structures and relational mechanisms in the organization that enable both business and IT people to execute their responsibilities in support of business/IT alignment and the creation of business value from IT-enabled business investments" (De Haes and Van Grembergen , p. 2). In fact, business/IT alignment is "the fit and integration among business strategy, IT strategy, business structures and IT structures" and is "an important driving force to achieve business value through investments in IT" (Van Grembergen and De Haes (2009, p. 6). According to Leonard and Seddon (2012), business/IT alignment is considered to be a key issue for organizations and is still the first top management concern for executives in organizations around the world based on the findings of the annual study of IT key issues and trends done by Society for Information Management in 2015 (Kappelman et al. 2016). Furthermore, Weill and Ross (2004, pp. 3–4) point out that "effective IT governance is the single most important predictor of the value an organization generates from IT", where by effective IT governance Weill and Ross (2004, pp. 2–3) mean "an actively designed set of IT governance mechanisms (e.g. committees, budgeting processes, approvals, IT organizational structure, chargeback, etc.) that encourage behaviour consistent with the organization's mission, strategy, values, norms and culture".

As we noticed, also the research in IT governance in public organizations has growth in importance and different research studies have been reported in this topic both in developed and developing countries (see, e.g., Parfitt and Tryfonas 2009; Nfuka and Rusu 2013). In a study done by Winkler (2013, p. 843) about IT governance mechanisms in the public sector in Germany, the author has found that "that structural and relational mechanisms are important means to achieve alignment between administration departments and IT units", but on the other hand, the findings "provide no clear evidence for the influence exerted by procedural mechanisms". Apart from these findings, Winkler (2013, p. 844) has mentioned "the importance of relational networks for IT alignment especially in a public sector context". Considering public sector investments in ICT-enabled services, the consequent innovations have different effects according to different governance mechanisms adopted in specific policy domains and governance settings, thus producing different types of change, spanning from technical/incremental change to transformative/disruptive/radical change through organizational/sustained change (Misuraca and Viscusi 2015).

Thus, different challenges are coming for researchers in studying IT governance in public organizations due to the differences between political, administrative and practices in these organizations. Moreover, Hoch and Payan (2008) have noticed that in the public sector the IT projects are complicated with requirements and goals that are including political objectives not only economical ones. Furthermore, the trend towards digital governance in public sector creates other challenges like those mentioned by Misuraca and Viscusi (2014) as the policy-maker's innovation dilemma. These challenges are related to governance processes and policy-making mechanisms change due to the application of information and communication technology (ICT)-enabled innovation. Hence, the dilemma is actually related to governance and alignment issues between policy ICT-enabled initiatives and the diverse stakeholders they involve. Indeed, as pointed out by Misuraca and Viscusi (2014, p. 146), we could imagine a government that does everything by this book (following the rule of law, managing by facts, being disciplined about costs and quality, etc.), but, for example, miss in listening to citizens and not being able to engage properly with them, not being capable of anticipating unexpected situations, or other, and thus can get blindsided by an "innovation" that rapidly takes away its sphere of power in the governance space, because it was doing everything right, but not coping with the transformations happening in the society surrounding its machinery.

Taking the above issues into account, the research in IT governance in public organizations has already captured the attention of researchers, policy-makers and IT practitioners due to the challenges we have mentioned above. This book's primary contribution will be to highlight the actual trends and challenges in research in IT governance in public organizations with the aim to report innovative research and new insights in the theories, models and practices in this research topic. In what follows an outline of the main contents of this book is discussed, in order to provide the reader with a "map" orienting his/her on the chapters better fitting his/her practice or research interests and needs. Obviously, the reader may also decide to go through the different arguments following the structure we have provided for this book.

Outline of the Book

IT governance as a research topic has been investigated from different disciplinary perspectives, whose contributions were most of the time parallel with some overlapping or integrations by the above-cited key authors. This characteristic of the research on IT governance has been inherited also by its study in public organizations as a specific domain of analysis. In this book, we have classified the diverse contributions in the following macro-areas: "Management", "Modelling" and "Cases", which represent the three parts of the volume. We now briefly discuss them through the topics of their chapters.

In Part I (Management) of this book, an introduction to IT governance in public organizations is provided by Edimara et al., discussing the diverse purposes with regard to private organizations, the specific needs, drivers and mechanisms. Subsequently, Rusu and Jonathan investigate a close and often complementary topic of IT governance: IT alignment in public organizations. Through a systematic literature review, the authors aim to clarify the key issues and difference of the subject when treated in a different domain than the business one, especially with regard to organizational performance and the role of organizational structure, culture and social interactions. Caffrey and McDonagh further analyse these issues, by focusing on the roles of middle managers in aligning strategy and IT in public service organizations. Then, Lundström and Edenius analyse alignment and governance with regard to IT-related policy decisions, providing insights into the impact of their implementation and how the consequent change of seemingly mundane activities creates the evolution of new structures and practices. Focusing on routines and practices at micro-level, this paper indirectly poses a set of questions for the role of modeling in IT governance in public organizations.

In Part II (Modeling) of this book, Rychkova and Zdravkovic consider the challenges faced by public administration, actually asked to respond to the increasing service demand and the need for co-production by the renewed and growing engagement of citizens and partner organizations due to the digitalization at societal level and the development of open government initiatives. To this end, the authors propose a model based on the theory of public value and the notion of capability suitable to support public organizations in positioning, justifying and governing their IT projects. Besides this model, the subsequent chapter by Gómez et al. discusses a framework for IT governance implementation suitable to improve alignment and communication between the stakeholders of IT services in public organizations and especially in public enterprises, totally or partially owned by a state, who control them through a public authority. Considering modelling challenges and benefits of IT governance in public organizations is then connected to what are key themes in IT practice and information systems engineering, that are (i) the design and implementation of IT architecture, analysed by Henkel et al., and (ii) the adoption of enterprise architecture in public organizations, whose root causes and suitable solutions are discussed by Dang and Pekkola.

Finally, Part III (Cases) of this book is dedicated to the discussion of case studies of IT governance in public organizations in order to provide an ideal yet contextual counterpart to perspectives presented in the first two parts of the volume. Thus, Bailey et al. discuss IT governance in the context of e-government strategies implementation in the Caribbean, providing a critical assessment through the discussion of successes, challenges and the adoption of new technologies in the area. Furthermore, Aasi et al. consider the relationship of IT organizational structure and IT governance performance, considering the case of the IT department of a public research and education organization in a developing country. The last two chapters consider the case of two managerial and organizational issues. First, Magnusson et al. investigate the relationship between organizational ambidexterity and IT governance through a case study of the Swedish Tax Authorities. The contribution aims to provide empirical insights on the phenomenon of ambidextrous IT governance, spanning the boundaries between disciplines such as organization science and information systems. Finally, Langsten and Nordström investigate the role of institutional logics in IT projects activities and interactions in a large Swedish hospital, thus questioning the implication of the institutional logics perspective for IT governance.

We hope that the reader will find interesting the journey through IT governance in public organizations, exploring the sketches of a still developing map made up on the arguments discussed by the chapters of this book.

Kista, Stockholm, Sweden   Lazar Rusu
Lausanne, Switzerland   Gianluigi Viscusi
February 2017

References

Brown, C. V., DeHayes, D. W., Hoffer, J. A., Wainright, M. E. & Perkins, W. C. (2012). *Managing information technology* (7th ed.). Pearson Education.

Campbell, J., McDonald, C., & Sethibe, T. (2009). Public and private sector IT governance: Identifying contextual differences. *Australasian Journal of Information Systems, 16*(2), 5–18.

De Haes, S., & Van Grembergen, W. (2015). *Enterprise governance of information technology: Achieving alignment and value, featuring COBIT* 5 (2nd ed.). Springer International Publishing Switzerland.

Hoch, D., & Payan, M. (2008, March). *Establishing good IT governance in the public sector, Transforming Government* (pp. 45–55). McKinsey & Company.

Kappelman, L., Johnson, V., McLean, E., & Torres, R. (2016). The 2015 SIM IT issues and trends study. *MIS Quarterly Executive, 15*(1), 55–83.

Leonard, J., & Seddon, P. (2012). A meta-model of alignment. *Communications of the Association for Information Systems, 31*(11), 230–259.

Misuraca, G., & Viscusi, G. (2014). Digital governance in the public sector: Challenging the policymaker's innovation dilemma. In *Proceedings of the 8th International Conference on Theory and Practice of Electronic Governance—ICEGOV2014*, pp. 146–154.

Misuraca, G., & Viscusi, G. (2015). Shaping public sector innovation theory: An interpretative framework for ICT-enabled governance innovation. *Electronic Commerce Research*. doi:10.1007/s10660-015-9184-5.

Nfuka, E., & Rusu, L. (2013). Critical success framework for implementing effective IT governance in Tanzanian public sector organizations. *Journal of Global Information Technology Management, 16*(3), 53–77.

Parfitt, M., & Tryfonas, T. (2009). Painless: A model for IT governance assessment in the UK public sector. *EDPACS: The EDP Audit, Control, and Security Newsletter, 39*(2–3), 1–25.

Van Grembergen, W., & De Haes, S. (2009). *Enterprise governance of it: Achieving strategic alignment and value*. New York, NY, USA: Springer Science+Business Media.

Weill, P., & Ross, J. W. (2004). *IT governance: how top performers manage it decision rights for superior results*. Boston, MA, USA: Harvard Business School Press.

Winkler, T. J. (2013). IT governance mechanisms and administration/IT alignment in the public sector: A conceptual model and case validation. In *Wirtschaftsinformatik Proceedings 2013*, p. 53.

Contents

Acronyms

ACM	Adaptive Case Management
API	Application Programming Interface
BSC	Balanced Scorecard
CEO	Chief Executive Officer
CIO	Chief Information Officer
COBIT	Control Objectives for Information and Related Technology
CRM	Customer Relationship Management
CSFs	Critical Success Factors
CTO	Chief Technology Officer
HER	Electronic Health Record
EA	Enterprise Architecture
EM	Enterprise Modelling
ERP	Enterprise Resource Planning
FEA	Federal Enterprise Architecture
GDP	Gross Domestic Product
ICT	Information and Communication Technology
IT	Information Technology
ITG	IT Governance
ITGI	IT Governance Institute
ITU	International Telecommunication Union
MBA	Master of Business Administration
MIS	Management Information Systems
MIT	Massachusetts Institute of Technology
MOOCs	Massive Open Online Courses
OECD	Organization for Economic Cooperation and Development
OECS	Organization of Eastern Caribbean States
P2P	Peer 2 Peer
ROI	Return on Investment
SCM	Supply Chain Management
SMEs	Small and Medium Enterprises

SOA	Service-Oriented Architecture
STA	Swedish Tax Authority
TOGAF	The Open Group Architecture Framework
UN	The United Nations
US	The United States of America
VOIP	Voice over Internet Protocol
WfM	Workflow Management System

Editors and Contributors

About the Editors

Lazar Rusu, Ph.D. is Professor at Department of Computer and Systems Sciences, Stockholm University, Sweden. He is involved in teaching and research in IT management and has a professional experience of over 30 years both industrial and academic in information systems area. His research interest is mainly in IT governance, business-IT alignment and IT outsourcing. The results of his research have been published in proceedings of top international conferences such as ECIS, HICSS, AMCIS, PACIS and ISD and journals such as Computers in Human Behavior, Industrial Management & Data Systems, Information Systems Management, Journal of Global Information Technology Management and Journal of Information Technology Theory and Applications, among others. He is associate editor of International Journal of IT/Business Alignment and Governance.

Gianluigi Viscusi, Ph.D. is research fellow at the Chair of Corporate Strategy and Innovation (CSI) of the EPFL. His areas of expertise include information systems strategy and planning, business modelling, e-Government, information quality and value and social study of information systems. Currently, he is specifically interested in four research streams: crowd-driven innovation, investigating how crowdsourcing affects organizations in different industries; cognitive economy and digital innovation impacts on business and society; translational research and science communication; policy and technology innovation. In 2010, he has co-authored with Carlo Batini and Massimo Mecella the book "Information Systems for eGovernment: a quality of service perspective" (Springer, Heidelberg).

List of Contributors

Parisa Aasi Department of Computer and Systems Sciences, Stockholm University, Stockholm, Sweden

Urban Ask University of Gothenburg, Gothenburg, Sweden; Westerdal Oslo School of Arts, Communication and Technology, Oslo, Norway

Arlene Bailey Sir Arthur Lewis Institute of Social and Economic Studies (SALISES), The University of the West Indies, Mona, Jamaica

Belén Bermejo Computer Science Dpt, University of the Balearic Islands, Palma, Spain

Eamonn Caffrey Trinity College Dublin, Dublin, Ireland

Dinh Duong Dang Laboratory of Industrial and Information Management, Tampere University of Technology, Tampere, Finland

Mats Edenius Department of Informatics and Media, Uppsala University, Uppsala, Sweden

Beatriz Gómez Computer Science Department, University of the Balearic Islands, Palma, Spain

Martin Henkel Department of Computer and Systems Sciences, Stockholm University, Kista, Sweden

Gideon Mekonnen Jonathan Kozminski University, Warsaw, Poland

Carlos Juiz Computer Science Department, University of the Balearic Islands, Palma, Spain

Jenny Lagsten CERIS, Department of Informatics, Örebro University, Örebro, Sweden

Dorothy Leidner Department of Management Information Systems, Baylor University, Waco, USA

Edimara M. Luciano Pontifical Catholic University of Rio Grande Do Sul, Porto Alegre, Brazil

Jenny Eriksson Lundström Department of Informatics and Media, Uppsala University, Uppsala, Sweden

Marie Anne Macadar Pontifical Catholic University of Rio Grande Do Sul, Porto Alegre, Brazil

Johan Magnusson University of Gothenburg, Gothenburg, Sweden; Westerdal Oslo School of Arts, Communication and Technology, Oslo, Norway

Joe McDonagh Trinity College Dublin, Dublin, Ireland

Indianna Minto-Coy Mona School of Business and Management, The University of the West Indies, Mona, Jamaica

Malin Nordström Information Systems, Department of Management and Engineering, Linköping University, Linköping, Sweden

Samuli Pekkola Laboratory of Industrial and Information Management, Tampere University of Technology, Tampere, Finland

Gabriela V. Pereira Danube University Krems, Krems an der Donau, Austria

Erik Perjons Department of Computer and Systems Sciences, Stockholm University, Kista, Sweden

Lidija Polutnik School of Business, Economics and Law, University of Gothenburg, Gothenburg, Sweden; Babson College, Wellesley, USA

Lazar Rusu Department of Computer and Systems Sciences, Stockholm University, Kista, Stockholm, Sweden

Irina Rychkova Centre de Recherche en Informatique, University Paris 1, Pantheon-Sorbonne, Paris, France

Eriks Sneiders Department of Computer and Systems Sciences, Stockholm University, Kista, Sweden

Dhanaraj Thakur Alliance for Affordable Internet, The Web Foundation, Washington DC, USA

Jacob Torell University of Gothenburg, Gothenburg, Sweden

Guilherme C. Wiedenhöft Pontifical Catholic University of Rio Grande Do Sul, Porto Alegre, Brazil

Jelena Zdravkovic Department of Computer and System Sciences, Stockholm University, Kista, Sweden

Part I
Management

Chapter 1
Discussing and Conceiving an Information and Technology Governance Model in Public Organizations

Edimara M. Luciano, Guilherme C. Wiedenhöft,
Marie Anne Macadar and Gabriela V. Pereira

Abstract Over the past decades, the role of Information Technology (IT) has changed significantly, from office and process automation to value aggregation and innovation through its use. This set of changes also includes citizen profile, government positioning and openness. They generate many new demands, such as fast, reliable IT solutions, information, and services that are enhanced by IT solutions. Considering this scenario, managing IT is no longer enough; it is necessary to go one step further to a governance process. This chapter aims to propose a guide for discussing and conceiving an IT Governance (ITG) model in public organizations. In order to verify its suitability, a multi method approach was adopted, combining various data collection and analysis techniques. A case study was conducted in the State Government of Rio Grande do Sul (Brazil), aiming to verify the suitability of the guide in a certain context. The results presented in this chapter combine multiple data sources such as non-participant observation, document analysis and focus groups. The findings show that the following aspects are essential when discussing an ITG model: business needs, managing pillars, organizational governance principles, regulations, common issues related to IT, business needs related to IT, ITG goals, ITG principles, ITG mechanisms, key decisions, decision rights, organizational structure, Critical Success Factors and monitoring indicators. Our findings have revealed that by applying the proposed guide it was possible to conceive an ITG model related to the specific criteria of the studied case.

E.M. Luciano (✉) · G.C. Wiedenhöft · M.A. Macadar
Pontifical Catholic University of Rio Grande Do Sul, Porto Alegre, Brazil
e-mail: eluciano@pucrs.br

G.C. Wiedenhöft
e-mail: Guilherme.wiedenhoft@pucrs.br

M.A. Macadar
e-mail: Marie.macadar@pucrs.br

G.V. Pereira
Danube University Krems, Krems an der Donau, Austria
e-mail: gabriela.viale-pereira@donau-uni.ac.at

© Springer International Publishing AG 2017
L. Rusu and G. Viscusi (eds.), *Information Technology Governance in Public Organizations*, Integrated Series in Information Systems 38,
DOI 10.1007/978-3-319-58978-7_1

1.1 Introduction: Why Public Organizations Need IT Governance?

The role of IT has changed significantly from office and process automation to value aggregation and innovation through its use. This means that the IT role is no longer primarily technical and reactive, but has become proactive and focused on the core activities of organizations (Walsham 2001). Among the motivations for adopting new technologies are the necessity of supporting the changes in the organizational scenario, the intensive use of instantaneous and portable devices and the growing importance of IT in supporting management (Castells 2011).

The situation is no different in public organizations. In addition to sharing the most common changes in scenario as private organizations, there is a significant change in the management style, which is moving from internally-oriented and bureaucratic to externally-oriented and focused on citizens' needs (Bloomfield and Hayes 2009).

The efforts toward electronic government confirm the important role of IT in the improvement of the relationship with citizens, mainly through the delivery of public e-services and accountability activities. The use of IT in governments has been considered as a driver for social, economic and political changes such as government administrative reform, social transformation and organizational change (Yildiz 2007). As a result, new models of the relationship between state and society have been rising, bringing opportunities to transform the connection between government and citizens (Cunha and Miranda 2013).

Amid this process, gradual changes in citizens' profiles have also occurred. A larger number of passive citizens, who considered themselves weak compared to the almighty state, are becoming more interactive and actively participating in decisions about their country. Although participation of citizens in government decisions is still incipient in many parts of the world, this has shown an upward curve at three levels of an electronic participation model developed by the United Nations (UN 2012), namely access to public information, public consultations and electronic decision-making process.

As the discussion about a new model of relationship between citizens and government evolves, it is possible to observe a gradual shift in the government initiatives from tools that improve services to those that support citizens' participation (Yildiz 2007). This set of changes—citizen profile, government positioning and openness—generates new demands for fast, reliable IT solutions that can be accessed from highly available platforms, and for data, information, and services.

Considering this scenario of change, only management of IT is no longer enough; it is necessary to go one step further towards a governance process. The differences between management and governance are related to time and business orientation: management involves short term and internal aspects, while governance deals with long-term and external aspects (Van Grembergen and De Haes 2009). Governing IT, consequently, can assist organizations in meticulous IT decision-making processes, increasing or maintaining the alignment between IT and stakeholders' expectations (Juiz and Toomey 2015).

For a public organization, considering long-term questions is mandatory, because they are part of a complex actors' network where it is usually necessary for several organizations working together to render a project or service for citizens operational (Al Qassimi and Rusu 2015). One important challenge for public organizations is making state IT decisions rather than government IT decisions, so they are retained for more than one political mandate. This is especially important in countries where democracy is not mature enough.

As shown by Meijer and Bolívar (2016), the necessities of the population should be considered over the long-term. IT decisions that do not change with every administration tend to be more consistent, and their implementation is more likely to be kept over the years within an Information and Technology Governance (ITG) process. Thus, it is possible to increase and guarantee the responsiveness of governments, which is related to the extent that they meet the needs of citizens (Agrawal et al. 2014).

Considering that, it is necessary to put in place a formalized process for governing these initiatives, in order to avoid the non-organized growth of IT solutions. It is also necessary in public organizations to reduce the amount of ad hoc solutions (Rusu et al. 2009). Without a governance process it is easy to have duplication of technologies and solutions and an unnecessary increase in complexity. The greater the complexity, the higher the transaction costs. More transaction costs mean more financial costs that may compromise future investments on new e-government initiatives, and also increase the difficulties in planning new initiatives while managing the currents ones.

This chapter aims to propose a guide for discussing and conceiving an IT Governance model in public organizations. The research question that leads this study is—which are the aspects that need to be discussed when conceiving an organizational ITG model?

The chapter is organized in six sections. We first describe the current state of research in the field of IT Governance. We used a disciplined process for conducting our literature review, as suggested by Webster and Watson (2002)—using keyword searches in ProQuest and Google Scholar for IT Governance, IT Governance in Public organizations, as well as following forward and backward citations. Thus, Sect. 1.2 discusses the theoretical background related to IT Governance in Public organizations. Section 1.3 addresses why a public organization needs its own ITG model. Section 1.4 details a set of steps that emerged from the literature review and was the basis for the discussion and conception guide. Section 1.5 presents the results on the suitability of this guide in a case study. Section 1.6 provides concluding remarks.

1.2 Conceptualizing IT Governance

The main issues related to IT have been moving gradually from the types of technology that are to be adopted, to the definitions and policies regarding how these technologies and resources should be used to generate a competitive advantage for organizations (Nfuka and Rusu 2011; Bartenschlager and Goeken 2010) and increase the level of alignment between IT and business. IT Governance is part of these new issues in pursuing long-term IT, and not just managing but governing IT as well. This change occurs because IT has become a way to competitively leverage the organizations, and at the same time there is a need to govern IT for achieving the expectations of different stakeholders.

According to Weill and Ross (2004), IT Governance can be understood as the specification of the decision rights and the accountability framework that encourage desirable behaviour in IT use. ITG involves specifying decision-making structures, processes and relational mechanisms for the direction and control of IT operations (Sambamurthy and Zmud 1999). It is further characterized as a set of mechanisms associated with the structure, processes, and relationships, which must be related to one or more objectives of the organization (Van Grembergen et al. 2004). These mechanisms can contribute to organizational performance and efficiency, for example in cost reduction or better use of IT infrastructure (Lunardi et al. 2014).

Based on this, e-governance initiatives must encompass ITG mechanisms as a way to achieve long-term solutions and to increase their effectiveness. Governance may be considered as a set of organizational arrangements and patterns of authority for IT decisions, and is characterized as a set of mechanisms that defines the decision-making structure, rights and responsibilities (Van Grembergen and De Haes 2009). Figure 1.1 shows the needs and the options, considering a long-term

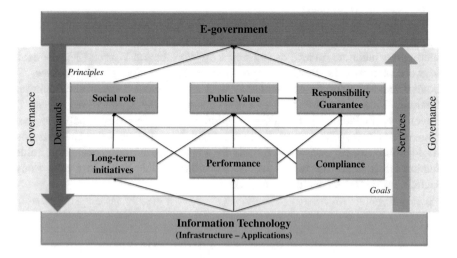

Fig. 1.1 IT Governance variables in public organizations. *source* Luciano et al. (2016)

view and the stakeholders' expectations, in order to add organicity and transparency throughout the process.

Numerous technologies (bottom of Fig. 1.1) are necessary to implement the diverse e-government initiatives (top of Fig. 1.1) that are in operation or under development, being an interface between the governance process that brings e-government demands and the IT infrastructure and applications. IT, in turn, provides services that are a part of e-government strategies. The governance process encompasses goals, such as obtaining performance, having long-term initiatives, and matching compliance with regulations. The goals need to be achieved, while principles like public value generation, preserving the social role of public organizations, and pursuing responsibility and guarantee (involving effective use of resources) must be respected.

ITG is considered part of the scope of corporate governance (Weill and Ross 2004; Peterson 2004). It is related to organizational effectiveness, compliance with laws and regulations, meeting stakeholder necessities, and adequately reacting to the pressures for demonstrating good returns on IT investments. Tiwana et al. (2013) represent IT Governance as a specification about what is governed, who governs and how it is governed.

ITG involves a set of high-level definitions, such as principles, values, and goals, operationalized through mechanisms that are incorporated in the day-by-day activities as a means to making ITG feasible (Wiedenhoft et al. 2014). But what are the differences between ITG in private and public organizations? Although the ITG concept is applicable to both, there are some particular differences in terms of principles, dimensions, perspectives, purposes, and scope, which are discussed below. When analysing the **principles** of Corporate Governance, and considering that they may also be applied to Organizational Governance (in non-profit organizations), it is possible to perceive that the difference is the emphasis, or the weightage given to each principle. In public organizations, for example, the emphasis is on principles such as accountability and transparency (Fox 2007), especially considering the performance, constitution and mission of public organizations.

Regarding the ITG **dimensions**, both public and private organizations aim to meet compliance (related to liability and guarantee), performance (related to the use of resources) and continuity (related to the social role of an organization). The difference is the emphasis or understanding of each dimension. Public organizations are more focused on long-term issues, as an effort to concentrate the initiatives on state necessities related to citizens regardless of political parties' mandates (Dawes et al. 2004). As regards the performance dimension, the issue of resource use involves not only the best possible use of resources but also the related legal issues.

In terms of ITG **perspectives**, both control and behaviour are addressed in private and public organizations (Campbell et al. 2009). Once again, the difference is the emphasis or understanding of each perspective. In public organizations the control is usually performed by departments external to the governance structure, which control all offices and issues, including IT. In private organizations, usually

Table 1.1 IT Governance purposes in private and public organizations. *source* based on Campbell et al. (2009); Dawes et al. (2004); Khalfan and Gough (2002)

IT Governance purposes	Private organizations	Public organizations
Focus	Control, stakeholders needs	Control, citizens needs
General goals	IT contribution to management improvement	
	IT contribution to outcome increase	IT contribution to citizens services improvement and improving their quality of life
Effectiveness monitoring variables	Specific, like profit margins, cost reduction or market share increase	Diffuse, focused on projects aiming public welfare
Governance structures	New structures— or changes in the role of the current ones— created by necessity, respecting the regulations	New structures— or changes in the role of the current ones— following the decision structure provided by legislation
Decisions	New decision-making roles (or changes in the current ones) according to necessity, respecting the regulations	New decision-making roles (or changes in the current ones) according to necessity, respecting the regulations an the legal limits of each role
Organizational role	Predominantly focused on the financial sustainability	Predominantly the social role
Stakeholders	Owners, shareholders and other stakeholders related to each field and organization	Citizens and the whole society and also multiple stakeholders, related to each field and organization, which often have competing goals.

the control is developed within the governance structure, frequently making use of market frameworks focused on control.

Some of the differences between private and public organisations with reference to their ITG approach are related to the **ITG purpose**, as shown in Table 1.1.

Another important difference is the **scope** of ITG processes. A public organization such as a state or a national government is a complex system formed by autonomous organizational entities connected to each other, sometimes under an implicit hierarchy or without a clear coordination responsibility. The necessity to respect this network, where organizations are at the same time autonomous and dependent, seems to be the major challenge that differentiates public and private organizations. This occurs due to the necessity of considering that property resources, labour and information are distributed, and they need adequate coordination and governance in order to improve the quality of services and create public value (Al Qassimi and Rusu 2015).

In order to meet this challenge, it is necessary to contemplate the inter-institutional ITG, considering both the organization and its specificity, and the organizational environment, meaning the network and the synergy of its nodes. Inter-institutional ITG is a dynamic process characterized by the integrated action of organizational and human forces (Grant and Tan 2013). In aiming to be effective, this process needs to build trust, foster cooperation and establish a relationship between the involved organizations (Chong and Tan 2012). This type of arrangement is most commonly applied to public organizations, even though it is not exclusive to this sector.

1.3   Why a Public Organization Needs its Own ITG Model

Considering the particularities of organizations, internally and in their scenario, it is important that they develop their own ITG model. Among the internal characteristics that can impact ITG adoption are size (Alreemy et al. 2016), main activities (Juiz et al. 2014), organizational focus (Wilkin and Chenhall 2010), and organizational culture (Grant and Tan 2013). These characteristics can determine, drive or influence the goals of a particular organization related to the ITG process, the governance principles and the mechanisms that will be adopted, as well as the indicators that will be used to measure ITG effectiveness. As an example, a large organization might have different goals regarding its ITG model when compared to a larger multinational organization. The same occurs with public organizations: city governments could have different goals, compared to state or federal governments.

Considering the context of a public organization such as the government of a state or country, an office or a ministry, there is a distributed ecosystem formed by independent organizations connected to each other through different types of hierarchy (Campbell et al. 2009). The challenges are higher, because these organizations contemplate the distributed property of resources, work and information, and also because they pursue ways to protect and enhance the quality and value of services delivered by the ecosystem. In order to face this challenge, it is important to consider inter-organizational ITG, encompassing both the organization itself and its related network, including the synergy among its nodes (Grant and Tan 2013).

The scenario, in turn, can especially determine, drive or influence the ITG model because of some regulations and pressures from the organizational field. The regulations applied to a specific industry should drive the ITG models, because these regulations need to be part of the ITG model in order to avoid a situation where the governance process contributes to a non-compliance situation. As an example, a state-owned bank needs to strictly follow the banking industry regulations regardless of its ownership or administration.

Market pressures influence the ITG model, since organizations accept market institutionalization pressures as a way to be legitimated by other entities, especially those from the same field. According to Pereira et al. (2013), the adoption of ITG practices is influenced by external factors, especially to minimize the uncertainty regarding governance processes.

Another important issue concerning ITG in public organizations is related to capturing a good and comprehensive perspective, which could include principles as investigated by Juiz et al. (2014): Strong commitment to integrity, ethical values, and the rule of law; Openness and comprehensive stakeholder engagement; Defining outcomes in terms of sustainable economic, social, and environmental benefits; Determining the interventions necessary to optimize the achievement of intended outcomes; Developing the capacity of the entity (e.g. leadership); Managing risks and performance through robust internal control and strong public financial management; and Implementing good practices in transparency and reporting to deliver effective accountability.

In short, each organization needs its particular ITG model due to its internal characteristics and contextual facts, but also because each organization is different from others and its ITG model needs to capture and address any particular variables that make organizations unique despite their similarities. A specific ITG model is more precise, because it is based on the organizational particularities and considers the pressures resulting from all the external variables, but especially because it addresses the high-level goals related to the ITG process that is noticeably different. As a consequence, the ITG model becomes more effective.

1.4   A Guide to Discuss and Conceive an ITG Model

A lot of literature has discussed the benefits for organizations that govern their IT, as well as the challenges, intervenient factors, and the potential results. But one important question remains: how to adopt IT Governance? There are several issues related to this aspect that should be better investigated, such as:

- The set of steps to define both the governance model and its adoption;
- The aspects that need to be discussed in the organization;
- The organizational basis that provides support for the ITG process;
- The evidences that the ITG model would create and increase the alignment between IT and business;
- The variables to consider, when choosing market models to assist ITG adoption.

To contribute to the issues mentioned above, this research proposes a guide to help organizations create their own ITG model. This guide is made up of a set of blocks and components that need to be identified and discussed within the organization. Several aspects must be discussed when preparing an organization's ITG model. Four blocks that need to be deeply analysed were defined: (a) the organizational fundamentals, (b) the drivers for ITG, (c) ITG operationalization, and (d) effectiveness monitoring. The two first blocks were created considering that background information about organizational and IT governance is necessary before choosing ITG mechanisms and specification of decision rights, which is the third one. The verification of the effectiveness of this model is the last block. The authors intensively discussed several versions of this guide, based on both the literature review presented in the previous sections and also their practical experience.

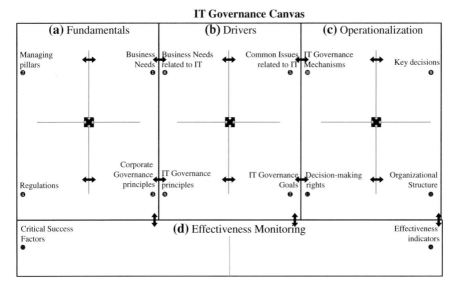

Fig. 1.2 A canvas to discuss and conceive an ITG Model

To facilitate the comprehension of this guide, the main blocks (letters "a" to "d") and components (numbers 1 to 14) are graphically presented as a Canvas, as shown in Fig. 1.2. The arrows illustrate the interplay between the main elements of the Fig. 1.2.

1.4.1 Fundamentals

This block encompasses the organisations' basis, which provides support and is the guide for the ITG model. It is identified in the Corporate Governance and Organizational Governance Models, for private or public/non-profit organizations, respectively. In case an organization does not have a formal model, it can be identified in the non-formalized governance definitions and purposes. It can also be identified by the strategic plan, especially in the strategic map and strategic goals. Four different components need to be identified:

1. Business Needs: defined from Managing Pillars, they involve the necessities of an organization in terms of operation, strategies, targets, and future plans (Juiz and Toomey 2015);
2. Managing Pillars: constitute the organizational management operating focus and a few elements into which an organization puts its efforts (Weill and Ross 2004);
3. Corporate Governance Principles: involve the identification of those corporate or organizational principles that act as a background in all organizational decisions and actions (Juiz et al. 2014);

4. Regulations: involve the identification of laws, standards and other regulations with which the organization needs to be compliant (Wilkin and Chenhall 2010).

This block (Fundamentals) is the only one totally based on business perspective. So, it is an important base on which the ITG model will be developed. The components of this block will be the guide for the discussion of the next elements.

1.4.2 Drivers

This block covers the motivation for this process, and where an organization wants to reach as a result. The ITG process involves the ITG model discussion, its implementation and the evaluation of effectiveness. Four components need to be identified:

5. Common Issues Related to IT: Issues related to the planning, acquisition or use of IT. It brings insights to the discussion in order to verify whether the mechanisms list is complete, i.e., if the planned mechanisms deal with the necessary issues (Ali and Green 2012);
6. Business Needs Related to IT: involve the necessities of an organization related to IT in terms of operation, strategies, targets and future plans (Juiz and Toomey 2015);
7. IT Governance Goals: represent the intentions and the desired results from the ITG process. They are defined from the Business Needs and guided by ITG Principles (Weill and Ross 2004);
8. IT Governance Principles: derived from the Corporate or Organizational Governance Principles and from the Managing Pillars; they represent a background for all decisions and actions related to ITG in an organization (Weill and Ross 2004);

The discussion of this block generates important information for the remaining steps of the process.

1.4.3 Operationalization

After identifying the organizational basis and the drivers of the process, the next step is to reflect about how the principles and the ITG objectives will be operationalized, by discussing the following:

9. Key Decisions: list of decisions related to IT that are vital to the achievement of IT goals and to the alignment with business. Governance design and analysis requires stepping back from day-to-day decision making and focusing on identifying the fundamental decisions to be made (Weill and Ross 2004). Normally, key decisions are just a few high-level decisions;

10. Mechanisms: introduce a set of practices by which the high-level settings (from previous blocks) are operationalized day-to-day (Sambamurthy and Zmud 1999). They are defined from the ITG Goals, but common issues related to the planning, acquisition, and use of IT are also considered. The ITG mechanisms must meet the ITG Goals and respect the ITG Principles (Wiedenhöft et al. 2014).

11. Organizational Structure: List of positions, roles, and line responsibilities that need to be considered when discussing an ITG model. It provides important insights, especially as to the specification of decision-making rights, and it is mandatory for public organizations provided that they have functional roles stated by law (Sambamurthy and Zmud 1999).

12. Decision-Making Rights: the decision-making rights state explicitly what roles each role can take in key decisions, being also accountable for them. They are defined from the ITG Goals, but it is also important to consider the organizational structure, such as positions, roles, and process responsibilities. The organizational structure provides important insights into this step, but it is mandatory for public organizations that have functional roles stated by law (Xiao et al. 2013).

By finishing the discussion of ITG Principles and goals, ITG mechanisms, key decisions and decision-making rights, the ITG organizational model will be ready. This model then goes into a thorough discussion and review within the organization, followed by the implementation of each mechanism or decision-making structure. This implementation is extremely particularized, and needs to be defined by and for each organization.

1.4.4 Effectiveness Monitoring

Once the ITG model is ready and the implementation strategy has been defined by each organization, it becomes important to monitor the effectiveness of each mechanism and practice adopted through the use of indicators. According to Westerman, Mitra and Sambamurthy (2010), measuring IT Governance mechanism effectiveness helps to increase stakeholder confidence as a result of increased compliance with the governance principles.

13. Critical Success Factors: are limited to a few areas in which satisfactory results ensure success in effective IT governance implementation (Nfuka and Rusu 2011). The Critical Success Factors assist the definition of effectiveness indicators;

14. Effectiveness Monitoring Indicators: enable the monitoring of the ITG model effectiveness, particularly the key mechanisms and decision-making structures. Indicators are defined (or selected from previous sources such as literature) from the mechanisms and the key decisions and decision-making rights (Wiedenhöft et al. 2014).

It is important to remember that the ITG model must be unique to each organization, because of the different objectives related to ITG adoption, and also the particularities of each organization considering its market activity, size, or intervenient aspects like political or cultural ones.

1.5 Verifying the Suitability of the Proposed Guide

Burrell and Morgan (1979) state that every social scientist tackles their discipline through explicit or implicit assumptions about the nature of the social world and how this can be investigated. In this study, we assumed a functionalist paradigm, whereby a unit of analysis is understood through the functions that this phenomenon plays, so the focus is to understand the society in such a way as to generate knowledge that may be used by organizations (Burrell and Morgan 1979).

In order to verify the suitability of the proposed guide, a multimethod approach (Mingers 2001) was adopted, combining various data collecting and analysis techniques in a qualitative approach. Participant and non-participant observation, document analysis and focus groups were used to collect data and achieve data triangulation (Dubé and Paré 2003). These techniques were applied in a case study in the executive power of the State Government of Rio Grande do Sul (Brazil), more specifically in the IT Governance Steering Committee (ITGSC). High-level IT decisions are made by this Committee. It has the responsibility to establish policies, which regulate the decision making process related to IT artifact acquisition (hardware, software and services delivery). The ITG Steering Committee is also responsible for the development and implementation of an ITG Model by the executive state branch. This organization was selected because they were starting the discussion of the ITG model at the time the data collection of this research was planned. As such, it was possible to apply all the steps of the guide in order to verify its suitability for an ITG model discussion.

Nowadays, the ITGSC has 13 members, including its president. They act on behalf of different government bureaus, and the members' profiles can be observed in Table 1.2. Data were collected between Jun 2015 and May 2016. During this period, researchers participated in weekly meetings with the IT Governance Steering Committee (ITGSC).

This group represents ten State Offices and one IT semi-public company. Four of these offices have up to 50 civil servants, three have between 100 and 500 civil servants, two have between 500 and 1,000, and two offices, including the semi-public company, have more than 1,000 civil servants. The size of each IT local team is up to 25 civil servants in eight offices, between 26 and 50 in two offices and more than 1,000 civil servants in the semi-public company

First and foremost, we organized a workshop in order to homogenize and comprehend basic concepts related to ITG. This event ensured that further discussions occurred at the same level of understanding when specific concepts were used. Afterwards, the same team started working on the construction process in

Table 1.2 ITG steering committee members' profile

Gender	Education	Current Position	Average experience in IT (years)	Average experience in the position (years)
Male (12)	Master's degree (2); MBA (8)	IT Director (5); IT Manager (4);	16,5	5,7
Female (1)	Graduate (3)	ITG Coordinator (2); ITG Analyst (2)		

order to develop its own ITG Model, which will be presented in the following section.

1.5.1 Fundamentals

With the purpose of identifying the organizational basis that supports and guides the ITG model, as mentioned at Item 4, we conducted non-participative and participative observations and document analysis. At the outset, the Strategic Plan and specially the Balanced Scorecard of the executive branch and also the ICT Policy were read and discussed. Additionally, relevant documents such as decrees, administrative rules and other legislative acts were also examined.

Next, principles and Managing Pillars were identified in the aforementioned documents. During the participant observation, the participants identified key words related to the fundamentals of the organizations. The observations occurred during three meetings of the IT Steering Committee, and the participants grouped the similar answers, deciding which of them could be considered as principles of organizational governance, managing pillars, business needs and regulations. The answers were categorized, and finally grouped and prioritized, achieving the results shown in Table 1.3.

The Principles of Organizational Governance are those that act as a background in all organizational decisions, processes and actions. They need to be respected and considered in all the following discussions as a means to contribute to the alignment between IT and business.

Meanwhile, the Managing Pillars should form the main focus of the organizational management—a small set of elements that an organization needs to put a lot of effort into. They are a starting point to achieve the strategic goals.

The Business Needs are defined from the Managing Pillars, including IT organization needs such as high-level demands to anticipate solutions for management issues that need to be addressed.

Table 1.3 Principles of organizational governance, managing pillars, business needs and regulations

Principles of organizational governance	Managing pillars and business needs	Regulations
Transparency	Simplicity	ICT Policy—executive branch
Resource optimization	Service orientation	Access to information law
Citizens' orientation	Agility	IT Steering committee normative resolution—regulates the composition of the committee, structure, roles and responsibilities
	Efficiency	
Sustainability	Financial sustainability	Regulatory Decree—regulates the ICT Policy
Collaboration between offices and sectors	Access to public information	
Integration between offices and sectors		
Equity among stakeholders		
Privacy		

The Regulations influence the other three elements of the Fundamentals block, because their attendance is mandatory and non-negotiable.

This is the only block in which business elements are directly identified. It is an important discussion, because these elements act as pillars for the following variables and also contribute to IT-business alignment.

1.5.2 Drivers

The importance of identifying the Business Needs related to IT is because they are the translation of Business Needs and show the requirements of an organization related to IT in terms of operation, strategies, targets and future plans. When defining ITG Mechanisms (see item 1.5.3), it is important to verify if the mechanisms are addressing the IT needs. Through a Focus Group, four Business Needs were identified: (a) articulate and facilitate the local IT Managers' decision-making and (b) align the IT actions to the Government strategy, (c) stay compliant with culture, policies, guidelines and procedures and (d) Shared understanding of the ICT objectives and the Government.

Common Issues related to IT are important because they are fundamental for verifying if the planned mechanisms deal with necessary issues. They were discussed in the same focus group that discussed the Business Needs related to IT. The following problems were identified: duplication of IT solutions, non-standardized acquisition decision-making process, investments in non-finished projects, and investments in projects or acquisitions not aligned with business or IT priorities.

The Principles of IT Governance are derived from the Principles of Organizational Governance and the Managing Pillars. They represent a background for all organizational ITG decision processes and actions. Their function in the whole process is very similar to Principles of Organizational Governance, Managing Pillars and Business Needs (see item 1.5.1), but focused on IT issues and decisions.

In order to define Principles, we organized a focus group with ITGSC members. They worked in pairs to list several potential principles on post-its. A set of 11 principles was identified. After this, each group presented their vision, and all participants discussed the appropriateness or otherwise of each principle of ITG, considering as a reference their own Organizational Governance. The 11 principles were grouped or removed from the list, and, after four rounds of discussion, a final set of principles was established, as shown below. They mentioned ICT (Information and Communication Technology) instead of IT, because this is the most common term for them.

Principles of IT Governance:

- Rational and coordinated use of ICT assets;
- Citizen-oriented electronic services;
- Integration and interoperability;
- Consistency, reliability and security of data and information;
- Transparency and access to public information;
- Promotion of collaborative networks and diffusion of knowledge on ICT.

Different organizations will present different principles, since they probably are based on different Organizational Governance Principles and Managing Pillars. Consequently, they could have different Business Needs and Regulations. Additionally, the organizational maturity level and the ITG savvy of members (that make important decisions) might differ between organizations.

The focus group was also used to discuss and create a list of goals when adopting IT Governance. ITG Objectives represent what a government office wants to achieve with the ITG process and what are their intentions. The objectives are defined by the Business Needs and oriented by the Principles of IT Governance.

Considering that this is a more complex discussion, some objectives presented in literature (especially from Weill and Ross 2004) were shown to the group. The participants worked in pairs and listed 19 potential ITG goals on post-its.

After the discussion in pairs, each group presented their vision, and all participants discussed each potential ITG objective, considering as a reference the Organizational Governance Principles, and the Managing Pillars. The answers were grouped, separated, removed from the list and prioritized, achieving the results shown below.

IT Governance Objectives:

- Articulate the coordinated use of ICT resources;
- Strengthen the agility and efficiency when supporting changes;
- Support the strategy and government management;

- Propose technological solutions to the government management;
- Promote technological solution analysis based on cost-benefit variables;
- Enable simple and effective technological solutions;
- Promote ICT Governance;
- Encourage the use of innovative technological solutions;
- Disseminate ICT knowledge and qualify ICT management.

These objectives show why the ITG process has been conducted and what the desirable performance is.

1.5.3 Operationalization

IT Governance Mechanisms

The ITG mechanisms are the main operationalization of the ITG Model in the organization. In order to define them, a focus group with five discussion rounds was carried out based on the 24 mechanisms proposed and validated by Wiedenhoft et al. (2014). Initially, the researchers explained each mechanism by using the mechanisms concepts presented in the aforementioned research.

The list of mechanisms was extensively discussed in order to select the appropriate ones. This selection was based on: (a) mechanisms that enable the operationalization of the ITG objectives; (b) mechanisms that respect the ITG principles; (c) mechanisms aligned with the reality of their organizations, both in terms of ITG maturity and IT savvy. Finally, the group identified 13 mechanisms and also created four new mechanisms, as shown in Table 1.4.

Organizational Structure

The identification of the organizational structure was based on the Policy of ICT identifying the main actors in the guiding document, as well as the role of each actor for IT and Business. The understanding of the functioning of IT decisions in the State of Rio Grande do Sul (State of RS), obtained through observation, was also extremely important for identifying the organizational structure behind management and IT governance in the State of RS.

The executive power consists of many different sectors, divided into departments and agencies, which include Governorship, Departments, Local Authorities, Foundations and Economic Foundations. The Department of Information and Communication Technology, associated to the Main Secretariat of Government, has the responsibility of coordinating, monitoring and regulating the actions and internal policies of ICT from state public administration through the ICT Steering Committee (CGTIC) and the Executive Committee of ICT (CETIC). The definition and implementation of strategies for IT are held through the following organizational structures:

Table 1.4 IT Governance mechanisms

Kind of mechanism	Mechanism	Source
Structure	State ITG Steering Committee	Adapted[a]
	State ITG Executive Committee	New
	Local ITG Steering Committee in each office and agency	Adapted[a]
	The President of the ITGSC as part of the General Government Secretariat Staff	Adapted[a]
	A formalized Organizational Structure of ICT Management	Adapted[a]
Process	Definition and update of an ICT Policy	New
	ICT Strategic Planning	New
	Formal process of Strategic Alignment of ICT/Government	Adapted[a]
	Formal process of ICT Control and Measurement	Adapted[a]
	Formal process of ICT Financial Investments Prioritization	Adapted[a]
	Formal process of Information Security	Adapted[a]
	Formal process of Project Management	Adapted[a]
	Formal process of Processes Management	Adapted[a]
	Formal process of ICT Services Management	Adapted[a]
Relationship	ICT Managers' network	New
	IT Governance Office	Adapted[a]
	Formal practices to define/communicate the ICT value	Adapted[a]

[a] From Wiedenhöft et al. (2014)

- CGTIC—Defines the strategies and guidelines regarding the application of the ICT-RS Policy and establishes governance standards (PGOV) and technical standards (PTEC);
- CETIC—Supporting the CGTIC in promoting the application of the guiding principles and pursuing the objectives of the ICT-RS Policy; Analyse compliance with governance standards and the technicians responsible for issuing recommendations and determine actions for the implementation of ICT-RS Policy.
- GGTIC—Defines strategies, policies and guidelines for the application of the ICT-RS Policy and the establishment of rules and recommendations for the development of ICT actions in an integrated and systematic way within the scope of its authority;
- RGTIC—It is a network of all ICT managers in the entire organization with the goal of sharing and discussing issues related to the use of ICT, proposing technical and governance standards, as well as rules on the use of ICT.

All actors have goals and relationships with each other, which are levelled in the spheres of Strategic Management and Administrative Technical Operations. The Strategic Management sphere includes actors that somehow impact ICT-related decision-making and support the senior management, filtering the fundamental and highly strategic information. In addition, these actors act in managing, organizing and making decisions about standards and policies. The administrative, technical and operational sphere consists of actors whose roles include supporting, administratively and technically, the key decision makers from the first sphere.

Key Decisions and Decision-Making Rights

In an oriented way, decisions were divided according to the macro decisions on: Infrastructure, Business Applications, Investment and Contracts. These dimensions emerged from literature, and are concatenated to micro decisions from the business. Each macro decision was indicated in the matrix using post-it with distinct colours. In order to relate the micro decisions with the macro decisions, the same colours were used. The matrix include three columns: Decides, participates (which have direct connection with the decision-making process) and informed (which relates to the outcome of the decision). The description of the columns was presented to the participants as follows:

- Decides—has the responsibility to make the decision.
- Participates—is consulted or participates in some decision-making stage
- Informed—Actors that are informed about some decision taken.

After some rounds of discussion, they defined as main decisions the following: infrastructure, business applications, investments and contracts. These decisions were recognized as the most important from the perspective of the ICT Steering Committee and are also referenced by Weill and Ross (2004).

1.5.4 Monitoring Effectiveness

After identifying the organizational and IT bases—fundamentals and drivers, respectively—and the way these high-level definitions will be put into practice (operationalization), it is necessary to define how to monitor the effectiveness of these mechanisms and the model itself. A focus group was conducted in order to identify the Critical Success Factors (CSF) and the indicators.

The Critical Success factors are the key areas where the company should achieve the best results to be successful. This discussion was based on the list of CSF provided by Nfuka and Rusu (2011). After three rounds of discussion, 9 CSF previously identified by the aforementioned authors were found applicable in the context. The analysed and prioritized list of CSFs is available in Table 1.5 as follows:

In order to define the indicators for monitoring ITG effectiveness, another Focus Group was organized. Based on effective dimensions and indicators defined by Wiedenhöft et al. (2014), the ICT Steering Committee discussed each indicator considering their relevance especially to the ITG Mechanisms and ITG Goals. Through a content analysis, 213 codes were identified and categorized. After six rounds of discussions, a set of 24 indicators (themes) related to 10 measurement criteria were identified. Table 1.6 shows the relevant indicators that emerged from the case analysis, grouped by dimension of effectiveness.

Table 1.5 Prioritized Critical success factors

Priority	Critical success factors
1	IT leadership to understand the business goals and IT contribution and bring it to the attention of management
2	Involve and get support from senior management
3	Define and align IT strategies to corporate strategies and cascade them down in an organization
4	Encourage and support IT/Business communication and partnership
5	Consolidate IT structures to ensure responsiveness and accountability
6	Consolidate Performance measures and benchmarks to track and demonstrate success
7	Engage key stakeholders
8	Consolidate, communicate and enforce policies and guidelines for cost effective IT acquisition and use across the organization.
9	Consolidate, standardize and manage IT infrastructure and applications to optimize costs and information flow across the organization

After all these steps, the main components of an ITG Model are identified, so that a document formalizing the model should be written and submitted for appreciation and approval at the Organizational Governance Committee level. After the model gets approved, it is time to start its implementation. At this moment, market models can be especially useful.

1.5.5   Final Remarks Related to the Guide Application

When dealing with IT Governance, it is important to consider that the ITG model must be unique to each organization, because of different objectives related to the business and ITG adoption, and also considering the particularities of each organization. Such particularities can be its market activity, size, and regulatory context or intervenient aspects like political or cultural ones. The presented guide was proposed in order to assist organizations to conceive their own model considering all the contextual elements, needs and future expectations. The result of application of this guide can also be useful when choosing market models to assist the ITG adoption.

We consider that the guide is useful for discussing an IT Governance model that is specific to each organization, provided that it was possible to discuss all blocks and components in the selected case in order to verify the suitability of the guide to its proposal, i.e., discussing and conceiving an ITG Model.

It was possible to perceive that some items such as ITG Goals, IT Principles, Critical Success Factors, Decision Rights and Effectiveness Monitoring Indicators, that were gathered from Weill and Ross (2004), Van Grembergem and De Haes (2009), Nfuka and Rusu (2011), and Wiedenhöft et al. (2014) were not totally

Table 1.6 ITG effectiveness indicators

Criterion	Indicator
Economic and financial	Average rate of return on investment
	IT expenses
	Compliance of the IT budget-planned x executed
Internal and external compliance	IT actions addressing the corporate governance model
	% of compliance with external audits
	% of compliance with internal audits
Resource management	Balance between the demand and capacity
	Performance level of management and executive teams
	IT staff turnover
	IT service continuity
	IT Investment
Risk management	Occurrence of identified risks
	Projects with risk analysis
	Total preventive measures against risks
	Total measures of risk mitigation
Stakeholder satisfaction	Satisfaction of shareholders and sponsors
	Satisfaction of users and customers
	IT employee satisfaction
	Satisfaction with IT vendors
Strategic alignment	Objectives of IT complying with strategic objectives of business
	Participation of IT in business
	Total new business implemented by IT
Training and knowledge	Sharing knowledge between business and IT
	Participation of stakeholders in IT decisions

adequate for the studied organization. This shows the importance of discussing items like those presented in this guide, in order to consider the specificities and the context of each organization.

1.6 Concluding Remarks

This research developed a guide for discussing and conceiving ITG in public organizations and verified its suitability through analysis in the State Government of Rio Grande do Sul (Brazil), considering the specifics of the context. The findings show that Organizational Governance Principles, Managing Pillars and Business Needs; ITG Principles and Objectives; and ITG Mechanisms are necessary when discussing an ITG model.

The results presented in this chapter combine multiple data sources such as non-participant observation, document analysis and focus groups. The guide was initially tested in the ITG Steering Committee of the State of Rio Grande do Sul (Brazil) in order to explore the adoption of ITG in public organizations in a specific context. Considering this, contextual variables can be a limitation. The context involves factors like national and organizational culture, laws and regulations, which tend to have a positive or negative influence, hindering, facilitating or accelerating the IT Governance adoption.

However, all organizations that use IT to support their operations adopt an ITG model, even if this sometimes occurs without a clear understanding of its benefits, or not recognizing its practical use by adopting formal models (Weill and Ross 2004). Understanding and interpreting an IT governance model brings benefits to organizations, such as better decisions for the use of IT assets (Van Grembergen et al. 2004).

Our findings have revealed that, by applying the proposed guide to a State Government initiative, it was possible to conceive an ITG Model related to the specific criteria of the studied case. Therefore, the resultant model that emerged from the application of the proposed guide cannot be applied as such in any situation, since it was conceived for (and by) a specific context. This might be a limitation of this research, although it is not possible to conceive a general model for every single context given the fact that environment particularities, such as policies, structure, and economy, need to be deeply analysed and considered. That is the reason why we are proposing this guide, discussing our results in a particular situation and offering inspiration for those who are searching for an ITG Model for public organizations. The practical contribution of this research is that the guide might be used by public organizations that are in the process of creating their ITG model. More specifically, the guide proposes a set of items that need to be considered when discussing an ITG initiative. However, managers should perceive different contexts and adapt it depending on their own needs. Regarding the results in terms of principles, the most common aspects that emerged from the studied case were related to transparency, collaboration and citizen-oriented processes, emphasizing the interest of governments in the needs of their citizens (Agrawal et al. 2014). Considering the main objectives when governing IT through the proposed guide, they can be split into internal and external dimensions. On the one hand, rational and coordinated use of IT assets, citizen oriented electronic services, integration and interoperability, consistency, reliability and security of data and information are some internal benefits from ITG Models. On the other hand, transparency, access to public information, and promotion of collaborative networks and diffusion of knowledge in IT appear as benefits that encompass external aspects and stakeholders.

A limitation of this study is that the findings are illustrated by only one case study in Brazil. The case was very rich and the collected data helped verification of the suitability to an ITG model discussion. However, we do also believe that there is a need to go forward. The next steps will include the concept of inter-organizational governance, in order to encompass both the organization itself and its related network, including the synergy among its nodes. We also intend to identify how the IT governance model helped the achievement of goals, the respect for the principles and alignment with management pillars and business needs.

Finally, is important to emphasize that without a governance process it is easy to have duplication of technologies and solutions, which provoke an unnecessary increase in complexity. The higher the complexity, the higher the transaction costs. More transaction costs mean more financial costs that may compromise future investments on new initiatives, and also increase difficulties in planning new initiatives while managing the currents ones. In the end, it could compromise the reach of the government role of creating public value and social contribution.

References

Agrawal, D., Kettinger, W. J., & Zhang, C. (2014). The openness challenge: why some cities take it on and others don't. In: Savannah GA (ed) *Proceedings of the Twentieth Americas Conference on Information Systems*, (USA), AIS, Paper 14. Retrieved September 09, 2015, from http://aisel.aisnet.org/amcis2014/Posters/eGovernment/14/.

Ali, S., & Green, P. (2012). Effective information technology (IT) governance mechanisms: an IT outsourcing perspective. *Information Systems Frontiers, 14*, 79–193.

Alreemy, Z., Chang, V., Walters, R., et al. (2016). Critical success factors (CSFs) for information technology governance (ITG). *International Journal of Information Management, 36*(6), 907–916.

Bartenschlager, J., & Goeken, M. (2010). IT strategy implementation framework-bridging enterprise architecture and IT governance. In: *Proceedings of the Sixteenth Americas Conference on Information Systems,* Lima (Peru), AIS, Paper 400. Retrieved January 05, 2015, from http://aisel.aisnet.org/amcis2010/400.

Bloomfield, B. P., & Hayes, N. (2009). Power and organizational transformation through technology: hybrids of electronic government. *Organization Studies, 30*(5), 461–487.

Burell, G., & Morgan, G. (1979). *Sociological paradigms and organisational analysis. Elements of the sociology of corporate life.* London: Heinemann.

Campbell, J., McDonald, C., & Sethibe, T. (2009). Public and private sector IT governance: identifying contextual differences. *Australasian Journal of Information Systems, 16*(2), 05–18.

Castells M. (2011). *The rise of the network society: The information age: Economy, society, and culture* (Vol. 1). Wiley, London.

Chong, J. L. L., & Tan, F. B. (2012). IT governance in collaborative networks: a socio-technical perspective In: *Proceedings of the Nineteenth Pacific Asia Journal of the Association for Information Systems* (Vol. 42, Article 3). Retrieved October 15, 2016, from http://aisel.aisnet.org/pajais/vol4/iss2/3.

Cunha, M. A., & Miranda, P. R. (2013). O uso de TIC pelos governos: uma proposta de agenda de pesquisa a partir da produção acadêmica e da prática nacional. *Organizações Sociedade, 20* (66), 543–566.

Dawes, S., Pardo, T. A., & Simon S., et al. (2004). Making smart IT choices: Understanding value and risk in government IT investments. Retrieved May 12, 2016, from https://www.ctg.albany.edu/publications/guides/smartit2/smartit2.pdf.

Dubé, L., & Paré, G. (2003). Rigor in information systems positivist case research: current practices, trends, and recommendations. *MIS Quarterly, 27*(4), 597–636.

Fox, J. (2007). The uncertain relationship between transparency and accountability. *Development in Practice, 17*(4–5), 663–671.

Grant, G., & Tan, F. B. (2013). Governing IT in inter-organizational relationships: Issues and future research. *European Journal Information System, 22*(5), 493–497.

Juiz, C., & Toomey, M. (2015). To govern IT, or not to govern IT? *Communications of the ACM, 58*(2), 58–64.

Juiz, C., Guerrero, C., & Lera, I. (2014). Implementing good governance principles for the public sector in information technology governance frameworks. *Open Journal of Accounting, 03* (01), 9–27.

Khalfan, A., & Gough, T. G. (2002). Comparative analysis between the public and private sectors on the IS/IT outsourcing practices in a developing country: a field study. *Logistics Information Management, 5*(3), 212–222.

Luciano, E. M., Macadar, M. A., & Wiedenhöft, G. (2016). Information Technology Governance enabling long-term electronic Governance initiatives. In: Scholl, H.J., Glassey, O., & Janssen, M., et al. (eds.) *The Dual IFIP EGOV ePart 2016 Conference*, Guimarães, September 2016 (Vol. 23, pp. 390–391). IOS Press, Amsterdam. Retrieved October 7, 2016, from http://ebooks.iospress.nl/ISBN/978-1-61499-669-9.

Lunardi, G. L., Becker, J. L., Maçada, A. C. G., et al. (2014). The impact of adopting IT governance on financial performance: an empirical analysis among Brazilian firms. *International Journal of Accounting Information Systems, 15*(1), 66–81.

Meijer, A., & Bolívar, M. P. R. (2016) Governing the smart city: a review of the literature on smart urban governance. *International Review of Administrative Sciences* 82(2):392–408 [first published on April 29, 2015].

Mingers, J. (2001). Combining IS research methods: towards a pluralist methodology. *Information systems research, 12*(3), 240–259.

Nfuka, E. N., & Rusu, L. (2011). The effect of critical success factors on IT governance performance. *Industrial Management & Data Systems, 111*(9), 1418–1448.

Pereira, G. V., Luciano, E. M., & Macadar, M. A., et al. (2013). Information technology governance practices adoption through an institutional perspective: the perception of Brazilian and American CIOs. In: *Proceedings of the Forty-seventh Hawaii International Conference on System Sciences (HICSS)*, Wailea, Maui (HI USA), January 2013, pp. 4446–4455. IEEE. Retrieved February 15, 2016, from https://www.computer.org/csdl/proceedings/hicss/2013/4892/00/4892e446-abs.html.

Peterson, R. (2004). Crafting information technology governance. *Information Systems Management, 21*(4), 7–22.

Al Qassimi, N., & Rusu, L. (2015). IT Governance in a Public Organization in a Developing Country: A Case Study of a Governmental Organization Procedia Computer Science *64* (2015): 450–456.

Rusu, L., Nfuka, EN., & Mutagahywa, B., et al. (2009). The state of IT governance in organizations from the public sector in a developing country. In *Proceedings of the Forty-second Hawaii International Conference on System Sciences (HICSS), Waikoloa, Big Island (HI USA), January 2009, IEEE, p. 1–12*.

Sambamurthy, V., & Zmud, R. W. (1999). Arrangements for information technology governance: a theory of multiple contingencies. *MIS Quarterly, 23*(2), 261–290.

Tiwana, A., Konsynski, B., & Venkatraman, N. (2013). Special issue: information technology and organizational governance: the IT governance cube. *Journal of Management Information Systems, 30*(3): 7–12.

Un, E. (2012). Government Survey 2012: E-Government for the people. Department Economic and Social Affairs, United Nations, New York.

Van Grembergen, W., & De Haes, S. (2009). *Enterprise governance of information technology: achieving strategic alignment and value*. US: Springer.

Van Grembergen, W., De Haes, S., & Guldentops, E. (2004). Structures, processes and relational mechanisms for IT governance. *Strategies for Information Technology Governance 2*(4): 1–36.

Walsham, G. (2001). *Making a world of difference: IT in a global context*. London: Wiley.

Webster, J., & Watson, R. T. (2002). Analyzing the past to prepare for the future: Writing a literature review. *MIS Quarterly*, 26(2), xiii–xxiii.

Weill, P., & Ross, J. W. (2004). *IT governance: How top performers manage IT decision rights for superior results*. Boston: Harvard Business School Press.

Westerman, G., Mitra, S., & Sambamurthy, V. (2010). Taking charge of the IT value conversation. *Center for Information Systems Research. MIT Sloan School of Management, Boston.*

Wiedenhöft, G., Luciano, E. M., & Testa, M. G. (2014). A indicators-based approach to measure information technology governance effectiveness: a study with Brazilian professionals. In: *Procedings of the Twenty-second European Conference on Information Systems*, Tel Aviv (Israel), AIS, Paper 20, 9–11 June 2014. Retrieved October 15, 2015, from http://aisel.aisnet.org/ecis2014/proceedings/track15/20.

Wilkin, C., & Chenhall, R. (2010). A review of IT governance: a taxonomy to inform accounting information systems. *Journal of Information Systems, 24*(2), 107–146.

Xiao, J., Xie, K., & Hu, Q. (2013). Inter-firm IT governance in power-imbalanced buyer–supplier dyads: exploring how it works and why it lasts. *European Journal of Information Systems, 22* (5), 512–528.

Yildiz, M. (2007). E-government research: Reviewing the literature, limitations, and ways forward. *Government Information Quarterly, 24*(3), 646–665.

Author Biographies

Edimara M. Luciano is an MIS Professor and Head of the IT Management and Governance Research Group at Pontifical Catholic University of Rio Grande do Sul (PUCRS, Brazil). She holds a PhD. from Federal University of Rio Grande do Sul (Brazil). Visiting Research Scholar in the IS and Innovation Research Group at the LSE (UK, 2016), AMCIS IT Governance and Architecture Minitrack Co-Chair, ECIS IT Governance and Business-IT Alignment Track Associate Editor, and MIS Program Co-Chair at the main Brazilian Conference on Administration. Her research interests include IT Governance, eGovernance mechanisms to reduce the levels of corruption, Open Data Government and Open Government, especially through the lens of culture and organizational and individual behavior.

Guilherme C. Wiedenhöft is an Assistant Professor in the School of Informatics at Pontifical Catholic University of Rio Grande doSul (PUCRS, Brazil). He holds a Master and a PhD. from the Graduation Program in Business Administration at PUCRS. He holds a bachelor's degree in Information Technology Management at the same University. He regularly serves as reviewer to ECIS, AMCIS, CONFIRM and also to several Brazilian conferences and journals. His research interests include Information Technology Governance in private and public organizations, especially through the lens of culture and organizational behavior.

Marie Anne Macadar is an Associate Professor of Management Information Systems in the Business Administration Graduation Program at the Pontifical Catholic University of Rio Grande doSul (PUCRS, Brazil). She holds her PhD. at University of São Paulo (Brazil). Visiting Research Scholar at Center for Technology in Government (State University of New York, USA). She is Minitrack Co-Chair at Conf-IRM and Healthcare Information Systems Minitrack Co-Chair at the main Brazilian Conference on MIS. Her research interests are related to e-Government, Smart Cities, e-Participation and citizen engagement, healthcare information systems and ICT for Development.

Gabriela Viale Pereira is Senior Scientist at the Department for E-Governance and Administration at Danube University Krems and visiting Post-doc at FundaçãoGetúlio Vargas (EAESP/FGV). She holds a doctoral degree in Business Administration (PUCRS, Brazil) in addition to her Master's degree in the field of Management Information Systems. She is Connected Smart City Minitrack Co-Chair at CeDEM. Her experience covers research at national (Brazil, Austria) and EU-funded project in electronic government, smart governance and smart city topics. She has background and interest in smart cities and open government data focusing in how ICT contribute increasing the quality of citizens' life.

Chapter 2
IT Alignment in Public Organizations: A Systematic Literature Review

Lazar Rusu and Gideon Mekonnen Jonathan

Abstract IT alignment is one of the widely researched topics in the information systems research area and continue to be a top management concern. However, IT alignment in the context of public organizations is still less explored. A systematic literature review is conducted to provide an overview of the current status of the research in this area and the possible future research directions. Major databases and top conference proceedings in information systems and e-government area were searched by using key words to collect articles for analysis. Finally, a total of 58 articles were identified and included in the literature review. The findings of this study indicate case study research as the most preferred research method. But due to the small numbers of public organizations explored in these studies the results are problematic for generalisation. Apart from these findings we have identified and discussed the research concepts addressed in IT alignment in public organizations studies that were categorized using the dimensions of Strategic Alignment Maturity model. The findings of this study have revealed some potential future research directions that have been less explored like organizational culture, organizational politics, social interaction, and informal organizational structure influence on IT alignment in public organizations.

2.1 Introduction

Information Technology (IT) alignment is a topic which has attracted the attention of scholars and practitioners and has been researched extensively for the last decades. Review of academic literature reveals that IT alignment has been described

L. Rusu (✉)
Department of Computer and Systems Sciences,
Stockholm University, Kista, Stockholm, Sweden
e-mail: lrusu@dsv.su.se

G.M. Jonathan
Kozminski University, Warsaw, Poland
e-mail: gideon@kozminski.edu.pl

© Springer International Publishing AG 2017   27
L. Rusu and G. Viscusi (eds.), *Information Technology Governance in Public Organizations*, Integrated Series in Information Systems 38,
DOI 10.1007/978-3-319-58978-7_2

and defined differently by different authors. Such terms as '*fit*' (Henderson and Venkatraman1993), '*harmony*' (Luftman 2000), and '*linkage*' (Henderson and Venkatraman1993) are used to refer IT alignment. Chan and Reich (2007) argue that the variations in the terms as well as the conceptualization of the phenomenon are attributed to the differences in academic disciplines. For instance, the term 'fit' is used in strategic management discipline while 'alignment' is almost exclusively used in Information Systems literature. However, most of the definition of IT alignment tend to refer towards commercial organizational settings. According to Luftman et al. (2015, p. 2) alignment activities are defined as "*IT-business, and business-IT related managerial behaviours that can enable and promote the coordination and 'harmonization' of activities across the business and the IT domain in ways that add business value*". However, McKeen and Smith (2003) conceptualise IT alignment broadly as a situation where organizational goals as well as the information systems that support them are in congruence. In public organizational settings, Winkler (2013, p. 834) define IT alignment as "*the degree to which the IT goals support the strategic goals of a public agency, and to which administration and IT stakeholders are committed to support these goals*".

In opinion of Leonard and Seddon (2012) information systems managers consider IT alignment to be a key issue for their organizations. In fact, according to Kappelman et al. (2016) IT alignment continues to be the first top management concern for executives in organizations around the world. However, despite the frequent and wide investigations in the area with different viewpoints suggesting different future research directions, there are still areas that have not been addressed. For instance, previous studies have provided different definitions and characteristics, and identified various factors that could influence IT alignment (Luftman et al. 2004; Sposito et al. 2016). Several models have also been proposed to help in addressing the challenge of achieving IT alignment in organizations (Tapia 2009; Avison et al. 2004) like the strategic alignment model proposed by Henderson and Venkatraman (1993) that remains to be one the most widely known and used among IS researchers (Renaud et al. 2016). More than two decades on and after various models and frameworks built based on strategic alignment model, achieving IT alignment remains to be a challenging endeavour for organizations' management.

On the other hand, IT alignment in specific types of organizations such as public organizations have not attracted the attention of researchers as they deserve (Winkler 2013; Vander Elst and De Rynck 2014) and there is a lack of research of IT alignment in public administration (Walser et al. 2016). In order to uncover the less explored areas and provoke further discussion on the topic, a systematic literature review of the previous studies is necessary (Webster and Watson 2002). According to Webster and Watson (2002) literature review contributes to the advancement of knowledge in an area of study by helping the development of theories and less studied areas are revealed while extensively explored topics are synthesised and analysed. This literature review is intended to contribute to research in IT alignment in public organizations area in three ways. The first aim is to provide an overview of the IT alignment research activities in the domain of public sector organizations. The second aim is to structure studies in such a way that those interested can easily draw a link and compare the contributions of past studies. This will also make it easier for other researchers to easily identify studies that are relevant to their research area of interest. The third aim is to provide a systematic presentation of research literature review that helps to point out issues that have been explored while uncovering areas that have attracted less attention from researchers. The intention here is to show the research gap and indicate opportunities for future research in this area.

There are several reasons to attract researchers' attention on IT alignment in public organizations. A comparison of surveys conducted with managers from public and private institutions revealed "many similarities between the two sectors but also some pronounced critical differences" (Caudle et al. 1991, p. 172). The underlying factors for these differences were pointed out by different scholars (Muhammad 2009a, b; Meijer and Thaens 2010; Winkler 2013; Vander Elst and De Rynck 2014). The presence of stakeholders with competing or opposing interests, the wide variety of services delivered, and complex institutional structure with both political and administrative management powers are found to present a challenge for IT alignment in public organizations. Chan and Reich (2007) further argue that the differences between the private and public sectors make the need, use and application of IT different which in turn justifies the need for IT alignment studies in variety of organizational settings. Furthermore, information technology has become an important resource to improve the variety and quality of services provided by public organizations (Heintze and Bretschneider 2000; Garicano and Heaton 2010; Winkler 2013) which makes IT alignment studies relevant and timely appropriate.

The remainder of the paper is structured as follows. The detailed research method appears in the following section. The third and fourth sections present the results and the findings of the existing research on IT alignment in public organizations and in the last section are the conclusions that provide a summary of the main findings and suggestions for further research.

2.2 Research Method

This study was done through a systematic literature review that is a rigorous review of research results (Kitchenham et al. 2009; Okoli and Schabram 2010). The research questions and research process including the procedures in the search of the research literature and the method of analysis of the collected articles are presented in the following sub-sections.

2.2.1 Research Questions

In order to make sure the number of articles collected would be relevant and manageable for analysis, limiting the focus of the review was deemed necessary. For this purpose, a number of research questions were formulated. The research questions are:

RQ1: What research has been conducted on IT alignment in public organizations? Which publication channels (journals and conference proceedings) were used?
RQ2: What are the research goals and the research concepts studied in the area of IT alignment in public organizations?
RQ3: What research design was used in the research studies concerning IT alignment in public organizations?
RQ4: What are the main findings of research in IT alignment in the public organizations?
RQ5: What conclusions can be drawn from the findings of previous studies and what are the potential future research directions?

2.2.2 The Research Literature Review Process

IT alignment is one of the most researched topics within the information systems research area in the past three decades (Gerow et al. 2014; Vander Elst and De Rynck 2014; Coltman et al. 2015) and there are several sources of scientific literature. The literature search process was carried by following the guidelines as suggested by Webster and Watson (2002), Kitchenham et al. (2009), and Okoli and Schabram (2010). A total of six scientific databases were chosen to search for publications. These widely used databases were selected based on the variety of collection of scientific papers with breadth of research topics they index. According to Weber and Watson (2002), leading journals are sources of articles that could contribute significantly to the area of study. Thus, direct phrase search was conducted in the eight IS Senior Scholars' Basket of Journals, and the four reputable information systems conference proceedings. Apart from these top IS journals and conference proceedings, Government Information Quarterly journal and International Conference on Electronic Government proceedings were also included in the search of the research literature in IT alignment in public organizations due to their strong relevance to the topic of the review. The table of contents of these journals and conference proceedings were also manually scanned to find articles that were not caught by the search of combinations of keywords. In order to complete the literature selection, the citations of the articles found in the direct search were reviewed manually. Forward search was also carried out using Google Scholar to determine if the articles that cite the previously identified articles are

Table 2.1 Databases, journals and conference proceedings used in the research literature review

Databases	ACM Digital library
	AIS eLibrary
	EBSCO Host
	Emerald
	IEEEXplore
	ISI web of knowledge
	SpringerLink
Journals	European Journal of Information Systems
	Government Information Quarterly
	Information Systems Journal
	Information Systems Research
	Journal of Association of Information Systems
	Journal of Information Technology
	Journal of Management Information Systems
	Journal of Strategic Information Systems
	MIS Quarterly
Conference proceedings	AMCIS—Americas Conference on Information Systems
	ECIS—European Conference on Information Systems
	eGov—International Conference on Electronic Government
	HICCS—Hawaii International Conference on System Sciences
	ICIS—International Conference on Information Systems
	PACIS—Pacific Asia Conference on Information Systems

Table 2.2 Combinations of keywords used in the research literature review

"IT alignment"	and	"public organization"
"strategic IT alignment"		"public sector organization"
"alignment"		"public sector"
"strategic alignment"		
"strategic IS alignment"		
"IS alignment"		
"business-IT alignment"		
"business/IT alignment"		
"IT-business alignment"		
"IT/business alignment"		
"strategic fit"		

relevant for the literature review. The databases, journals and conference proceedings used in the literature review are shown in Table 2.1.

Since the conceptualization and definitions have been various in academic literature, different terms have also been coined to refer IT alignment (Chan and Reich 2007). This would make it difficult to capture all of the relevant articles by searching only the title, abstract and keywords. The different combinations of key words used during the literature search are presented in Table 2.2.

Many case studies in IT alignment have been carried out and published in different trade publications (Chan and Reich 2007) as well as academic journals/conference proceedings (Coltman et al. 2015; Gerow et al. 2014). However, only peer reviewed articles investigating IT alignment in public

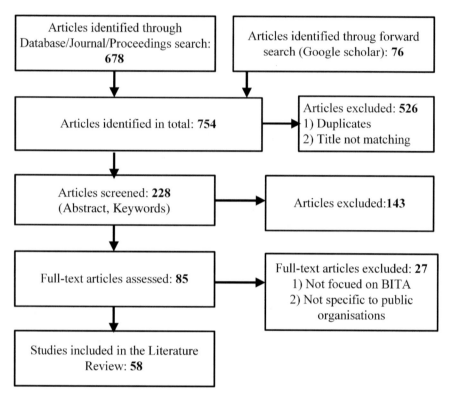

Fig. 2.1 The research literature review process

organizational settings were target for this literature review. Both conceptual and empirical studies published in English are included in the literature review process. Since little attention has been given to IT alignment research in the context of public organizations (Meijer and Thaens 2010; Muhammad 2009a, b; Winkler 2013), the year of publication is not restricted during the literature search in order to capture reasonable number of articles for analysis. Sub-topics of research were specified in order to gather all studies related to IT alignment. However, articles presenting research in progress as well as studies investigating both private and public organizations at the same time are excluded. The literature review process is shown in Fig. 2.1.

After capturing articles in journals and conference proceedings by searching both databases as well as the search functions of the selected journals and conference proceedings, a forward search was also carried out using Google Scholar. After the duplicates were removed, the evaluation of relevance of the studies to IT alignment in public organizations was done using the inclusion and exclusion criteria as is shown in Table 2.3. In the literature review process first, only the titles, the abstracts and key words of the articles were evaluated to make sure the inclusion criteria are met. If the studies were found to be within the scope of the research

Table 2.3 Inclusion/exclusion criteria in the literature review

Inclusion criteria	Exclusion criteria
Complete articles investigating IT alignment issues in public organizations	Research-in-progress articles
	Articles not published in peer-reviewed journals or conference proceedings
	Articles published as book chapters
	Articles on IT alignment not specific to public organizations
	Duplicate articles
	Articles written in languages other than English

topic, then these were selected for the second-round evaluation. In the second stage of the evaluation we have gone through the full text of the articles in order to find the articles which might contain inconsistencies between the abstract and its full content. The same inclusion/exclusion criterion as shown in Table 2.3 was used to arrive at the final list of articles chosen for the review.

The data collection in this literature review was manually extracted from each of the articles that were selected after the inclusion and exclusion criteria. The data collected from the selected articles is including the followings: Publication Type (journal or conference proceeding); Authors; Research Method; Main Research Concepts; Research Questions/Hypotheses/Objective; Findings and Conclusions.

2.3   Results

This section presents the results and discussions on the answers to the research questions.

2.3.1   What Research has been Conducted on IT Alignment in Public Organizations? Which Publication Channels were used like Journals and Conference Proceedings?

The literature search resulted in the identification of 58 relevant studies on IT alignment in public organizations which contains 33 journal articles and 25 conference articles that are presented in Table 2.4 and Table 2.5. A presentation of these papers selected for the review that were published between the years 1993 and 2016 is also shown in Fig. 2.2. As we noticed from Fig. 2.2 the first article investigating IT alignment in public organizational setting was published in 1993. The same journal (Journal of Strategic Information Systems) has published two more articles one in 1994 and another a year later. However, articles did not start to

Table 2.4 Research on IT alignment in public organizations published in journals

Journals	Articles
Business Process Management Journal	Ebrahim and Irani (2005); Koh et al. (2006)
Government Information Quarterly	Andrade and Joia (2012); Fedorowicz et al. (2009); Gil-García and Pardo (2005); Kim et al. (2007); Larsson and Grönlund (2014); Luna-Reyes et al. (2007); Meijer and Thaens (2010); Mergel (2016); Sawyer et al. (2008)
Health Care Management Review	Iveroth et al. (2013)
Information Polity: The International Journal of Government and Democracy in the Information Age	Vander Elst and De Rynck (2014)
Information Systems Frontiers	Klievink et al. (2016); Tonelli et al. (2015)
Information Systems Journal	Bannister (2001); Irani et al. (2005); Rose et al. (2015)
Information Technology and People	Wiredu (2012)
Journal of Information Technology	De Marco and Sorrentino (2007); Pang et al. (2014); Thorogood et al. (2004)
Journal of Information Technology Teaching Cases	Mu and Stern (2015)
Journal of Management Information Systems	Dulipovici and Robey (2013)
Journal of Strategic Information Systems	Broadbent et al. (1994); Flynn and Goleniewska (1993); Hasan and Lampitsi (1995); Lee-Partridge et al. (2000); Teo and Ranganthan (2003)
MIS Quarterly	Silva and Hirschheim (2007)
Records Management Journal	Asprey (2004)
Scandinavian Journal of Information Systems	Simonsen (1999)
TELKOMNIKA	Amali et al. (2014)

be published every year until 2003 except the year 2011. As it is shown in Fig. 2.2, the number of journal articles picked in 2014 (6 articles).

We also noticed that most of the journal articles were published in the Government Information Quarterly between 2005 and 2016 (9 articles) while the Journal of Strategic Information System is the second most publisher (5 articles) of IT alignment studies in public organizations followed by Information System Journal and Journal of Information Technology with 3 articles each (see Table 2.4).

The highest numbers of conference papers were published in the proceedings of the Hawaii International Conference on System Sciences (6 articles) and International Conference on Electronic Government (5 articles) as it can be seen from Table 2.5. Furthermore 3 articles were published in proceedings of Americas Conference on Information Systems and in proceedings of European Conference on e-Government (2 articles). All of the remaining conferences have published one article each.

The first two conference articles were published four years apart; the first in 1997 by Americas Conference on Information Systems followed by the second article

Table 2.5 Research on IT alignment in public organizations published in conference proceedings

Conference proceedings	Articles
Americas Conference on Information Systems	Papp (1997); Vargas et al. (2010); Walser et al. (2016)
Electronic Government International Conference	Christiansson et al. (2015); Iribar-ren et al. (2008); Isomäki and Liimatainen (2008); Mkude and Wimmer (2015); Van Veenstra and Zuurmond (2009)
European Conference on e-Government	Muhammad (2009); Ojo et al. (2009)
European Conference on Information Systems	Wastell et al. (2001)
Hawaii International Conference on System Sciences	Birkmeier et al. (2013); Chongthammakun and Jackson (2010); De Souza Bermejo and Tonelli (2011); Denford and Schobel (2012); Dulipovici and Robey (2012); Vogt and Hales (2010)
International Conference on Digital Government Research	Estevez et al. (2011)
International Conference on Electrical Engineering and Informatics	Seman and Salim (2013)
International Conference on Financial Theory and Engineering	Maidin and Arshad (2010)
International Conference on Model and Data Engineering	Doumi et al. (2011)
International Enterprise Distributed Object Computing Conference Workshops	Valtonen et al. (2011)
International Technology Management Conference	Tapia (2009)
Pacific Asia Conference on Information Systems	Hsu et al. (2006)
International Conference on Wirtschaftsinformatik	Winkler (2013)

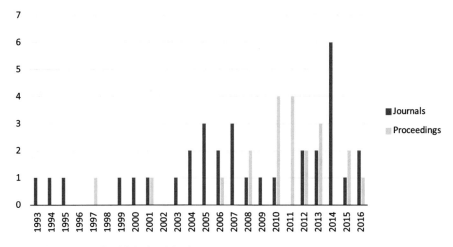

Fig. 2.2 Number of published articles by year

appearing in European Conference on Information Systems in 2001. It took another five years for the next article to be published in a conference proceeding. However, as shown in Table 2.5, conference articles were published every year since then except the years 2007, 2009, and 2014 by reaching a pick in 2010 and 2011 (four studies on each year). As we could see the number of articles published in conference proceedings are higher than the journal articles in the years 2008, 2010, 2011, 2013 and 2015.

2.3.2 What are the Research Goals Addressing IT Alignment in Public Organizational Settings?

Responding to the concerns of practitioners, where it has been identified as one of the top concern for many executives, researchers have extensively studied IT alignment. IT alignment has been described in many ways and scholars attempted to address the different issues that could influence it. However, the relationship between IT alignment and organizational performance was rarely questioned (Chan and Reich 2007). On the other hand, according to Luftman (2000) the main concern for both practitioners and researchers gravitate toward the three frequently asked questions: How can IT alignment be assessed?; (2) How can IT alignment be improved?; (3) How can IT alignment maturity be achieved?

The analysis of the current literature review also indicates that the conceptual as well as the empirical studies have attempted to answer one or combinations of these three questions by focusing on different factors that are related to IT alignment in the context of public organizations. The previous literature reviews indicate, the state-of-the-art of measuring IT alignment was considered to be one of the priorities of researchers leading to plethora of empirical studies (Gerow et al. 2014; Coltman et al. 2015). A presentation of the reviewed articles categorized on research goals is presented in Table 2.6.

As indicated in Table 2.6, the research goals of the articles reviewed indicate that the exploratory studies have been the primary choice of IT alignment researchers. A number of 37 articles were set out to further our understanding of IT alignment in public organizational setting. Moreover, we noticed that 11 studies have the objective of proposing different approaches and best practices to address different issues of IT alignment faced by public organizations. While the development, assessment and suggestion of models and frameworks was the research goal of 9 studies and the remaining 3 studies have proposed different assessment tools. A discussion of the articles reviewed in each research goal and also of the research topics is included below.

Table 2.6 Articles on IT alignment in public organizations categorized according to research goals

Research goals	Articles
Assessment tools	Klievink et al. (2016); Vander Elst, S., and De Rynck, F. (2014); Vogt and Hales (2010)
Best practices/approaches	Bannister (2001); Birkmeier et al. (2013); Broadbent et al. (1994); De Souza Bermejo and Tonelli (2011); Estevez et al. (2011); Sawyer et al. (2008); Simonsen (1999); Tapia (2009); Teo and Ranganthan (2003); Tonelli et al. (2015); Wastell et al. (2001)
Exploratory/understanding	Andrade and Joia (2012); Asprey (2004); Papp (1997); Chongthammakun and Jackson (2010); Christiansson et al. (2015); De Marco and Sorrentino (2007); Denford and Schobel (2012); Doumi et al. (2011); Dulipovici and Robey (2013); Fedorowicz et al. (2009); Flynn and Goleniewska (1993); Gil-García and Pardo (2005); Hasan and Lampitsi (1995); Hsu et al. (2006); Isomäki and Liimatainen (2008); Iveroth et al. (2013); Kim et al. (2007); Koh et al. (2006); Larsson and Grönlund (2014); Lee-Partridge et al. (2000); Luna-Reyes et al. (2007); Maidin and Arshad (2010); Meijer and Thaens (2010); Mergel (2016); Mkude and Wimmer (2015); Mu and Stern (2015); Muhammad (2009); Pang et al. (2014); Rose et al. (2015); Seman and Salim (2013); Silva and Hirschheim (2007); Thorogood et al. (2004); Tonelli et al. (2015); Van Veenstra and Zuurmond (2009); Vargas et al. (2010); Walser et al. (2016); Winkler (2013); Wiredu (2012)
Frameworks/models	Amali et al. (2014); Doumi et al. (2011); Ebrahim and Irani (2005); Irani et al. (2005); Iribarren et al. (2008); Ojo et al. (2009); Valtonen et al. (2011); Vander Elst and De Rynck (2014)

2.3.2.1 Assessment Tools

The literature review has identified three studies presenting different assessment tools that could be used to help organizations make judgements on different variables that are relevant for IT alignment. For instance, one of the studies (Vander Elst and De Rynck 2014) has explored how the political and institutional variables come into play with the alignment process in public organizations. The proposed assessment tools are designed to assess IT alignment in different levels. How organizations could use big data to significantly monitor their activities so that IT alignment is maintained is proposed by the second study (Klievink et al. 2016). In order to make sure public organizations maintain the objective of delivering valuable services and 'public goods' to their citizens, IT alignment needs to be maintained only when it has strategic significance (Vogt and Hales 2010). Community value estimation is meant to make sure public organizations focus on valuable endeavours for their communities (Vogt and Hales 2010).

2.3.2.2 Best Practices/Approaches/Methods

Several methods and approaches related to IT alignment were identified (11 studies). Contrary to the rational top-down approach, Simonsen (1999) presented a strategic alignment approach which is inspired by Scandinavian approach to system design. This approach is consistent with one of the exploratory studies (Fedorowicz et al. 2009). A different approach of IT alignment by integrating the 'unintegrated' information systems in public organizations is also proposed (Bannister 2001). The different methodologies in the studies were all meant to help organizations in their attempt to: identify and configure activities (Birkmeier et al. 2013; Sawyer et al. 2008; Teo and Ranganthan 2003) integrate systems (Bannister 2001), configure organizational structure and IT infrastructure (Broadbent et al. 1994; Wastell et al. 2001), assess readiness (Estevez et al. 2011), plan and implement IT governance (De Souza Bermejo and Tonelli 2011; Teo and Ranganthan 2003; Tonelli et al. 2015) in order to achieve and maintain IT alignment.

2.3.2.3 Exploratory Studies

A closer look into the exploratory studies shows the diversity of research topics. Even though previous findings of literature reviews indicate that the relationship between IT alignment and performance of organizations is rarely challenged, there were few studies which were set out to explore how IT alignment can influence the performance of public organizations. However, performance was studied from different angles. The questions raised address: how the different dimensions of IT alignment rather than IT alignment as a whole can influence organizational performance (Seman and Salim 2013); how antecedents of IT alignment can affect organizational performance; whether IT alignment improves user or employee satisfaction (Walser et al. 2016); whether lack of IT alignment could influence the success of e-government initiatives (Gil-García and Pardo 2005); and if achieving and maintain IT alignment is considered as a success of managing IT and if it contributes in gaining competitive advantage (Lee-Partridge et al. 2000).

Researchers have shown interest in investigating the different factors that could influence IT alignment in public organizations. The common factors studied include: organizational structure (Andrade and Joia 2012; Dulipovici and Robey 2013; Irani et al. 2005; Mergel 2016; Sawyer et al. 2008; Thorogood et al. 2004) and organizational culture (Dulipovici and Robey 2013; Irani et al. 2005). In addition to trying to identify organizational structures that would be conducive towards reaching IT alignment (Broadbent et al. 1994), studies have also attempted to investigate if such organizations that are considered as impediment can hinder organizations from achieving IT alignment (Andrade and Joia 2012).

The relationship between different IT governance practices and IT alignment has also caught the attention of researchers (Hasan and Lampitsi 1995; Maidin and Arshad 2010; Mu and Stern 2015; Tonelli et al. 2015). For instance, several studies have investigated whether IT alignment or strategic alignment planning should be planned, initiated and led by the IT department (Flynn and Goleniewska 1993). On the other hand, the role of IT executives and business leaders to achieve IT alignment has been raised by researchers. How the relationship between IT leaders and other top management team (Denford and Schobel 2012; Luna-Reyes et al. 2007) and how the IT use of executives helps to achieve strategic alignment (Hasan and Lampitsi 1995) were also studied. Furthermore, the values and beliefs of leaders of public organizations and how this affects the way they support, lead and clarify vision that would create shared objective across the aisle which in turn brings about IT alignment was also one of the topics of a study (Rose et al. 2015).

Beyond the internal organizational variables, external environments were also addressed. The different changes in technology and political landscape or even events such as elections and how these could affect IT alignment are also some of the topics of research (Silva and Hirschheim 2007). Studies have also raised the issue of outside providers as well as collaborators and how their needs and objectives affect the existing internal routines and strategic alignment in public organizations (Fedorowicz et al. 2009; Mergel 2016). Authors have also carried out studies with the aim of proposing best practices and approaches that could help in achieving IT alignment in public organizations. The suggested methods, however, differ among studies. For instance, the introduction of the position of Government Chief Information Officer (GCIO) in order to demonstrate the attention given to IT in public organizations is considered to contribute toward the alignment process. The development of assessment model on how organizations can gauge their readiness to embrace this function is among the research goals (Estevez et al. 2011). A programme was also proposed to help in improving the link between IT leaders and administrative executives (Dulipovici and Robey 2013).

Unlike many private organizations, the public organizations do not carry out robust strategic IT planning (Vargas et al. 2010). How public organizations plan to achieve IT alignment in a different way than public organizations (Papp 1997) and the importance of readiness to engage in robust planning and efficient communication (Vargas et al. 2010) are two of the studied topics. Public organizations' IT strategic readiness (Koh et al. 2006); the robustness and effectiveness of enterprise architecture types in achieving IT alignment (Isomäki and Liimatainen 2008; Valtonen et al. 2011; Van Veenstra and Zuurmond 2009); relative importance of components of Unified Strategic Alignment (Vargas et al. 2010) and theory formulation in order to influence IT alignment dimensions (Iveroth et al. 2013; Seman and Salim 2013) are other issues addressed. There were also studies that were set out to challenge the current prominent body of research. For instance, the fact that IT alignment remains to be difficult to achieve in the public healthcare domain (Koh et al. 2006) was pointed out as a sign that new approaches have to be brought into light to further our understanding to the phenomenon. One study (Meijer and Thaens 2010) raises the question on whether different configuration types of public organizations are necessary to reach alignment that is suited to match the specific operational strategies of organizations. Other studies further raised and attempted to investigate if other disciplines could help us to understand IT alignment better. For instance, can disciplines such as public administration together with strategic IT management possess the tools to shade light and lead us to achieving alignment by clarifying public bureaucracy and public value (De Marco and Sorrentino 2007); Pang et al. 2014; Wiredu 2012).

2.3.2.4 Frameworks/Models

Eight of the studies reviewed have attempted to either develop new models or frameworks (Amali et al. 2014; Doumi et al. 2011; Ebrahim and Irani 2005; Irani et al. 2005; Iribarren et al. 2008; Valtonen et al. 2011) or evaluated the already existing frameworks and models to propose new process models (Ojo et al. 2009) that could be applied in public organizations. On the other hand, researchers have also proposed new approaches on how IT alignment is assessed using the existing models (Vander Elst and De Rynck 2014). The evaluation of the Strategic Alignment Maturity (SAM) model of Luftman (2000) and how different approaches could be followed in order to make the model suited to be applied in public organizations is the goal of two studies (Ojo et al. 2009; Vander Elst and De Rynck 2014). Furthermore, enterprise architecture and how it could be used to enhance alignment is also a topic for researchers (Doumi et al. 2011; Ebrahim and Irani 2005; Valtonen et al. 2011). The aim of the studies focusing on frameworks and models could be grouped into two categories: evaluation of different variables influencing IT alignment (Irani et al. 2005; Iribarren et al. 2008), and different dimensions of IT alignment or IT alignment at different levels (Doumi et al. 2011; Vander Elst and De Rynck 2014) and proposing models and frameworks to design, organise, implement and manage resources in such a way that IT alignment is achieved (Amali et al. 2014; Doumi et al. 2011; Ojo et al. 2009; Valtonen et al. 2011).

2.3.3 What Are the Research Concepts Addressing IT Alignment in Public Organizational Settings?

As pointed above, there are several constructs and models proposed to help us further our understanding and help organizations assess, improve, reach and maintain IT alignment (see Coltman et al. 2015 for a list of IT alignment models). For the purpose of this review, Luftman et al. (2015) Strategic Alignment Maturity (SAM) model with its six dimensions (Communication, Value Analytics, IT Governance, Partnering, Dynamic IT Scope, and IT and Business Skills Development) that promotes alignment was used as a IT alignment model to group the research concepts covered in the articles reviewed (Table 2.7).

The SAM model of Luftman et al. (2015) was chosen as it was validated by a survey across 16 different industries thus making it not specific to a particular industry, business function or company. Furthermore, SAM model is considered to

Table 2.7 Research concepts found in the selected articles categorized according on the six dimensions of SAM model of Luftman et al. (2015)

SAM dimensions	Communication			Value Analytics				IT Governance			
Research concepts	Knowledge management	Organizational learning	Shared domain knowledge	Assessment	Perception of value of IT	Public value	Value of IT	Best practices	IS/e-Gov. implementation	Levels of alignment	Managing risk
Articles											
Ebrahim and Irani (2005)											
Koh et al. (2006)	✓							✓			
Gil-Garcia and Pardo (2005)			✓						✓		
Luna-Reyes et al. (2007)			✓								
Kim et al. (2007)	✓							✓	✓		
Sawyer et al. (2008)											
Fedorowicz et al. (2009)											
Meijer and Thaens (2010)											
Andrade and Joia (2012)											
Larsson and Grönlund (2014)											
Mergel (2016)											
Iveroth et al. (2013)		✓		✓	✓		✓				
Vander Elst and De Rynck (2014)		✓								✓	
Tonelli et al. (2015)				✓			✓				
Klievink et al. (2016)				✓				✓			
Bannister (2001)	✓	✓				✓					
Irani et al. (2005)				✓							
Rose et al. (2015)	✓		✓			✓	✓				
Wiredu (2012)						✓					
Thorogood et al. (2004)						✓	✓				

(continued)

Table 2.7 (continued)

SAM dimensions	Communication			Value Analytics				IT Governance			
Research concepts	Knowledge management	Organizational learning	Shared domain knowledge	Assessment	Perception of value of IT	Public value	Value of IT	Best practices	IS/e-Gov. implementation	Levels of alignment	Managing risk
De Marco and Sorrentino (2007)											
Pang et al. (2014)						✓					
Mu and Stern (2015)		✓						✓			
Dulipovici and Robey (2013)	✓										
Flynn and Goleniewska (1993)					✓						
Broadbent et al. (1994)					✓						
Hasan and Lampitsi (1995)					✓						
Lee-Partridge et al. (2000							✓				
Teo and Ranganthan (2003)											
Silva and Hirschheim (2007)											
Asprey (2004)											
Simonsen (1999)											
Amali et al. (2014)											✓
Papp (1997)											
Vargas et al. (2010)								✓			
Walser et al. (2016)								✓			
Isomäki and Liimatainen (2008)											
Iribarren et al. (2008)				✓							
Van Veenstra and Zuurmond (2009)		✓					✓				

(continued)

Table 2.7 (continued)

| SAM dimensions | Communication | | | Value Analytics | | | | IT Governance | | | |
Research concepts	Knowledge management	Organizational learning	Shared domain knowledge	Assessment	Perception of value of IT	Public value	Value of IT	Best practices	IS/e-Gov. implementation	Levels of alignment	Managing risk
Mkude and Wimmer (2015)									✓		
Christiansson et al. (2015)											
Muhammad (2009)			✓								
Ojo et al. (2009)											
Wastell et al. (2001)		✓									
Vogt and Hales (2010)						✓	✓				
Chongthammakun and Jackson (2010)											
De Souza Bermejo and Tonelli (2011)						✓			✓		
Denford and Schobel (2012)											
Dulipovici and Robey (2012)		✓	✓								
Birkmeier et al. (2013)				✓							
Estevez et al. (2011)				✓							
Seman and Salim (2013)										✓	
Maidin and Arshad (2010)								✓			
Doumi (2011)				✓				✓			
Valtonen et al. (2011)								✓		✓	
Tapia (2009)		✓						✓			
Hsu et al. (2006)				✓							
Winkler (2013)							✓				✓

Table 2.7 continued

IT Governance			Partnering			Dynamic IT scope				Business and IT skills Development	
Organizational structure	Public bureaucracy	Vertical/ horizontal alignment	Participatory design method	Stakeholder involvement	Top management involvement	Enterprise architecture	External environment change	Organisation/ tech change	Integrated/ unintegrated IS	Employee satisfaction	Readiness for change
		✓				✓		✓	✓		
			✓		✓						✓
✓				✓				✓	✓		
							✓	✓			
✓				✓							
✓			✓				✓	✓	✓		
✓			✓	✓				✓			
						✓			✓		
✓	✓					✓					
✓	✓		✓	✓				✓			
			✓	✓				✓			
					✓					✓	
✓					✓						
✓	✓				✓				✓		
✓		✓					✓		✓	✓	
✓										✓	

(continued)

Table 2.7 (continued)

IT Governance			Partnering			Dynamic IT scope				Business and IT skills Development	
Organizational structure	Public bureaucracy	Vertical/ horizontal alignment	Participatory design method	Stakeholder involvement	Top management involvement	Enterprise architecture	External environment change	Organisation/ tech change	Integrated/ unintegrated IS	Employee satisfaction	Readiness for change
			✓		✓					✓	
							✓				
	✓										
									✓		
✓		✓									
						✓				✓	
				✓		✓					
				✓							
						✓			✓		
✓				✓							
								✓			
								✓			
								✓			
✓			✓		✓	✓			✓		
									✓		
											✓
✓	✓		✓			✓					
✓			✓								
				✓							
✓			✓			✓					
✓											

be the most utilised IT alignment model both in research literature and among practitioners (Renaud et al. 2016).

Communication has been pointed out to be one of the most important enablers of IT alignment in public organizations (Koh et al. 2006; Tapia 2009). The research topics, in the identified articles, however were mainly presented in the form of knowledge management (Asprey 2004; Dulipovici and Robey 2013), organizational learning, or knowledge not shared and kept in a 'silo' (Bannister 2001). Different frameworks, models and processes proposed to help in achieving IT alignment have also reiterated the significance of communication (Bannister 2001; De Souza Bermejo and Tonelli 2011; Irani et al. 2005; Sawyer et al. 2008). There are 9 studies that have explored the issue of communication in relation to IT alignment.

IT governance which refers to how organizations allocate the decision-making authority in relation to IT (Luftman et al. 2015) and how it is related to IT alignment has attracted the attention of many of the studies reviewed. Studies have investigated on whether there are efficient IT governance frameworks that might lead to IT alignment or attempted to design new IT governance structures (e.g., Amali et al. 2014; Estevez et al. 2011; Hasan and Lampitsi 1995; Maidin and Arshad 2010; Tonelli et al. 2015; Winkler 2013). A total of 22 studies have IT governance as their main topic of research.

The second most studied dimension of IT alignment is *partnering* which refers to relationship between the two sides of organisation—business and IT (Luftman et al. 2015). The relationship between IT executives and the rest of top management team is widely studied (e.g., Broadbent et al. 1994; Denford and Schobel 2012; Hasan and Lampitsi 1995; Luna-Reyes et al. 2007; Mu and Stern 2015; Simonsen 1999) along with how a collaborative approach involving the business and IT staff in planning of shared strategies (e.g., Broadbent et al. 1994; Isomäki and Liimatainen 2008; Muhammad 2009a, b; Simonsen 1999). A total of 20 studies have addressed the issues related to the two IT alignment dimensions.

Both *value analytics* which describes how metrics can be used to measure the contribution of IT in a language that would be understood by the business- and IT organisation, and *dynamic IT* scope referring to the adaptability or flexibility in terms of emerging technologies and provision of tailored solutions (Luftman et al. 2015), have gained attention in the IT alignment research. Since the measurement IT alignment might be challenging due to the intangible nature of services provided by public organizations (Vogt and Hales 2010), new ways of assessing different levels of alignment were proposed (Klievink et al. 2016; Vander Elst and De Rynck 2014; Vogt and Hales 2010). On the other hand, how organizational change should be planned and implemented so that it could be aligned with the changes in technology (e.g., De Marco and Sorrentino 2007; Koh et al. 2006; Van Veenstra and Zuurmond 2009; Walser et al. 2016) and other external environments (De Marco and Sorrentino 2007; Koh et al. 2006; Larsson and Grönlund 2014; Mergel 2016; Vander Elst and De Rynck 2014) were explored as well. While the number of studies addressing the dimension of value analytics was 14, the number of dynamic IT scope stands at 17.

The literature review also reveals that human resource practices which are referred as '**business and IT skills development**' (Luftman et al. 2015) have not caught the attention of the IT alignment researchers so far (7 studies were identified). Even though IT governance studies have touched upon human resource related practices (e.g., Tonelli et al. 2015; De Souza Bermejo and Tonelli 2011), only five studies have focused on addressing the issues (Asprey 2004; Dulipovici and Robey 2013; Silva and Hirschheim 2007; Teo and Ranganthan 2003; Walser et al. 2016). Few studies have also researched organizational readiness for change (Ojo et al. 2009; Estevez et al. 2011).

2.3.4 What Research Design has been used in the Research Studies Concerning IT Alignment in Public Organizations?

In a literature review process, authors might choose to restrict the studies based on specific research design or methodology (Okoli 2015). However, the author also cautions against setting narrow including criteria based on particular research design which might limit the number of articles that could satisfactorily provide an overview of the research in the field being investigated. No restriction was placed on the research design used while searching for articles for this review.

The research design followed by the authors of the articles reviewed are broadly categorized into conceptual and empirical (Table 2.8). The analysis follows the scheme as suggested by Orlikowski and Baroundi (1991) for categorising information systems research literature. The articles under the category of conceptual are those ones which have used literature reviews and previous theoretical frameworks to draw theories, models and frameworks. Hence, the articles categorized under empirical are those ones who have used case study, survey, and mixed methods as is shown in Table 2.8.

From the research studies, we have reviewed and presented in Table 2.8, only 4 are conceptual studies. As indicated in Table 2.8, the analysis of the studies has shown that empirical studies are by far the dominant group of IT alignment studies in the context of public organizations. On the other hand, case studies are the most widely applied research method with 40 of the 54 studies conducted using the research method. This is consistent with most studies in the field of information systems (Oates, 2005). On the other hand, studies on IT alignment investigating public organizations which are known to have complex organizational structure, various stakeholders with competing or even opposing interests (Winkler 2013) call for using case study research method. According to Yin (2014), case studies are appropriate for studying complex concepts involving multiple actors, processes and goals in depth while maintaining the overall characteristics of real-life events. Concerning the other research methods used and shown in Table 2.8 we noticed

Table 2.8 Articles in IT alignment in public organizations categorized according to research design

Research design		Journals	Proceedings	Total	Articles
Conceptual		4	0	4	Ebrahim and Irani (2005); Gil-García and Pardo (2005); Larsson and Grönlund (2014); Pang et al. (2014)
Empirical	Case study	25	15	40	Asprey (2004); Bannister (2001); Chongthammakun and Jackson (2010); Christiansson et al. (2015); De Marco and Sorrentino (2007); De Souza Bermejo and Tonelli (2011); Denford and Schobel (2012); Doumi (2011); Dulipovici and Robey (2012); Dulipovici and Robey (2013); Fedorowicz et al. (2009); Hasan and Lampitsi (1995); Irani et al. (2005); Iribarren et al. (2008); Isomäki and Liimatainen (2008); Iveroth et al. (2013); Kim et al. (2007); Klievink et al. (2016); Koh et al. (2006); Lee-Partridge et al. (2000); Luna-Reyes et al. (2007); Meijer and Thaens (2010); Mu and Stern (2015); Muhammad (2009); Ojo et al. (2009); Rose et al. (2015); Sawyer et al. (2008); Silva and Hirschheim (2007); Simonsen (1999); Tapia (2009); Teo and Ranganthan (2003); Thorogood et al. (2004); Van Veenstra and Zuurmond (2009); Vander Elst and De Rynck (2014); Vogt and Hales (2010); (Walser et al. 2016); Wastell et al. (2001); Wiredu (2012)
	Survey	3	5	8	Broadbent et al. (1994); Flynn and Goleniewska (1993); Hsu et al. (2006); Maidin and Arshad (2010); Papp (1997); Tonelli et al. (2015); Vargas et al. (2010); Winkler (2013)
	Mixed methods	1	5	6	Birkmeier et al. (2013); Estevez et al. (2011); Mergel (2016); Mkude and Wimmer (2015); Seman and Salim (2013); Valtonen et al. (2011)

survey to be the second in the category of empirical research design while a number of six articles have used mixed methods.

2.4 Findings

The summary of the main findings of the reviewed studies on IT alignment in public organizations is presented below.

2.4.1 A Holistic View that Should Focus on Relationship Between Organizational Structure, IT Infrastructure as Well as Overall Organizational Objective is Needed in Order to Achieve IT Alignment in Public Organizations

The complexity of organizational structure in public organizations coupled with the public bureaucracy makes it daunting task for leaders in their attempt to reach strategic alignment. On the other hand, studies have shown that achieving IT alignment will not be problematic if simultaneous adjustments are made to the IT infrastructure, organizational structure as well as business objectives (Thorogood et al. 2004; Wiredu 2012).

2.4.2 Public Administration Studies Need to Inform Researchers and Practitioners on how IT Alignment Should be Approached to Enable Public Value

Findings suggest that sustaining IT alignment for long period of time is more challenging than achieving it in the first place and should be viewed as a continuous process (Vander Elst and De Rynck 2014). However, other disciplines such as public administration studies can inform both IT and business leaders to gain realistic grasp of the relationship between technological as well as organizational changes in public organizations (De Marco and Sorrentino 2007). IT alignment will have little value for organizations and the citizen unless it enables to advance public value (Vogt and Hales 2010) by utilising the available resources and overcoming competing objectives from different stakeholders (Pang et al. 2014).

2.4.3 IT Alignment in Public Organizations is Found to be Correlated with Organizational Performance

The empirical studies investigating organizational performance in different forms have shown that IT alignment is correlated with a positive organizational performance. For instance, among the factors affecting the success of e-Government initiatives, misalignment between business and IT was placed before the competing or opposing goals from different stakeholders (Gil-García and Pardo 2005). IT alignment is also considered to be one of the top four IT management success factors in public organizations (Lee-Partridge et al. 2000). On the other hand, empirical studies have also indicated that IT alignment is associated with employee and IT users' satisfaction (Walser et al. 2016) as well as positive IT governance practices. IT alignment is also found to contribute to the establishment of strategic directions in public organizations (Kim et al. 2007).

2.4.4 Organizational Structure Plays an Important Role on Influencing IT Alignment in Public Organizations

Previous literature reviews have shown that organizational structure plays an important role on influencing IT alignment. The findings of the studies reviewed also indicate that this is also the case in public organizational settings. The topic is among the widely-discussed factors that could influence IT alignment in public organizations (Andrade and Joia 2012; De Souza Bermejo and Tonelli 2011; Irani et al. 2005; Mu and Stern 2015; Muhammad 2009a, b; Tapia 2009; Thorogood et al. 2004; Wiredu 2012). However, studies have also shown that the external environment have an influence on how public organizations are structured. For instance, abrupt change in external events such as elections followed by organizational restructuring may lead to misalignment as it poses a risk of failure in the introduction of planned information system (Silva and Hirschheim 2007).

2.4.5 Public Organizations have Different Choices of Paths Toward IT Alignment

One of the characteristics that make public organizations from others is the large size of stakeholders as well as variety of services they provide to their citizens (Winkler 2013). This requires different public organizations to follow different strategies that may lead to different outcomes. However, studies also indicate that even those organizations which have similar tasks may possess different resources, different organizational structure, as well as different alignment strategy choices (Hsu et al. 2006; Sawyer et al. 2008). On the other hand, organizations may also have different approaches in the way they go about reaching IT alignment. For instance, unlike the common top-down approach where strategic alignment is formulated at the top and cascaded down to the tactical and operational level, IT alignment may be planned using a participatory approach (Simonsen 1999). Such approaches are found to be effective in the public organizational setting (Fedorowicz et al. 2009; Luna-Reyes et al. 2007).

2.4.6 Organizational Culture and Social Interactions Play an Important Role in Shared Understanding of IT Alignment

Findings of studies indicate that lack of shared understanding for IT alignment is associated with organizational culture coupled with obsolescence and IT personnel operating in silos (Mu and Stern 2015). Even though communication between various discipline experts, social interactions is found to be conducive for knowledge sharing and IT alignment, interaction outside the formal organizational structure might lead to different social representations (Asprey 2004; Dulipovici and Robey 2013) which eventually can lead to misalignment (Dulipovici and Robey 2013).

2.4.7 Relationships Between Executive Leaders, Involvement of Executive Leaders and IT Use by Executive Leaders is Influencing IT Alignment

The role of leaders in influencing IT alignment in public organizations is demonstrated through empirical studies. For instance, the perception of the strategic role of the CIO by the CFO and vice versa is affects the relationship the two executives will have. This relationship in turn determines the outcomes of their respective roles in reaching IT alignment (Denford and Schobel 2012). On the other hand, studies show that the involvement of executive leaders facilitates the success of IT alignment in different levels (Asprey 2004). The executive use of IT is also found to contribute on improving the communication between the business and IT departments which in turn helps in IT alignment.

2.5 Conclusions

The conclusions that can be drawn from the findings of the reviewed studies and the potential future research directions are presented below.

This study has presented a systematic literature review on IT alignment in public organizations. The aim of this study was to identify the main findings of the studies related to IT alignment in public organizations in the last 23 years. For this purpose, we have used in our literature review a large number of information systems databases, journals and conference proceedings as well as e-Government journals and conference proceedings to identify the most relevant studies. Following a systematic research review the literature search process was rigorous and has due to identification of the articles that are relevant to provide an overview of the state-of-the-art. The analysis of the findings of the reviewed studies indicates that IT alignment in the public organizations remains to be one of the challenging phenomena for leaders in these organizations. The studies also had shown the growing awareness of leaders on the issue. The *common theme among the studies include the complex organizational structure, the challenges of measuring the value of IT, the IT governance mechanisms, IT infrastructure, public bureaucracy, and enterprise architecture and how these all affects IT alignment in public organizations.* Different enablers and inhibitors of IT alignment and how public organizations could tackle them were also addressed by both empirical and conceptual studies. *Some of these factors such as organizational structure, different enterprise architecture types, IT governance frameworks are studied widely* which has resulted in suggestions of appropriate choices. However, *other factors such as organizational culture, organizational politics, social interaction, and informal organizational structure influence on IT alignment in public organizations have been less studied.* Many studies have acknowledged the effects of the configuration of organizational structures, IT infrastructures and business objectives with the goal of strategic alignment. However, external factors which might have influence on IT alignment have not attracted the attention of many researchers. For instance, public organizations are the users of external information systems of different service providers and collaborators. But as we noticed only a few studies have explored how the objectives, priorities or values of these external providers interfere with the strategic alignment endeavour of public organizations. The effects of political events and unexpected external environment changes on IT alignment could also be studied further.

The role of executive leaders' in IT alignment has garnered also researchers' attention. Different themes standout in the research studies surrounding IT and business leaders. The relationship between IT leaders and the rest of top management team as well as the values and beliefs of IT leaders in affecting IT alignment might be further investigated to reveal deeper insights. A possible further research direction might be how the relationship between political leaders, IT leaders and public organisation's employees is influencing IT alignment. For example, the organizational politics influence on IT alignment could be a relevant topic to be studied in a further research. Concerning the most preferred choice of research method we have found that in most of the studies reviewed this is case study research which is consistent with other studies in the information systems discipline. This has presented some implications on the findings of most of the studies. The models, frameworks and best practices proposed are constructed based on only on one or a few cases which could be problematic in terms of generalisation of the results. Apart from the studies attempting to validate the Strategic Alignment Maturity model in some public organizational settings and the proposed modification of the model, we have found studies that were aimed at solving specific problems for a few public organizations. The study of different IT alignment approaches challenging the traditional top-down strategy planning such as participative approach (if this will be replicated and validated) might bring a new insight concerning IT alignment in public organizations.

References

Amali, L. N., Mahmuddin, M., & Ahmad, M. (2014). Information technology governance framework in the public sector organizations. *TELKOMNIKA (Telecommunication Computing Electronics and Control), 12*(2), 429–436.

Andrade, A., & Joia, L. A. (2012). Organizational structure and ICT strategies in the Brazilian judiciary system. *Government Information Quarterly, 29*(1), 32–42.

Asprey, L. (2004). Information strategies: are we aligning the business case with enterprise planning? *Records Management Journal, 14*(1), 7–13.

Avison, D., Jones, J., Powell, P., & Wilson, D. (2004). Using and validating the strategic alignment model. *The Journal of Strategic Information Systems, 13*(3), 223–246.

Bannister, F. (2001). Dismantling the silos: extracting new value from IT investments in public administration. *Information Systems Journal, 11*(1), 65–84.

Birkmeier, D. Q., Gehlert, A., Overhage, S., & Schlauderer, S. (2013). Alignment of business and IT architectures in the German federal government: A systematic method to identify services from business processes. In: *Proceedings of Hawaii International Conference on System Sciences (HICSS)*, IEEE Computer Society (pp. 3848–3857).

Broadbent, M., Butler, C., & Hansell, A. (1994). Business and technology agenda for information systems executives. *International Journal of Information Management, 14*(6), 411–426.

Caudle, S. L., Gorr, W. L., & Newcome, K. E. (1991). Key information systems management issues for the public sector. *MIS Quarterly, 15*(2), 171–188.

Chan, Y. E., & Reich, B. H. (2007). IT alignment: what have we learned? *Journal of Information Technology, 22*(4), 297–315.

Chongthammakun, R., & Jackson, S. J. (2010). Extending virtual organizations in the public sector: lessons from CSCW, STS, and organization science. In: *Proceedings of Hawaii International Conference on System Sciences (HICSS)*, IEEE Computer Society (pp. 1–10).

Christiansson, M. T., Axelsson, K., & Melin, U. (2015) Inter-organizational public e-service development: Emerging lessons from an inside-out perspective. In: *Proceedings of the IFIP International Conference on Electronic Government (EGOV)* (pp. 183–196).

Coltman, T., Tallon, P., Sharma, R., & Queiroz, M. (2015). Strategic IT alignment: Twenty-five years on. *Journal of Information Technology, 30*(2), 91–100.

De Marco, M., & Sorrentino, M. (2007). Sowing the seeds of IS cultivation in public service organisations. *Journal of Information Technology, 22*(2), 184–194.

De Souza Bermejo, P. H., & Tonelli, A. O. (2011). Planning and implementing IT governance in Brazilian public organizations. In: *Proceedings of Hawaii International Conference on System Sciences (HICSS)*, IEEE Computer Society (pp. 1–10).

Denford, J. S., & Schobel, K. B. (2012). The chief information officer and chief financial officer dyad—how an effective relationship impacts individual effectiveness and strategic alignment. In: *Proceedings of Hawaii International Conference on System Sciences (HICSS)*, IEEE Computer Society (pp. 5072–5081).

Doumi, K., Baïna, S., & Baïna, K. (2011). Modeling approach using goal modeling and enterprise architecture for business IT alignment. In: *Proceedings of the First International Conference on Model and Data Engineering* (MEDI 2011) (pp. 249–261).

Dulipovici, A., & Robey, D. (2012). Strategic alignment and the implementation of a knowledge management system: a social representation perspective. In: *Proceedings of Hawaii International Conference on System Sciences (HICSS)*, IEEE Computer Society (pp. 4062–4071).

Dulipovici, A., & Robey, D. (2013). Strategic alignment and misalignment of knowledge management systems: A social representation perspective. *Journal of Management Information Systems, 29*(4), 103–126.

Ebrahim, Z., & Irani, Z. (2005). E-government adoption: architecture and barriers. *Business Process Management Journal, 11*(5), 589–611.

Estevez, E., Janowski, J., & Ojo, A. (2011). Establishing Government Information Officer systems-readiness assessment. In: *Proceedings of the 12th Annual International Conference on Digital Government Research* (pp. 292–301).

Fedorowicz, J., Gelinas, U. J., Gogan, J. L., & Williams, C. B. (2009). Strategic alignment of participant motivations in e-government collaborations: the internet payment platform pilot. *Government Information Quarterly, 26*(1), 51–59.

Flynn, D. J., & Goleniewska, E. (1993). A survey of the use of strategic information systems planning approaches in UK organizations. *The Journal of Strategic Information Systems, 2*(4), 292–315.

Garicano, L., & Heaton, P. (2010). Information technology, organization, and productivity in the public sector: evidence from police departments. *Journal of Labour Economics, 28*(1), 167–201.

Gerow, J. E., Grover, V., Thatcher, J. B., & Roth, P. L. (2014). Looking toward the future of IT-business strategic alignment through the past: a meta-analysis. *MIS Quarterly, 38*(4), 1059–1085.

Gil-García, J. R., & Pardo, T. A. (2005). E-government success factors: mapping practical tools to theoretical foundations. *Government Information Quarterly, 22*(2), 187–216.

Hasan, H., & Lampitsi, S. (1995). Executive access to information systems in Australian public organizations. *The Journal of Strategic Information Systems, 4*(3), 213–223.

Heintze, T., & Bretschneider, S. (2000). Information technology and restructuring in public organizations: does adoption of information technology affect organizational structures, communications, and decision making? *Journal of Public Administration Research and Theory, 10*(4), 801–830.

Henderson, J., & Venkatraman, N. (1993). Strategic alignment: leveraging information technology for transforming organizations. *IBM Systems Journal, 32*(1), 472–484.

Hsu, F. M., Hu, P. J. H., & Chen, H. (2006). Examining the business-technology alignment in government agencies: A study of electronic record management systems in Taiwan. In: *Proceedings of Pacific Asia Conference on Information Systems (PACIS)*, Paper 98.

Irani, Z., Love, P. E., Elliman, T., Jones, S., & Semistocleous, M. (2005). Evaluating e-government: learning from the experiences of two UK local authorities. *Information Systems Journal, 15*(1), 61–82.

Iribarren, M., Concha, G., Valdes, G., Solar, M., Villarroel, M. T., Gutiérrez, P., & Vásquez, Á. (2008). Capability maturity framework for e-Government: A MULTI-dimensional model and assessing tool. In: *Proceedings of the International Conference on Electronic Government (EGOV)* (pp. 136–147).

Isomäki, H., & Liimatainen, K. (2008). Challenges of government enterprise architecture work–stakeholders' views. In: *Proceedings of the International Conference on Electronic Government (EGOV)* (pp. 364–374).

Iveroth, E., Fryk, P., & Rapp, B. (2013). Information technology strategy and alignment issues in health care organizations. *Health Care Management Review, 38*(3), 188–200.

Kappelman, L., Johnson, V., McLean, E., & Torres, R. (2016). The 2015 SIM IT issues and trends study. *MIS Quarterly Executive, 15*(1), 55–83.

Kim, H. J., Pan, G., & Pan, S. L. (2007). Managing IT-enabled transformation in the public sector: A case study on e-government in South Korea. *Government Information Quarterly, 24*(2), 338–352.

Kitchenham, B., Brereton, O. P., Budgen, D., Turner, M., Bailey, J., & Linkman, S. (2009). Systematic literature reviews in software engineering—a systematic literature review. *Information and Software Technology, 51*(1), 7–15.

Klievink, B., Romijn, B. J., Cunningham, S., & de Bruijn, H. (2016). Big data in the public sector: uncertainties and readiness. *Information Systems Frontiers*, 1–17. doi:10.1007/s10796-016-9686-2.

Koh, C. E., Prybutok, V. R., Ryan, S., & Ibragimova, B. (2006). The importance of strategic readiness in an emerging e-government environment. *Business Process Management Journal, 12*(1), 22–33.

Larsson, H., & Grönlund, Å. (2014). Future-oriented eGovernance: The sustainability concept in eGov research and ways forward. *Government Information Quarterly, 31*(1), 137–149.

Lee-Partridge, J. E., Teo, T. S., & Lim, V. K. (2000). Information technology management: The case of the Port of Singapore Authority. *The Journal of Strategic Information Systems, 9*(1), 85–99.

Leonard, J., & Seddon, P. (2012). A Meta-model of Alignment. *Communications of the Association for Information Systems, 31*(1), 231–259.

Luftman, J. (2000). Aligning business-IT alignment maturity. *Communications of Association for Information Systems, 4*(14), 1–50.

Luftman, J., Lyytinen, K., & Zvi, T. (2015). Enhancing the measurement of information technology (IT) business alignment and its influence on company performance. *Journal of Information Technology*. doi:10.1057/jit.2015.23.

Luftman, J., Sledgianowski, D., & Reilly, R. (2004). Identification of IT-business strategic alignment maturity factors: an exploratory study. In *AMCIS 2004 Proceedings* (Vol. 470, pp. 3717–3725).

Luna-Reyes, L. F., Gil-Garcia, J. R., & Cruz, C. B. (2007). Collaborative digital government in Mexico: some lessons from federal Web-based interorganizational information integration initiatives. *Government Information Quarterly, 24*(4), 808–826.

McKeen, J. D., & Smith, H. (2003). *Making IT happen: critical issues in IT management.* Chichester, Hoboken, NJ: Wiley.

Maidin, S. S., Arshad, N. H. (2010). Information technology governance practices in Malaysian public sector. In *Proceedings of the Financial Theory and Engineering (ICFTE)* (pp. 281–285).

Meijer, A., & Thaens, M. (2010). Alignment 2.0: Strategic use of new internet technologies in government. *Government Information Quarterly, 27*(2), 113–121.

Mergel, I. (2016). Social media institutionalization in the US federal government. *Government Information Quarterly, 33*(1), 142–148.

Mkude, C. G., & Wimmer, M. A. (2015). E-government systems design and implementation in developed and developing countries: results from a qualitative analysis. In *Proceedings of the IFIP International Conference on Electronic Government (EGOV)* (pp. 44–58).

Mu, E., & Stern, H. A. (2015). The City of Pittsburgh goes to the cloud: a case study of cloud solution strategic selection and deployment. *Journal of Information Technology Teaching Cases, 4*(2), 70–85.

Muhammad, M. R. (2009a). Antecedents of IT alignment in public sector: Case of E-Syariah implementation in Malaysia. In *Proceedings of the UK Academy for Information Systems Conference* (Vol. 36, pp. 1–11).

Muhammad, M. R. (2009b). IT alignment in Malaysian public sector: e-Syariah as a case of study. In *Proceedings of the 9th European Conference on eGovernment* (pp. 501–509).

Oates, B. J. (2005). *Researching information systems and computing.* Thousand Oaks, California: Sage Publications.

Ojo, A., Janowski, T., & Shareef, M. (2009). Aligning electronic government and public administration reform programs-process, tool and case study. In: *Proceedings of the 9th European Conference on eGovernment* (pp. 510–521).

Okoli, C. (2015). A guide to conducting a standalone systematic literature review. *Communications of the Association for Information Systems, 37*(1), 879–910.

Okoli, C., & Schabram, K. (2010). A guide to conducting a systematic literature review of information systems research. *Sprouts: Working Papers on Information Systems, 10*(26):1–49.

Orlikowski, W. J., & Baroudi, J. J. (1991). Studying information technology in organizations: research approaches and assumptions. *Information Systems Research, 2*(1), 1–28.

Pang, M. S., Lee, G., & DeLone, W. H. (2014). IT resources, organizational capabilities, and value creation in public-sector organizations: a public-value management perspective. *Journal of Information Technology, 29*(3), 187–205.

Papp, R. (1997). Strategic alignment: Firm/Industry assessment. In: *Proceedings of 22nd Americas Conference on Information Systems (AMCIS 2016)*, Paper 242.

Renaud, A., Walsh, I., & Kalika, M. (2016). Is SAM still alive? A bibliometric and interpretive mapping of the strategic alignment research field. *The Journal of Strategic Information Systems, 25*(2), 75–103.

Rose, J., Persson, J. S., Heeager, L. T., & Irani, Z. (2015). Managing e-Government: value positions and relationships. *Information Systems Journal, 25*(5), 531–571.

Sawyer, S., Hinnant, C. C., & Rizzuto, T. (2008). Pennsylvania's transition to enterprise computing as a study in strategic alignment. *Government Information Quarterly, 25*(4), 645–668.

Seman, E. A. A., & Salim, J. (2013). A model for business-IT alignment in Malaysian public universities. *Procedia Technology, 11,* 1135–1141.

Silva, L., & Hirschheim, R. (2007). Fighting against windmills: Strategic information systems and organizational deep structures. *MIS Quarterly, 31*(2), 327–354.

Simonsen, J. (1999). How do we take care of strategic alignment? *Scandinavian Journal of Information Systems, 11*(1), 1–20.

Sposito, M., Neto, A., & Barreto, R. (2016). Business-IT alignment research field: a systematic literature review. In: *Proceedings of the 18th International Conference on Enterprise Information Systems* (pp. 549–558) doi:10.5220/0005832005490558.

Tapia, R. S. (2009). Converging on business-IT alignment best practices: Lessons learned from a Dutch cross-governmental partnership. In: *Proceedings of the International Technology Management Conference* (ICE) (pp. 1–9).

Teo, T. S., & Ranganathan, C. (2003). Leveraging IT resources and capabilities at the housing and development board. *The Journal of Strategic Information Systems, 12*(3), 229–249.

Thorogood, A., Yetton, P., Vlasic, A., & Spiller, J. (2004). Raise your glasses–the water's magic! Strategic IT at SA water: a case study in alignment, outsourcing and governance. *Journal of Information Technology, 19*(2), 130–139.

Tonelli, A. O., Bermejo, P. H. S., dos Santos, P. A., Zuppo, L., Zambalde, A. L. (2015). IT governance in the public sector: a conceptual model. *Information Systems Frontiers* (pp. 1–18). doi:10.1007/s10796-015-9614-x.

Valtonen, K., Mäntynen, S., Leppänen, M., & Pulkkinen, M. (2011). Enterprise architecture descriptions for enhancing local government transformation and coherency management: case study. In: *Proceedings of the IEEE 15th International Enterprise Distributed Object Computing Conference Workshops* (pp. 360–369).

Van Veenstra, A. F., & Zuurmond, A. (2009). Opening the black box: Exploring the effect of transformation on online service delivery in local governments. In *Proceedings of the International Conference on Electronic Government (EGOV)* (pp. 234–244).

Vander Elst, S., & De Rynck, F. (2014). Alignment processes in public organizations: an interpretive approach. *Information Polity, 19*(3, 4):195–206.

Vargas, N., Johannesson, P., & Rusu, L. (2010). A unified strategic business and IT alignment model: A study in the public universities of Nicaragua. In: *Proceedings of 22nd Americas Conference on Information Systems (AMCIS 2016)*, Paper 212.

Vogt, M., & Hales, K. (2010). Strategic alignment of ICT projects with community values in local government. In: *Proceedings of Hawaii International Conference on System Sciences (HICSS)*, IEEE Computer Society (pp. 1–10).

Walser, K., Weibel, D., Wissmath, B., Enkerli, S., Bigler, N., & Topfel, M. (2016). Business-IT alignment in Municipalities—The Swiss Case. In: *Proceedings of 22nd Americas Conference on Information Systems (AMCIS 2016)* (pp. 1–10).

Wastell, D., Kawalek, P., & Willetts, M. (2001). Designing alignment and improvising change: experiences in the public sector using the SPRINT methodology. In: *Proceedings of European Conference on Information Systems (ECIS)*, Paper 106.

Webster, J., & Watson, R. T. (2002). Analysing the past to prepare for the future: writing a literature review. *MIS Quarterly, 26*(2): xiii–xxiii.

Winkler, T. J. (2013). IT governance mechanisms and administration/IT alignment in the public sector: A conceptual model and case validation. In: *Proceedings of International Conference on Wirtschaftsinformatik* (pp. 831–845).

Wiredu, G. O. (2012). Information systems innovation in public organisations: An institutional perspective. *Information Technology and People, 25*(2), 188–206.

Yin, R. (2014). *Case study research: design and methods* (5th ed.). Thousand Oaks, California: Sage Publications.

Author Biographies

Lazar Rusu Ph.D., is Professor at Department of Computer and Systems Sciences, Stockholm University, Sweden. He is involved in teaching and research in IT management and has a professional experience of over 30 years both industrial and academic in information systems area. His research interest is mainly in IT governance, business-IT alignment and IT outsourcing. The results of his research have been published in proceedings of top international conferences like ECIS, HICSS, AMCIS, PACIS, ISD and journals like Computers in Human Behavior, Industrial Management & Data Systems, Information Systems Management, Journal of Global Information Technology Management, Journal of Information Technology Theory and Applications, among others. He is associate editor of International Journal of IT/Business Alignment and Governance.

Gideon Mekonnen Jonathan is a Ph.D. candidate at Kozminski University in Warsaw, Poland. He earned the degree of Master of Business Administration (MBA) as well as M.Sc. in Computer and Systems Sciences from Stockholm University, Sweden. His research interest includes business-IT alignment in public organizations, business intelligence and decision support systems.

Chapter 3
A Perspective on the Roles of Middle Managers in Aligning Strategy and Information Technology in Public Service Organizations

Eamonn Caffrey and Joe McDonagh

Abstract The paper presents theoretical findings in relation to the roles of middle managers in strategic alignment situated in public service organizations based on a study of the Irish public healthcare system. Middle manager roles in strategic alignment is an area of under-represented interest and the paper aims to make a contribution to bridge that gap by offering a perspective based on gaining insight into the strategy process as it relates to information technology (IT) management and strategy-making. A process-oriented study traced a longitudinal case-series of five episodes of IT strategy-making which formed the basis for data collection and analysis. The study revealed six distinct roles as being relevant to middle managers in aligning strategy and IT. The findings are discussed as they relate to IT middle manager roles in strategic alignment, and middle manager strategic agency in public service.

3.1 Introduction

The alignment of strategy and IT, commonly referred to as strategic alignment, has persisted as a key issue for the field of IT management for some thirty-five years now. It was reported to be the top European key issue for IT management in 2013 (Derksen and Luftman 2014). Strategic alignment has proven to be a "*long-standing pervasive conundrum*" (Luftman and Ben-Zvi 2010: 265) for IT managers and business leaders alike. A review of the scholarly literature on strategic alignment revealed that there was an under representation for the role of middle managers, particularly in relation to the process that deals with aligning strategy and IT. Even though the IT management literature on strategic alignment advocates

E. Caffrey (✉) · J. McDonagh
Trinity College Dublin, Dublin, Ireland
e-mail: ecaffrey@tcd.ie

J. McDonagh
e-mail: jmcdongh@tcd.ie

© Springer International Publishing AG 2017
L. Rusu and G. Viscusi (eds.), *Information Technology Governance in Public Organizations*, Integrated Series in Information Systems 38,
DOI 10.1007/978-3-319-58978-7_3

strongly that managers have an important role to play, the emphasis is mostly on senior managers. In terms of the role of middle managers, there was a distinct gap to fill. Furthermore, the public service context was lacking in terms of past scholarly interest into this complex IT management domain. Therefore, the study turned to the broader strategy-making literature as it relates to the roles of middle managers in strategizing for insightful advice on what middle managers actually do.

By way of building on and extending extant literature, this paper offers the fruits of a longitudinal case study that focused on the process of aligning strategy and IT across multiple strategy initiatives. The study was situated in the Irish public healthcare system, a system made up of many public service organizations. Process analysis led to findings that describe the roles of IT middle managers in strategic alignment. The dominant activities for each role are described. A high level discussion then follows that considers the findings in terms of middle manager roles in strategic alignment, and middle manager strategic agency in public service. Finally, the contribution made by this paper is discussed, followed by concluding comments.

3.2 Literature Review

3.2.1 Definition of Middle Manager

Traditionally, middle managers have been described as a level of management in an organization responsible for the detailed running of business affairs (Willcocks and Griffiths 2010). From a scholarly perspective, middle managers hold positions situated somewhere between the strategic apex and the operating core of an organization (Mintzberg 1989). Focus is further sharpened by defining who not to include insofar as middle management rules out top-level executives, first-line management and junior supervisors (Dutton and Ashford 1993). Further expansion on middle managements' position within the organizational hierarchy shows that consideration could be given to include any manager situated two levels or more below the CEO and above line managers (Huy 2001). Middle managers hold positions below corporate vice presidents or major division and department heads. "*In government, this would include those below assistant secretaries or major bureau heads, such as managers in GS13—15 positions in the* [U.S.] *federal government*" (Rainey 2009: 177). Moreover, Mintzberg (2009) regards those reporting to a manager(s) and have other managers reporting to them as middle managers. In consideration of the above, the operational definition of middle manager that applied to this study was defined as "*any manager two levels or more below the CEO, above the level of junior manager, reports to manager(s) and has other manager(s) reporting to them.*"

3.2.2 An Evolving Role

One of the earliest associations between the research literature and middle manager involvement in strategy-making was made by Bower (1970). Up until this point, the conceptual belief was that senior managers were wholly responsible for decision-making on matters of strategic interest and that middle managers pursued a course of action aligned to senior management decisions and can be described as a top-down analytical process (Andrews 1971; Ansoff 1965; Chandler 1962; Child 1972; Hambrick and Mason 1984; Porter 1980). This model of strategy-making is known as the 'choice perspective' with its intellectual roots embedded in economics and organizational theory. The role of middle manager under the choice perspective is limited to providing some level of input to the formulation of strategy but, for the most part, the primary role is concerned with strategy execution (Floyd and Wooldridge 2000).

Middle managers are considered to be key actors in the generation, mobilization and application of organizational resources (Burgelman 1983a). Kanter stated that *"middle managers have their fingers on the pulse of operation, they can also conceive, suggest and set in motion new ideas that* [senior] *managers may not have thought of"* (1982: 96). This concept of strategy-making is seen as a 'social learning' process with middle managers mediating between organizational boundaries in response to a continuously changing environment (Wooldridge et al. 2008).

3.2.3 Middle Managers and Strategic Level

The middle managers' role in strategy-making is predominantly located at the functional- or business-level. Middle managers *"make resource-allocation decisions that are central and strategic, though they do so at a lower level with much less visibility"* (Osterman 2008: 71). The role in strategy-making is largely attributable to functional expertise given their strong sense of the problems and issues. Middle managers have a role in the early stages of the strategy-making process that warrants distinct inputs based-on demonstrable functional expertise and sound industry knowledge (Thakur 1998). Middle managers respect the senior management agenda, while senior managers bow to the competency and knowledge of middle managers that assume responsibility for making it happen (Mantere 2008). In terms of strategy-making in public organizations, middle managers *"interpret and represent their work unit's interest; lend or secure assistance; develop organizational relationships; and leverage other's time"* (Morgan et al. 1996: 360). Subsequently, role expectations have been enlarged linked to educational development, management experience and specialist competencies (Harding 2003).

3.2.4   Role Types

Past empirical studies have revealed a range of role configurations for middle managers in strategy-making. These include: championing alternatives; synthesizing information; facilitating adaptability; and implementing deliberate strategy (Floyd and Wooldridge 1992). Middle managers were described by Huy (2001) as radical change agents by practicing the roles of: entrepreneur; communicator; therapist; and tightrope artist. A set of strategic role types were identified by Thompson et al. (2008) that include: follower; champion; collaborator; listener; and director.

By synthesizing insights from the empirically-derived strategic roles mentioned, it was possible to distil a set of tentative roles that captured what middle managers do in relation to strategizing. "*A successful literature review constructively informs the reader about what has been learned*" (Webster and Watson 2002: xviii). The tentative roles are general categories derived to present the core activities practiced by middle managers and these comprised of: co-creator; intrapreneur; champion; collaborator; change-agent; and implementer.

Each category can be described as mutually exclusive. The *co-creator* is concerned with involvement and participation at the middle and senior management levels to generate relevant strategy content. The *intrapreneur* fulfils the role by way of generating new ideas that can alter the way things get done. The *champion* is focused on selling issues and influencing strategic direction, along with promoting and gaining support for particular initiatives. The *collaborator* aims to rally support throughout the organization for strategizing activity, to learn about issues and to promote ideas. The *change-agent* is focused on providing support and guidance to facilitate some level of business transformation. The *implementer* is largely concerned with the execution of strategic plans by way of aligning organizational action with the planned direction. For the purpose of the literature review, the categories helped to shed light on middle manager roles in strategizing and each is described more fully next.

3.2.4.1   Co-creator

Strategy-making is a powerful tool in the hands of middle and senior management. Strategy-making is a process of co-creation between middle and senior management towards building relevance and commitment. The change in strategic approach from the time when middle managers' only contribution to strategy-making was to appease 'wishful thinking' on the part of the executive board, to that of a new direction involving the extensive participation of middle managers, leading to a "*sense of ownership, commitment and professional business culture among the firm's managers*" (Vila and Canales 2008: 278). From a senior management perspective, strategy-making is only relevant when it is co-created with the active and committed participation of middle managers. Co-creation is based on the exchange and sharing of knowledge, building consensus around core priorities, forming agreements to act, remaining mindful of changing conditions and maintaining flexibility throughout.

3.2.4.2   Intrapreneur

In an organizational context where middle managers are encouraged to support and develop diverse entrepreneurial activities, middle managers thereby assume responsibility for setting the strategic context. Burgelman (1983b) argued that the role of senior management in strategy-making is that of strategic recognition by ensuring strategic activities are aligned with the organizational vision. This perspective parallels with Andy Grove's sense of middle manager as the purveyor of 'strategic dissonance' (Grove 2015). The role of middle manager is to support the development of strategic activities by "*combining these with various capabilities dispersed in the firm's operating system, and by conceptualizing strategies for new areas of business*" (Burgelman 1983c: 1349). Burgelman posited that strategic choices about the organizational approach to corporate intrapreneurship should be governed by a process of "*experimentation and selection*" (1983c: 1360). The organization's capacity to undertake such a process is determined by the availability of middle managers who can conceptualize strategies for new business areas based on the results emerging from the autonomous strategic activities at the functional-level. Middle manager strategic agency is strengthened when senior management show legitimacy for middle management efforts to experiment and develop autonomous business practices (Mantere 2008). Middle managers focus on challenging all known product design paradigms, thus middle managers practice a critical role in the "*process of abandoning the old and generating the new*" (Nonaka 1988: 12). Middle managers' influence on strategy by way of intrapreneurship is considered in two parts. *First*, selectively align organizational capabilities with the external environment. *Second*, such alignment requires middle managers to be exposed to the demands of the external constituents, and thereby in a position to recognize opportunities for the organization to seize aligned with the strategic direction (Floyd and Wooldridge 1997). Middle managers' close proximity to frontline business provides a strong sense of the problems and issues facing the organization. This enables them to see new opportunities for solving problems and encouraging growth (Huy 2001).

3.2.4.3   Champion

Championing occurs when middle managers attempt to influence the decisions of senior managers. Middle "*managers champion the needs of their unit, lobby for its causes, promote its products, advocate on behalf of its values—and just plain peddle influence for it*" (Mintzberg 2009: 78). Middle managers act as the communication link for providing information to senior management along with transforming their views on strategic vision. Only middle managers have a complete sense of the daily business and work realities while simultaneously maintaining a strong grasp of the big picture. Bourgeois and Brodwin (1984) argued for an approach to strategy-making that would encourage middle managers to come forward as champions of new strategies. "*If he* [CEO] *is to exploit the fact that they* [middle managers] *can see strategic opportunities which he cannot, he must allow them discretion in the commitment of resources*" (Bourgeois and Brodwin 1984: 257). The next best strategy championed by someone capable and determined (middle manager) might well supersede an optimum strategy supported with only lukewarm feeling. The role involves the recommendation of strategic options to senior management (Floyd and Wooldridge 1992). Middle managers collect and present information to key stakeholders and based-on expertise communicate strategic options. Middle managers can provide a wide range of alternatives (Mantere 2008). There is continuous discourse between vision and reality and middle managers develop business concepts and sound working practices that were proven to distinguish between naïve romanticism and hard realism (Nonaka 1988). Involving middle managers in strategy-making serves to improve the quality of decisions; initiate and assess alternative courses of action; and challenge strategic decisions made by senior management.

3.2.4.4   Collaborator

Collaboration is described as the intent to seek understanding and influence actions among peers. The ability of middle managers to collaborate in order to "*build relationships, identify problems and shared interests, and provide each other with support and resources is vital to organizational success*" (Thompson et al. 2008: 66/7). Middle managers can bring peers on board because they usually have the best social networks (Huy 2001). Middle managers collaborate with employees to gain a better understanding of issues and ideas. Middle managers are the 'linking pin' between organizational levels in the form of generating feedback, ideas, suggestions and even dissent (Baldoni 2005). Effectively, middle managers are the '*linking pin*' in orchestrating strategy-making efforts.

3.2.4.5   Change-Agent

Middle management behavior can contribute to greater organizational flexibility in the form of less formality, encouraging new approaches or reacting differently to changing situational circumstances, even sometimes in an unofficial capacity and unbeknownst to senior management. Crafting flexible organizational arrangements to bring about some level of business transformation is the role of 'change-agent' (Floyd and Wooldridge 1992). The role revolves around four inter-related sets of activities involving: personal change; helping others through change; implementing necessary organizational changes; and maintaining business as usual (Balogun 2003).

Middle managers shoulder substantial responsibilities during periods of major change (Huy 2001). Middle managers manage the chaotic nature of change to keep individuals and groups focused and motivated and to continue performing well throughout.

3.2.4.6 Implementer

Senior management visionary content and translated strategic aims are often met with middle management approval however; middle managers are usually concerned with how to translate intention into tangible deliverables. The role is concerned with implementing senior management plans by aligning organizational action with strategic aims and to deliver against expectations (Floyd and Wooldridge 1992). The degree of middle manager involvement in deliberate strategy implementation is significantly higher than any other aspect of the strategy-making process. Without the support and assistance of middle managers, translation of strategy into realistic achievements is most unlikely to happen. This is something senior managers regard as a persistent problem (Thakur 1998). Senior managers view strategy-making as a process of identification, formulation, implementation and evaluation, and middle managers are considered by many to be exclusively responsible for implementation. Middle managers are described as problem solvers insofar as they figure out how to make things happen (Huy 2001). Middle managers motivate and inspire the troops, guiding employee participation and commitment toward the execution of strategy. Organizational capabilities are aligned with strategic aims under the direction and influence of middle managers.

3.2.5 Public Service Perspective

In the context of strategy-making in public service, middle managers have an extended role to enact with potential policy-making implications insofar as there is good potential to create public value. Nevertheless, the public service management literature has not fully added its support for an enlarged strategic role (Currie 2000). Public service organizations place strong emphasis on agenda-setting and introducing strategy initiatives from the top-down rather than by placing any kind of special emphasis on middle management participation (McGurk 2009). Individualized leadership is the norm for many public service organizations (Lawler 2008). However, when given a supportive context, middle managers can transition to make a greater strategic contribution (Currie and Procter 2005). Under the new public management model that aims to improve efficiency, curtail expenditure, and reduce bureaucracy and dependency on expert power (Farrel and Morris 2003), some organizations have looked to the private sector for insight into potentially helpful business practices (Haveri 2006). Private sector practice illustrates features such as innovation, creativity, and competency. In corporate environments, middle managers are known to demonstrate a spirit of entrepreneurship, be highly driven, motivated and responsible (Exworthy and Halford 1999).

Under the public management model, the ideal manager is one who visions, leads via ideas and sets example, and strives toward adding strategic value (Viitanen and Konu 2009). Arguably, the traditional control-approach no longer prevails and has been replaced by an approach that is both human- and client-centered (Clarke and Newman 2000). By becoming more assertive, middle managers can make a greater contribution to the strategic agenda in public organizations (Bergin 2009).

To summarize, the central focus of this study was to explore the roles of IT middle managers in strategic alignment in public service; an enduring critical management issue for many organizations. The literature review described the diverse roles of middle managers in strategy-making. This was important later on in the study when comparing the findings and searching for empirically derived parallels.

3.3   Methodology

By way of an exploratory study focused on the roles of middle managers in aligning strategy and IT, the research methodology adopted the process method to trace and inquire into five episodes of IT strategy-making in the Irish public healthcare system.

This required an approach that facilitated the collection of data within its natural setting where "*participants experience the issue or problem under study*" (Creswell 2007: 37). By adopting from the interpretative paradigm, this helped to reveal the complex middle manager actions to provide an account of what was seen and heard based on participant experience of past episodes of IT strategy-making. By exploring the social and historical context, understanding about how the present situation came about was shared (Klein and Meyers 1999).

3.3.1   Process Research Method

The research method embedded a process-orientation in order to "*describe life as it unfolds in its natural setting with intimate first-hand observations from a particular subject's frame of reference*" (Van de Ven and Poole 2002: 869). The interpretive paradigm connected the researcher with a range of traditional IT management research methods. The study adopted a case-based process-oriented design well suited to studying the strategy construct (Caffrey and McDonagh 2015). Key features of the research methodology endorsed a commitment to: spend extensive time in the field; engage in complex, time-consuming data analysis; write long passages of narrative to substantiate claims; and participate in social science research that does not have firm guidelines but is constantly evolving (Creswell 2007). Application guidelines are recommended by Pettigrew (1990, 1992, 1997) when using the process method. The guidelines are based on past research concerned with inquiry into strategy and organizational practice (Pettigrew 1985; Pettigrew and McNulty 1995; Pettigrew and Whipp 1991, Pettigrew et al. 1992). The method distinguishes between process method inputs and outputs (Pettigrew 1997). On the input side, choices need to be made about practical issues concerning the following areas: ethics and contracting; purpose; themes; research questions; time; and data source types. Ethics and contracting are especially important to process method studies because of the close links between researcher and the host case organization. Consideration requirements include issues such as respect for all persons and points of view; gaining organizational access and publication of findings; negotiation and agreement about matters of confidentiality, and anonymity. The need for foresight about research purpose, themes, and core questions anchor the study in extant scholarly literature. The method entails the constant iteration of deductive and inductive reasoning to logically structure, organize and present the recognizable patterns that emerge through the creative cycle of analysis. A series of steps are recommended when conducting research using the process method and these are presented in Fig. 3.1.

The "*bounded system*" (Simons 2009: 29) chosen for the case was the Irish public healthcare system. The 'system' comprised of many public service organizations and government departments. Some members of the "*bounded system*" at the time of the field research included: Department of Health; Department of Finance; Health Service Executive; Health and Information Quality Authority; Central Statistics Office; and the Institute of Public Health. The system embodied a complex multi-organizational environment where structures, management arrangements and accountabilities frequently changed over time.

During the timeline of 1999–2010 when the strategy episodes unfolded (and continue to do so today), frequent structural changes to the system took place. The five strategy episodes of significance included: (i) Dublin Academic Teaching Hospitals (DATHs) ICT Convergence Strategy (2003); Health Boards Executive (HeBE) ICT Strategy (2004); National Health Information Strategy (NHIS) (2004); Primary, Community, and Continuing Care (PCCC) ICT Strategy and Action Plan (2005); and Health Service Executive (HSE) ICT Strategy (2008). A single case design was chosen to support the theory building nature of the research (Benbasat et al. 1987). The overall design was that of a single case but it was highly plausible for this to contain multiple sub-elements (Simons 2009). Each sub-element explored a particularity of the issue of interest, namely, an episode of IT strategy-making and each episode was written up as part of the overall singular case structure.

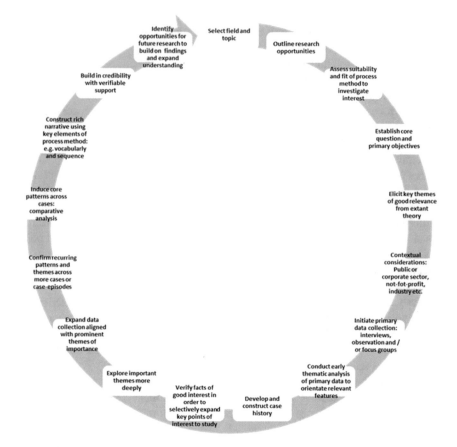

Fig. 3.1 Process method in action

3.3.2 Data Collection

The approach to data collection was aligned with the interpretive belief that to fully understand the worldly settings within which IT middle managers are engaged then it is necessary to gather and analyze data based on their point of view and experience. A semi-structured open-ended style to interviewing was adopted. Additional input sources included a wide range of secondary data that referred specifically to the episodes of IT strategy-making. A single case design was chosen to support the theory building nature of the research (Benbasat et al. 1987). Each episode of IT strategy-making constituted a 'sub-element' (Simons 2009) within the singular case structure. The research embellished a process-orientation that traced the sequence of events by way of exploring the actions and interactions as told by the research informants in relation to each episode of IT strategy-making. The informants were largely made up of IT, clinical and business managers and advisors at the middle

Table 3.1 Interview participants

Management group	Episodes of IT strategy-making					
	DATHs	HeBE	NHIS	PCCC	HSE	Total
Management consultant (Strategy and IT)		1	1		1	3
Middle manager (Business)			1		3	4
Middle manager (Clinical)			1		1	2
Middle manager (IT)	2	2	2	2	5	13
Senior manager (Business)		1				1
Senior advisor (IT)				1	1	2
Senior manager (IT)	1				1	2
Total	3	4	5	3	12	27

and senior management level. All informants held first-hand insights into at least one of the five IT strategy-making episodes. Primary data was sourced through a series of 27 interviews; see Table 3.1 for a profile of participants.

The aim was to collect relevant processual data pertinent to the episodes of IT strategy-making, which "*consist*[ed] *largely of stories about what happened and who did what when—that is events, activities, and choices ordered over time*" (Langley 1999: 692). The in-depth nature of inquiry provided insight into what was on the participants' mind based on the lived experience of past strategizing events. This provided an opportunity to listen, engage and probe the interviewee on particular themes of interest and to explore issues more deeply. Interviews facilitated the collection of longitudinal data that would not otherwise have been revealed in an observatory manner. Acclimatizing the participant through various subtleties (e.g. icebreakers) helped to put the interviewee at ease and to talk openly about their participative experience of strategizing events.

3.3.3   Data Analysis

Data analysis was undertaken at the individual (i.e. sub-element) level, followed by sub-element comparison to identify patterns among case elements. Narrative analysis was chosen to make sense of the process data given its particular suitability to the research aim. A rich narrative (Van de Ven and Poole 2002) required the "*construction of a detailed story from raw data*" (Langley 1999: 695). This began by writing up the case history in chronological form for each episode of IT strategy-making (Pettigrew 1997). The approach aided the discovery of meta-level themes, preliminary patterns and dominant analytical themes (Pettigrew 1997). Coding involved the segmentation of data into units and "*rearranging them into categories that facilitate insight, comparison, and the development of theory*" (Kaplan and Maxwell 2005: 42). The exploratory quest sought out holistic patterns for the roles of IT middle managers within the longitudinal case-series (Pettigrew 1997).

The narrative report was organized into two sections. *First*, a high-level overview provided an historical account covering three important areas: (i) Irish Public Healthcare System; (ii) Policy Statements on the Role of IT; and (iii) Evolutional Perspective on IT development. Providing an historical account as part of the narrative was considered important because it helped to provide descriptions of events by taking a retrospective view of the past. *"The past is alive in the present and may shape the emerging future"* (Pettigrew 1997: 341). *Second*, an individual account of the five episodes of IT strategy-making was presented. This reported specifically on the key events and process activities as they related to the roles of middle managers. The headings selected to describe each episode were inductively derived in order to capture the essence of the key events as they related to the strategy process. The events were sequentially ordered however, some events occurred simultaneously. The key event headings are described in Table 3.2.

After writing up the narrative, the next stage turned to the process of intellectual pattern recognition. The narrative was constructed to present an account of the researcher's interpretation of reality based-on the data gathered. The narrative revealed the range of actors that participated in the episodes of IT strategy-making who operated with a range of interests and perceptions (Pettigrew 1990). By distilling the evidence as presented in the narrative by way of meta-level themes, it was possible to identify preliminary patterns that were taken to yield deeper insights into the interview data. By distilling the underlying logics in the form of dominant theme analysis, this led to the identification of middle manager role categories. To develop greater insight into middle manager actions it was necessary to follow the

Table 3.2 Key events featured in episodes of IT strategy-making

Key event	Description
Starting out	This event described the beginning of the episode and pointed to the initial activities enacted to get the event underway
Assessment of healthcare IT environment	This event described the activities that were enacted to gather a sense of the current state of the healthcare IT environment
Engaging with the irish health system	This event highlighted stakeholder engagement activities that were enacted by IT middle managers during the process
Distilling priorities	This event accounted for the activities enacted by IT middle managers to categorize the major issues and themes into the high-level priorities that required further attention in terms of strategic IT development
Planning considerations	This event pointed to some of the key considerations given attention during the process
Crafting technological solutions	This event described many of the technical aspects considered as part of the process and the activities enacted by IT middle managers around these
Building support	This event described activities enacted by IT middle managers to gain support and commitment, usually at a senior management level
Implementing strategy	This event dealt with the executional activities enacted as part of the strategy process

themes through an iterative process involving the narrative accounts, interview data and the extant literature. Or as Pettigrew put it, *"does one stop peeling the layers from the onion only when the vapors inhibit all further sight?"* (1990: 272). The process supported Pettigrew's view in that *"interpretative theoretical cases move the analysis and writing beyond the analytical chronologies"* (1990: 280). This required a more explicit need to interpret the narrative but to also link emerging conceptual themes inductively derived to stronger analytical themes within the data set. In this particular case, role types were denoted by categories and the related role attributes and activities were shown as a set of subcategories arrived at by way of inductive and deductive analysis iteratively driven.

3.4 Findings

An ideal set of IT middle manager roles emerged from the analysis. The purpose of which was to provide a theoretical understanding grounded in original data that did not betray the richness, complexity and dynamism of the data (Langley 1999). The roles came about through the identifiable middle manager actions across the five episodes. Through an iterative process of pattern recognition, a theoretical framework that comprised of six middle manager roles emerged. The six roles associated with strategic alignment in public service organizations were: *Initiator*; *Orchestrator*; *Planner*; *Technologist*; *Broker*; and *Executor*. For each role, a set of dominant activities was identified and shown in Table 3.3.

A brief discussion on each role is presented along with supporting data samples to embed integrity. A high-level illustration of the roles is presented in Fig. 3.2.

3.4.1 Initiator

Around the focus of ideas, the Initiator aims to shift the mind-set of the middle management level by enthusing lateral thinking towards new possibilities that will extend the level of IT—enablement. As one participant responded, it's about *"Setting out a vision where properly supported service delivery becomes enabled by effective IT systems."* Based-on the generation of ideas, the Initiator visualizes a new state, which centers positively on future IT developments to transform the current system to a system that is technologically integrated and fully-enabled. *"Vision has got to be born out of knowledge of what has happened, what is happening, influenced by best judgement as to what will or might happen."* The strategic context is set out showing the guiding assumptions and parameters upon which to base the strategic IT agenda. *"Define and set out the strategic context upon which to base major ICT decisions."* The Initiator identifies key elements of the strategy formation process and organizes middle managers into roles and responsibilities, and instils a strong sense of coherence amongst the management actors. Ensuring that effective

Table 3.3 IT middle manager roles and dominant activities in strategic alignment

Dominant activities	Roles					
	Initiator	Orchestrator	Planner	Technologist	Broker	Executor
	Idea generation to externalize potential for IT-enablement	Outline scope of stakeholder involvement	Priority identification and selection	Focus on strategic fit of potential technological solutions	Champion strategic IT initiatives among executive ranks	Plan implementation program of activities
	Translate ideas into a vision for the future	Develop processes for active involvement	Collaborate with stakeholders to build consensus	Eliminate fragmentation and silo structures by focusing on integration	Promote potential benefits of wholly enabled-IT environment	Translate intent into executable action
	Set out strategy formation process	Promote purpose and reasons for fully inclusive process	Identify capability and capacity requirements	Focus on architectural design to build capacity	Establish realistic expectations to secure funding commitments	Realize strategic IT aims, deliver expected outcomes and full range of benefits

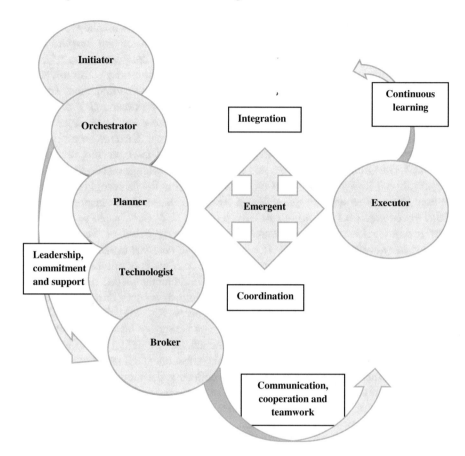

Fig. 3.2 High-level illustration of middle manager roles in strategic alignment

communication processes are embedded into the process enshrines clear and transparent sharing of information. The Initiator designs communicative processes to ensure the effective collection and dissemination of information between individuals and groups. The underlying tenet of an effective process in strategic alignment is to establish mutual understanding among all paricipants. *"Consult with colleagues to form recommendations for this country to move forward in time."*

3.4.2 *Orchestrator*

The role identifies all stakeholders that are relevant to a comprehensive strategy-making process. A stakeholder analysis is performed, followed by stakeholder tours to learn about the business issues and challenges. The process of generating active involvement requires a comprehensive effort to schedule, arrange and stage such events (open-discussions, meetings, forums, workshops, seminars etc.). *"To develop an IT strategy independently, without including hospital organizations and related service delivery organizations is a complete waste of time."* Essential to the process is developing and building relationships with the various business areas to actively gain their support and to encourage participation. The role focuses on gaining support from the bottom/up and top/down. *"It's absolutely critical the process is bottom/up but there is also a strong top/down element to it, there is also a need for the Minister, the Secretary General, the Assistant Secretaries, they all have to participate, support and promote the strategizing agenda."* The Orchestrator realizes that much of the knowledge can be held at lower organizational levels and is intent on tapping into this for its recognizable contribution. *"Very often most people will say, 'we'll get an academic institution or the ESRI or management consultants to have a look at this issue', when very often the best people to look at it are ourselves, but devoting frontline commissions to support the development process is a real tangible cost but development is futile without this support."* One of the challenges to overcome is in rallying professional support mainly due to the urgent and substantive demands placed on professional time. The role places strong emphasis on building awareness throughout for the importance of a comprehensive engagement process. The role aims to build consensus among members on the future direction. Only by bringing together key stakeholders can common agreement be reached. A key activity is to ensure all issues are raised and made known, and that the subsequent solutions are aligned to those same issues, all the while ensuring that collective decision-making determines the most appropriate way forward. *"Focus on the communities of interest, everybody wants the same thing and it's important that people don't feel threatened."* The Orchestrator role is one of the most active by way of boundary spanning.

3.4.3   Planner

The main activity is to isolate major priorities from the catalogue of issues identified. The various stakeholder groups must reach a harmonious view on priorities and participate in the goal setting task for each. This process includes agreeing on priority action plans along with assigning responsibility for the management participants involved. *"The big challenge is that there is no point in having actions that are not attributable to the individual organizations that will be responsible for implementing them."* The IT, functional and business managers collaborate in the form of a joint intellectual effort, organized in a timely manner, which offers up detailed information that forms the basis for reaching conclusions on priority status. *"Given the constraints that we're operating under, time and money, we have to adopt an approach that prioritizes and we're not good at doing that so we need to get better at generating key priorities that need to be worked on."* Given the end-to-end complexities by way of multiple stakeholder interests, the context for IT development is viewed as a gradual process that penetrates over time. Key considerations include resource allocation, management competencies, skill capacity, and project accountability. The fundamental purpose is to advance the level of IT capability and thus, improve overall quality of public service delivery. The planning process is governed using various methodologies and mechanisms (issue scoring methodology; priority rating methodology; information library database of global initiatives etc.). *"Important to have a control framework because without it things will happen that shouldn't, it needs to provide a national approach to IT development, so the strategy considered the various governance structures to plan, develop, and implement the strategy."* A process of collaborative deliberation determines what key issues become business priorities for development. Once priorities are defined, all possible IT development initiatives are considered. As part of the process, the planner outlines constitutional expectations and responsibilities, such as development responsibilities, core objectives, timelines, actionable goals aligned to strategic priorities and so on. *"From working on strategy the last number of years, you've got to know two things, you've got to know your business and you've got to know those you're dealing with in the business."* A critical undertaking is made by the Planner to estimate around core areas essential to effective IT development such as capacity and capability (headcount, skills; technology etc.) requirements.

3.4.4 Technologist

The Technologist is focused on developing technological solutions to meet the information requirements for the various functional and business areas. The development of technological solutions involves the application of knowledge and expertise along with using techniques, systems and methodologies with the purpose of designing and implementing appropriate solutions. The role focuses on the development of IT solutions aligned with priorities. *"Got to design your technical solutions to address the needs of a number of stakeholders, not just one of them."* Mindful is the need to develop solutions that provide deeply embedded integrity. On the one hand, developing a single IT solution to address a specific functional or business requirement is standard-in-approach. On the other hand, developing a solution that spans any multiple of units, functions and organizations, and highly dependent on external support, requires a much higher degree of integrative capability. *"The question of integration, how to link fifteen disparate sets of information? Healthcare systems is made up of primary care, emergency care, hospital care and community care, and information can move up and down within a hospital reasonably well but it can't move across, it's the poor old patient who has to do all this integration."* Information architecture is the mechanism by which to approach the issue of integration Information architecture is designed with a view to develop and expand IT interoperability, connecting infrastructure and applications architecturally from the top down, but also based on operational and service process. *"We focused particularly on information architecture as the mechanism by which to develop capacity, joining up the dots architecturally is the challenge."* Users must be involved in the development cycle; discussion between technical experts and user groups holds unambiguous meaning. Development takes shape in the form of co-creation at the technical-, functional- and/or business-level where process is learned, ideas are exchanged, and issues are worked through together. *"People want to sign off on a 400- page blueprint for a financial system who have no idea, not even interested, it's the people who actually have to configure it that revel in this level of detail."* The development of new solutions is aligned to certain fundamentals that endorse an enterprise- or system-level perspective. *"If they're going to link up systems outside the organization into areas such as revenue or social protection, we need to know, then you're talking about interdependencies, it might not be on the radar of the other organizations."* Such fundamentals include an alignment with the IT systems environment (e.g. fragmented or tightly integrated), information architecture, technical infrastructure, flexibility, standardization, and interoperability.

3.4.5 Broker

The Broker's aim is to secure support from senior management to invest in the development of IT solutions. Reaching agreement is reflected in senior management commitment to support an IT strategy by way of providing financial resources at 3–5% of revenue for IT investment. *"The major challenge we have with IT strategy is in resourcing it. Funding for IT in Ireland is pretty poor, less than 1%, compared to the U.S. where it is 3–6%. Previous strategies were unrealistic in terms of timeframes, funding and staffing—we need more resources to make it happen."* The Broker acts as champion of the strategic plan to senior management. In championing the plan, the Broker makes recommendations and agrees to continual reviews as deemed appropriate by the senior management. *"I made recommendations to the CEOs and boards; presented the IT strategy to the management advisory council."* It is part of the Broker's remit to promote the importance of IT by illustrating the potential gains. In so doing, the Broker educates senior management about the enabling possibilities along with raising awareness at the executive level. *"The major challenge is to build political awareness of the fact that IT will have to be resourced, challenge number one, two and three—the board will accept it, the senior management team will not accept it, it won't happen and then it will get killed."* It is the act of influential behavior that the Broker uses to steer support for the IT strategy. *"You need good working relationships and need to keep all those relationships well maintained, it's the role."* This type of influential behavior involves raising senior management awareness; broaden their understanding for its potential; build trust; and secure commitment to support the strategy. *"Moving in political management and governance circles, lots of experience, lots of depth."* Expectations are set whereby IT investment is not necessarily tied to monetary savings or reduced operating cost. Essentially, IT-enablement, particularly in public service, results in improved service delivery by way of greater information flow leading to productivity gains. *"By making the information flow better and become more accessible and readily available is not going to save money, it means that the latent demand that is out there will result in greater throughput of patients and greater quality of healthcare."* Further, timelines in relation to strategic IT are extensive; expectations are set accordingly.

3.4.6 Executor

The Executor role oversees the implementation of strategic IT solutions. Implementation is organized with deliberate intent. The role oversees the challenge of translating intent into action that results in making meaningful change. *"There are strategies and then there are plans for implementation of strategies, two very separate things."* In effect, the Executor is accountable for bringing about IT-enabled transformation that fulfills on the promise of the strategic aims. This means realizing the stated benefits that can often go beyond getting IT to work. Realizing the full set of benefits requires enduring persistence and a relentless focus. The role regards a successful implementation to include delivery of IT solutions, but also achieve the expected outcomes. *"A big focus of IT strategy must go beyond delivering the systems at the end but actually delivering all of the benefits that were planned, traditionally we've tended to ignore that."* The role charts the path to follow by navigating activities from beginning to end. The Executor assigns roles, responsibilities and accountabilities. The Executor ensures a high degree of recipient involvement. The role organizes individuals and groups to focus on specific elements of the program. *"Team members operate at different levels, you might find the smartest people are actually down at the lowest levels, that's got to be recognized."* Common goals and aims are set out, aligned to the development of a new state through a process of direction, persuasion, consensus-building and unity of action. During the course of implementation, obstacles and disruptions emerge. *"People have to click as well so you have to select the knowledge base, the skill base, and team membership and coordination of implementation events will only happen with the right people involved."* The Executor is expected to persevere and overcome such challenges. The role demonstrates a strong sense of determination, obstinately focused on realizing the aims. *"You keep working at it, you're persistent. They can put in years of effort before they actually get to the stage where they might have a system that they can deploy."* At various intervals during the process, it is necessary to consult and engage with all stakeholder parties to discuss and review challenges as they arise. *"Quick wins in this environment just don t happen."* Reaching collective agreement on appropriate action is critical to keeping the momentum going.

3.5   Discussion

Observations made in relation to the role of middle managers in strategic alignment are discussed next, followed by findings made in relation to middle manager strategic agency in public service. It is only possible to discuss findings at a very high-level.

3.5.1   Middle Manager Role in Aligning Strategy and IT

It was shown by Nonaka (1988) that senior management have strong expectations in terms of what they hope to achieve. But in relation to IT strategy-making, the findings revealed that senior management hold little idea about the potential for IT impacts at the functional- and business-level. Subsequently, senior management is highly reliant on middle managers to set the contextual picture for the potential of IT-enablement. Furthermore, Nonaka (1988) pointed out that senior management have strong awareness about the enabling possibilities that can result from involving middle managers in strategy-making. This was not found to be the case in relation to the study's findings.

Middle managers provide the impetus whereby strategizing emerges at the middle management level. Middle managers demonstrated acute awareness of the need to act strategically. Top-down direction was seldom forthcoming or essentially necessary. Middle managers are greatly involved in option generation and selection activities to ensure a high-level of consistency in terms of strategic fit.

It was discovered that IT middle managers continuously struggle to find a suitable balance between day-to-day operational activities and the need to focus on strategy-related activities (Huy 2001). It was shown that some managers relish the challenge but the evidence supported a dual-role in terms of managing daily routines coupled with the need for strategizing. It was found that for the most part, middle managers sought the opportunity for greater strategic enactment but the pressing environmental demands prevent this from happening and thus, the essential need to resource a comprehensive IT strategy-making process is crucial.

A notable finding made and in contrast to the roles posited by Thompson et al. (2008) was that IT middle managers are content to assume responsibility for setting the long-term agenda in aligning IT development with the organizational direction. The role is less that of 'follower' and more akin to initiate than imitate whereby middle managers lead on the process to develop a vision that will guide IT development. With that being said however, it was evident that senior management were aware of the need for a comprehensive IT strategy but what this should entail was determined at the middle management level.

According to Pappas and Wooldridge (2007), middle managers with boundary spanning responsibilities play a greater role in strategy-making. However, the significance is not necessarily around the degree of boundary spanning responsibility but in how middle managers work as a group toward a unified aim. Some roles were required to span boundaries extensively (e.g. Orchestrator) and some less so (e.g. Initiator). The overarching importance was found to center on the degree of integrative effort made by middle managers in working together as a collective toward realizing strategic aims. Essentially, while managers with boundary spanning responsibilities make sizable strategic contributions, outcomes are strongly contingent on the level of 'collectivism' that exists among middle managers in terms of coordinating and integrating strategic activities.

3.5.2 Middle Manager Strategic Agency in Public Service

The findings support Kelly et al. (2002: 10) in that middle managers "*play an active role in steering networks of deliberation and delivery and maintain the overall capacity of the system.*" The findings suggest that middle managers do just that; steer networks of deliberation in determining major business priorities and align IT development to match. An inhibitor to good strategy-making in public service is the lack of involvement at the middle management level (Currie 2000). Currie argued that middle managers can have a significant impact by way of altering the intended strategy to reflect contextual realities that are otherwise overlooked by senior management. It is contended that middle managers can strongly intervene and help to overcome such obstacles.

Deliberate strategy intended to align IT development with core priorities is determined by a process of engagement to elicit core issues and chart a plan for the future. Senior management involvement is confined to supporting the recommendations, sanctioning resources and providing commitment to support the process. Currie argued that middle managers can play a greater role in strategy-making in public service and the findings embrace this point.

Middle managers make the greatest contribution to public service strategy-making in the areas of boundary spanning opportunities and center-periphery relations (Currie and Procter 2005). This paper endorses that view. Implicit in each strategy episode was the "*lack* [of] *resources and support to do useful things, such as rewarding excellent subordinates or pursuing promising initiatives*" (Rainey 2009: 177). To overcome this constraint, Rainey argues for senior management to bestow more power onto middle managers insofar as the sharing of power expands power which would enable middle managers to do good work. The findings support the view that senior management must "*relax rules, increase participation, assign important tasks, and reward innovation*" (ibid.) in order to strengthen the levels of middle manager strategic agency.

3.6 Contribution

The study presented a diverse set of roles for IT middle managers. The findings hold the potential to meaningfully aid the middle management level when aligning strategy and IT. For each role, a set of dominant activities was presented. It is at the level of functional and business strategy-making that IT middle managers have an expanded role to enact. The findings showed that IT middle managers can lead on the alignment of strategy and IT by working conjointly across boundaries and up and down organizational levels.

In aligning strategy and IT, senior management support occurs by way of full commitment in support of major IT initiatives. A deficit in senior management support and understanding can have impeding consequences. A key issue noted in scholarly literature refers to the high degree of psychological separateness between middle and senior managers in public organizations. There is potential to considerably reduce this gap whereby senior management act to expand the level of middle management power in support of IT strategizing.

Public service organizations, no less than private sector, are challenged by social, cultural, economic, and political influences that "*leave managers muddling through, betting, and tinkering*" (Chan and Reich 2007: 298). In response to overcoming such challenges, Lehmann (1993) proposed a 'unified process' whereby IT strategy is continual on learning from 'below' (Galliers 2001). The findings support this notion of a 'unified process' whereby IT middle managers (below senior managers) craft and steer strategizing events.

Essentially, the presence of all six roles in IT strategizing can potentially lead to better outcomes. However, this is something that will require further investigation in order to verify.

3.7 Conclusion

The study explored a major theme of practical interest to the field of IT management. The aim of the study was to learn about the roles of middle managers in strategic alignment in public organizations. The research approach adopted a process-oriented methodology to conduct a longitudinal study of multiple episodes of IT strategy-making. The research was carried out within the contextual setting of the Irish public healthcare system, a system made up of many public organizations and government departments. Process analysis aided the identification and description of IT middle manager roles in strategic alignment in public service, namely: Initiator; Orchestrator; Planner; Technologist; Broker; and Executor. The paper described the dominant activities enacted by middle managers in aligning strategy and IT. The findings revealed that strategic alignment is a complex set of ongoing, continuous and dynamic activities contingent on middle manager action purposely focused on raising the level of congruency between functional and business priorities and IT development. Effectively, middle managers' can be described as key activists in aligning strategy and IT in public organizations and have important roles to play. Finally, the findings speak strongly in favor of the view that the middle manager role in aligning strategy and IT is a "*process of abandoning the old and generating the new*" (Nonaka 1988: 12).

References

Andrews, K. (1971). *The concept of corporate strategy*. IL, Irwin: Homewood.

Ansoff, H. I. (1965). *Corporate strategy*. New York: McGraw Hill.

Baldoni, J. (2005). *Great motivation secrets of great leaders*. New York: McGraw-Hill.

Balogun, J. (2003). From blaming the middle to harnessing its potential: creating change intermediaries. *British Journal of Management, 14*(1), 69–83.

Benbasat, I., Goldstein, D. K., & Mead, M. (1987). The case research strategy in studies of information systems. *MIS Quarterly, 11*(3), 369–386.

Bergin, E. (2009). On becoming a manager and attaining managerial integrity. *Leadership in Health Services, 22*(1), 58–75.

Bourgeois, L. J., III, & Brodwin, D. R. (1984). Strategic implementation: five approaches to an elusive phenomenon. *Strategic Management Journal, 5*(3), 241–264.

Bower, J. L. (1970). *Managing the resource allocation process*. Boston, MA: Harvard University Press.

Burgelman, R. A. (1983a). A model of the interaction of strategic behavior, corporate context, and the concept of strategy. *Academy of Management Review, 8*(1), 61–70.

Burgelman, R. A. (1983b). A process model of internal corporate venturing in the diversified major firm. *Administrative Science Quarterly, 28*(2), 223–244.

Burgelman, R. A. (1983c). Corporate entrepreneurship and strategic management: Insights from a process study. *Management Science, 29*(2), 1349–1364.

Caffrey, E., & McDonagh, J. (2015). The theory and application of process research to the study of it strategy-making. In S. Hai-Jew (Ed.), *Enhancing qualitative and mixed methods research with technology* (pp. 392–427). IGI Global: Hershey PA.

Chan, Y. E., & Reich, B. H. (2007). IT alignment: What have we learned? *Journal of Information Technology, 22*(4), 297–315.

Chandler, A. D. (1962). *Strategy and structure: chapters in the history of the american industrial enterprise*. Cambridge, MA: MIT Press.

Child, J. (1972). Organizational structure, environment and performance: The role of strategic choice. *Sociology, 6*(1), 1–22.

Clarke, J. & Newman, J. (2000). *The managerial state. power, politics and ideology in the remaking of social welfare*. London: Sage.

Creswell, J. W. (2007). *Qualitative inquiry and research design*. Thousand Oaks, CA: Sage Publications Inc.

Currie, G. (2000). The role of middle managers in strategic change in the public sector. *Journal of Public Money and Management, 20*(1), 17–22.

Currie, G., & Procter, S. J. (2005). The antecedents of middle managers' strategic contribution: The case of a professional bureaucracy. *Journal of Management Studies, 42*(7), 1325–1356.

Derksen, B. & Luftman, J. (2014). European key IT and management issues and trends. (pp. 1–36) CIONET. http://blog.cionet.com/wp-content/uploads/2014/02/ITTrends_2014print.pdf. Accessed 5 June 2015.

Dutton, J. E., & Ashford, S. J. (1993). Selling issues to top management. *The Academy of Management Review, 18*(3), 397–428.

Exworthy, M., & Halford, S. (1999). Professionals and managers in a challenging public sector: conflict, compromise and collaboration? In M. Exworthy & S. Halford (Eds.), *Professionals and new managerialism in the public sector*. Buckingham, UK: Open University Press.

Farrel, C., & Morris, J. (2003). The Neo-bureaucratic State: Professionals, managers and professional managers in schools. *General Practices and Social Work. Organization, 10*(1), 129–156.

Floyd, S. W., & Wooldridge, B. (1992). Middle management involvement in strategy and its association with strategic type: A research note. *Strategic Management Journal, 13*(1), 153–167.

Floyd, S. W., & Wooldridge, B. (1997). Middle management's strategic influence and organizational performance. *Journal of Management Studies, 34*(3), 465–485.

Floyd, S. W., & Wooldridge, B. (2000). *Building Strategy from the Middle: Reconceptualizing Strategy Process*. Thousand Oaks, CA: Sage.

Galliers, R. D. (2001). Rethinking information systems strategy: Towards an inclusive strategic framework for business information systems management? Paper presented at the EGOS Colloquium, Lyon, France.

Grove, A. S. (2015). *High output management: With a new foreword by Ben Horowitz*. London: Vintage Books Editions.

Hambrick, D. C., & Mason, P. A. (1984). Upper echelons: The organization as a reflection of its top managers. *Academy of Management Review, 9*(2), 193–206.

Harding, N. (2003). *The social construction of management: texts and identities*. London: Routledge.

Haveri, A. (2006). Complexity in local government change: limits to rational reforming. *Public Management Review, 8*(1), 31–46.

Huy, Q. N. (2001). In praise of middle managers. *Harvard Business Review, 79*(8), 72–79.

Kaplan, B., & Maxwell, J. A. (2005). Qualitative research methods for evaluating computer information systems. In J. G. Anderson, C. E. Aydin, & S. J. Jay (Eds.), *Evaluating the organizational impact of health care information systems*. Thousand Oaks, CA: Sage.

Klein, H. K., & Myers, M. D. (1999). A set of principles for conducting and evaluating interpretive field studies in information systems. *MIS Quarterly, 23*(1), 67–94.

Langley, A. (1999). Strategies for Theorizing from Process Data. *Academy of management review, 24*(4), 691–710.

Lawler, J. (2008). Individualization and public sector leadership. *Public Administration, 86*(1), 21–34.

Lehmann, H. (1993). Core competence and learning alliances—The new face of information management. *Journal of Information Technology, 8*(4), 149–174.

Luftman, J., & Ben-Zvi, T. (2010). Key issues for IT executives 2010: judicious IT investments continue post-recession. *MIS Quarterly Executive, 9*(4), 263–273.

Mantere, S. (2008). Role expectations and middle manager strategic agency. *Journal of Management Studies, 45*(2), 294–316.

McGurk, P. (2009). Developing "Middle Leaders" in the Public Services? *International Journal of Public Sector Management, 22*(6), 464–477.

Mintzberg, H. (1989). *Mintzberg on management*. New York: Free Press.

Mintzberg, H. (2009). *Managing*. London: Prentice Hall.

Morgan, D., Bacon, K. G., Bunch, R., Cameron, C. D., & Deis, R. (1996). What middle managers do in local government: Stewardship of the public trust and the limits of reinventing government. *Public Administration Review, 56*(4), 359–366.

Nonaka, I. (1988). Toward middle-up-down management: Accelerating information creation. *Sloan Management Review, 29*(3), 9–18.

Osterman, P. (2008). *The truth about middle managers*. Boston: MA, Harvard Business Press.

Pappas, J. M., & Wooldridge, B. (2007). 'Middle Managers' divergent strategic activity: An investigation of multiple measures of network centrality. *Journal of Management Studies, 44* (3), 323–341.

Pettigrew, A. M. (1985). Context and action in the transformation of the firm. *Journal of Management Studies, 24*(6), 649–670.

Pettigrew, A. M. (1990). Longitudinal field research on change: Theory and practice. *Organization Science, 1*(4), 267–292.

Pettigrew, A. M. (1992). The character and significance of strategy process research. *Strategic Management Journal, 13*(S2), 5–16.

Pettigrew, A. M. (1997). What is a processual analysis? *Scandinavian Journal of Management, 13* (4), 337–348.

Pettigrew, A. M., Ferlie, E., & McKee, L. (1992). *Shaping strategic change: Making change in large organizations, the case of the NHS*. London: Sage.

Pettigrew, A. M., & McNulty, T. (1995). Power and influence in and around the boardroom. *Human Relations, 48*(8), 845–873.

Pettigrew, A. M., & Whipp, R. (1991). *Managing change for competitive success*. Oxford, UK: Basil Blackwell.

Porter, M. E. (1980). *Competitive strategy*. New York: Free Press.

Rainey, H. G. (2009). *Understanding and managing public organizations*. San Francisco, CA: Jossey-Bass.

Simons, H. (2009). *Case study research in practice*. London: Sage.

Thakur, M. (1998). Involving middle managers in strategy making. *Long Range Planning, 31*(5), 732–741.

Thompson, T., Purdy, J., & Summers, D. B. (2008). A five factor framework for coaching middle managers. *Organization Development Journal, 26*(3), 63–71.

Van De Ven, A. H., & Poole, M. S. (2002). Field research methods. In A. C. Baum (Ed.), *Companion to organizations*. Oxford: Blackwell Publishers.

Viitanen, E., & Konu, A. (2009). Leadership style profiles of middle-level managers in social and health care. *Leadership in Health Services, 22*(2), 108–120.

Vila, J., & Canales, J. I. (2008). Can strategic planning make strategy more relevant and build commitment over time? The case of RACC. *Long Range Planning, 41*(3), 273–290.

Webster, J., & Watson, R. T. (2002). Analyzing the past to prepare for the future: Writing a literature review. *MIS Quarterly, 26*(2), xiii–xxiii.

Willcocks, L. P., & Griffiths, C. (2010). The crucial role of middle management in outsourcing. *MIS Quarterly Executive, 9*(3), 177–193.

Wooldridge, B., Schmid, T., & Floyd, S. W. (2008). The middle management perspective on strategy process: Contributions, synthesis, and future research. *Journal of Management, 34*(6), 1190–1221.

Chapter 4
Governing Is in the Details—The Longitudinal Impact of IT-related Policy Management for Public Boards

Jenny Eriksson Lundström and Mats Edenius

Abstract Decision makers increasingly enforce policies of digitalization of everyday activities. The aim of this study is to examine, at the micro level, the practices and their impact of people transforming the way they conduct their public board work due to an IT-related policy decision. We argue for analysis of the seemingly small, slow, yet fundamental interactions with which humans shape and reinvent organizational life. Our approach provides insights into the impact of implementation of policy decisions and how change of seemingly mundane activities creates the evolution of new structures and practices of importance. Our study highlights a reconstitution of routines and change of anchoring practices of a public board that (a) anchors new material to a board member's responsibilities without utilizing its inherent advantages, (b) anchors new conflicting routines while abandoning well established ones, and (c) results in new routines that weaken fundamental goals of the board member's role and work counterproductive to human cognition.

4.1 Introduction

Publicly owned companies in Sweden are grounded in the idea that government should be open to public scrutiny. It allows for maintaining a democratic dialogue; with its pillars set in the thoughts of enlightenment such as democracy, transparency, and communicative actions as cooperative action, i.e. mutual deliberation and argumentation (Habermas 1984). Often, information technologies (IT) is seen as a tool for this pursuit. To implement new IT, the characteristics of the organization as well as its context must be taken into account (Rainey 2003). Change in work practices that emerge as the introduction of different technologies is shown to

J.E. Lundström (✉) · M. Edenius
Department of Informatics and Media, Uppsala University, Uppsala, Sweden
e-mail: jenny.eriksson@im.uu.se

M. Edenius
e-mail: mats.edenius@im.uu.se

© Springer International Publishing AG 2017
L. Rusu and G. Viscusi (eds.), *Information Technology Governance in Public Organizations*, Integrated Series in Information Systems 38,
DOI 10.1007/978-3-319-58978-7_4

be both unanticipated and to go in different, often undeterminable directions. Research shows that different kinds of practice models, implemented poorly or not sustained, will fail to achieve intended goals despite research evidence supporting their effectiveness (Bond et al. 2009). Despite a multitude of implementation approaches research has found that an effective implementation approach to be crucial to the successful practice. In this, both structural and procedural models of implementation influence the outcome (Orlikowski 1996, 2000). The art of government and IT-implementation is indeed a complicated matter.

More research is needed to investigate in more detail the impact of implementation of new technologies, how it influences change processes and in what way it shapes the possibilities for ongoing organizational change (Vaast and Walsham 2005, p. 66). This chapter takes on the call of Vaast and Walsham. It aims at examining, at the micro level, the impact of people transforming the way they conduct their work due to an IT-related policy decision within a public owned company, and in particular with respect to its demand for maintaining democratic values.

We have studied how people in a board of one of the municipally owned companies of a large Swedish Municipality uses tablets instead of paper packs to prepare themselves for the board work. Despite high ambitions of the policy makers to utilize new IT-devices in new and innovative ways, due to the way the new IT-devices are used, the search for drama may be a misleading term to describe the impact of the IT-policy. We aim to show that this doesn't mean that modest variations of rudimentary activities are of less importance in understanding digitalization of organizations related to its values. In this chapter we empirically illustrate how such processes over time are affected and constrained by the digitalization of everyday activities. To support our arguments, we draw on a model (Eriksson Lundström and Edenius 2014) to further explain how such processes can be understood.

Our argumentation is based on a perspective where organizations can be regarded as constituted by the ongoing agency of organizational members and artefacts and how actions taken by the members of the organization (intentionally or not) reproduce or alter organizational properties. In line with prominent IS-researchers, e.g. Orlikowski (2000) we recognize that technology is always situated and emergent and people tend to enact technologies-in-practice over time. We call for a dynamic perspective where practices are understood in the context of their circuits of reproduction and shed light on recurrent and (quite) modest reciprocal variations in organizational practices over time, where each shift in practice creates its own condition for different outcomes.

We have built our perspective on Giddens's (1984) structuration theory, and in particular on Sewell's (1992) extended analysis of this theory. Hence, as support for the analysis we take our departure in the reflexive dualities of resources, practices and schema. In this way we are to illustrate the mechanism on how IT-policy invokes, and impacts on organizational change via dynamic interplay, inherent relations and performative enactment.

Our empirical study and arguments are grounded in a longitudinal case study. The setting is a Swedish municipality and we lay our focus on a policy decision taken in the Municipal Council as part of its Vision 2030—a World-Class City. Via document analysis, observation and interviews originating from the period of 2007 to 2015, we examine the impact of a policy decision concerning digitalization of board packs and memoranda in a board of the municipality-owned Housing Corporation (HC).

We focus on the local interpretation of the policy decision enacted and defined technological devices and its relation to social relations of the board. These findings may have implications for other implementation areas of digitalization, and in particular for policy-governed and hierarchically structured organizations.

This chapter is structured in the following way: In following section, the context of the study is presented and our theoretical approach is discussed in more detail. This is followed by some methodological considerations for the study. In the next part of the chapter the empirical material is presented and interpreted. It is followed by a discussion. The chapter ends with concluding remarks.

4.2 The Context of the Study

We discern three different, but interrelated roles, of a board: First, the board members monitor executives; second, the board is responsible to define, create and implement a corporate strategic plan; third, the board members represent the company and legitimize the business to its environment (see Ruigrok et al. 2006). As the power of the board members is vested in them by their respective political party, no formal regulation besides from the country jurisprudence is set to govern their acts. Instead, the manifestation of democracy largely lies with the responsibility of its practitioners:

> ...it ought to be the happiness and glory of a representative to live in the strictest union, the closest correspondence, and the most unreserved communication with his constituents. Their wishes ought to have great weight with him; their opinion, high respect; their business, unremitted attention. It is his duty to sacrifice his repose, his pleasures, his satisfactions, to theirs; and above all, ever, and in all cases, to prefer their interest to his own. But his unbiased opinion, his mature judgment, his enlightened conscience, he ought not to sacrifice to you, to any man, or to any set of men living.

> These he does not derive from your pleasure; no, nor from the law and the constitution. They are a trust from Providence, for the abuse of which he is deeply answerable. Your representative owes you, not his industry only, but his judgment; and he betrays, instead of serving you, if he sacrifices it to your opinion. (The Works of the Right Honourable Edmund Burke. Volume I. London: Bohn 1854, pp. 446–8).

Correspondingly, in Sweden, The Swedish Companies Act (ABL) is the formal statute for controlling board responsibilities. This gives rise to the duty of the board member to use their own judgment when exercising their power. Viewing this discourse; transparency, communication, competency to act; preparedness, atten-tiveness, critical analysis and partaking in discussions, all become key activities for the manifestation of democracy in publicly governed corporations.

4.3   Theoretical Approach

Structure is perhaps the most used metaphor in the Social Sciences. Inspired by Giddens (1979, 1984) and Bourdieu (1999), and based on Sewell (1992) we focus on this inquiry in terms of discourses and practices in which rules, activities and resources are enacted into routines, a semiotic system of interrelated meanings that constitute structured practices can be discerned. In other words, for our empirical setting, the board of a large publicly owned housing company, with their recurrent activities, e.g. reading, writing motions, participating in meetings etc., the board members partake in and relate to both the social collective that "constructs" the board, and partake in and relate to the social structuring of the board as part of the structured practices of this particular discourse. In this continuous interplay the new IT-devices employed as means for enacting policy decisions are merely come to being by being imprinted by schemas. In our case a schema that embodies the above presented manifestations of democracy may be the following legal statute (but not necessarily restricted to such formal rules):

> ...all members of a board need to be well informed before the board makes its decision. (The Swedish Companies Act 8:17).

Thus thanks to these schemas, the observable discourse and practices are reproduced. Conversely, the reproduction of discourse and practices caters for the robustness of the schema.

We follow the processual focus put forth by Sewell (1992) who argues that structures can be seen as composed simultaneously of schemas and of resources. Hence, also schemas are by definition capable to be exchanged, switched or transferred to other environments. And this may be introduced by resources (for example a new IT-device). Consequently, despite that a discourse, e.g. a board, can seem quite robust, this means that the schemas governing the discourse are never entirely robust, not even for a seemingly unchanged context. For enacting a schema, a meeting routine, electing a person to serve as attestant (to approve the minutes), which make sense in a board meeting may appear strange, and thus interpreted differently in a family dinner setting, which means that schemas will work differ-ently when they are put into practice and therefore they may be subjected to modification.

Hence, structured practices are dynamic, because they are a continually evolving outcome of processes of social interaction and resourceful agencies. Together with the affordance and constraints of resources, actions give rise to ways of enactment of schemas as reproductions or transformations of organizational practices (i.e.

practices are constantly changing), albeit some changes are very small (Nicolini 2007).

It is within this context and schema a new technology is introduced and thus, we ask the question; what is the impact of the policy decision when agents transform their work the way they do?

4.4 Method

Sewell (1992) states even though activity only can be understood as composed by schemas, the extent to which these are brought into being can only be understood when enacted for a resource. This directs our ambition to study practices via close observations in a micro-level setting. These practices can be defined as the "recurrent, materially bounded and situated action engaged in by members of the community" (Orlikowski 2002, p. 256). Thus, the board can be conceived as consisting of context, a site of structured practices. Action taken by the organizational members is continually reproduced, and the board and its recurrent, materially bounded and situated actions seems to be quite robust.

4.4.1 Empirical Setting

Our study draws on a longitudinal single in-depth case study to obtain rich and naturalistic data.

The municipality of our study is one of the largest municipalities in Sweden. It houses the capital of Sweden as its regional capital and home to the Municipal Council. In accordance a policy decision in 2007 the Municipal Council decided that IT was to be treated as a strategic means of its overall business development.

HC is one of the municipality's publicly owned housing corporations. It was established 1937. It services one of the largest municipalities in Sweden with publicly owned housing. Today approximately 50000 people are living in the 26000 apartments of HC, and 3500 business facilities. HC has 300 employees and a yearly overturn of 2 billion SEK.

The board of HC consists of seven regular members and seven deputy members. They are elected by the Municipal Council. The board serves the indirect democratic system, and thus, the board of HC reflects the balance of political power of the Municipal Board. The Chairperson is appointed by the political majority and the deputy Chairperson is appointed by the opposing political parties of the Municipal Board. The term of office is four years, coinciding with the Swedish municipality election terms. To be elected as representative of this particular board is an important political responsibility, as the board serves as the representation of the people of the municipality. As a consequence, the board members that take office are very experienced in board work. In addition, three official representatives are elected into the board.

The regular members of the board are four males and three females and three official representatives, two females and one male. In addition, the board has seven deputy members, six males and one female. The ages of the full board range from 26 to 71, with a median age of 57 and an average age of 54. Regardless of role in the board, the members all are experienced computer users in the sense that they are using or have been using computers for work and for political assignments on a daily basis. Their earlier experiences of tablets were very varying, ranging from no previous experience to having incorporated a tablet into their everyday doings in leisure and work (i.e. both for the board activities as well as other work assignments unrelated to the board work).

4.4.2   The Policy Decision

The decision to digitalize board packs and memoranda was part of implementing the Vision 2030—a World-Class City of the municipality and its IT-policy for digital renewal and green-IT. The policies state that IT should be seen as a tool in the daily work of the municipality and used in a new and innovative way. Prior to the introduction of tablets, the introduction of tablets in sister organizations of HC had been conducted. Some of the board members have also been part of a board of a sister organization, and these board members hold first-hand experience from these projects. The choice of tablets was made based on existing procurement contracts, and hence, the choice of hardware and particular software was already pre-made. Regardless of earlier experience or access to an existing tablet, all board members received a new tablet, a preinstalled software package for accessing the board pack, an email account and alias, and security codes. A short introduction on how to use the tablet and software was given to the board members. After one of the planned board meetings, an introduction for half an hour on how to use the tablet and software was given to the board members from an external IT-consultant. The focus of the introduction was twofold; how to download and work with the board pack, and how to log into the software styrelsemöte.se. Largely, no additional instructions on how the implementation was to be executed accompanied the tablets.

4.4.3   Data Collection

The research project was granted access to the board via a joint decision at one of the regular meetings. To ensure trust in the board we choose to conduct overt observations (e.g. Creswell 2012). The empirical material is collected during the period 2012–2015, via document analysis, observation and interviews. The material includes four years of Practitioner-Researcher participation (going native) as a board member prior to the introduction of the tablets, participant in the education on the tablets, and ongoing. It is complemented by in situ Complete-Observer participation at board meetings 12 and 30 months after the introduction of the tablets. Even if doings of the board members were the focus of this study, in order to gain a deeper understanding of the routines, observations were complemented with interviews with the board members of HC (including the board member researcher). During the period of data collection, interviews with all regular board members and officials of the public housing corporation were carried out by a research assistant skilled in interview technique. All regular board members were approached twice. This approach, triangulation with practitioner-researcher observations, might have mitigated any effect the research project might have had on the board members. In this way changes in the activities could be interpreted with more confidence.

4.4.4 Data Analysis

Inspired by grounded theory (Strauss and Corbin 1998), we conducted an iterative textual analysis of the interviews transcripts and field notes. This process was proceeded by multiple readings and coding of the empirical material. Different data were identified and put into different sub-themes of classified patterns. From such a standpoint, a case study is both the process of learning about the case and the product of our learning. So, even if triangulation has been of importance in the data gathering, the data analysis is based on making clear a complex empirical material. However, it is important to notice that the aim with the empirical material is not primarily to verify some clear theories or hypotheses but to illuminate and elaborate on practices as these relates to IT-related policy decisions in public organizations. The method is therefore to be regarded as abductive (Hanson 1958, Alvesson and Sköldberg 2000).

4.5 Digitalization of a Board and Its Practices

In this chapter we focus our attention to the empirical material that concern the policy decision and its impact. For a comprehensive presentation of the empirical material of the study see Edenius and Eriksson Lundström (2016). In summary, three years into the study, all but two of the board members express they are very positive to the tablets, and state that it simplified their board work activities. There are indications on barriers and problems, mainly concerning the possibility to write on the tablet, the difficulty of getting a view of the material and switching between documents. Some also report issues with reading outdoors, and issues concerning connectedness and power supply routines. We also note that even though all board members have received the same kind of equipment, two board members have experienced serious malfunctioning of the tablet or the software. One board member has had several periods with malfunctioning software and lack of access. The tablet has been sent to service and software has been checked, without any improvement. A remaining situation, the board member cannot access the board packs without external support in the form of an email containing a link to each document being sent, via which the board member can access one document at a time.

> It's just that when you get and pick them up one by one, so it's just a bit more work than it was when you had that other [app]. It works. BJ II, p. 3

Another board member has had similar issues, but also due to private reasons, had low attendance at the meetings.

> … For quite a long time, during the last year I did not have the tablet started up at all. It was just on a shelf somewhere. And then I did not start it. So when I started it said that it would take several million minutes before it could restart. And then I handed it in, and then I have not downloaded it again. LG II p. 1

These two board members have handled the breakdowns of the tablets in completely different ways. Clearly, it is not simply the a priori affordances or constraints of resources that forms and maintains new practices. So what is it that results in activities that lead to different outcomes for their role as a board member?

We can tentatively discern two different outcomes, in which the enactment of schemas via situated activities result in barriers for the material, and, when the tablets become resources incorporated within processes of structuration, at the expense of other resources not taken into practice or even into consideration. By means of our theoretical underpinnings the orthogonal outcomes may be explained as the natural outcome of continuously ongoing dynamic processes of normalization of activities into structured practice, processes that draws on social interaction and resourceful agency (Sewell 1992).

With this backdrop, we direct the inquiry to the social. From the empirical material we note that the board members hold a firm idea of their role as a member of the board. The three interrelated roles that signify board work are present, even though the role of representing HC is less pronounced. As they view their responsibility as pertaining to indirect democracy; transparency, competency to act; preparedness, attentiveness and critical analysis and partaking in the discussion are highlighted:

> Yes, I have the same role as all the other board members. I shall assess the documents, I will evaluate the CEO's proposal, I will ask relevant questions when I'm not really clear on some issues. When I think something is missing or something I do not think is good or declare that there is an argument which I think is not relevant. DB II, p. 7

Often the board members explicitly refer to the Swedish Law formalization of the democratic function when they describe their responsibility (see Fig. 4.1 (1) and (2) respectively):

> I think it's important to read thoroughly and ask questions. Somehow. After all, I am responsible under the Companies Act. And have some sort of individual responsibility for the company and will ensure the company's best. And I still think it's pretty important that I

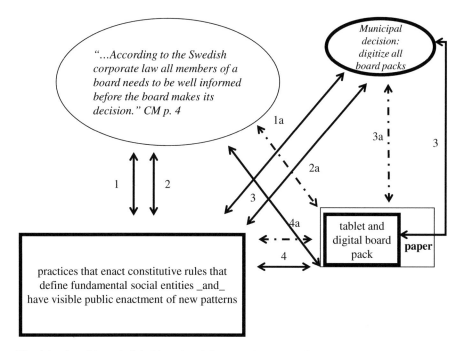

Fig. 4.1 The tablet and digital board pack is constrained to the functionality of paper substitute-two constitutive rules, the formal statute of the board member's responsibility (*1*) and the mandatory municipal board decision (*1a*) influence the enactment of practice. Practices that ensure that all board members are able to keep up with the changes in accordance to the formal statute of the board member's responsibility (*2*) and that also acknowledge the mandatory municipal board decision as it is interpreted (*2a*) causes tablet and digital board pack to be a legitimate resource only for enacting practices related to the board pack (*3, 4*) and ONLY as a mere paper substitute, while physical paper and practices that enact it are weakened as a legitimate resource (*3a*) or legitimate practices but uphold the very possibility of its digital replacement (*4a*)

am well read into the material and to place relevant questions and not just making time pass. Then, you must be aware that the influence of the individual in this kind of board is relatively small. Directives come from the group company which in turn got them from the Municipal Council and then the daily routine is handled by the Chairman and the CEO. Most of the board is a kind of democratic control function, that is. LG II p. 4

…we can never put ourselves in the position in which one of the board members hasn't gotten enough information so that a decision cannot be taken. Formally it is the case that such a decision can be challenged and nullified, and thus the decision needs to be read-dressed. According to the Swedish Companies Act all members of a board needs to be well informed before the board makes its decision. DN p. 4

So, what happened to the goals of the policy vision? In the following we use an analytical model to illuminate and elaborate on how this responsibility is enacted in relation to the policy decision. In this way we unfold three themes of consequences what such rudimentary changes in practices may entail.

4.5.1 The Policy Is Different but Practices Shouldn't Change

Replacing paper as the bearer of information with tablets and digital board packs and memoranda was part of implementing the Vision 2030—a World-Class City of the Municipality (see Fig. 4.1 (1a)). The main goal of the policy was to ensure that "IT should be seen as a tool in the daily work of the municipality and used in a new and innovative way". We recall that the choice of tablets and the software was made based on existing procurement contracts, and no recommendations on the implementation long-term goals accompanied the decision of the Municipal Board to implement the policy decision via tablets. The main point of such communication to each board member was the introduction to the tablet given in 2012.

> Observation: The board meeting was running a bit late. It ends with a half-hour instruction to the tablets. A relatively young woman, a consultant at an IT company, is the course leader. The woman gives a professional and friendly impression. She says that it is a short time for an introduction, but that it will be ok. There are two functions she focuses on; how to download and work in the documents of the board pack, and how to log into the area styrelsemöte.se (Instruction Session 2012-10-28).

In this case, despite all other functionality of a tablet, the consultant communicates the tablet as a mere replacement of the paper version of the board pack, and how the board members are to take notes in this paper substitute. No one voices the question of the policy, whether the tablet could or should facilitate new routines, processes, functionality etc. Instead the idea of the physical paper as an ideal resource for social practice is enforced, and that it is endorsed from the Municipal Board as part of the consequence of the policy "all board packs should be digitalized" (see Fig. 4.1 (2a)):

> [Interviewer:] Do you feel that the documents you get, that they have changed or anything in relation to before when you had them on paper?
>
> No. They look the same. Only that they are uploaded to the tablet. That's the difference. They look the same and they should do. There is no reason to change them. This is just a tool. Without the thing, there, their content is supposed to be the same and the layout is the same, you should not start rationalizing the papers because it is located on an app on a tablet, you should not change the document's appearance in relation to what you had before if you are happy with it. If you are not happy with it then you should change the look but it should be done regardless of the manner in which they, transmit, send, and read the documents. BD II, p. 3

Throughout the study, we observe that the paper as an ideal stays as part of the practices in the board. It may be seen as manifested via e.g. the following examples/practices:

> Observation: The CEO presented the plans for a new building. To give everyone access to these, she sends her tablet around the table (Meeting 2013-11-28).

> Observation: The agenda is updated and a paper version of the updated agenda is placed at each seat the table. No update is sent out via the tablets (Meeting 2014-01-30).

In these observations the ongoing dynamics, inherent relations and performative enactment in the local setting, the new technology, i.e. tablet and digital board pack, are given only a limited scope and legitimacy from the schemas (see Fig. 4.1).

As the explicit activity following the mandatory municipal decision, the instruction, is the only visible public enactment of the new policy sanctioned by the Municipality and the activities in the board, only endorse an interpretation of the new schema with the view of the tablet as a mere paper substitute as the allowed meaning in enacted practices (see Fig. 4.1 (3, 4)). Then contrary to the main goal of the policy (that IT should be used in new and innovative ways) all other legitimate uses of the tablet than as a paper substitute are gated out (see Fig. 4.1 (3a)) (Schultz and Boland 2000). This interpretation of the tablet (as a resource) is constitutive of the tablet in the board work in the sense that the (legitimate) use of the tablet in the board work is constituted in part by acting in accord with the tablet as a mere paper substitute, sometimes interchanged for a physical paper (3a). However, we also acknowledge the possibility that, by paraphrasing Searle (1983, p. 28): as some rules also create the very possibility of certain activities, rather, the interpretation of the tablet as solely a paper substitute creates the very possibility of using the tablet in the board setting as part of legitimate practice (see Fig. 4.1 (4a)).

With reference to disciplinary power, we might say, that the introduction of the digital devices combines both the deployment of force and the establishment of truth (Foucault 1977). It combines the deployment of policy and new technology and the establishment of its success.

4.5.2 Practices are Different but Nothing Should Change

In the beginning of our observations, the board members stated the need of writing down thoughts and notes in the actual board pack. One board member voiced the view of the majority of the board members of the value and importance of the notes to be written in immediate proximity to the issue, and directly on the actual paper the note concerned:

> If you write on two papers, a separate paper, the risk is that it disappears. RV I p. 5 2013

Later on in the study, the same board member voices that he/she has adopted a new way of working, a change that also several of the other board members voice. Clearly, now the note-taking seldom occurs during reading, and never in the board pack (see Fig. 4.2 (3a)). The way of working indicates a preference to taking notes on paper, however, as the board pack is in digital form, the problem of making digital notes in the digital board pack (see Fig. 4.2 (5)) and possibly the importance of keeping the notes in direct proximity to the agenda item, has made the note-taking occur more and more seldom (see Fig. 4.2 (4a)).

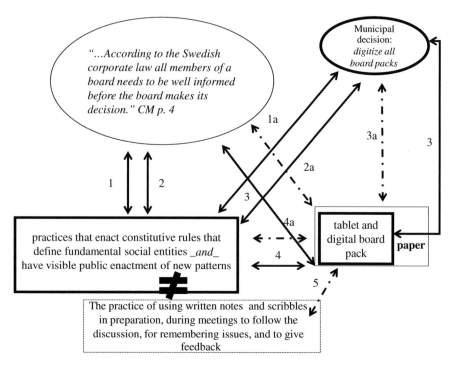

Fig. 4.2 Normalization process of new practices into a new schema. Two constitutive rules, the formal statute of the board member's responsibility (*1*) and the mandatory municipal board decision (*1a*) influence the enactment of practices. Interpretations of the constitutive rules that define fundamental social entities and have visible public enactment of new patterns help establish patterns of new practices (*4*). This entails a weakening of the practices that were connected to paper (*4a*). This entails a weakening of the practices that were connected to paper (*4a*), which in turn makes paper more obsolete (*3a*) in favour of the tablet (*3*). Due to its barriers for making notes (*5*) ongoing, the practice of using written notes is neither a practice that enacts the schema of digitizing board packs (*2a*) nor longer a practice that enacts the schema of being well informed as part of a board member's responsibility (*1*)

[Interviewer:] But when you read, do you [take notes]?
…if I make notes?
Yes, I surely do sometimes. Now it happens rarely. There is such a thing that stopped when, it is not on paper, then one can highlight in a way. No, but I do, of course, I read that and I have some comments so I can take a little note about it…Yes, when I write, then I have a note book I write in. I can obviously write in the tablet too but I write, I take out my note book only. On a piece of paper. Now it is not so often it is much like that. Without having to read through e.g. a, well, whatever it may be, when it is in response to a letter, or if it's a construction issue or something. You probably remember what you had questions on, so to speak, when you take up the actual document again. So it's not so often it occurs, it is actually not.

[Interviewer:] As you read, if you make a note, then do it in a paper on the side?
Yes, I do.
[Interviewer:] Do you underline anything in the document?
Yes, I know, you can do it, it can of course be done.
[Interviewer:] Yes, but I mean you do not do it when you read?
No. No. RV II p 11 2014

Correspondingly, a new schema on how to conduct preparations appears to be forming. The memory of previous ways of preparation via written notes in the material is still vivid, however, it is not affecting the preference of the tablet as the only (reasonable) tool for the activities and subsequent preparations (see Fig. 4.2 (2a)).

[Interviewer:] How did you do it before when you had paper documentation?
Well, then, I wrote on the document sometimes. Made notes in the margin. Hieroglyphs only I could interpret. Now it is rarely there are any matters that you need, then, to go through, then it goes all the way through but it is often as good a basis that's rarely there are some difficult issues, I think where you have to write very much. Make many notes. I think actually. I think the documents of the board pack in general are good.
Is it the same as before?
Yes, I think that was good in the past too. I think they had good track of stuff can I say.
RV II p 11 2014

The motivations that are presented for the new way of working include the quality of the board pack, and an indication of support for the view that in society paper is outdated (see Fig. 4.2 (4)). In addition, another way of working that circumvents the issue of digital notes is presented.

If you were to discard of a tool, which would you opt out?

Now I have the tablet so I choose not to get rid of it. Would it be paper again, no, then I feel probably almost no to it. Despite what I say in certain situations. It depends on how you are used to working with it. And if you look at the children and grandchildren, I think not at all. They wonder, paper what is it?
[Interviewer:] Despite then these you mentioned, including this restriction, or that this particular difficulty to get an overview or this that one might not…
Yes, yes. But then one can if one thinks it, then one can print that part of the document and use it when you go through to find issues. But people are now used to working with it from birth, with tablets, so I do not think it will be a problem for anyone. I hope. RV II p 11

The same indications of this process from written notes in direct proximity to the issue in the board pack as part of the preparations to a more "memory based mental note" can be found in the majority of the board member interviews (see Fig. 4.2 (1)). This enforces the idea of paper as outdated (see Fig. 4.2 (3a)) and the importance of using digital board packs (see Fig. 4.2 (3)) and it also affects other well established practices that are directly affecting the key criteria of the board meeting (see Fig. 4.2 (2a)).

[Interviewer:] As you read, how do you do? Do you take notes, or?
I don't write much. I might make notes in the documents, it may happen that I do. But it is
not so common that I do it really, I probably have paper and pen handy, but above all, I will
of course remember what is there, different things that I react to. JUM II, p. 2
[Interviewer:] In the past when you had these final paper documents, it happened when you
went through them, that you quoted, wrote things in them?
Mm, I did. It happened.
[Interviewer:] And now…? Then do no such thing now?
Naeh, I do not.
Do you write on any paper next?
It can happen, I would say more often. When I do it. One can say that the sum [? 08:37] I
will trust more to my memory. If I have any questions I might write it down, but I will trust
more to my memory when I use the tablet. Than before. CK II p 3

Based on the above the following examples of snapshots of the resulting continuous interactions could be recognized with regards to the use of written notes
during preparation and board meetings (See Fig. 4.2 relations 1–5).

The material and the new policy decisions regarding the format of the board
packs (digital) and ways of enacting the schema concerning a board member's
responsibility (that before the decision in the municipal board would not have been
possible) together frame the new interpretations of board work activities. Still, only
as the result of people continuously working, individually and collectively to enact
practices, these become routinely embedded in social contexts (May et al. 2009).

In this way the policy decision and procurement agreements frames (i.e. makes
possible or restricts) the possible practices that the resulting meaning of the schema
can give legitimacy to, e.g. what activities to use to carry out the board work. As an
illustrative example of this ongoing, dynamic, and reflexive dualities of interactions
between practices, schema and resources, the results indicate an ongoing convergence towards conformity to the basic social relations as the 'natural' expression of
self (Foucault 1977).

4.5.3   Everything Is Different and Nothing Has Changed

We recall that the empirical material indicates an additional consequence, the view
of the tablet as a mere substitute for paper constrains the activities that may help
mitigate this restricting view of the tablet as a resource. Still, the empirical material
indicates that the tablet itself is no blank slate and it seems connected to other
schemas that influence what is to be considered acceptable behaviour. Thus, the
influences on the continuous interactions with regards to the use of tablets and the
particular procured software and minimal introduction may result in a more limited
and restricted definition of what constitutes a legitimate activity:

> Observation: During the presentation the tablets are placed on the table, or kept passively in the laps of the board members. Their focus is with the presenter or at the screen. This is to be compared to the paper versions of the presentation. Two board members have the presentation available in paper form. They use the papers very actively, turning pages with emphasis and interchangeably looks on the presenter, the screen and the papers. Almost as if the use of the digital version of the presentation (colour) is off-limits for use while the presenter speaks (Meeting 2014-08-27).

Correspondingly, we find that the board members who report issues with the tablet, attribute these issues (not supported by the tablet's existing functionality) to their own shortcomings.

> [Interviewer:] When you write, you're with the documents, you have the documents in the tablet and then that you write - you keep them parallel or?
> Yes, that's the problem. Because then I had to switch between pages… Yeah. I do not know, probably is it that there are very many good features that I do not master. That is about to switch sides and.
> [Interviewer:] How do you do when you switch page?
> Yes when I press the bottom button, so to speak, and then I open another page. BG II, p. 3

For the only board member that reports that one does not use the tablet, the board member still maintains a positive attitude to the improvements that the administration has gained from the digitalization of the board pack.

> Yes, but. Not in the work of the Board in the meetings, however, that during the preparations so I imagine that. If you are like me and have had, has not really taken me over this hurdle and started using this tool properly, I think it has become more accessible with the documents. But, and lighter as well. It is nevertheless true that these bundles of papers are often quite large and impractical in some way, to carry around. So I think that it has become, the information has become more available, and it is the course more quickly to the board. And you do not have postal service and so-so. But during the Board meetings so I cannot say that I have found a difference really. With the reservation that I then have had poor attendance and may not be the right person to judge it.
> [Interviewer:] But nothing that you [experienced], for it is your experience that we want to…
> For my part, it has of course made more difficult because I find it difficult to get access to it. Once I thought, regardless now I will go to this board and so, so the tablet had become crazy. And another time I couldn't get to the iPad because it was somewhere at home. After we moved. And another time, I lost the login information for the spouse moved the tablet and papers to a different place. All things. So for my part, it has hampered the whole. LJ II p. 4-5

The empirical material further gives indications as to an additional consequence, the view of the tablet as a mere substitute for paper constrains the board members from activities that may help mitigate this restricted use of the tablet. The interpretation in its site may even be said to constrain the legitimacy of suggesting an activity that may help mitigate the barriers of the tablet as a resource, despite that the activities in question are part of explicit focus areas in the policy (see the above presented section The Policy Decision, Focus areas 1–5). As the following example indicates: When asked if anyone has shared knowledge on how to use the tablet, none of the board members have done so. One of the board members who is an experienced user has advice on how to handle the issue of writing with the tablet:

> [Interviewer:] Is there anything you would add or do you want to tell us about?
> No, but I want to emphasize this with the difficulty of writing that may make one not to always be active. To acquire keyboards are not so expensive and so complicated that, it would give very positive effects, I think for those who sit on the Board.
> [Interviewer:] Is it something you've talked about or have expressed the desire?
> No, actually, I have not done that. JG II, p. 8

Subsequently this generates a negative loop with respect to the tablets as resources that are acceptable for accomplishments beyond providing a static paper substitute.

As a conceptual exercise, we may posit a simulation of the discourse of the board in which the dualities of the practices, legitimate interpretations of the schemas (norms and formal rules), and the acceptable definition and use of tablets in the board room discourse drive the board members into a vicious circle of ongoing reconstruction of the interactional patterns, in turn modifying the schemas that define a boarding meeting, to counter the very idea of board work as the exercise of democratic dialogue (Fig. 4.3).

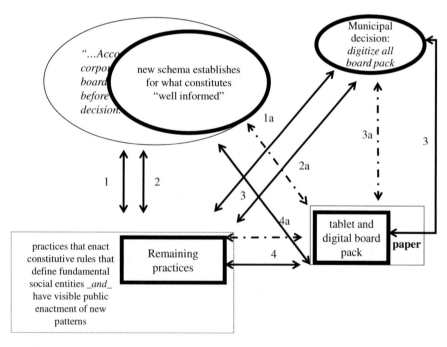

Fig. 4.3 The process of limiting and constraining the interpretation of the tablet to the point where the only legitimate interpretations are counterproductive for the policy and the practices of the board work

Practices are contextually constituted, and convey meaning in and as part of their discourse. Shedding light on practices gives casual priority to practices instead of, for example, different ideas board members might have on fulfilling different democratic values as being members in a municipality owned corporation. However, structure is always enabling as well as constraining.

Furthermore, the board members' may or may not be empowered by access to the tablets as resources. The reason is that as the dynamic dualities continuously shape the view of what constitutes "legal" practices, a negative loop may be entered with respect to the tablets as resources that are acceptable for accomplishments beyond providing a static paper substitute. This serves as an illustration not only that the transformative capacity of resources can go both ways, but that small sublime changes in rudimentary practices may lead to both abrupt/episodic outcomes (i.e. when two of the participants don't get their tablets to work) and radical change (the potential democratic dialogue related to board work and public owned companies. It is represented in our model as adjustments of the schemas as schemas for practices).

Practices that have earlier been considered fundamental for the constitution of the meeting and the role as a board member have quite easily become discarded. By means of our theoretical framework the orthogonal outcomes may be explained as the natural outcome of continuously ongoing dynamic processes of normalization of activities into structured practice, processes that draws on social interaction and resourceful agency in relation to the IT-devices, all happening below and beyond any deliberate intent of managers and policy makers (Orlikowski 1996, 2000, Schultz and Boland 2000).

4.6 Findings

Social practices have a complex relation with policies and IT, which may affect conflicting goals, to the detriment of successful routines invented for acknowledging human barriers as well as societal goals. As a result, one imminent challenge for policymakers is the view of a policy decision of implementing IT as a panacea for success. Our findings in the above presented study highlight that the acceptance of the tablet as the resource for digital board packs, the activities of the board members in core areas such as preparation and during the board meeting are changing due to the constraints posed by the material and existing fundamental social relationships. Thus, routines are reconstituted and anchoring practices of the board is subject to a change that (a) anchors new material firmer to board activities without utilizing its inherent advantages, (b) anchors new conflicting routines while weakening well established ones, and (c) results in new routines that weaken fundamental goals of the board work and work counterproductive to human cognition, leaving the individual to grapple with a situation where everything is different and everything has changed. At the same time as someone looking for a drama will be disappointed.

Even though the manner in which the board members take notes or not in preparation or during a board meeting might appear as small changes in rudimentary practices, such sublime practice (both for the board members who carry it out and a potential observer), our constructionist approach and micro-level-perspective bring into surface the importance of the sublime to further understanding its importance in a context of implementing new devices in the service of democracy.

The board meeting is dependent upon digital devices like the board packs. In general terms, our empirical material illuminates how new meanings arise and old meanings just seem to vanish into thin air. As Pinch (2008, p. 473) stresses by quoting Powell and DiMaggio (1983, p. 188), such an agenda resonates well with the critical agenda for institutional analysis that "... show how choices made at one point in time create institutions that generate recognizable pattern of constraints and opportunities at a later point". However, our study shows that the trick might not only be to illuminate such new patterns along a timeline but to recognize small, sublime, disruptive activities related to different practices.

By drawing attention to these practices on a micro level, we hope that policies can be assessed with greater confidence. Inspired and in line with Sewell we suggest that the empirical material illuminated and elaborated in the analytical model are not to be seen as reified categories that policy makers can invoke to explain the shape of organizational outcomes. For theory, we have called for an analysis and hopefully even inspired other researchers to focus on the seemingly small, slow, yet fundamental dialectical interactions with which human agents shape and even reinvent their organizational life, and how this ongoing process is enacted by new technologies that leads to emergent outcomes.

4.7 Concluding Remarks

Our discussion concerns implementation of policy decisions, and how the individuals involved can enact and decisions based on both formal statutes, norms and more fundamental social relations (Meyer and Rowan 1977).

However, of importance for practitioners aiming for successful implementation of IT, our analysis does not ignore the importance of how digital artefacts are implemented, how and not only to the degree consultants teach standard practices, but the way they introduce a particular device what they are and their potential in different contexts. In other words, we note that the consultant and her presentation may be an important force for homogeneity of both perception and practice (Leonardi and Barley 2008). Our perspective is more in line with Orlikowski's (2000) approach of a practice lens that only technologies-in-use, not technological artifacts, shape organizing processes. Furthermore, following Orlikowski's argumentation also tells us that people tend to enact the same or similar material arrangements over time. Still, our empirical material tells us much more.

We agree with Leonardi (2013, p. 64) who argues that at a macro-social level, "a technology-in-practice is really nothing more than a set of norms governing them, why, and how to use a technology in a specific setting". Nevertheless, our study supports the idea that technologies at a micro level seem to push practices in different directions but not more and solely as much that the social structure will allow for.

It must be noted that previous studies have shown that the appropriation of new technologies and the adjustments that different members of an organization enact over time may both facilitate the slow, sometime subtle, but also significant transformation of organizing practices (Orlikowski 1996). Nevertheless, of importance to policy makers, the fundamental practices related to maintaining a democratic dialogue is partly dissolving. Hence, also a possible venue for future work, we note that it is not just a question about that different separate organizational practices are transformed, but also what a board is.

References

Alvesson, M., & Sköldberg, K. (2000). *Reflexive methodology: New vistas for qualitative research*. London: Sage.

Bohn, H. G. (1854). *The works of the right honourable Edmund Burke* (Vol. I, pp. 446–448). London. http://en.wikipedia.org/wiki/Representative_democracy#cite_note-3. Accessed 20 April 2015.

Bond, G., Drake, R., McHugo, G., Rapp, C., & Whitley, R. (2009). Strategies for improving fidelity in the national evidence-based practices project. *Research on Social Work Practice, 19*(5), 569.

Bourdieu, P. (1999). *The logic of practice*. Stanford: Stanford University Press.

Creswell, J. W. (2012). *Qualitative inquiry and research design: Choosing among five approaches*. Sage.

Eriksson Lundström, J., & Edenius, M. (2014). Anchoring tablets in organizational practices—a practice based approach to the digitalization of board work. In *The Proceedings of the 34th International Conference on Information Systems (ICIS), Auckland, New Zealand, December 14–17, 2014.*

Edenius, M., & Eriksson Lundström, J. (2016). Technology-triggered change management as means for unintended reconstitution of board work (submitted manuscript).

Foucault, M. (1977). *Discipline and punish*. London: Penguin.

Giddens, A. (1979). *Central problems in social theory*. Macmillan, UK: Basingstoke.

Giddens, A. (1984). *The constitution of society: Outline of the theory of structure*. Berkeley: University of California Press.

Habermas, J. (1984). *The Theory of Communicative Action* (Vol. 1). Boston: Reason and the Rationalization of Society, Beacon Press.

Hanson, N. (1958). *Patterns of discovery: An inquiry into the foundation of science*. Cambridge: Cambridge University Press.

Leonardi, P. (2013). Theoretical foundation for the study of sociomateriality. *Information and Organization, 23,* 59–76.

Leonardi, P., & Barley, S. R. (2008). Materiality and change: Challenges to building better theory about technology and organizing. *Information and Organization, 18*(3), 159–176.

May, C., Mair F. S., Finch, T., MacFarlane, A., Dowrick, C., Treweek, S., Rapley, T., Ballini, L., Ong, B. N., Rogers, A., Murray, E., Elwyn, G., Legare, F., Gunn, J., & Montor V. M. (2009).

Development of a theory of implementation and integration: Normalization process theory. *Implementation Science 4*(29).

Meyer, J., & Rowan, B. (1977). Institutionalized organizations: formal structure as myth and ceremony. *American Journal of Sociology, 83*(3), 340–363.

Nicolini, D. (2007). Stretching out and expanding medical practices: the case of telemedicine. *Human Relations, 60*(6), 889–920.

Orlikowski, W. J. (1996). Improvising organizational transformation over time: A situated change perspective. *Information Systems Research, 7*(1), 63–92.

Orlikowski, W. J. (2000). Using technology and constituting structures: A practice lens for studying technology in organizations. *Organization Science, 11*(4), 404–428.

Orlikowski, W. J. (2002). Knowing in practice: Enacting a collective capability in distributed organizing. *Organization Science, 13,* 249–273.

Pinch, T. (2008). Technology and institutions: Living in a material world. *Theory of Sociology, 37,* 461–483.

Powell, W. W., & DiMaggio, P. J. (1983). The iron cage revisited: Institutional isomorphism and collective rationality in organizational fields. *American Sociological Review, 48*(2), 147–160.

Rainey, Hal G. (2003). *Understanding and managing public organizations* (3rd ed.). San Francisco: Wiley/Jossey-Bass.

Ruigrok, W., Peck, S., & Board, H. (2006). Board characteristics and involvement in strategic decision making: Evidence from Swiss companies. *Journal of Management Studies, 43*(5), 1201–1226.

Schultze, U., & Boland, R. J. (2000). Knowledge management technology and the reproduction of knowledge work practices. *Journal of Strategic Information Systems, 9,* 193–212.

Searle, J. (1983). *Intentionality: An essay in the philosophy of mind.* Cambridge: Cambridge University Press.

Sewell, W. (1992). A theory of structure: Duality, agency and transformation. *American Journal of Sociology* (98), 29.

Strauss, A., & Corbin, J. M. (1998). *Basics of qualitative research: Techniques and procedures for developing grounded theory.* Thousand Oaks, CA: Sage.

Vaast, E., & Walsham, G. (2005). Representation and actions: the transformation of work practices with IT use. *Information and Organization, 15,* 65–89.

Part II
Modeling

Chapter 5
Towards Decentralized IT Governance in the Public Sector: A Capability-oriented Approach

Irina Rychkova and Jelena Zdravkovic

Abstract Modern public organizations undergo an important transformation becoming a part of dynamic "innovative ecosystem" where they co-create value with citizens, government, policy makers and other institutions. Information Technology plays a central role in this transformation. Getting more value from IT becomes an intrinsic part of organizational mission. Information Technology Governance (ITG) is an important instrument that ensures that the organization will succeed in its mission. Efficient yet adaptive ITG is indispensable. To respond to the increasing service demand, public organizations require resources and capacities that lay outside the organization. Co-production, engagement of citizens and partner organizations, open innovation—are some of the major challenges. Meeting these challenges, public organizations need to master new governance styles to overcome the shortcomings of hierarchical structures and centralized decision making. In this work, we define a model where we adopt the theory of *public value* in order to reason about different contexts where ITG mechanisms are proposed as *capabilities*. We distinguish between three ITG styles: centralized, federated and decentralized and thereby provide a rationale allowing public organizations to identify an ITG style that fits best to their value-creation context and corresponding capability patterns as reusable ways for implementing governance of IT.

I. Rychkova (✉)
Centre de Recherche en Informatique, University Paris 1, Pantheon-Sorbonne,
90, rue Tolbiac, 75013 Paris, France
e-mail: irina.rychkova@univ-paris1.fr

J. Zdravkovic
Department of Computer and System Sciences, Stockholm University,
Borgarfjordsgatan 12, 164055 Kista, Sweden
e-mail: jelenaz@dsv.su.se

© Springer International Publishing AG 2017
L. Rusu and G. Viscusi (eds.), *Information Technology Governance in Public Organizations*, Integrated Series in Information Systems 38,
DOI 10.1007/978-3-319-58978-7_5

5.1 Introduction

Today, technologies are emerging and evolving at an ever-increasing rate—
e-Government, distance/hybrid education (e.g., MOOC), e-Health, e-Commerce are
just few examples of influential applications of Information Technologies
(IT) which shape strategies in both private and public sector. Getting more value
from IT is an increasingly important organizational competency (Weill and Ross
2004); in this view, Information Technology Governance (ITG) is an instrument
that can ensure that the organization will meet its strategic goals.

Weill and Ross (2004) defines IT governance as a part of corporate governance,
focused on *specifying the decision rights and accountability framework to
encourage desirable behavior in using IT*. ITG can be persisted in an organization
*as a set of organizational arrangements and patterns of authority addressing the
major areas in the organizational IT* (Sambamurthy and Zmud 1999). In De Haes
and Van Grembergen (2015), the authors emphasize the importance of IT governance in the organization, as *an integral part of the corporate governance, over-
seeing the definition and implementation of processes, structures and relational
mechanism in the organization that enable both business and IT people to execute
their responsibilities in support of Business/IT alignment and the creation of
business value from IT-enabled business investments.*

In this chapter, we examine IT Governance in the context of public organizations. According to Moore (1997), strategies in public sectors are (1) focused on
long-run over short; (2) attending to large issues with big impact on performance
rather than small issues with impacts on productivity; (3) concentrating on ultimate
ends rather than needs. Missions of public organizations are mostly associated with
important social outcomes and require long-term strategies and strong commitment
in all the operational areas, including IT. Whereas opportunities are limitless,
resources are scarce and complexities are growing. In order to be successful in
creating value from their IT, modern public organizations have to ensure: (i) continuous analysis of the aimed value, including social and political impact;
(ii) continuous engagement of beneficiaries (clients, customers, citizens) into setting
the objectives for the IT and evaluation of the results; (iii) continuous engagement
of partner organizations (co-producers) into standard creation and use (Weill and
Ross 2004); (Moore 1997); (Moore and Khagram 2004).

Meeting these requirements is challenging due to inherently hierarchical structure of public organizations and centralized decision making that also applies to
their IT. According to Mintzberg (1979), *"Centralization is the tightest means of
coordinating decision making in the organization. All decisions are made by one
individual, in one brain, and then implemented through direct supervision"*.
Whereas efficient in closed stable environment, centralized decision making shows
serious drawbacks in open environments driven by innovations. Modern public
organizations need to become a part of dynamic innovative ecosystem where *they
co-create value* with citizens, government, policy makers, other public and private

organizations and institutions. To succeed in their missions, *public organizations need to master governance styles that overcome the shortcomings of hierarchical structures and centralized decision making.*

Whereas centralized organizational structures have been long dominating in the past with their governance styles (Weill and Ross 2004); (Gordon 2014), organizations adopting federated and decentralized decision making are gaining attention over the last decade (Morgan 2014); (DuMoulin 2015). Decentralized style of ITG does not rely on traditional structures such as executive committees, boards and management hierarchies, but rather on a broad participation of stakeholders. Decentralization should not however be confused with anarchy that accepts neither structure nor control: modern decentralized organizations support hierarchies based on merit and experience (not on a position in an administrative ladder); *they adopt decentralized communication, coordination and control following the principles of social peer-to-peer.*

IT-enabled value creation depends strongly on the organizational context. To effectively develop its ITG structures, processes and relational mechanisms, the organizations need first to *define the context* of IT governance and to *identify the governance style* that fits best to this context. We adopt the public value approach for strategic management in public sector developed in Moore (1997), Moore and Khagram (2004). Public value describes the value that an organization contributes to society. For public organizations, it is the value developed for individual citizens, communities and organizations through provisioning new services and improving existing services, including IT services and services enabled by IT. Thus, we consider public value as an important concept for ITG creation. We propose to examine the following elements in order to define the ITG context: (1) *the public value* from the IT that the organization is going to produce (2) *the sources of legitimacy* and support that would authorize the organization to act and (3) *capabilities* the organization will need in order to deliver the result. We identify four context models and map these models on three ITG styles—centralized, federated and decentralized (Fig. 5.1).

To facilitate a value, and context-based formalization of ITG, we consider it as an *organizational capability*. In the context of business planning, it is becoming recognized as a fundamental component to describe what a core business does and, in particular, as an ability for delivering value, beneath the business strategy (Ulrich and Rosen 2011). The interest in reasoning about ITG in an organization in terms of capabilities is twofold: (a) ITG capabilities can describe the value from IT and an ability for delivering this value by encouraging context-specific relevant behaviors in using IT; (b) ITG capabilities support configurability of ITG structures, processes and relational mechanisms on a higher level. We distinguish between three ITG styles (centralized, federated and decentralized). These styles imply the use of different ITG capabilities. We define the corresponding *ITG capability patterns* as the regular and repetitive means for the implementation of the three ITG styles. These patterns can be used to simplify and to guide a context-specific description of

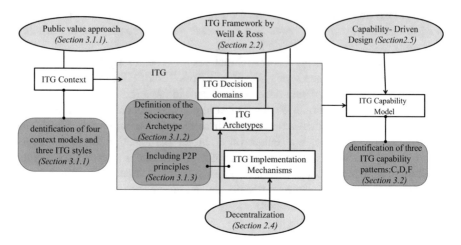

Fig. 5.1 Organization of this chapter. The rounded rectangles depict the main contributions of this chapter; the ellipses depict the main theories; the rectangles depict the main concepts we address

ITG structures and processes. Figure 5.1 presents a short overview of the chapter, linking together the underlying theories (ellipses), established concepts (rectangles) and our contributions (rounded rectangles).

The reminder of this paper is organized as follows: in Sect. 2 we present the relevant theoretical background; in Sect. 3 we discuss the results and in Sect. 4 we illustrate these results on a case of the Higher Education sector. Section 5 provides concluding remarks and directions of future work.

5.2 Theoretical Background

In this section, we present the main theories and concepts that leaded us to the definition of *IT governance capability* that will be addressed in the next section. First, we provide a definition of IT governance and acknowledge several frameworks in IT governance. In particular, we focus on the IT governance framework developed in the Center for Information Systems Research, Sloan School of Management of MIT (Sect. 2.2). This framework is widely recognized by both academics and practitioners and it provides an important foundation for our work. Than we discuss some challenges of IT governance in public organizations (Sect. 2.3). In order to understand the nature of these challenges, we discuss organizational structures (Sect. 2.4). Our experience and observations show that modern public organizations have complex structures and tend to exhibit the properties of centralized, federated and decentralized organizations. Thus, adopting relevant IT governance styles can be of a vital importance. Capacity and ability of an organization to execute various IT governance mechanisms depending on its value-creation context can be considered as an IT governance capability. We discuss the capability-driven approach in Sect. 2.5.

5.2.1 IT Governance and Related Frameworks

According to the Organization for Economic Cooperation and Development (OECD), corporate governance provides the structures for determining the organizational objectives, for attaining those objectives and for monitoring performance (OECD 2015). As a part of corporate governance (Weill and Ross 2004), IT Governance is focused on the management and use of IT to achieve corporate performance goals needing to address three questions:

1. What decisions must be made to ensure effective management and use of IT?
2. Who should make these decisions?
3. How will these decisions be made and monitored?

For implementing ITG, an organization has to identify the scope of IT and the main areas/issues where decisions have to be made; it has to define decision-making structures (i.e., organizational units, specific roles, committees) responsible for making these IT decisions; it has to design and implement processes for IT decision-making and IT monitoring to ensure the desired behaviors using IT; eventually, it has to specify the mechanisms supporting the active participation of, and collaborative relationship among entities appointed to defined governance structures, and according to an organizational governance style (Weill and Ross 2004); (De Haes and Van Grembergen 2015).

Over the years, a number of frameworks have emerged, such as: ISO 38500 (ISO/IEC 38500 2015) is an international standard for corporate governance of IT at the highest level of organizations to understand and fulfill their legal, regulatory, and ethical obligations in respect of their organizations use of IT; COBIT (ISACA/ COBIT 5 2012) provides a framework for governance and control process of IT with the focus of aligning it with business; IT BSC (Grembergen and De Haes 2005), where the theory of the balanced scorecard is used as a performance measurement system for IT governance enabling strategies for improvement. Once an ITG framework is designed and implemented, the effectiveness of ITG can be measured based on some indicators. For example, the effectiveness of ITG can be perceived through the (increased) effectiveness and efficiency of the organizational IT, improved business/IT alignment, risk management etc. (De Haes and Van Grembergen 2015); (Wiedenhöft et al. 2014).

In our study we focused on a single perspective of ITG, i.e., its patterns for different organizational governance styles ranging from centralized to decentralized. Not aiming to design a new framework, we ground our proposal on a well-established ITG theory of Weill and Ross provided in Weill and Ross (2004).

5.2.2 IT Governance Framework of Weill and Ross

Peter Weill and Jeanne W. Ross from the Center for Information Systems Research, Sloan School of Management of MIT, proposed an approach toward designing and implementing IT governance based on an extensive research and experience with a large number of organizations working in private and public sector (Weill and Ross 2004). The main concerns of their approach are the following:

IT Decision Domains: Five interrelated IT decision domains are: IT principles, IT architecture, IT infrastructure, Business application needs, IT investment and prioritization. IT principles define desirable behavior for IT professionals and users. IT architecture is an organizing logic for data application and infrastructure aiming to achieve a desired level of business and technical standardization and integration. IT infrastructure is the foundation of shared capabilities (both technical and human). Business application needs includes decisions about specific needs that directly generate value. IT investment and prioritization consist of choosing which initiatives to fund and how much to spend on them.

IT Governance Archetypes: they describe the combination of people or roles who have decision rights or who provide the input for one or several decision domains described above. Weill and Ross define six archetypes: Business Monarchy, IT Monarchy, Feudal, Federal, IT Duopoly and Anarchy. Except Anarchy, the archetypes strongly rely on the hierarchical structure of the organization (and its IT), requiring the involvement of CxO, BU leaders. They also imply that the decisions in main IT areas will be done within the organizational boundary and will not involve external stakeholders (e.g., partners, clients, government, employees). Besides the two "monarchy" archetypes that refer to a centralized organization already in their name, the three "non-monarchy" archetypes (i.e., federal, feudal, duopoly) also rely on leaders (business or IT) of the organization and do not specify further decentralization. The anarchy archetype specifies that the input will be provided or decision will be made by the business unit that owns the business process, by the project team or by the end users, supporting no structure or control. This is the reason why the anarchy archetype is rarely adopted by organizations. This corroborates with the empirical data collected by Weill and Ross and many other sources in the literature.

Implementation Mechanisms: The approach provides three categories of mechanisms to specify how the decisions made by the identified individuals (or groups) will be enacted: decision-making structures, alignment processes and communication approaches.

Decision-making structures clarify who is responsible and accountable for decisions. Examples of these structures are committees (IT project, IT security, Architecture, steering committee), executive teams, business unit leaders, IT leaders, heads of functional areas, key business process owners. Alignment processes ensure effective input to decision makers and implementation of their decisions. Examples of these processes are formal IT performance measurements, service-level agreements (SLAs), KPI, knowledge management. Communication approaches allow for disseminating governance processes and responsibilities to concerned actors. Examples of these approaches are CIO announcements, web portals, focused groups meetings, co-location, cross-training.

The implementation mechanisms reflect and fit the governance style defined by the archetypes. Thus, not much support for decentralized decision making and open innovation is defined.

5.2.3 IT Governance in Public Organizations

Public organizations deliver services that can be considered as a public good, or that are established by a government policy. Whereas for private organizations, value translates into the client satisfaction, public organizations are interested in achieving social outcomes, which are not always associated with client satisfaction (e.g., law enforcement, tax collection, etc.). The client of a public or governmental organization becomes a mean to an end rather than an end in itself (as for private organizations) (Moore and Khagram 2004). In both (Weill and Ross 2004) and (Moore and Khagram 2004) the authors recognize the following challenges of public organizations that need to be addressed when designing ITG:

Measuring performance and value from IT: the value from IT does not translate into revenues or customer satisfaction. Measurement of concrete outputs and activities (e.g., a number of customers visiting a web page, a number of submitted/closed demands etc.) is often used as an alternative but inefficient. Organizations need to study and measure *social outcomes from the IT*. This measurement requires continuous communication with beneficiaries (citizens) and their engagement into both setting up the objectives for the IT as well as for evaluation of the results.

Funding and prioritization of IT programs: Funding and prioritization decisions about IT programs are challenging as they can hardly rely on performance measurement due to above. Moreover, funding decisions are often made by political power holders who may not directly benefit from the program or service. To prioritize the investments into IT infrastructure and services, the analysis of their aimed value and their beneficiaries is required.

Interoperability and partner engagement: To create and to benefit from co-production opportunities, public organizations need to develop and promote interoperability. The main challenge is how to encourage external co-producers to participate in standard creation and to invest in standard compliant systems and processes? Strong engagement with partner organization is required.

More recently, dFogIT governance framework (CIPFA and IFAC 2014) which is based on the ISO/IEC 38500 emphasized the key principles of governance in public organizations—*commitment to integrity and ethical values* and *openness and comprehensive stakeholders' engagement*; followed as well by the need for outcomes in terms of economic, social and environmental benefits, management of risks and performances, implementing good practices, etc. The work presented in

Juiz et al. (2014) utilized this framework to illustrate a way to implement the ISO/IEC 38500 standard in a public high-education sector to assess maturity of organization's IT governance, as well as to and further refine the principles of governance in the public sector as suggested in dFogIT framework. In Janahi et al. (2015) the authors have proposed a conceptual approach to the management of ITG in the public sector, where *strategic/organizational objectives, human resources, IT resources* and *processes and activities* are seen as the main concepts having well defined interconnection relations between them. When proposing our capability-oriented ITG patterns we took in the consideration both the outlined principles and the concepts as it can be well seen in Sect. 3.2.

5.2.4 *Organizational Structures and Decentralization*

The terms centralization and decentralization often refer to the power over the decisions made in the organization. According to Mintzberg (1979), when *all the power* for decision making rests *at a single point* in the organization—the structure should be called *centralized*; to the extent that the power is dispersed *among many entities*, the structure should be called *decentralized*.

Military organizations are typically examples of centralized organizations. They have an explicit hierarchy, with responsibilities and decision making power clearly defined and fixed for the positions within this hierarchy. Many public organizations have a hierarchical structure with federated decision making, where decisions are made by a group of individuals (a board or committee) appointed by the authority or government. This also applies to their IT.

Centralized and Federated organizations are very stable and robust but they cannot respond easily to change and are slow to act (Mintzberg 1979).

Information flow in these organizations is also an issue: once the organization grows, all the decisions cannot be understood in one center (Mintzberg 1979). People who see new opportunities and who understand what needs to be done to adapt, are not always sitting at the top of the organization according to Morgan (2014). Following (Mintzberg 1979) and (Morgan 2014) we summarize the following reasons for decentralization in IT:

- Decision-making powers need to be shared. Power has to be placed where the knowledge is.
- Innovation through IT requires an extreme agility from organizations. Making decisions locally improves agility and reduces time needed to address the issue.
- Creative people require considerable room for maneuver. Resistance to new technologies due to the lack of understanding or fear to put at risk the existing position often comes from the center and jeopardizes new opportunities.

5.2.4.1 Decentralized Decision Making

A number of organizational structures supporting decentralized decision making have recently emerged and became used. These structures are often addressed as "post-modern" organizations. These organizations are often grounded on the principles of social P2P (Bauwens 2005), implementing *peer-production, peer-trust, peer-review*, and *peer-vote* mechanisms for decentralized communication and decision making. The examples of post-modern organizations include *Collaborative Network (CN), Virtual Organization, Coopetitions*, and *Sociocratic* organizations. They distinguish from both centrally and federally governed organizations and from anarchies.

Collaborative Network (CN) and *Virtual Organization* both refer to a group of independent business entities (or complete organizations) that share resources and skills to achieve their goals (Camarinha-Matos and Afsarmanesh 2005). *Coopetition* describes a complex relationship between two or more organizations that simultaneously are in competition and cooperate together (Bengtsson and Kock 2000).

Sociocracy is a method for governance *used by public, private, non-profit, and community organizations and associations*. It represents an alternative to the traditional organizational structure based on cybernetic principles (i.e., as a system with feedback loops) (Buck and Villines 2007). The decision-making power is distributed within the organization (Romme 2016). Three fundamental principles of sociocracy include: (1) Decisions are made when there is a consent from all participants (i.e., no objections); (2) A sociocratic organization is composed of a hierarchy of semi-autonomous circles; (3) Each circle is linked to one above and to one below via individuals acting as links functioning as full members in the decision-making of both (*double-linking*) (Endenburg 1998a, b). Compared to a regular committee or board, a sociocratic circle is self-managed. While committee members might be appointed by an authority, individuals are elected to roles in sociocracy circles in open discussion using the same consent criteria used for other policy decisions.

Currently sociocracy is used by public, private, non-profit, and community organizations and associations. It represents an alternative to the traditional organizational structure based on hierarchy on one hand and to the flat management on the other hand. New branches that incorporate some of Endenburg's principles of sociocracy include holacracy. The examples of holacratic organizations include Sun Hydraulics, Valve, GitHub, Zappos.

Among the core principles behind the post-modern organizations are *self-organization* and *peer-to-peer (P2P)* that were extensively studied in the literature.

The idea of a process based on *self-organization* of equipotent participants was proposed in computing: Peer-to-peer is a distributed application architecture where peers make a portion of their resources, such as processing power, disk storage or network bandwidth, directly available to other network participants, without the need for central coordination by servers or stable hosts (Schollmeier 2002).

Peer-to-peer architecture was also explored by social science, where the concept of commons-based peer-production (or social production) was proposed as an alternative mode of socioeconomic production (Benkler 2006). According to this principle, a large number of people work cooperatively, in contrast to traditional firm production, where the tasks are delegated by some central authority. Bauwens (2005) describes P2P as "a template of human relationships", a "relational dynamic" which is springing up throughout the social fields. The dynamics is based on free participation of equipotent partners, engaged in the production of common resources, without recourse to monetary compensation as key motivating factor. Social P2P does not deny 'authority', but only fixed forced hierarchy, and therefore accepts authority based on expertise.

Related concepts include *open innovation*. It is a paradigm that assumes that looking to advance in their technologies, organizations should use external ideas as well as internal ideas, and internal and external paths to market (Chesbrough 2003).

To conclude, we would like to illustrate organizational decentralization with examples of decisions that can be made in some of the five main IT domains defined by the IT governance framework of Weill and Ross (see Sect. 2.2 for details).

- Examples of *IT principles* supported by a decentralized organization can include: knowledge management, technology-supported open innovation, use of open standards/co-creation of standards, interoperability, compliance with (industry) standards.
- Examples of *IT architecture* decisions include: distributed (P2P) architecture, data integration, standard interfaces for communication, high cohesion/low coupling, SOA.
- Examples of *IT infrastructure* decisions include: use of cloud computing, grid computing; public infrastructure (e.g., the Internet, telecom networks); shared standard applications (ERP, CRM, SCM, etc.), shared standard application for communication and coordination (social networks, knowledge sharing platforms, groupware, VOIP etc.)

5.2.5   Capability-Driven Approach

The capability notion originates from competence-based management and military frameworks, further advancing the traditional enterprise modeling approaches *by representing organizational designs from a result-based perspective*.

From the business perspective, a capability describes what the business does that creates value for customers. It represents a design from a result-based perspective including various dimensions including organizational values, goals, processes, people, and resources. The notion has a growing presence in the current business and IT alignment frameworks starting from more business-oriented such as Business Architecture and Business Modeling, towards the alignment-oriented represented by Enterprise Architecture (EA), and Enterprise Modeling (EM). In brief, the emergence of the use of the capability notion seems having the following motivations:

(a) in the context of business planning, it is becoming recognized as a fundamental component to describe what a core business does and, in particular, as an ability for delivering value, beneath the business strategy (Ulrich and Rosen 2011);
(b) it supports configurability of operations on a higher level than services and process, and according to changes in operational business context (Bērziša et al. 2015).

Following the above, *we consider IT Governance capabilities as abilities and capacities of an organization to ensure maximum value from its IT in a given context.* We further define ITG capability patterns to provide guidelines for practical adoption of the governance styles (centralized, federated and decentralized) in public organizations.

5.3 ITG Capability for Public Organizations

5.3.1 Decentralization in IT Governance

Following (Weill and Ross 2004), we consider three distinctive IT governance styles: Centralized (C), Decentralized (D) and Federated (F).

- Centralized ITG relies on Business or IT monarchies in most of decision areas. This governance style is relevant when the high degree of standardization is required and cost-efficiency is one of the primary value sources.
- Federated ITG relies on duopolies and federal governance structures. This style can be beneficial for organizations seeking for cost-efficient use of the assets and IT-enabled innovation.
- Decentralized ITG fits to organizations focusing on innovation and time to market and with the tendency to delegate decision making from the center to local units or project teams.

Weill and Ross relate the ITG to the value an organization seeks to create from IT, but it does not provide an explicit link to the organization's environment where this value will be created. A modern public organization can be seen as a part of dynamic ecosystem, where it maintains the relationships of different nature with the other organizations and individuals (Fig. 5.2). In order to successfully achieve its goals in this complex environment, the organization needs to master different governance styles and use them according to the *context*.

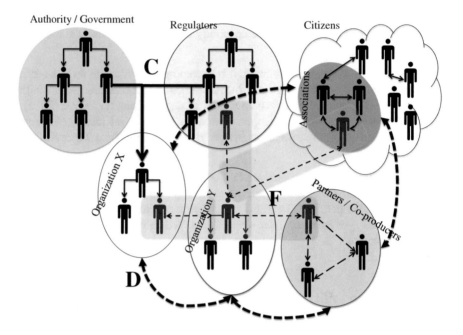

Fig. 5.2 Organizational ecosystem. C (centralized), D (decentralized) and F (federated) characterize the relationships between the organization and the other parts of its environment

5.3.1.1 Applying the Theory of Public Value for Defining the ITG Context

In order to identify the context for public organizations, we adopt the theory of Public Value proposed in Moore and Khagram (2004) identifying three main characteristics of public organizations: *public value, authorizing environment providing legitimacy and support*, and *core organizational capabilities* (*internal and external*) required to produce this value.

Public value describes the value that an organization contributes to society. Value for the public is a result of evaluations about how basic needs of individuals, groups and the society as a whole are influenced in relationships involving the public (Meynhardt 2009). Whereas private value is associated with satisfying individual desires, public value is mostly focused on achieving social outcomes.

The Center for Technology in Government published a report, where they studied five U.S. and international governments, examining the full value of government IT investments (Cresswell et al. 2006). The results of this research demonstrate that the IT investments generate public value of two distinctive types: value from improvement of internal government operations and processes (e.g., improving quality of service, cost reduction) and value from broader political and social outcomes (enabling new services, creating working places, contributing to individual and community well-being). We generalize these findings and propose to distinguish between:

1. *Value from delivering specific benefits directly to citizens*
2. *Value from improving the organization itself as a public asset*

Each of these value types can be associated with one or multiple *value sources*: cost saving, increase in quality of service, enabling new services, and intrinsic enhancements (i.e., changing environment providing political, social, cultural impact, improving general quality of life of an individual or a group).

Legitimacy (and support). Public organizations are not free to choose their market—they are *authorized* to provide their services by their environment that comprises government, customers, employees, suppliers, local communities, citizens, policy makers, controlling organizations etc. The authorizing environment provides the organizations with legitimacy and support and may vary depending on the scope of the IT project and its aimed value. For example, public organizations can be mandated by their authorizing environment to deliver a specific service, ensuring compliance with regulations, recommendations and standards. In return, they benefit from their support (financial and legislative) while providing their services.

Required core capabilities. Public organizations need to develop and manage their *core* capabilities (functionalities) in order to deliver results. Compared to private organizations, much of capacity required to produce public value lay outside the public organization and thus not under its direct control. To succeed in their missions, public organizations need not only to develop internal capabilities controlled by the organization itself, but also to explore co-production opportunities with external partners (e.g., other public and private organizations, volunteers, associations etc.) by means of external capabilities.

We examine the three elements above (public value, legitimacy, and core capabilities) in order to define the ITG context asking the questions:

1. What is the important public value you are seeking to produce with the IT?
2. What sources of legitimacy and support authorize the agency, or wider system, to take action and provide resources to create that value?
3. What core capabilities does the agency and service provider require to deliver this result?

We propose a model (Fig. 5.3) that represents four different situations (value-creation contexts) for ITG in public organizations and links them to the three ITG styles (C—Centralized, D—Decentralized, and F—Federated). We define the contexts based on two parameters: type of aimed public value (horizontal axis) and type of required core capabilities (vertical axis). The four models of value creation context are depicted as four quadrants on the plane separated by the dashed lines. For each of these four context models we give an example of a value source and a source of legitimacy and support:

Required core
capabilities

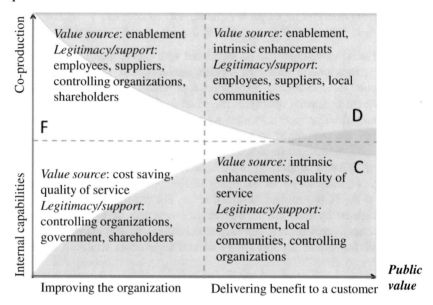

Fig. 5.3 A model that links the ITG context to the ITG style

Context Model 1 (bottom left): IT programs aiming at improving the organization through cost saving and/or efficiency of their services (ex.: electronic registration for residence permit, marriage certificate) are receiving legitimacy and support from authority (controlling organizations and government). Authorizing organizations also can be main clients/requestors of such programs and provide funding for them. The organization in this case has to focus on compliance with regulations and standards. It creates foundation for internal operational capabilities. Full value may comprise the increased transparency of the organization and improved reputation.

Context Model 2 (top left): IT programs aiming at improving the organization through enabling new services (ex.: on-line real time transport schedule and route planner) are receiving legitimacy and support from both authority (controlling organizations and government) and employees and external suppliers. Organization creates foundation for internal and external operational capabilities using co-production. Organization enables new capabilities both internally and externally (for community, co-producers etc.). Full value from the program can expand the organizational boundaries having an impact on society.

Context Model 3 (top right): IT programs aiming at delivering benefits to a customer through co-creation of value with external partners (ex.: MOOC) are receiving legitimacy and support from local communities. Organization creates foundation for shared operational capabilities using co-production. Intrinsic enhancements and enabling new services for communities is the main focus.

Context Model 4 (bottom right): IT programs aiming at delivering benefits to a customer through enhancing local capabilities (ex.: eTax, FATCA) are receiving legitimacy and support from authority (controlling organizations and government). Authorizing organizations typically are the main requestors (mandated services). Intrinsic enhancements and quality of service are the main focus.

The three ITG styles (C, D and F) correspond to the areas below, above and between the solid curves accordingly. These areas are overlapping and covering more than a single quadrant: this indicates that the same governance style can be appropriate in different context models in order to encourage some desired behavior in using IT. One can interpret the figure as follows: Context model 3 requires mostly decentralized ITG; Context model 4 requires mostly centralized ITG since high control is required and resources are provided by the authority. Context model 1 requires Centralized or Federated ITG. Context model 2—Federated or Decentralized ITG.

Whereas Centralized and Federated ITG are widely addressed in the literature and supported by empirical study in Weill and Ross (2004), governance arrangements, and mechanisms for Decentralized ITG are only gaining attention. As discussed in Sect. 2.2, the ITG framework proposed by Weill and Ross relies on (mostly) centralized governance archetypes. Considering the increasing interest of organizations in decentralized decision making, open innovation and co-creation of value, we find it justified to extend the list of governance archetypes proposed in Weill and Ross (2004) to cover the gap between monarchy, feudal, federal and anarchy archetypes.

5.3.1.2 Decentralized Decision Making: Extending the List of Governance Archetypes

Public organizations benefit from stability and robustness embedded into their centralized or federated structures. However, to meet the reality of a modern society where they are operating, public organizations need to master governance styles that overcome the shortcomings of centralized decision making.

Collaboration and innovation opportunities are driving factors for modern organizations. To foster the innovation, modern public organizations need to encourage different behaviors with respect to the IT by exploiting a wide range of IT governance structures. In particular, the archetypes surmounting hierarchical structures and supporting decentralized decision making are of a great interest.

Dismantling the (fixed) hierarchies does not necessarily lead to anarchy or absolute lack of control (Bauwens 2005). We introduce a sociocracy (Endenburg 1998a, b) governance archetype and consider that it can cover the gap between centralized (or monarchy-based) archetypes and anarchy.

In sociocracy, the inputs for the decisions can be provided by various stakeholders including project leaders, IT and domain experts, customers, employees, suppliers, local communities, representatives of controlling/regulating organizations, policy makers. Governance archetypes defined in Weill and Ross (2004) specify the decision making rights either as *appointed* to the specific (fixed) positions in the organization (ex.: C-level executives, business process owners) or *undefined*, where all the user can do as they please (anarchy archetype). Sociocracy specifies another way, where the stakeholders are *self-appointed* or *peer-appointed* (peer-voted) to provide the input or participate in the decision-making.

We consider that representatives of the controlling organizations play mostly advisory role providing an input for all the areas. The project teams, in contrast, can provide the input and make the decisions in all the areas. Partners and co-producers provide the input and can make decisions regarding IT architecture, infrastructure and business application needs. We consider that all the stakeholders can provide the input for the business application needs area and can participate in decision making regarding prioritization and funding.

5.3.1.3 Distributed Decision Making and P2P: Extending the List of Governance Implementation Mechanisms

Following the identification of decisions and the specification of input and/or decision rights, an organization must decide on detailed decision responsibility and accountability, how alignment will occur, and how information will be communicated throughout the organization.

To support decentralized ITG arrangements, specific alignment processes and communication approaches that go beyond traditional organizational structure need to be defined. For example, responsible/accountable relations formally defined by hierarchical organizations might need to be replaced with principles of self-organization and relations based on trust and reputation. P2P provides a foundation for governance mechanisms supporting decentralized decision making.

Practical implementation of sociocracy relies on the use of technology: application for cooperation, social software, groupware, and social networks are an integrated part of it. For example, to provide the input and facilitate the decision making in the business application needs area, an organization might need to create innovation labs (Magadley and Birdi 2009), define peer-review, peer-trust, peer-voting, and crowdsourcing (Howe 2006) processes.

We consider the decentralized ITG as relying upon decentralized structures and adopting P2P principles for decision making at least for one IT area where decision should be made. Business applications and IT funding and prioritization are primary candidates. Sociocracy describes the decentralized structures and P2P provides foundation for the mechanisms. Based on the context, federal, duopoly and IT monarchy archetypes can be used for decision making regarding IT principles, architecture and infrastructure.

In the next section, we explain how an organization can design its ITG capabilities by following three generic capability patterns reflecting the centralized, federated and decentralized IT governance.

5.3.2 ITG Capability Patterns

The idea behind ITG capabilities is to specify what a public organization should be able to do to ensure viability and adopt its IT Governance strategies.

We propose capability as a high-level functional concept (i.e., ability and capacity, Sect. 2.5), ensuring a set of organizational values which in turn determine a context, as well as set of goals realized by processes and resources. We have formalized the outlined concepts and relationships in a model (Fig. 5.4).

- *Context*: it represents the information that can be used to characterize the situational environment of a public organization. The context of an ITG capability is defined by analyzing the *public value* the organization aims to create, its sources of *legitimacy and support* and *core capabilities* (Sect. 3.1.1), which eventually lead to the goals to be achieved and the processes and resources to support the goals.
- *Goal*: it is a desired state of affairs that needs to be attained to realize established value(s). Goals can be refined into sub-goals forming a goal model refining desired behaviors in using IT, such as cost-effective use of IT, or effective use of IT for growth; and effective use of IT for business flexibility.
- *Actor*: it is a person or even a part of the organization holding the responsibility for the achievement of a goal; for ITG, these actors may be organization's executives, IT decision makers, etc.
- *Process*: it is a series of actions that are performed in order to support one or more of the established goals. In the ITG domain the processes concern decision making about IT, coordination of IT processes, IT monitoring, performance management and other.
- *Resource*: When initiated, a process is perceived to engage or consume resources—people, materials, software. ITG processes rely for example on the actors involved in IT decision-making enactment and monitoring, as well as on the needed entities—technology and infrastructure supporting processes' execution, as well as coordination and communication between involved actors.

We formalize ITG capability patterns that specify the elements from the model in Fig. 5.4 following centralized, federated and decentralized ITG styles. Based on a vision of its public value (i.e., improving the organization or direct delivering of benefit to a customer), sources of legitimacy and support and required core capabilities (i.e., internal or co-production), a public organization could specify the context, goals, actors, processes and resources required to define its ITG (Sect. 3.1).

ITG capability patterns presented above provide organizations with the practical guidelines and support configurability of their ITG structures, processes and relational mechanisms on a higher level. To efficiently design and adopt ITG mechanisms, an organization needs to:

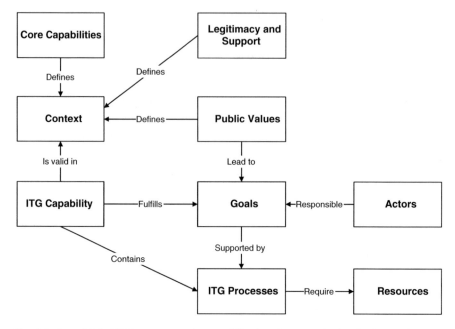

Fig. 5.4 A model for IT Governance using capability based on organizational values and context

1. Define its IT governance context using the context models shown in 3
2. Define its fitting governance style (C, F or D)
3. Adapt the IT governance design (specify "more centralized" or "more decentralized" governance structures and mechanisms)
4. Enact the IT governance by instantiating the IT governance pattern (fill in values and context from; determine goals/actors and processes and resources based on the generic types from Tables 5.1, 5.2 and 5.3).

The ITG capability patterns defined above are meant to provide guidelines and facilitate the application of ITG mechanisms. Whereas some elements vary strongly between patterns, some can remain very similar. For example, the need to respect regulations or follow standards (radio, telecom, IT development etc.) can be present in all three patterns, whereas the way these regulations will be met and the compliance control can be totally different.

5.4   Study of the Results

Over the last few years' higher education in Sweden was analyzed in Zdravkovic et al. (2015). The objective was to observe the alignment between the organizational structure and governance rules in use. As common, universities include a number of entities—faculties, faculty departments, and units. Nowadays, the

Table 5.1 Capability pattern: *centralized IT governance, public sector*

Context	*Using IT for delivering direct benefit to a customer or to a community*: value sources may range from improving user experience from the existing public services, to providing new services unavailable before, and to broader impact on the society via intrinsic enhancements (e.g., improving quality of life, ecology, economic growth, sustainability)
	Using IT for improving the organization (i.e., organizational business processes, applications, infrastructure): value comes from improving efficiency and effectiveness of the organization itself, resulting in the reputation and public opinion
	Government, controlling organizations and policy makers are the main funding source and the main client of the program/project. They authorize the program/project and support it in a form of appropriate recommendations, laws, directives, standards example: mobile and radio communication standards, regulations on privacy/security
	Partner organizations can provide some capacities for "non-core" operations
	For achieving the broader social impacts, individual citizens become "a means to an end"; customer satisfaction is not always a priority
Goals	*Cost-effective use of IT; compliance with the provided business and technology standards; high process standardization and/or high process integration; centralized data management; centralized change management and exception handling*
Actor	IT governance structures follow monarchy, feudal, federal archetypes—the relevant actors are *C-level executives, representatives from authority, corporate IT and/or unit IT leaders, heads of functional areas, key business process owners*
Process	*IT performance measurement based on KPIs, IT portfolio management, SLAs, formal communication/coordination processes based on hierarchy* (steering committees and boards)
Resource	*Actors* (see above), *enterprise-wide standard solutions providing centralized reporting, business intelligence, ERP, CRM, SCM*
ITG Capability	Organizational IT plays the role of a *backend* in the integrated value-creating system, supporting the business logic. The organization creates the foundation for its internal core capabilities

entities are becoming more independent than before, due to geographical dislocation, decentralization of management and because of formal as well as informal communication patters in use. Universities therefore show an obvious need to adjust governance of their IT according to the organizational structure and decision-making in place. *Providing education* and *conducting research activities* are two core missions where university creates (public) value. The following three cases illustrate how the ITG capability patterns from the previous section can be instantiated to support the first mission—*Education*:

Case 1: *Improving education management with IT*

A Swedish university delivers a standard education service to its students. IT infrastructure and systems for managing student subscription for the university, their curriculum, results are typical examples of IT investments in the university. The aimed public value from the IT in this case can be expressed as *improving the quality of educational service* as well as *intrinsic improvements* for the community

Table 5.2 Capability pattern: *federated IT governance, public sector*

Context	*Using IT for improving the organization*: value comes from improving efficiency and effectiveness of the organization itself (e.g., cost saving, improved processes, enabling new internal services), resulting in reputation and public opinion *Using IT for delivering direct benefit to a customer or to a community*: value sources include improving user experience from the existing services, enabling new services for citizens, enabling cooperation opportunities and partnerships for other organizations, and broader impact on the society via intrinsic enhancements *Government*, controlling organizations and *policy makers* are the main client of the program/project. They authorize the program/project and support it in a form of appropriate recommendations, laws, directives, standards example: mobile and radio communication standards, regulations on privacy/security *Communities and citizens* indirectly evaluate the outcomes expressing their opinion about the organization as a whole
Goals	*Cost-effective use of IT; effective use of IT for asset utilization; effective use of IT for growth; high process integration; centralized data management*
Actors	IT governance structures follow duopoly, feudal and federated archetypes—the relevant actors are: *C-level executives, representatives from authority, project leaders (internal and external), IT and domain experts (internal and external), representatives from controlling organizations*
Processes	*IT performance measurement based on KPIs, SLAs, processes for conflict resolution between local control (at co-producers) and global control (organization and authority), coordination between the central and local production, Semi-formal processes for communication and coordination on the horizontal level (focused groups, discussions, communities of practice) supported by technology*
Resources	*Internal production and co-production based on shared resources* (knowledge, technology, infrastructure, services): *Infrastructure and solutions supporting coordination within and between levels* (i.e., groupware, social networks); standard solutions providing centralized reporting, business intelligence, ERP, CRM, SCM
ITG Capability	Organizational IT plays the role of a mediator (service bus), coordinating and controlling the inter-organizational processes between partners. The organization itself provides the standards to ensure coordination/communication between co-producers. It also links the co-producers with the end users (citizens)

(i.e., social, cultural, financial impacts are envisaged). This corresponds to the *Context Model 1 (bottom left)* in Fig. 5.3.

The government and high education policy makers on the country level can be considered as an authorizing environment issuing directives related to learning objectives, degrees, and quality requirements. Local communities and professionals can provide directions indicating the skills "most needed". The university develops internal capabilities in order to create the aimed value. According to this context, *the centralized ITG* (Fig. 5.3) is relevant.

This implies the instantiation of the centralized ITG capability pattern presented in Table 5.1. Here *organizational IT takes the role of a backend, supporting a more effective management of studies and the followed documentation*. As for the

Table 5.3 Capability pattern: *decentralized IT governance, public sector*

Context	*Using IT for delivering direct benefit to a community*: value sources may range from enabling new capabilities (co-production and cooperation opportunities, innovative ways to service delivery) to broader impact on the society via intrinsic enhancements (e.g., improving quality of life, ecology, economic growth, sustainability)
	Using IT for improving the organization (i.e., organizational business processes, applications, infrastructure): value comes from improving communication and knowledge sharing in the organization itself and within the extended organizational environment (e.g., organizational learning, communities of practice, social networks), resulting in increased creativity, motivation and commitment of individual employees
	Government, controlling organizations and policy makers authorize the program/project and support it in a form of appropriate recommendations, laws, directives, standards. Example: mobile and radio communication standards, regulations on privacy/security
	In value creation, an organization cannot rely uniquely upon its internal operational capabilities (e.g., it cannot respond to the demand or it does not have required expertise). *Partner* (public and private) organizations, community, individual citizens or associations provide (external) operational capabilities and expertise required to (co)produce value (e.g., IT service providers, mobile service providers, other non-IT organizations etc.)
	Communities and individual citizens participate in evaluation of the program/project (i.e., providing their opinion, feedback, "liking", "sharing", discussing, browsing, using etc.) and its evolution
Goals	*Effective use of IT for growth and business flexibility; distributed data management; interoperability and (open) technology standards; peer-production, support for open innovation*
Actors	IT governance structures follow federated and sociocracy archetypes—the relevant actors are: *project teams or their representatives, representatives from controlling organizations, C-level executives, IT and domain experts* (internal and external)
Processes	Focus is on decentralized decision making mechanisms (P2P based) and efficient communication and collaboration processes (supported by technology). Processes include: *peer-voting, peer-trust management, peer-review*
Resources	Co-production based on *shared resources* (knowledge, technology, infrastructure, services): *infrastructure and solutions supporting cooperation* (i.e., groupware, social networks);
ITG Capability	Organizational IT plays the role of a frontend providing the means for information, knowledge and service discovery and sharing for the stakeholders defined by the context. Organization creates foundation for internal and external core capabilities based on P2P. It promotes interoperability and supports co-creation of standards, innovation in technology (internally and externally); as well as open innovation

IT-related goals, nowadays they target a cost-effective use of IT through centralization and standardization of software platforms and centralized data management, analytics and reporting. The actors at this level are the rector and a group of high-level administration officers centrally managing activities and making decisions which are then spread to faculties and departments. This corresponds to

Business monarchy archetype. The processes and the resources supporting the main service are standardized, and controlled from the top of the organization, such as IT performance measurement based on KPIs, or IT portfolio management.

Case 2: Enabling student mobility with IT

Another example illustrates the use of *federated ITG capabilities*. Universities in Sweden are actively involved in national and international programs that support mobility of undergraduate, graduate and doctoral students and faculty members: joint master programs, Erasmus exchange programs etc. The aimed public value is to improve service quality and to enable new capabilities for universities, students and communities. Co-creation of value with partners from another organizations (universities) is required in this context. To ensure comparable, compatible and coherent systems of higher education, the partners (co-producers) need to comply with Bologna Process (Wikipedia/Bologna Process 2016). This compliance requires significant changes in the organizational IT. Therefore, the sources of legitimacy and support in this context include university authorities and policy makers on the country and European level (for Bologna Process). This corresponds to the *Context Model 2 (top left)* in Fig. 5.3. The *federated ITG* is relevant.

This implies the instantiation of the federated ITG capability pattern (Table 5.2). Here *organizational IT plays the role of a mediator, coordinating and controlling the inter-organizational processes between partners*. It also links the (partner) universities with the students. Data integration between universities and standards for data exchange are of the main interest. The actors include university international office, head of faculties, program managers, faculty members, IT department. This corresponds to duopoly and federal archetypes. The processes and the resources supporting the main service are standardized, and controlled by the European representatives and university authorities in order to ensure the compliance. Examples of processes: SLAs, formal transformation of local grades to Bologna grading systems etc.

Case 3: Personalized educational program for everybody

Our last example illustrates the use of *decentralized ITG capability*. The concept of open education (Wikipedia/Open Education 2016) describes "institutional practices and programmatic initiatives that broaden access to the learning and training traditionally offered through formal education systems". Open education programs include distant learning, e-Learning, MOOC. Adoption of technologies and processes for developing these programs is a strategic goal for many universities.

The aimed public value is to provide a wider access to education. This is a direct service for customers. This implies an important social impact and intrinsic improvements. The source of legitimacy and support comprises communities and individual citizen willing to benefit from the program. Co-creation of capabilities is required. This corresponds to the *Context Model 3 (top right)* in Fig. 5.3. According to the context, we consider that the *decentralized ITG* is relevant.

This implies the instantiation of the decentralized ITG capability pattern (Table 5.3). Here the organizational IT can play the role of a frontend: OpenCourseWare (OCW) is an example where the courses and supporting materials created at universities and published for free via the Internet. Interoperability is the main focus. A university needs to use some open standard or co-create a standard with other universities for on-line course delivery (ex.: https:// studyinsweden.se/news/moocs-at-swedish-universities/- is a MOOC platform for Swedish HE). Organization creates foundation for internal and external operational capabilities based on P2P, e.g., peer-review, social platforms for discussions. Actors can include faculty teams creating the content and collaborating with web designers and IT experts; students, university authorities. Federal and sociocracy archetypes can be used for ITG. The processes and the resources supporting the main service are standardized. Compared to the previous example, the standards are not provided but peer-voted or co-created by the participants.

5.5   Conclusions

Values created by public organizations and their IT in particular, expand the boundaries of these organizations. Therefore, modern public organizations need to be seen as a part of dynamic ecosystem, where it maintains the relationships of different nature with individuals and other organizations. To fulfill their goals, public organizations need to adapt to their context, exhibiting as consequence various behavior in using IT. In this study we proposed a value-driven solution for IT governance in public organizations distinguishing from centralized and federated, to decentralized structures.

Whereas centralized and federated governance structures are well covered by a palette of governance archetypes proposed in Weill and Ross (2004), we observed a lack of decentralized governance structures—only *anarchy* is mentioned and, as empirical studies demonstrate, very rarely used by the organizations. To narrow the gap between the business and IT monarchy, feudal, duopoly, federal archetypes and anarchy, we defined a *sociocracy* governance archetype. Sociocracy and its variants (e.g., holacracy) are used by public and private organizations, some examples are Valve, W. L. Gore, Morning Star, GitHub, Zappos. Sociocracy supports self-organization and decentralized decision making.

Next, the organization needs to examine its *context*: what public value it desires to provide, what its authorizing environment is (i.e., who will authorize and support the value provisioning, who will benefit from it), and, eventually, what kind of core organizational capabilities will be required. These elements are interrelated and provide an understanding of a context where the IT governance will be enacted. We suggested that the *model of IT governance* can become "more centralized" or "more decentralized" according to this context. We considered IT governance as an organizational capability and defined three *ITG capability patterns* that reflect centralized, decentralized and federated ITG styles accordingly.

An ITG capability pattern can be seen as a guideline on how to define IT governance to support desired public values driving different context situations. We illustrated how the IT governance patterns can be instantiated on the case of the Higher Education public sector in Sweden.

Our motivating assumption was that public organizations need to master a wide range of ITG mechanisms and to deploy them depending on their value-creation context. In particular, we identified and discussed such mechanisms for decentralized ITG. We consider that our findings can be interesting for the organizations (public or private) that already experienced negative effects of centralized IT governance and decision making (e.g., project failures due to lack of commitment, poor adoption, bad user experience, etc.). This work can also interest the organizations that explicitly move towards decentralization in their IT and are seeking to adjust their ITG.

The model proposed in Fig. 5.4 provides an organizing logic that can help organizations to position, justify and govern their IT projects in a consistent way, based on the public value concept. However, we deliberately show that the ITG styles are not mutually exclusive and that several styles can be used in the same value-creation context. We plan to elaborate the guidelines and recommendations in the future, by conducting multiple empirical studies and collaborating with practitioners. The ITG capability patterns presented in Tables 5.1, 5.2 and 5.3 are intended to facilitate the application of ITG mechanisms. They provide a general idea; the concrete "recipe" has to be elaborated for each particular organization.

In our future work, we envisage to design an approach for measurement of efficiency of ITG with respect to the ITG style. Relevant KPIs can be integrated into ITG capability patterns presented in this work.

References

Bauwens, M. (2005). Peer to peer and human evolution (Vol. 15). Integral Visioning.

Bengtsson, M., & Kock, S. (2000). Coopetition in business networks—to cooperate and compete simultaneously. *Industrial Marketing Management, 29*(5), 411–426.

Benkler, Y. (2006). *The wealth of networks: How social production transforms markets and freedom*. New Haven: Yale University Press.

Bērziša, S., et al. (2015). Capability driven development: An approach to designing digital enterprises. *Business and Information Systems Engineering (BISE), 57/1*. doi:10.1007/s12599-014-0362-0.

Buck, J., & Villines, S. (2007). *We the people: Consenting to a deeper democracy: A guide to sociocratic principles and methods*. Washington, DC: Sociocracy.Info.

Camarinha-Matos, L. M., & Afsarmanesh, H. (2005). Collaborative networks: A new scientific discipline. *Journal of Intelligent Manufacturing, 16*(4–5), 439–452.

Chesbrough, H. W. (2003). *Open Innovation: The new imperative for creating and profiting from technology*. Boston: Harvard Business School Press. ISBN 978-1578518371.

CIPFA and IFAC. (2014). Good Governance in the public sector. Retrieved September 01, 2016, from http://www.ifac.org/publications-resources/international-framework-good-governance-public-sector.

Cresswell, A. M., Burke, B., & Pardo, T. (2006). Advancing return on investment, analysis for government IT: A public value framework. Center for Technology in Government, University at Albany, SUNY.

De Haes, S., & Van Grembergen, W. (2015). *Enterprise Governance of information technology.* Heidelberg: Springer.

DuMoulin, T. (2015). Governance of enterprise IT missing in action. *Information Technology and Information Systems Research (ISACA) forum.* Retrieved September 7, 2016, from http://www.isaca.org/Knowledge-Center/Research/Documents/COBIT.

Endenburg, G. (1998a). *Sociocracy: The organization of decision-making.* Eburon. ISBN 90-5166-605-5.

Endenburg, G. (1998b). *Sociocracy as social design.* Delft: Eburon. ISBN 90-5166-604-7.

Grembergen, W. V. & De Haes, S. (2005). Measuring and improving IT Governance through the balanced scorecard. *Information Systems Control Journal (ISACA), 2.*

Gordon, F. R. (2014). Information technology Governance structures on strategic alignment. School of Business at DigitalCommons@ Liberty University, Open Publications. Retrieved September 7, 2016, from http://digitalcommons.liberty.edu/cgi/viewcontent.cgi?article=1026&context=busi_fac_pubs.

Howe, J. (2006). The rise of crowdsourcing. *Wired magazine, 14*(6), 1–4.

ISACA/COBIT 5. (2012). Control practices: Guidance to achieve control objective for successful IT Governance. Retrieved April 15, 2016, from http://www.isaca.org/Knowledge-Center/Research/Research-Deliverables/Pages/COBIT-Control-Practices-Guidance-to-Achieve-Control-Objective-forSuccessful-IT-Governance-2nd-Edition.aspx.

ISO/IEC 38500. (2015). Governance of IT for the organization. Retrieved June 11, 2016, from https://webstore.iec.ch/preview/info_isoiec38500%7Bed2.0%7Den.pdf.

Janahi, L., Griffiths, M., & Al-Ammal, H. (2015). A conceptual model for IT Governance in public sectors. In *The Proceedings of the 4th International Conference on Future Generation Communication Technologies (FGCT 2015)* (pp. 1–9). IEEE. http://ieeexplore.ieee.org/document/7300242/.

Juiz, C., Guerrero, C., & Lera, I. (2014). Implementing good Governance principles for the public sector in information technology governance frameworks. *Open Journal of Accounting, 3*(1). http://www.scirp.org/journal/OJAcct/.

Magadley, W., & Birdi, K. (2009). Innovation labs: an examination into the use of physical spaces to enhance organizational creativity. *Creativity and innovation management, 18*(4), 315–325.

Meynhardt, T. (2009). Public value inside: what is public value creation? *International Journal of Public Administration, 32*(3–4), 192–219.

Mintzberg, H. (1979). The structuring of organizations: A synthesis of the research. University of Illinois at Urbana-Champaign's academy for entrepreneurial leadership. (Historical Research Reference in Entrepreneurship).

Morgan, J. (2014). *The future of work: Attract new talent, build better leaders, and create a competitive organization.* New Jersey: Wiley. ISBN: 978-1-118-87724-1.

Moore, M. H. (1997) *Creating public value: Strategic management in government.* Cambridge: Harvard university press. ISBN 9780674175587.

Moore, M., & Khagram, S. (2004). On creating public value: What business might learn from Government about strategic management. Corporate Social Responsibility Initiative Working Paper no. 3. Retrieved May 05, 2016, from https://www.hks.harvard.edu/m-rcbg/CSRI/research/publications/workingpaper_3_moore_khagram.pdf.

OECD. (2015). *Principles of corporate Governance.* Paris: OECD Publishing. http://dx.doi.org/10.1787/9789264236882-en.

Romme, G. (2016). *The quest for professionalism: The case of management and entrepreneurship.* Oxford: Oxford University Press.

Sambamurthy, V., & Zmud, R. W. (1999). Arrangements for information technology Governance: A theory of multiple contingencies. *MIS Quarterly, 2*(23), 261–290.

Schollmeier, R. (2002). A definition of peer-to-peer networking for the classification of peer-to-peer architectures and applications. In *Proceedings of the First International Conference on Peer-to-Peer Computing.* IEEE.

Ulrich, W., & Rosen, M. (2011). The business capability map: Building a foundation for business/IT alignment. cutter consortium for business and enterprise architecture. Retrieved February 28, 2016, from http://www.cutter.com/content-and-analysis/resource-centers/enterprise-architecture/sample-our-research/ea110504.html.

Wiedenhöft, G., Mezzomo Luciano, E., & Gregianin Testa, M. (2014). An indicators-based approach to measuring Information Technology Governance effectiveness. A Study with Brazilian Professionals.

Wikipedia. (2016). Bologna process. In Wikipedia, The Free Encyclopedia. https://en.wikipedia.org/w/index.php?title=Bologna_Process&oldid=724628455.

Wikipedia. (2016). Open education. In Wikipedia, The Free Encyclopedia. https://en.wikipedia.org/w/index.php?title=Open_education&oldid=720754185.

Weill, P., & Ross, J. W. (2004). *IT Governance: how top performers manage IT decision rights for superior results*. Boston: Harvard Business School Press.

Zdravkovic, J., Rychkova I., & Speckert, T. (2015). Requirements for IT Governance in organizations experiencing decentralization. In *Proceedings of the Post-CAiSE 2014 Forum*. LNBIP (Vol. 204, pp 269–285). Springer.

Author Biographies

Irina Rychkova is Associate Professor of Information Technology at University Paris 1, Pantheon Sorbonne and researcher at Centre de RechercheenInformatique of Paris 1 since September 2009. Her research interests include strategic alignment, enterprise and business process modeling, model analysis. Irina holds a PhD in System modeling and Enterprise Architecture from Suisse Federal Institute of Technology at Lausanne (Ecole Polytechnique Federale de Lausanne), and MSc in Applied Mathematics and Physics from Moscow Institute of Physics and Technology, in Russia. Prior to joining CRI—Paris 1, Irina was a research assistant at the Ecole Polytechnique Federale de Lausanne, Laboratory of Systemic Modeling (LAMS).

Professor Jelena Zdravkovic is the Head of the Information Systems unit of the Department of Computer and Systems Sciences at Stockholm University. She has a PhD in Computer and Systems Sciences at Royal Institute of Technology (KTH) from 2006, as well as the MBA in E-commerce. Jelena has published research results in international conferences and scientific journals on the topics of business/IT alignment, enterprise modeling and requirements engineering. She has participated in several national and international projects on the interoperability, service modeling, and lately—capability-driven IS engineering. In her department, Jelena is the head of the study program "Enterprise systems and Service Design". She is in the Editorial Board of Springer's RE and BISE Journals, as well as a regular reviewer for several other international journals including Elsevier's Journal of Systems and Software, and Information & Software Technology journal, as well as the IEEE Computing journal. She serves in the program committees of more than 10 international conferences and workshops.

Chapter 6
IT Governance and Its Implementation Based on a Detailed Framework of IT Governance (*dFogIT*) in Public Enterprises

Beatriz Gómez, Belén Bermejo and Carlos Juiz

Abstract IT governance in public organizations and enterprises has encountered challenges due to internal and external factors. Most of these challenges are related to strategic alignment issues involving governance bodies and their communication with stakeholders. Furthermore, public organizations are now more concerned about receiving the most value from IT services. This requires effective IT governance that enables IT alignment and creates business value from IT investments. The contribution presented in this chapter is to depict the evolution in the IT-business relationship over the last years and highlight the challenges in IT governance. Second, the current IT governance standardization and its consequences in public enterprises will be reviewed. Finally, *dFogIT* is presented as real case of involving the implementation of the IT governance framework in a public organization.

6.1 Introduction

At present, there are a number of assets within organizations that enable the development of business activities to obtain value. Within organizations, assets related to human resources, financing, physical structures, public relations and intellectual property have traditionally been taken into account for governance activities and frameworks as Weill and Ross (2004) suggested. Information Technology (IT) has become an important asset in organizations, evolving from a

B. Gómez · B. Bermejo · C. Juiz (✉)
Computer Science Dpt, University of the Balearic Islands,
Carretera de Valldemossa, Km. 7.5, 07122 Palma, Spain
e-mail: cjuiz@uib.es

B. Gómez
e-mail: b.gomez@uib.es

B. Bermejo
e-mail: belen.bermejo@uib.es

© Springer International Publishing AG 2017
L. Rusu and G. Viscusi (eds.), *Information Technology Governance in Public Organizations*, Integrated Series in Information Systems 38,
DOI 10.1007/978-3-319-58978-7_6

133

type of service provider to a business enabler. Due to IT, the core activities of a company are developed based on business and IT jointly, fostering the discovery of new market opportunities.

Consequently, the boards of most companies have realized the significant impact that IT has on the success or failure of its business activities. Therefore, company boards need to know if the management of its computer systems serves and achieves its objectives, whether IT is easily learned and adaptive to changes in the company, and whether it meets with potential risks judiciously while also helping to recognize new business opportunities. Because IT is a new and important asset within companies, boards expect IT to offer business value, that is, to provide rapid solutions and safer and more quality services. In addition, this asset should generate a reasonable Return on Investment (ROI), and it must move the company from a stage of profitability due to efficiency and productivity to a stage of value creation and effective business strategy.

Currently, the expectations in many companies regarding IT and the reality do not meet. Thus, boards face business losses, reputational damage or a weakened competitive position. It is also not possible to obtain or even measure the ROI of IT investments and IT initiatives that are undertaken for the purpose of innovation and other benefits fail. However, there are also other companies that understand the risks and explore the benefits of IT. These companies have found the means to align IT strategy with business strategy, staggering IT strategy and objectives throughout the entire organization (Juiz and Toomey, 2015). They also provide the organizational structure that facilitates the implementation of this strategy and its goals. Additionally, these successful companies or organizations have constructive and communicative relationships between IT staff and the rest of the company, as they have adopted and implemented a direct/control framework with which they can measure the performance of IT.

Given that IT supports and extends business strategies and objectives, governance is essential. In response to this need, in 2008, the standard ISO/IEC 38500 was published, and it was revised in 2015 (Juiz, 2011). This standard outlines IT governance in the form of three activities: evaluate, direct and monitor. Six principles are applied in these activities. In addition, the standard provides an informal model to distinguish IT governance activities from traditional IT management tasks. However, the implementation of this model may be difficult precisely because of the simplicity of the standard. As a result of the adaptation of the standard, enterprises should create their own governance framework, one that offers an easy understanding of IT governance but that is compatible with ISO/IEC 38500. *dFogIT* (detailed Framework of Governance for IT) was developed at the University of the Balearic Islands (UIB); it connects the four layers related to IT in the company: corporate governance, IT governance, IT management and IT operations. Thus, *dFogIT* is a governance framework that can be implemented in any type of company and was used in the University of the Balearic Islands for several years.

In this chapter, the creation of *dFogIT* and the reasons for its creation are revealed. First, the reasons for governing IT and the different standards and practices that have arisen as a result of these requirements are explained. Then, *dFogIT* is described, and its characteristics and advantages are shown. *dFogIT* application samples from public and private companies are also reviewed, as well as its role in the creation of other IT governance frameworks. Finally, the last extension of this framework is presented; it can be extended to make the external stakeholders of public enterprises more visible, taking into account citizenship and the source of the authority that is delegated to public governors in a democratic system.

6.2   IT-Business Relationship Evolution Within Companies

Traditionally, in companies where the IT asset is becoming necessary for the development of business activities, there are two distinct domains: the domain of IT and the domain of business units (see Fig. 6.1). The concern of the business units is the development of their operations, in other words, how IT will enable these activities; IT is concerned with how services are managed and supplied. These two domains have a classical relationship of supply and demand, where IT only plays the role of service provider, and the business units are its customers.

Thus, in this traditional view, IT acts as a service provider, which can be easily outsourced. At the same time, this view shows the lack of strategic alignment between business units and IT within the institution, as the supply-demand relationship exists in terms of management and operations (although the business envisages the strategic business future). When IT has addressed the demand of the

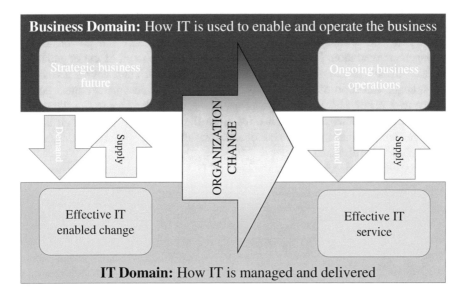

Fig. 6.1   Vision of IT as a service provider [Adapted from Toomey (2009)]

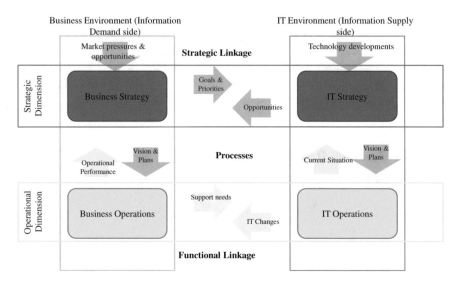

Fig. 6.2 Vision of IT separated into two dimensions [Adapted from Mueller et al. (2008)]

business units, organizational change processes and procedures are deployed by the company, meaning new services and operations have to be supported and maintained by IT.

From the traditional view of supply and demand of IT within organizations, it is necessary to evolve into a more mature vision, where IT becomes an asset that creates value for the company. Figure 6.2 shows the next stage in the evolution of IT within the company (Mueller et al., 2008). Although two distinct domains remain, IT and business, this evolution involves each domain being separated, in turn, into two dimensions, the strategic dimension and the dimension of management/operation. It also shows that the top management of the organization has to withstand external pressures related to stakeholders. Thus, having a vision of the strategic direction of the company is necessary. Business units expect performance as a result of these strategic plans. The same is the case in the domain of IT; IT strategic plans can be generated from the business vision, which is then implemented by management and operations; afterward, performance measurements should be obtained.

According to this view, the alignment of IT with business units occurs when business units provide strategic plans to IT that include the mission and vision of the organization, and IT responds with initiatives to bring out such plans (see Fig. 6.2). Therefore, the dialogue that takes place between these two domains is strategic, not simply operative. In the management/operation dimension, there is still dialogue about supply and demand, as services require the support of IT. The core of this vision rests on the communication between strategy and operations as well as between IT and the business units.

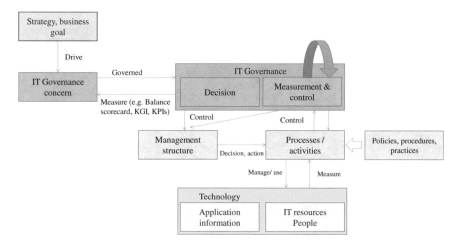

Fig. 6.3 View of the related processes of governance, management and operations [Adapted from Mueller et al. (2008)]

Although the second view is more mature than the previous one, companies that have reached this stage still have difficulties integrating IT within the company, as they are still divided into two distinct domains despite being increasingly connected. Communication between domains is becoming more important than the domains themselves.

In Fig. 6.3, the communication flows are more important than the different dimensions of business; in fact, a new dimension is introduced: IT governance. Senior managers have a strategy and business goals, and these areas should be at the forefront of IT governance. The purpose of IT governance should be to drive the alignment between business objectives and IT goals. IT governance involves making decisions about this alignment while at the same time implementing control mechanisms to verify that management is implementing these decisions. Consequently, there are two flows within an organization, direction and control. These flows should be the responsibility of managers who make decisions at the tactical level. Thus, IT governance is merely the transformation of strategic objectives into a viable direction for the firm, and the overall direction of the company cascades to the lower layers of the organization, whereas the act of controlling goes in the opposite direction.

As shown in Fig. 6.4, from an even more modern perspective of organizational IT, IT resources should be governed like physical assets, human resources, intellectual property resources and financial resources. They should be governed using the same instruments used to govern other assets, i.e., defining strategic plans and controlling desirable behavior by means of measurable Key Performance Indicators (KPI). The responsibility for the implementation of these activities falls on the executive members that govern the organization, that is, those structures that have

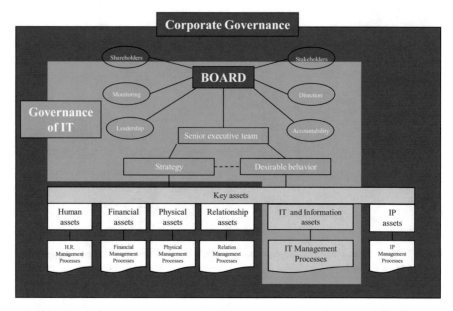

Fig. 6.4 Framework linking corporate and IT governance [Adapted from Weill and Ross (2004)]

the authority and accountability toward stakeholders. They will be held accountable for IT assets, which are becoming increasingly important and are creating more value for organizations than other traditional assets.

One of the main challenges of evolving toward a more mature approach is the resistance to change within organizations, particularly public enterprises. IT governance involves structural and cultural changes in the daily life of organizations. Therefore, it is essential that the organization has the desire to be governed before trying to implement techniques, tools, methods or frameworks to govern IT.

In Fig. 6.5, a layered view of the organization that governs IT is shown (Fernández and Piattini, 2012). As in the previous view, there are two vertical flows between the different layers: a direction flow and a control flow. To operate these flows, a clear definition of the layers and their scope within the overall objectives of IT governance should be clarified to all stakeholders.

In this layered view of organizational governance, each layer communicates with its lower and upper neighbors through direction and control, but the end result of these processes, i.e., what is delivered and returned in response, is undefined. In fact, throughout the evolution of IT governance within the company, communication within the layers of the organization was considered more relevant than the methods of this communication. However, the method of communication is crucial for the proper alignment of IT, business units, executive teams and the board. Communication between company layers must be depicted in a more accurate way to determine the method of direction and control. The scope of IT governance is

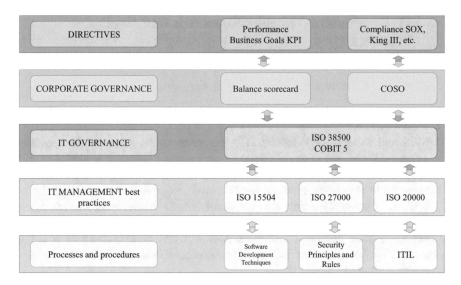

Fig. 6.5 ISO/IEC 38500: 2008 as operating framework [Adapted from Fernández and Piattini (2012)]

closely related to strategy alignment, as it is necessary to understand the extent to which the delegation of authority, functions or any kind of activity belongs to a particular layer and not to another one. It is important to know the functional aspect of a certain layer as well as the services provided to it by the lower and upper layers within the IT governance framework. Transparent and fluid communication is a key issue in the success or failure of IT governance within a company.

All topics referred to in this section are applicable to both private companies and public enterprises. But nevertheless, IT governance in the public sector is considered as the government services delivery to the citizens. Particularly, Elpez and Fink (2006) characterized IT governance in public sector as a service provided to the people through the execution of power, and authorities aimed at delivering public needs and interests. There are several studies about public universities: Juiz et al. (2014) compared a framework of good governance of the public sector with a framework of IT governance in a public university in Spain, whereas Hotzel et al. (2015) explained the role of the Chief Information Officer (CIO) in German Universities. There are other works from Sethibe et al. (2007) and Khalfan and Gough (2002), about the differences between private and public sector. Case studies about public sector and IT governance in developing countries are included in Al Qassimi and Rusu (2015). Other authors as Gomes et al. (2016) related IT governance and some aspect of IT management as IT risks and IT security. In fact, this chapter proposes an IT governance framework for public enterprises connecting the corporate public governance, the IT governance, the IT management and the IT operation with the main stakeholders, i.e., the citizens, from the governance of IT viewpoint.

6.3 IT Governance Through Standards and Good Practices

Thus far, the evolution of the IT strategic vision has been addressed, as well as the need to govern IT. This section shows that different definitions and functions of IT governance have emerged because of this need and because of the standardization of IT governance.

Weill and Ross (2004) defined IT governance as the practice of controlling behavior, activities and processes by creating a control mechanism; defining roles and responsibilities as well as rights and obligations; establishing rules and policies; defining the limits to behavior and reactions to change; and setting new limits.

In short, IT governance answers three questions effectively. First, what decisions should be taken to ensure the effective management and use of IT. Second, who should make these decisions, and third, how will they be executed and how will their execution be monitored. Below, the five decisions that fall within the realm of IT governance are highlighted:

1. IT principles: high-level statements regarding the use of IT.
2. IT architecture: an organizing logic that encompasses data, applications, and infrastructure within a set of policies, relationships, and technical choices to achieve the desired business and technical standardization and integration.
3. IT infrastructure: centrally coordinated, shared IT services that provide the foundation for IT capability on a firm-wide basis.
4. Business application needs: the business need for purchased or internally developed IT applications.
5. IT investment and prioritization: decisions regarding IT investments, including project approvals and justification techniques.

Regarding the second question, the decision can be made based on a series of analogous structures presented by Weill and Ross (2004), including monarchy business, IT monarchy, feudal system, federal system, IT duopoly or anarchy. As for the third question, it should be noted that each organization has to define its own mechanisms of monitoring and control. Two of the most widely used are project portfolio selection and IT investments and management of SLAs (Service Level Agreements).

In 2008, the standard for IT governance, ISO/IEC 38500, was published. Subsequently, the standard of governance COBIT 5 emerged (ISACA, 2012), which is also considered a de facto standard for management and IT governance.

The ISO/IEC 38500 standard provides good governance practices, providing a fluid and transparent communication structure between governance and management. These best practices are based on three main activities:

1. Evaluate: to examine and judge the present and future use of IT, including strategies, proposals and supply agreements (internal and external).

2. Direct: directing the preparation and implementation of plans and policies and assigning responsibilities to the purpose. Ensure the correct transition of projects to production, considering the impacts on the operation, business and infrastructure. Promote a culture of good governance of IT in the organization.
3. Monitoring: through measurement systems, monitoring the performance of IT, ensuring that it adjusts to plan.

Moreover, the six principles on which these good practices are based are as follows:

1. Responsibility: all members of the organization must understand and accept their responsibilities in both the supply of and demand for IT. Responsibility for actions carries with it the authority to implement those actions.
2. Strategy: the business strategy of the organization takes into account the current and future capabilities of IT. IT strategic plans meet current and projected needs derived from the business strategy.
3. Acquisition: IT acquisitions are made for valid reasons based on an appropriate and ongoing analysis, with clear and transparent decisions. There is an appropriate balance among benefits, opportunities, costs and risks in both the short and long term.
4. Performance: IT is dimensioned to support the organization, providing services with adequate quality to meet current and future needs.
5. Conformance: IT function complies with all applicable laws and regulations. Policies and practices in this regard are clearly defined, implemented and required.
6. Human behavior: IT policies, practices and decisions demonstrate respect for human behavior, including the current and emerging needs of all people involved.

As shown in Fig. 6.6, the model of IT governance proposed by the ISO/IEC 38500 includes the three activities mentioned above. The IT governance layer and IT management layer are also distinguished. These two layers are connected by plan and policy measures and proposal and performance measures, thus fulfilling the control and direction flows. The governance layer provides principles and policies to the management layer, which is responsible for returning solutions to meet the established objectives. In addition, performance measures for IT activity within the enterprise reach the layer of governance.

This bond between the layers of management and governance demonstrates that they should be aligned, so that IT meets the objectives of the organization. Communication conflicts should be resolved, so bridges between management and IT governance should be built, and these bridges have to be provided by the organization. Governing is about making decisions but also communicating them. Thus, this standard brings about more effective communication by creating bridges within the governance and the management.

ISO/IEC 38504 (2014) also argues that if the organization has governance principles, they should be applied in a way that aligns IT with these principles. The

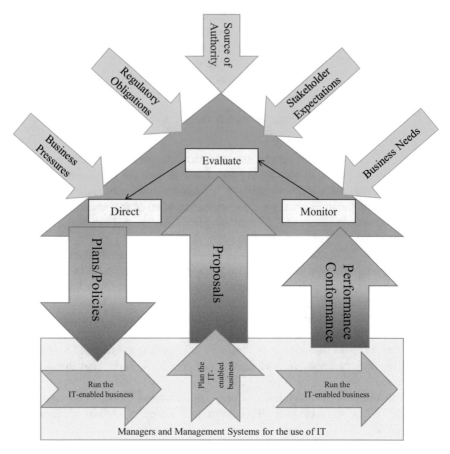

Fig. 6.6 IT Governance model in the ISO/IEC 38500 standard [Adapted from Juiz and Toomey (2015)]

aligned governance principles should result in management that is in conformance with IT governance, with the result that IT produces the expected results from the point of view of alignment. Based on these elements, IT becomes an enabler of business and board strategy, as they have certain principles and metrics associated with them.

To govern IT—not simply link the strategic plans of the company with IT staff but connect corporate governance with IT management and the operation of IT and business units—the organization has to construct a framework of IT self-governance because of the simplicity of the current IT governance standard. In any case, if the organization has to create an IT governance framework, a number of guidelines related to the design of IT governance frameworks should be taken into account as follows in Applegate et al. (2008):

1. Minimalist design: The framework does not have to be overly expensive in terms of bureaucracy.
2. Leadership: The framework has to be led by someone that has governing authority. Without the participation of the board, IT governance fails. If the board believes that IT is not part of corporate governance, IT will be externalized.
3. Implication: Within the organization, a senior executive must be involved and engaged in IT governance.
4. Generalization: The governance framework is not a particular aspect of IT; it is necessary to clarify that the whole institution is part of the framework.
5. Discipline: Once the framework is implemented, the organization should be consistent with discipline so that behavior is in line with strategy. In addition, exceptions should be detected and accommodated within the framework.
6. Objectives: Before implementing the framework, what objectives of the framework have to be known and what is expected from them.
7. Evolution: The implementation of the framework does not have to be a revolution within the organization but an evolution of the current environment. As a result, employees and senior management are motivated to play a role in cultural change.

6.4 Reasons for Building the *dFogIT* Framework

dFogIT corresponds to an implementation based on the ISO/IEC 38500 standard as Juiz (2014) suggested. The core of the framework takes into account three activities (direct, evaluate and monitor) and reinforces the six principles from this standard.

This IT governance framework was originated from several experiences administering public organizations:

- *No IT governance process, structure or communication.* Governance of IT does not exist at all and either the board or the IT staff is not aware of its necessity. Thus, no process for controlling the IT staff from the board is ever implemented in a formal way. The result of this absence of control process means having no regular agenda for directing the IT management. There is not any structure or committee to communicate the board strategy, either.
- *Outsized power of IT management in IT decision-making.* The consequence of no control over the IT staff is the outsized power of IT department in the institution, e.g., the IT department negotiates the project portfolio directly with the stakeholders.
- *CIO and CTO roles not clarified.* Since IT manager may be acting as CIO and Chief Technology Officer (CTO) during years, the creation of the CIO office (as brand new governing structure) usually provokes fighting in a turf battle between the CIO and the IT managers.

- *Absence of reporting, control and accountability.* Since there is no formal communication for the IT-business alignment from the board during years, the IT department remains uncontrolled and then there is no motivation for IT staff for building accountability processes, either.
- *Lack of confidence in IT assets and IT staff from the board.* The absence of formal and proper communication between the board and the IT staff always causes low confidence from board members in any situation in which IT assets are involved. Every activity of the IT department is ever under the suspicion of bad performance from the board viewpoint.
- *No strategy for IT, just short-term tactics.* Due to the lack of communication and confidence from board to the IT department, the latter implements its own vision of IT assets, resulting biased decisions about the IT deployment at the institution.
- *IT investment based on cash-flow availability for infrastructure.* IT management spends most of the time fighting for money with CFO or other stakeholders with their own IT budget.
- *Architecture decisions based on IT staff knowledge, not user interests or institutional strategy is considered.* Architecture decisions are usual belonging to IT profile managers, but these decisions must be supervised and controlled for superior layers of the organization.
- *No consideration for compliance, which is different from technical issues.* For example, IT department may be usually concerned with conformance issues, but only as a defensive argument in new projects or services demanded by the institution stakeholders.
- *No participation by users, IT personnel, business units, board members or any stakeholder in IT decisions unlike during the requirements phase of project management.* The project management methodology is ad hoc without using any kind of standardization for the stakeholders' participation on project decisions. Thus, sponsors of the projects together with IT staff decide the direction of the IT innovation instead of implementing a general strategy.
- *Communication with stakeholders by demand or by claim.* The communication of IT staff with the stakeholders is reactive and defensive. Firefighting in IT department remains as a busy activity, leaving no time for tactics and less for strategy issues.
- *Non-IT departments view the IT staff as an obstacle of their mission.* The reactive communication and the absence of control of the IT staff collaborate on seeing them as sidelined employees from the institution concerns.
- ...

Thus, UIB suffered most of these last situations, as a public organization, not only from a lack of governance practices but also from a complete absence of adequate IT asset governance, meeting few of the principles found in the overview of the ISO/IEC 38500 above.

After several years of complaints coming from any kind of stakeholders in the UIB, the Vice rector for IT propose to other board members, especially the Rector and the Chief Financial Officer (CFO), the implementation of a governance framework for IT assets.

Therefore, during the period 2011–2013, *dFogIT* was implemented at the University of the Balearic Islands, following the principles explained in previous sections.

6.5 Implementing ISO/IEC 38500: The *dFogIT* Framework

The framework consists of four layers; two are equivalent to the ISO/IEC 38500 standard, i.e., the IT governance layer and the IT management layer (see Fig. 6.7). However, the top and bottom layers (corporate governance and IT operation layers, respectively) are added in the framework because as announced in the ISO/IEC 38500, it is necessary to involve the entire organization in IT governance.

The arrows in Fig. 6.7 indicate either supply (produce) or demand (need) of something related to IT, as in previous models (see Figs. 6.1, 6.2, 6.3, 6.4 and 6.5), but now, every layer provides demand and supply in a different way. At first glance, the layer of corporate governance demands tangible results, that is, applications (IT solutions) that add value to the organization. The IT governance layer produces a direction from evaluating the monitoring of the lower layers. The IT management layer develops projects that enable business processes through ulterior operations or

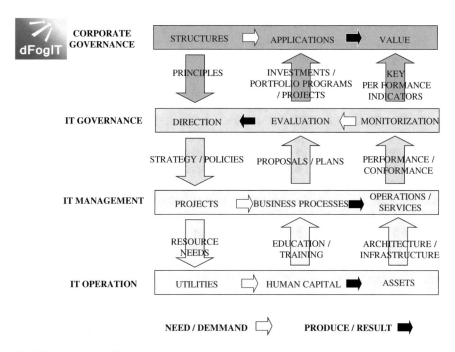

Fig. 6.7 *dFogIT* (detailed Framework of governance for IT)

services. In the operational layer, commodities are transformed into assets through the training and motivation of IT personnel. Therefore, from the point of view of the governance of IT, the operational layer is viewed as a collection of resources that build technology assets.

Thus, the model of Fig. 6.7 represents an organizational hierarchy with a layered separation of concerns about Information Technology. However, every layer is connected to their neighbors in the model. Corporate governance has the responsibility of developing strategic goals and plans. Then, the IT governance framework ensures that IT management goals are aligned with corporate strategy, and proposals from business processes and IT staff are considered for inclusion in portfolios dedicated to future projects and investments (follow vertical arrows in Fig. 6.7). Additionally, corporate governance also expects a series of progress indicators for IT services, i.e., the daily value of IT activities in the form of operations and services within the enterprise.

Therefore, IT governance members make plans and determine strategic principles for IT; strategy is generated at the corporate layer and is sent to the management layer. In addition, proposals provided by the management layer are evaluated, and IT performance is monitored to ensure that it is compliant (see again vertical arrows in Fig. 6.7).

In the management and operation layers, responsibility focuses on the knowledge of the resources needed to implement projects, i.e., how IT personnel become human capital and support business processes and how technology assets are based on infrastructure and architecture that support the service catalogue of daily operations (see vertical arrows from the bottom to the top in Fig. 6.7).

From an IT governance viewpoint, the *dFogIT* implementation model only considers how strategy becomes tactical, how tactics becomes operational and how this is translated into key performance indicators. Furthermore, *dFogIT* serves to depict and understand communication between different layers while also identifying the role of IT within the organization.

In *dFogIT*, direction and control flows are vertical within the communicating layers. On the one hand, it is necessary to know the organization's direction in order to translate business strategy into IT strategy, so that alignment may occur between the two strategies (see Fig. 6.8). On the other hand, the investment portfolio and the project portfolio should be controlled, which produces the required applications (see Fig. 6.9). Services and operations should also be controlled by means of performance indicators. To perform this control, the corporate governance layer has to inform IT governance about the appropriate performance indicators, goals and targets using balance scorecards. The IT governance layer should translate the measurements used by management into these performance indicators, thus measuring the value of IT assets. If the direction flow and the control flow links are not achieved by the implementation of IT governance, the corporate layer should not govern IT, and the latter will fail.

Within the framework of IT governance, there are two other virtuous cycles that affect organizational productivity through IT, the product cycle (see Fig. 6.10) and service cycle (see Fig. 6.11). IT products are the result of the implementation of

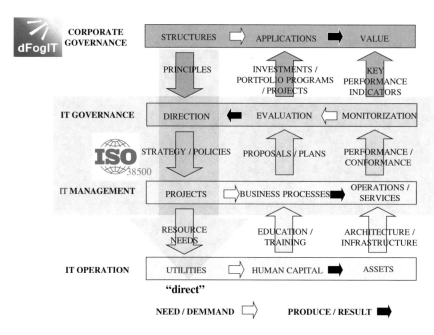

Fig. 6.8 Direct flow in *dFogIT*

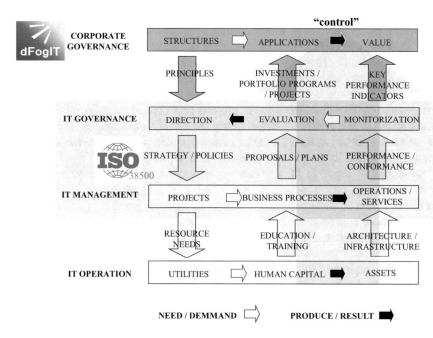

Fig. 6.9 Control flow in *dFogIT*

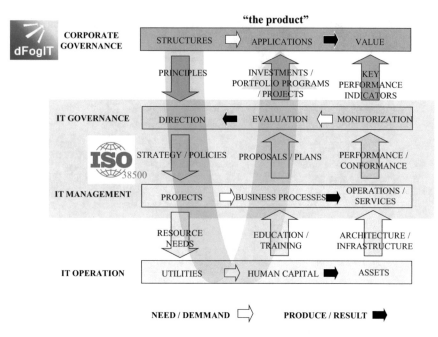

Fig. 6.10 Product cycle in *dFogIT*

approved projects from the project portfolio. Therefore, IT products must be rooted in the strategic plan and, as a result of tactical and operational activity, be a part of the project portfolio. These products should come from the corporate layer, enter the operating layer and return to its origin as corporate governance demands. That is, IT products should be the result of corporate governance principles and plans. Services do not have the same value as projects that enable business processes. It is more difficult to assess services because they are already implemented. The value of the services must be shown by obtaining corresponding performance measures and demonstrating that they add value to the company (see Fig. 6.11).

As shown in Fig. 6.6, IT governance supports a number of business-related flows. In *dFogIT*, these pressures are depicted as well as the pressures in the remaining layers of the governance framework, whether internal or external (Juiz 2011). Corporate governance has to manage pressures belonging to the design of the company, cultural change that involves the implementation of a governance framework, current legislation, the state of the market and value discipline developed by the organization. Second, IT governance has to support the pressure brought about by business activity and the pressure that arises from the risk involved in the use of IT. Regarding the management layer, pressure is brought to bear as a result of business processes and IT services management and delivery. In the operational layer, the pressures that come to bear are those related to the field of technology, such as product development and technical training of human

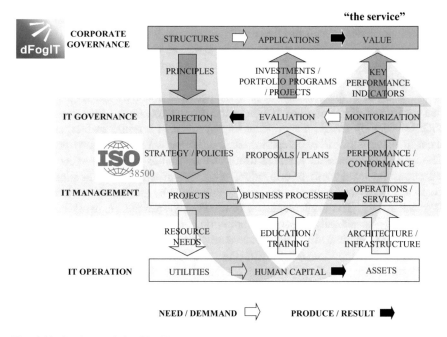

Fig. 6.11 Service cycle in *dFogIT*

resources. Thus, the success or failure of the implementation of the *dFogIT* framework depends on how the different structures in the four layers support these pressures.

6.6 *dFogIT* Case of Use

The *dFogIT* framework has a number of advantages. First provides visibility of the governance structures, strategy alignment and communication among the different layers of the company. Secondly, the five IT governance decisions, proposed by Weill and Ross (2004), are also included but shared in different layers; so that decisions more technical will be taken by lower layers and strategic decisions by higher layers. In turn, *dFogIT* is based on ISO/IEC 38500 governance standard.

In short, business results from product and services cycles are obtained as a result of the alignment of strategic principles and IT governance plans. Additionally, communication flows in *dFogIT* cascade to all organizational layers. Herein lays the difference with previous models of communication between business and IT, as seen in Figs. 6.1, 6.2, 6.3, 6.4 and 6.5. Moreover, the direction and control flows and the product and service virtuous cycles can be adapted to the reality of each company. That is, the instruments of IT governance, which are reflected in the arrows connecting the layers, can be replaced by those that are best suited to the current situation of the company, its governance maturity and its business processes related to IT assets.

To show the *dFogIT* framework and its use in an organization, the maturity of corporate governance for the IT assets at the UIB during 2007–2013 was reviewed by Juiz (2014) and Fernández et al. (2012).

The analysis of the maturity process that occurred in this period at UIB suggests that the impact of the implementation of the *dFogIT* framework (and consequently ISO/IEC 38500) reveals a significant improvement in scoring. In fact, any increment in value is positive, comparing 2011–2013 period with the previous period. The major improvements were the result of the virtuous cycle of project portfolio selection and investment prioritization, processes in which the intentions of the board and behavioral changes are strongly influenced by the strategic objectives and IT plans at UIB. The implementation of the IT governance framework had shown less impact—specifically IT services monitoring and KPI measurement—due to the premature finalization of the board mandate period (Juiz et al., 2014).

Prior to the adoption of *dFogIT*, the problems explained in Sect. 6.4 were exacerbated until the direction taken by the board and IT staff practices seemed irreconcilable. However, the board of a public organization, e.g., UIB, cannot continue operating without explicitly considering the public interest or enacting a desirable strategy for IT assets. Thus, the work explained in Juiz et al. (2014) not only illustrates the maturity of the UIB in terms of IT governance during this three-year period but also how IT was aligned with the principles of good governance in the public sector. This is a major improvement in the results back to the original focus, which is the inspiration to create the ISO/IEC 38500 standard; i.e., public organizations must act in the public interest of their stakeholders at all times.

6.7 Extension of *dFogIT* Framework to External Stakeholders

Every public sector entity or public service spends public money; how this money is spent and the quality of services it provides is critically important as citizens, users and taxpayers. Therefore, we need governance of public services to be of a high standard. Good governance leads to good management, good performance, and good investment of public money, good public behavior and good outcomes. Since IT has become an essential asset in any enterprise, including the public sector, good governance principles should be also implemented on IT governance practices in public organizations (Juiz, 2014).

One of the characteristics of *dFogIT* framework is that it can be implemented in any organization. Thanks to the experience during the implementation of the IT governance framework at the UIB (a public university); it was found that *dFogIT* should be modified to include the key external stakeholders of a public company, who are in most cases citizens. That is, *dFogIT*, as described so far, is an implementation framework for IT governance where the main stakeholders are external to the model; i.e., they are not explicitly reflected in the model in the same way that in the ISO/IEC 38500 standard are not.

There are two important aspects of the current model of that should be changed to adopt the model to include external stakeholders (Juiz et al., 2015). First, a new layer on top that considers the users should be added (Juiz, 2014). This means that the new framework model has to determine who the key stakeholders are, what their main demand is and what is the expected result of that demand (just as we did with each of the layers of the *dFogIT* framework). Second, the new specifications of ISO/IEC 38500 standard version 2015 (ISO/IEC, 2015) propose a model in which the present and future use of IT is directed and controlled by key stakeholders, who are external to the governance framework itself. Hence, the definition of IT governance based on the modification of behavior in terms of IT usage should not include business strategy as one of the main drivers; the organization's policies and evaluation and redirection of policy are used to achieve better IT governance, with clear accountability and responsibility (Juiz and Toomey, 2015). Third, the objective of applying a framework for IT governance to public governance is derived from the need to implement the seven principles of good governance in the public sector, as IFAC and CIPFA discussed (CIPFA and IFAC, 2014):

1. Strong commitment to integrity, ethical values and the rule of law.
2. Openness and broad participation of stakeholders.
3. Definition of the results in terms of economic, social and environmental benefits, all of which are sustainable.
4. Determination of the interventions that are needed to optimize the expected results.
5. Capacity development in the company, including company leadership.
6. Risk management and performance through robust internal control and strong public financial management.
7. Implementation of good practices on transparency and reporting to deliver effective accountability.

Therefore, expanding *dFogIT* to include external stakeholders involves adding a layer in which compliance with these seven principles of good governance is required for the public sector. In addition, the pressure from citizens, who pay their taxes to support the budget of the public enterprise, should be considered (see Fig. 6.12).

This new top layer indicates that the policies and strategies of the public enterprise, which are performed by the executive team, have to be communicated to citizens, who are the key stakeholders for public organizations. Therefore, in this new layer, citizens demand transparency, which is transformed into real democracy as a result of openness and accountability in the exchange of value for money (taxes). Thus, citizens use their power (direct or indirect) and at the same time legitimize the executive team in a particular public organization.

As in the original *dFogIT*, the extension of the framework has served as a basis for research related to IT governance in public enterprises (Coertze and Von Solms, 2015);

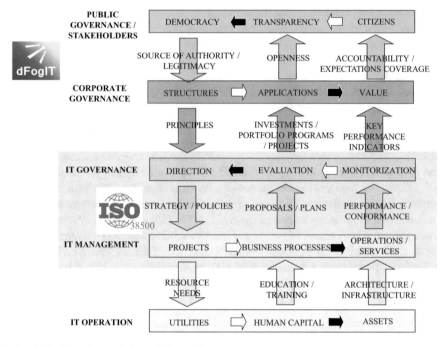

Fig. 6.12 *dFogIT* extended to public entities

(Pereda-Pérez, 2016). These studies show that the external stakeholder layer changes depending on the nature of the business, private, public or cooperative, and the implications for the affected instruments for IT governance. Thus, *dFogIT* framework was originally designed to be used in the internal IT governance and IT management aspects of any institution, public or private. However, in order to encourage more transparency at the public organizations through the implementation of the afore-mentioned cycles (Juiz et al., 2015), the *dFogIT* framework is extended with the main stakeholders in public enterprises: the citizens. Thus, the IT may be required to the same behavior as the other business assets, especially if those assets are financed through taxes from those citizens.

6.8 Conclusions and Open Problems

This chapter addressed the origins of the IT governance framework, namely, *dFogIT*. The vision of the relationship between IT and the rest of the enterprise differs based on the maturity of its IT governance. The IT asset should evolve from being a service provider to a business enabler. Thus, IT requires governance as do other traditional assets in the enterprise. As a result, there have been a number of management standards that claim to represent the standards of IT governance, but the only international IT governance standard is the current ISO/IEC 38500.

Due to the simplicity of the standard, CIOs need guidelines on how to implement the governance of IT within a company, so it is necessary to implement a governance framework for this purpose. Governing IT basically involves directing, evaluating and monitoring IT. This implies that the entire company, from senior management to IT staff, has to know the strategy of the company and the performance expected from their execution of IT assets. Therefore, the governance framework should include more detailed and adapted organizational layers and more precise instruments of IT governance to adopt ISO/IEC 38500 easily.

dFogIT complies with these characteristics because it has four layers in which all areas of the enterprise related to the governance of IT are represented. The key success factor of *dFogIT* is the explicit communication instrumentation between these layers, which creates alignment between IT strategy and the rest of the organization. The flows of direction and control, proper governance activities, and the product and service cycles are also provided by the implementation of the governance framework.

In particular, the implementation of *dFogIT* was shown in its place of origin, the University of the Balearic Islands (UIB). After the implementation of the governance framework in the institution, despite the organization resistance to change, significant strides in maturity have been observed. Moreover, after the analysis of the results of *dFogIT* deployment at UIB, the requirement to extend the framework to external key stakeholders arose—with a particular focus on the public sector –to determine whether the citizens (users) are crucial for the implementation of good governance best practices in public enterprises.

The task of governing IT has been easier because of the implementation governance frameworks that are compatible with the ISO/IEC 38500 standard, as in the case of *dFogIT*. However, major challenges for IT governance remain. One of the main challenges is the sustainability of the governance framework and the enforcement discipline of the governance structures involved in its application. That is, any governance framework should not only be supported and led by the corporate governance structures but also organized by the CIO office. These challenges remain unresolved in many organizations even after the implementation and execution of IT governance frameworks. Clearly, there are some root causes in the resistance to change in public organizations and the unwillingness to be governed in immature enterprises.

References

Al Qassimi, N., & Rusu, L. (2015). 'IT Governance in a public organization in a developing country: A case study of a Governmental organization'. In *Conference on Enterprise Information Systems/International*. HCrist, 05 October 2015. Procedia Computer Science. http://www.sciencedirect.com/science/article/pii/S1877050915026769.

Applegate, L., Austin, R., & Soule, D. (2008). *Corporate information strategy and management: Text and cases* (8th ed.). New York: McGraw-Hill, Inc. http://www.hbs.edu/faculty/Pages/item.aspx?num=34426.

CIPFA and IFAC. (2014). *Good Governance in the public sector*. New York: IFAC. ISBN 978-1-60815-181-3, http://www.ifac.org/publications-resources/international-framework-good-governance-public-sector.

Coertze, J., & Von Solms, R. (2015). Towards a cybernetics-based communication framework for IT Governance. In *48th Hawaii International Conference on IEEE: System Sciences (HICSS)* (pp. 4595–4606).

Elpez, I., & Fink, D. (2006). Information systems success in the public sector: Stakeholders perspectives and emerging alignment model. In *Issues in Information science and information technology*. Australia. http://connection.ebscohost.com/c/articles/21975732/information-systems-success-public-sector-stakeholders-perspectives-emerging-alignment-model, ISSN: 1547-5840.

Fernández, A., Barro, S., Llorens, F., & Juiz, C. (2012). Segunda fase del proyecto de arranque del Gobierno de las TI en el SUE, in UNIVERSITIC (ed.) *Descripción, gestión y gobierno de las TI en el Sistema Universitario Español*. ISBN 978-84-938807-4-3: CRUE, (pp. 88–114). http://www.gti4u.es/pdf/arranque-gobiertoti-universidad.pdf.

Fernández, C. M., & Piattini, M. (2012). *Modelo para el gobierno de las TI basado en las normas ISO. AENOR ediciones*. http://www.aenor.es/aenor/normas/ediciones/fichae.asp?codigo=9918#. WAhuiuCLRtQ, ISBN: 978-84-8143-764-5.

Gomes, J., de Macedo, N., Kussam, L. Y., Nogueira, R. M., & Arima, C. H. (2016). Gestão de riscos de segurança da informação e governança de TI no setor público, X Workhop de E pós-graduaçao e Pesquisa do Centro Paula Souza: ENGEMA. São Paulo, 07 October 2015 (pp. 753–763).

Hotzel, H., Wimmer, M., von der Heyde, M., & Lang, U. (2015). IT Governance—role of a CIO in German Universities. *PIK- Praxis der Informationsverarbeitung un Kommunikation, 38*(3-4), 121–126, doi:10.1515/pik-2015-0019.

ISACA. (2012). *COBIT 5: A Business Framework for the Governance and Management of Enterprise IT*. http://www.isaca.org/cobit/documents/cobit-5-introduction.pdf, ISBN: 978-1-60420-237-3.

ISO/IEC. (2014). *PDTR 38504 The structures of principles-based standards in the governance of IT*. Geneva: ISO/IEC. http://www.iso.org/iso/catalogue_detail.htm?csnumber=56638.

ISO/IEC. (2015). *38500: Governance of information technology for the organization*. Geneva: ISO/IEC. http://www.iso.org/iso/catalogue_detail?csnumber=62816.

Juiz, C. (2011). New engagement model of IT Governance and IT management for the communication of the IT value at enterprises. In E. Ariwa & E. El-Qawasmeh (Eds.), *Communications in Computer and Information Science Series* (pp. 129–143). Berlin: Springer. ISBN: 978.3.642-22602-1.

Juiz, C. (2014). La Rendición de Cuentas en las Entidades Públicas a través del Gobierno de las Tecnologías de la Información, *Novática, 229*. http://www.ati.es/novatica/2014/229/nv229sum.html#art26.

Juiz, C., & Toomey, M. (2015). To govern IT or not govern IT? *Communications of the ACM, 58* (2), 58–64. doi:10.1145/2656385.

Juiz, C., Bermejo, B., Guerrero, C., & Lera, I. (2015). Modelos de Gobierno de TI en empresas públicas, privadas y cooperativas para la mejora de comunicación de los objetivos empresariales y los resultados de rendimiento con diferentes partes interesadas, Gobernanza Empresarial de las Tecnologías de la Información. In A. Cobo & A. Albert (Eds.), *Gobernanza Empresarial de Tecnologías de la Información* (pp. 13–27). Santander: Editorial Universidad de Cantabria. ISBN 978-84-8102-760-0.

Juiz, C., Guerrero, C., & Lera, I. (2014). Implementing good governance principles for the public sector in information technology governance frameworks. *Open Journal of Accounting, 3*, 9–27. doi:10.4236/ojacct.2014.31003.

Khalfan, A., & Gough, T. G. (2002). Comparative analysis between the public and private sectors on the IS/IT outsourcing practices in a developing country: A field study. *Logistics Information Management, 15*(3), 212–222. doi:10.1108/09576050210426760.

Mueller, L., Magee, M., Marounek, P., & Phillipson, A. (2008). (ed.). *Rational software IBM IT Governance approach business: Performance through IT Execution.* http://www.redbooks. ibm.com/abstracts/sg247517.html, ISBN 978-07-384859-0-4.

Pereda-Pérez, F. J. (2016). *Análisis de las habilidades directivas. Estudio aplicado al sector público de la provincia de Córdoba.* Ph.D. thesis. Cordoba. http://helvia.uco.es/xmlui/handle/ 10396/13398.

Sethibe, T., Campbell, J., & McDonald, C. (2007). IT Governance in public and private sector organizations: Examining the differences and defining future research directions. In *18th Australasian Conferences on Information Systems.* Toowoomba, 05 December 2007. http:// www.canberra.edu.au/researchrepository/file/f33bed1a-dfed-0982-2f89-e60282e798c2/1/ fulltext_published.pdf.

Toomey, M. (2009). *Waltzing with the elephant: A comprehensive guide to directing and controlling information technology.* http://trove.nla.gov.au/version/45114006, ISBN: 9780980683004.

Weill, P., & Ross, J. W. (2004). *IT governance: How top performers manage IT decision rights for superior results.* Harvard Business Press. http://dl.acm.org/citation.cfm?id=1014896, ISBN: 9781591392538.

Author Biographies

Beatriz Gómez received the B.Sc. and M.Sc. degrees in Informatics on 2011 and 2013 respectively from the University of the Balearic Islands (UIB), Spain. Currently, she is Assistant Lecturer at the UIB teaching in the area of Architecture and Computer Technology. Before joining the Department of Computer Sciences of the UIB, she served for two years as an analyst and programmer and thereafter participated as an engineer and researcher at the Chair Telefónica—UIB of Digital Health and Sustainable Tourism. She is member of the ACSIC research group in the Department of Computer Science at UIB. Currently, she is the project manager of the Erasmus + K2 project IT Governance for Tunisian Universities (ITG4TU).

Belén Bermejo received her B.Sc. and M.Sc. degrees in Computer Sciences at the University of the Balearic Islands (UIB), Spain, in 2014 and 2016, respectively. She is a researcher at the ACSIC research group (http://acsic.uib.es) in the Department of Computer Science (UIB). She is PhD candidate in the field of cloud computing and resource management. She has authored some conference papers during her master period and in the first stages of the doctoral studies. She is a technician of the Erasmus+ K2 project IT Governance for Tunisian Universities (ITG4TU).

Carlos Juiz received the B.Sc., M.Sc. and Ph.D. degrees in Informatics respectively from the University of the Balearic Islands (UIB), Spain. He is Associate Professor of Computer Technology and Architecture at UIB. He has a postgraduate degree on Office automation from the Polytechnic University of Madrid, Spain. He had several positions related with the computer systems industry. He was visiting researcher at Department for Computer Science and Business Informatics, University of Vienna, in 2003 and Visiting Associate Professor at Biomedical Informatics Research, in 2011, at Stanford University. Carlos Juiz is heading the ACSIC research group (http://acsic.uib.es) and his research interest mainly focuses on performance engineering, green computing and IT governance. He is the coordinator of the IT Governance WG within SC 40 at AENOR, the Spanish representative in ISO/IEC.

Chapter 7
Business and IT Architecture for the Public Sector: Problems, IT Systems Alternatives and Selection Guidelines

Martin Henkel, Erik Perjons and Eriks Sneiders

Abstract Digitization is seen as a central force in order to transform the public sector to become transparent, participative, collaborative as well as efficient. In order to realize the digitalization, a public organization need to have an IT architecture that can support such a transformation. Therefore, decision makers in a public organization need to make informed decisions when governing, designing and implementing an IT architecture. This require that they have an understanding of the alternatives available to them in terms of possible IT systems and their roles in the organization's overall IT architecture. However, there is a lack of concrete descriptions providing such an understanding. In this chapter we present a number of types of IT system that public organizations could or need to have as part of their IT architectures; the problems these types of IT system address; what alternative IT systems and technology solutions are available for each type of IT system; and guidelines on what alternative solutions to select given the situation or condition at hand in a public organization. The chapter also includes a description of the relationships between the various types of IT systems and clarifies their roles by means of a business and IT architecture. The business and IT architecture, the different alternatives and guidelines are based on experiences from a number of research projects within the public sector. Real-life examples from the projects illustrate the alternatives proposed.

M. Henkel (✉) · E. Perjons · E. Sneiders
Department of Computer and Systems Sciences, Stockholm University,
Forum 100, SE-164 40 Kista, Sweden
e-mail: martinh@dsv.su.se

E. Perjons
e-mail: perjons@dsv.su.se

E. Sneiders
e-mail: eriks@dsv.su.se

© Springer International Publishing AG 2017
L. Rusu and G. Viscusi (eds.), *Information Technology Governance in Public Organizations*, Integrated Series in Information Systems 38,
DOI 10.1007/978-3-319-58978-7_7

7.1 Introduction

The digitization is seen as one of the main drivers of change in our time and affects all parts of society, not least the public sector. The digitalization is often defined as the process of making everything digital that can be digitalized in order to transform businesses and everyday life (Fors 2012), and for the public sector, the digital-ization is sometimes presented in terms of e-government. The digitalization is often seen as a necessary means to transform the public sector to become simplified, and efficient (Riksrevisionen 2016), but also to become transparent, participative, and collaborative, often together referred to as open government (Wirtz and Birkmeyer 2015). Such a transformation will benefit the citizens and private organizations as they are consumers of public sector services. To succeed with this transformation, questions about business and IT governance, financing, privacy and security issues need to be answered (Riksrevisionen 2016). In this chapter, we focus on gover-nance, design and implementation of the IT architecture.

An efficient, flexible and business aligned IT architecture is often seen as a necessary condition for successfully transforming the public sector to become simple, open and efficient. Today, public organizations employ a wide range of IT systems, such as case management systems for managing formal cases (i.e., applications) from citizens, workflow systems for efficient routing of documents, web applications and e-services for interaction between citizens and the public administration. If these types of IT systems are not integrated, and/or are not business aligned, the business processes of the organizations are not as efficient and/or of as high quality as they could be. Moreover, if new types of promising technologies are not used in full, this may also result in non-optimal business processes.

In order to successfully govern the IT architecture, decision makers need to make informed decisions. This requires that decision makers have an overview of the options available to them, both in terms of the individual IT systems and their relationships. Such overview will support the decision makers to select appropriate IT system solutions and to gradually design and implement their IT architecture.

Today, however, there is a lack of descriptions that provide an overview over the IT architecture of public organizations and that clarify the options available for the decision makers so that they can make concrete IT system selections. Therefore, the problem addressed in this chapter is the lack of support for decision makers to make informed decision regarding IT systems and IT architecture.

In this chapter, we present a business and IT architecture model supporting business and IT managers to select appropriate IT systems in public organizations. The model is based on several research projects involving public organizations (these projects are further described in Sect. 7.3). The main goals of the chapter are to present:

- A high-level business and IT architecture model of public organizations showing roles, main information flows and possible types of IT systems that can be introduced in a public organization. The focus of the model is on describing

the interaction with citizens, for example, the handling of citizen service requests and the management of more formal cases related to the citizen.
- A number of alternative IT systems and/or technologies to select among when developing an IT architecture as well as a number of guidelines for selecting an appropriate IT system given the situation or condition at hand for a public organization.

The high-level business and IT architecture model of public organizations has been introduced in an earlier paper when presenting the existing and future use of language technology in public organization (Henkel et al. 2016). In this latter version presented in this chapter, the model is used to present alternative IT systems and technologies for public organizations supporting the requests from—and interactions with—citizens and the daily operational work within the public organization for managing these requests and interactions.

The chapter is structured as follows: Sects. 7.2 and 7.3 presents related research and the research approach. Section 7.4 present the business and IT architecture model. Section 7.5 contains the alternative IT systems and technologies. Finally, Sect. 7.7 concludes the chapter.

7.2 Related Research

E-government refers to the use of ICT to improve the quality of public organizations in the form of efficiency, transparency and improved interaction with citizens (Yildiz 2007). In this chapter we examine e-government in the form of models of e-government, supporting IT architectures and IT systems within the architecture. Generally, models of e-government explain how e-government can be performed and how to improve it. IT architecture is related, since it helps to fulfill the promises of e-government.

A well-known *model for e-government* is the four stage model proposed by Layne and Lee (2001). The four stage model, and other similar theoretical models, describe how e-government can start from an initial web presence and develop into an ICT supported interaction between citizens and public organizations (Layne and Lee 2001). In this development, ICT is seen an enabler that improves efficiency and administration capabilities (Coursey and Norris 2008). One example of ICT as an enabler is that e-government service platforms may provide the opportunity to create open markets of services (Henkel et al. 2007). However, ICT development within e-government programs has been criticized for the use of generic "universal strategies" when trying to reach efficiencies (Cordella and Iannacci 2010). In this chapter, we do not apply a specific prescriptive e-government model, we rather examine and describe the current practices with regards to citizen services and case handling in public organizations. We do this based on our previous model, (Henkel et al. 2016) that we extend to describe IT systems and their alternatives. Furthermore, we avoid prescribing universal strategies, and, instead, we are focusing on concrete practical problems and practical solution supported by IT systems to overcome them.

Some authors have suggested *IT architectures* that may help public organizations to select appropriate IT systems. As a starting point, Pardo et al. (2011) point towards the specific needs of IT architecture for publics organizations, such as for supporting cross-boundary collaboration as part of open government efforts. Other authors propose concrete architectures. For example, Dias and Rafael (2007) and Batini (2010) suggest a division into a front-office and a back-office system that has similarities to our model since they show the needs to manage both general citizen questions and more formal case request. Another example is Salhofer and Ferbas (2007) that propose a new architecture that allow the use of process descriptions that is similar to what existing commercial case handling systems are offering. The reference architecture for e-government presented by Batini (2010) provides a coarse grained overview of potential e-government applications. However, the reference architecture works mostly as an example of what applications, or IT systems, that may exists, rather than providing any information of how they are interconnected. Similarly, Ebrahim and Irani (2005) presents an architecture framework for e-government. This framework contains four general layers: access, government, business and infrastructure, including IT systems, such ERP, CRM, data warehouse systems, in the different layers. However, the relationships between the IT systems are not presented or discussed, nor are alternative IT systems to select among. Thus, as exemplified above, many authors present a general architecture view, they document the IT architecture of pilot e-government projects or they suggest completely new architectures. In contrast to previous research our focus in this chapter is to describe the main building blocks that public organizations use in their IT architectures today. The presented architecture is grounded in several case studies. For the constituents parts of the IT architecture we also describe alternative implementations, which could help a public organization to tailor the architecture to their needs given the situation or condition at hand.

7.3 Research Approach

The research presented in this chapter can be described as knowledge integration, including information from previous research and our own experience of participating in a number of IT related research projects within the public sector. First, we present a business and IT architecture model of public organizations. This model is based on a number of research projects that we have participated in, and public documents from the public sector. Second, for each type of IT system in the business and IT architecture, we present alternative IT system and technology solutions, and provide guidelines for selecting a solution given the situation or condition at hand for the public organization. These descriptions of solutions are based on our experiences of customer services and case management processes in

Swedish public organizations. The result is thus based on our work as action and design researchers within a number of research projects, presented below:

IMAN2 project aimed to develop innovative e-government solutions for customer service and case management processes by the use of language technologies, with the aim to simplify and improve the interaction between public organizations and the actors they serve, such as citizens and organizations, both private and public (Henkel et al. 2016). The project was a collaboration between researchers in language technology at Stockholm university, Sweden, Royal Institute of Technology, Sweden, the business intelligence company Gavagai, the process improvement company Visuera, and the IT consultant company Cybercom. Moreover, the project includes a number of Swedish public organizations on national as well as local level: the Swedish Transport Administration, the Swedish Pension Agency, and the municipalities of Klippan, Kungsbacka, Nacka, and Söderhamn. The overall research strategy was action research. Data was collected via workshops and interviews with public administrators, both managers and operational personnel, all working with customer service and case management. Data were analysed and structured into models, such as business process models, business use cases, and models of cost-benefit analysis.

The Swedish Tax Agency project aimed at analyzing an existing e-service in order to create a better design for the customer (i.e. companies declaring taxes) (Goldkuhl 2009; Henkel and Perjons 2011). One of the problems investigated in the project was that an e-service developed by the Swedish Tax Agency was not used as much as expected. The e-service was aiming at supporting companies to send in tax declarations to the Swedish Tax Agency electronically. However, a large group of companies were continuing to use paper forms and traditional channels instead of using the e-service. In order to analyse the limited use of the e-service, we investigated the e-service design as well as the IT and business context on both the service provider's and service consumers' sides. The project was a collaboration between Stockholm University, Linköping University and the Swedish Tax Agency. The overall research strategy was action research. Data were generated from interviews with public administrators. Data were analyzed and structured into models such as business process models. The project was a subproject within a larger research project about e-service design called SAMMET, including also Skövde University, Scandinavian Airline Systems and Ericsson (SAMMET 2010).

Open Mobile Data project aimed at designing mobile services based on open or public data for immigrants (Henkel et al. 2016). A common theme among immigrants is that they do not know the obligations of citizens, legislation and rules, responsibility and role of the different public organizations, and the case handling processes within the organizations. The designed services aimed at supporting the immigrants to find information helpful in different situations related to public organizations. The project was a collaboration between Stockholm University, the municipality of Nacka and the company Mobilearn. The overall research strategy was design science. Data were generated from interviews with public administrators, both managers and operational personnel. Data were analyzed and structured into models such as business use cases.

IMAIL project aimed at creating an email client prototype for a Swedish Social Insurance Agency that should automatically answer a large part of simple questions in the incoming email flow; improve the quality of the semi-automatic answers (i.e. answer templates); and finally, reduce the workload for the handling officers. The development of the prototype was grounded in an empirical study comprises the analysis and clustering of 10,000 citizens emails and the working activity of 15 case handling officers that were collected through questionnaires, interviews and workshops. The project was a collaboration between Stockholm University and the Swedish Social Insurance Agency (Cerratto-Pargman et al. 2011).

7.4   The Business and IT Architecture of Public Organizations

In this section, a business and IT architecture model of public organizations is presented. The model describes citizens' requests and interactions with public organizations. Generally, there are two types of requests from citizens to public organizations:

- **General question**. A general question is a request for information about the public organization and its services. For example, a citizen can ask which plans exist to build block of apartments or highways in the neighborhoods of the citizen, or how to apply for a driving license.
- **Formal case request**. A formal case request is a request for access to certain services that require some form of formal investigation at the public organization. For example, a citizen can request a permission to build a house on a certain property, or request extra support at home for a person that is not able to manage cooking and cleaning. This type of request is regulated by national legislation as well as regional rules. This type of request commonly starts a formal case process in which a handling officer investigates the request and checks if it is compliant with the national laws and/or regional rules, and then make a decision about the citizen's right to have access to the service.

These two types of requests need to be managed by public organizations. Figure 7.1 describes somewhat simplified how a traditional public organization manage these two types of request. General questions are often managed by a customer (or citizen) service unit within the public organization. For example, a citizen contacts the customer service via telephone. The service officer at the customer service can answer the question, or make use of domain experts in the public organization if the service officer does not have the skillset to answer the questions. In many organizations, the citizens can also contact the domain expert directly, often via a telephone operator that direct the citizen to the right expert. Some general questions result in a formal case requests, see bottom part of Fig. 7.1. The citizens can also directly contact the public organization for a formal case request,

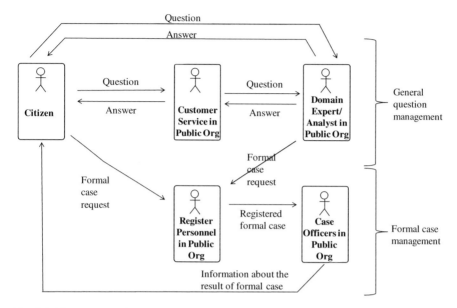

Fig. 7.1 The two type of requests that a public organization needs to manage: general questions and formal case requests

via phone or email. Formal case request are registered in a register system of the public organization, and the management of these formal request are usually supported by a case management systems. Formal cases are often carried out by case worker (or handling officer), a role that can be played by the same person as is playing the role of domain expert, mentioned above. The case worker will also contact the citizen via phone or mail to inform the result of the formal request. The process of managing formal cases is described in Fig. 7.1.

The management of the two types of requests in a traditional public organization, described above, is often not optimal. To address this, different type of IT solutions can be introduced for a more effective management of the requests, see Fig. 7.2:

Web info system. A public web site with info, for example Frequently Asked Questions (FAQ), can give the citizens easy access to answers of often asked questions (see Fig. 7.2). An example of a web info system is the extensive information that the Swedish Tax Agency has published on their web site.

eMail system. Questions from citizens can be sent to the customer service via email (see Fig. 7.2). These questions via email can be forwarded to a domain expert. For example, the Social Security Agency receives requests on issues related to parental leave and sickness leave via email.

Web forms. Web forms on a public web site can be used for formal case requests (see Fig. 7.2). For example, tax declarations can be filed to the Tax Agency by using their online forms.

Register system. This system is used to have a formal registry of all formal cases that are handled. Usually, each case is given a unique case number that is

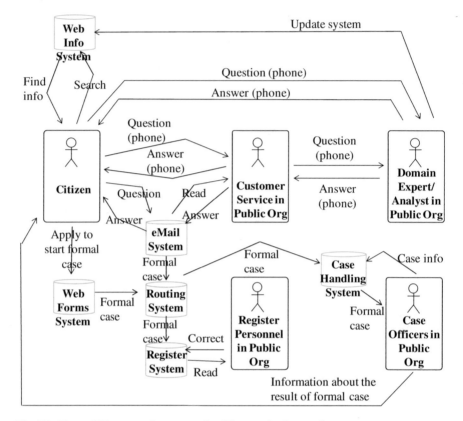

Fig. 7.2 Type of IT support that an actual public organization can have

public. All Swedish public organization is required to have a registry that contains the formal cases.

Case handling system. This system supports the handling of the cases, for example by providing workflow and/or content management support (see Fig. 7.2). For example, most Swedish municipalities, such as Klippan and Nacka, have a case handling system that support the operational handling of cases.

Routing system. A routing system can be introduced to integrate the web forms, the register system and the case handling systems, so that a case can automatically be registered in the register system as well as automatically be routed to the case management systems when a citizen post a formal case request via a public web form (see Fig. 7.2). This type of system is more seldom used, instead routing is done manually. For example the Transport Administration performs manual routing of 2000 request per month.

7.5 Alternative IT Systems and Technologies

In this section, alternative solutions for public sector are presented in form of IT systems and technologies. For each type of IT system presented in Sect. 7.4, a pattern is used in this section to describe the type:

- *Description of the IT system*—this part of the pattern describes briefly the type of IT system in focus.
- *Problem or need to be addressed by the IT system*—this part of the pattern describes why the type of IT system is needed in a public organization
- *Alterative IT/Technology solutions*—this part of the pattern describes alternative IT and/or technology solutions for addressing the problem that the type of IT system needs to address.
- *Situation-based selection of alternatives*—this part provide guidelines for selecting alternative IT/Technology solutions given the situation or condition of the public organization.

7.5.1 Web Info System

Description of IT system: Web Info System is a system using the web to provide citizens with public info about public organizations, their services as well as citizens' obligations. For example, a web site can provide the citizens with easy access to answers of often asked questions (i.e. Frequently Asked Questions).

Problem or need to be addressed by the IT system: A web page has become the standard way of providing information to citizens 24/7. The information provided is both in the form of stable information—such as information about legislations and rules, and of more event-driven kind—for example when a certain situation occurs, planned or unplanned. A typical example of a planned event is when the Swedish Tax agency provides comprehensive information about rules and procedures about tax declaration (i.e. tax return) on their web page in May each year when citizens need to file tax declarations. An example of an unplanned event is if the Swedish Pension Agency is late with sending out the yearly information about the citizens' pension prognosis due to, for example, IT problems. Such an incident will result in a number of telephone calls from citizens but can be partly avoided if information about the incident is swiftly published on the web site of the Swedish Pension Agency. A special issue for web info system here is that many times citizens need to gather web information from several public organizations, for example when starting a company, such as a restaurant.

To summarize, from the citizens' perspective the problem addressed by the web info system is the citizens' need to access public information 24/7, both planned and unplanned, and sometime the need to access compiled information from several organizations and sources. From the public organizations' perspective the problem addressed by the web info system is the need to lower the amount of resources needed for answering citizens' requests by providing the information on the web.

Alterative IT/Technology solutions: All Swedish municipalities and government agencies have a web page. Mostly, these are updated by the information department of the organization at hand, sometimes based on information from domain experts. We refer to this alternative as *in-house provisioning* of information.

There are also cases where the creation and maintenance of public information are distributed among several public organizations. This can be seen as a *federated* alternative to in-house provisioning of information. An example of the federated provisioning alternative is the Swedish web site "Verksamt.se", where several governmental agencies provide information on one web site describing what citizens need to do to start a new company. Thereby, citizens do not need to search for information of how to start a company on all these agencies web sites, and compile the information themselves, since all information is compiled on one web site (verksamt.se 2016).

A special case of the federated provisioning alternative is the use of open data. Open data is, according to the Swedish e-delegation (The Swedish e-delegation 2015), information from organizations that are available to all actors without restriction in terms of cost, intellectual property or legal obstacles. These types of data can be used by private or public service providers to supply the citizens with useful information in form of compiled, aggregated, and/or summarized data from different public organizations.

An example of this kind of use of open data is the app Mobilearn by the service provider with the same name (Mobilearn 2016). The purpose with the Mobilearn app is to provide public information to immigrants in their own native language. The provider of the app collect web info from for example the Swedish Migration Board's, the Swedish Tax Agency's, the Employment Service's and municipality's web pages through special scripts and occasionally via APIs. This information is then aggregated and translated to several languages. Mobilearn business model is to provide subscriptions to the service for a monthly fee, the paying customers being municipalities, which, thereby, can provide immigrants with public information supporting the immigrants in their interaction with public organizations (Henkel et al. 2016).

Situation-based selection of alternatives: The *in-house* information provisioning alternative is a good starting point when the information is mostly coming from the public organization itself. Furthermore, this provisioning alternative relies on the facts that the organization know, at least roughly, what the information needs of citizens are and have the in-house resources to handle it. In contrast to this, the *federated* provisioning alternative is better suited for handling situation where the information provided covers a large body of knowledge spread across several organization and sources. Furthermore, the use of open data let public organizations leverage the know-how and resources of external private organizations that may provide additional value to the data by carry out data compilation and data aggregation.

7.5.2   eMail System

Description of IT system: An email system of a public organization is a system that can handles questions from citizens as well as answers from public organization electronically. For example, questions can be sent via an email by a citizen to a public organization's customer service (sometimes called "citizen service") that can answer the question or forward it to be answered by a domain expert of the organization.

Problem or need to be addressed by the IT system: Answering email is a substantial part of the customer support in the municipalities and governmental agencies that we have contacted. The issues with email handling can be described as the issues of volume and quality. Volume concern the large amount of email that the organization receive. Even if all organizations that we have had contact with utilize some form of systematic support (such as case management systems) for answering emails, there is still a need to employ a number of persons just to answer requests via email. Even simple emails can take time to answer and the citizens may not get any answers at all during weekends. The issue with quality regards the quality of the answers. Similar questions may get different answers depending on the knowledge of the case handler.

To summarize, from the citizens' perspective the problem addressed by the email system are the need to receive high quality answers and to receive the email answers as quickly as possible. From the public organizations' perspective the problem addressed is the need to lower the amount of resources needed for answering citizens' emails.

Alterative IT/Technology solutions: Currently the used (IT) alternatives to tackle the issues of volume, speed and quality are the use of *automatic answering* systems and the creation of message *answer templates*. An example of the potential for using answering templates is the Swedish Pension Agency (Henkel et al. 2016). The Swedish Pension Agency estimates that it takes around 10 min on average to answer an email. They want to lower that time to 5 min with the introduction of a semi-automated message answering system. The message answering system will suggest templates to the service agent with different answers given the type of questions in the email. The service agent will then choose a *template* and adapt it given the question from the citizen, before sending the answer to the citizen. The Swedish Pension Agency is in the state of introducing such a system. The agency estimates that in the long run up to 90% of the email questions should be able to be answered using templates. Today, 110,000 emails are answered by the Swedish Pension Agency, and the use of templates is estimated to lower the costs of answering email to close to 50%. The agency also believes that the quality of the answers will be higher since the template includes quality assured information. An important part of the semi-automated message answering system is to maintain the templates. However, no organization has been designed for that yet by the agency, but at least one employee will be responsible for maintaining the templates.

An example of the potential with using total *automatic answering* is the Swedish Social Security Agency (Cerratto-Pargman et al. 2011). The Swedish Social Security Agency get a large amount of emails asking questions about compensation for sickness leave, parental leave and so forth. In a pilot case it was shown that at least 5% of the incoming emails could be correctly answered automatically. Besides lowering the load on the customer service the automatic answering of email also led to a quicker response time.

Situation-based selection of alternatives: Even if they can be used in combination, automatic answering and the use of answer templates have different purposes. Automatic answering is mainly targeting a high volume of frequently asked questions. That is, routine questions. The use of templates is more targeting the quality of the answers and is more suited to answer complex questions were the case handler may answer the email question by picking one or more template answers and modifying them. A difference is also the need for maintenance since templates continuously need to be updated.

7.5.3 Web Forms System

Description of IT system: Web forms systems on a public web site can be used for formal case requests. For example, tax declarations can be filed to the Swedish Tax Agency by using their online forms, "forcing" the citizens to provide all necessary information to the Tax Agency.

Problem or need to be addressed by the IT system: Web forms can range in complexity from very simple forms to forms that support complex interactions between a case manager and a citizen. A typical simple form use is similar to that of sending an email. However, web forms can also provide a more structured way to provide information and give immediate feedback. For example, Nacka municipality has a fairly advanced web based system where the citizens can browse available schools, and finally select a school for their children. The drawback here is that complex web forms can be expensive to create. This is especially true if the forms should be available in multiple channels, such as web pages as well as applications for mobile devices. Moreover, our experiences from the research projects are that expectations from the citizen are high—it not enough to have a service online, it needs to be good from a usability point of view as well.

To summarize, from the citizens' perspective the problem addressed by the web form system is the citizens' need of interacting with the public organisation in an advanced and user-friendly way. From the public organizations' perspective the problem addressed is the need to lower the amount of resources needed for managing advanced interaction with citizens, but also to be resource efficient when develop advanced web forms.

Alterative IT/Technology solutions: We have the experience of three alternatives when it comes to the deployment of web forms: *custom made*, *form platform* and vendor *portlets*. Many governmental organizations have forms that are *custom made*, that is, they are built by the organizations themselves or by consultants hired by the organizations. These solutions though are not built from scratch—they are built using web development platforms. For example, the Swedish Tax Agency and the Pension Agency have both made a large investment in custom made forms based on web development platforms (Henkel and Perjons 2011; Henkel et al. 2016). While custom made forms offers high flexibility, there are also organizations that use more standardized *form platforms* to create simpler forms. These platforms could best be described as information (rather than process) centred in that they provide an easy way to map on-screen forms to a database structure. This type of functionality is similar to that of traditional tools such as Oracle forms and Microsoft access forms. For example, Nacka municipality uses the Abou platform for developing simpler form entries (Henkel et al. 2016). The last alternative, vendor *portlets*, is a solution where vendors provide small applications, portlets that can be used by citizens. This solution is also applied in Nacka municipality (Henkel et al. 2016).

Situation-based selection of alternatives: While many organizations have excellent IT departments, they also have a limited IT budget. Thus, the organizations often strive to use standard solutions to minimize the amount of system development that is needed. This means that the use of vendors systems is preferred. However, for cases where the handling could be complex, or were the cost of errors could be substantial, custom made solutions are used. An example of a high customized solution is the Swedish Tax agency online declaration. It goes far beyond what can be built on a standard form platform since it provide ample support for the tax declarations process (rather than just supporting information entry). For example, when filling in the forms, the total numbers are calculated based on the tax regulations, and forms to be filled in are suggested based on the citizens type of employment (self-employed or by a company).

7.5.4 Case Handling System

Description of IT system: Case handling system supports the handling of formal cases, for example by providing workflow and/or content management support. Most Swedish municipalities, such as Klippan and Nacka, have a case handling system that supports the operational handling of formal cases.

Problem or need to be addressed by the IT system: Public organizations need to handle request by having procedures that are ranging from straight-forward standardized procedures to highly personalized procedures. Standardized request may be handled by a single case handler by following a strictly defined process. Other request may involve several case handlers, each with their own expertise. The issue here is to differentiate between the different types of cases so that proper system support can be applied.

An example of workflow management is the Swedish Social Insurance Agency that handles request via ordinary paper-based mail, email and phone via a workflow management approach. For example, a type of case that the agency handles is applications for housing supplementary allowances. This is a highly regulated process and thus suitable for a workflow approach. In contrast to this approach, the health care area commonly gathers different types of experts in a ward round, where the investigations and treatments of patients are discussed. This is an example of where an adaptive case management approach would be beneficial instead (Henkel et al. 2015).

To summarize, from the public organizations' perspective the problem addressed by the case management system is to lower the amount of resources needed for managing formal cases.

Alterative IT/Technology solutions: We here differentiate between two alternative solutions: support in the form of a *workflow management* system (WfM) or a system that support *adaptive case management* (ACM). The first alternative, workflow management, support work that are structured according to a pre-defined order of activities. However, public organizations also need to handle many requests that are non-standardized and knowledge intensive, meaning that public agents need to interact with each other and with the requesting citizen in order to manage the request. These requests are not well supported by traditional WfM approaches. Instead, adaptive case management is aimed to handle these kind of requests (Herman and Kurz 2011; White 2009). In contrast to WfM, ACM does not focus on following a strictly defined order of activities in a process; the focus is rather to support a knowledge worker to select and perform appropriate activities by providing well-structured information (Herman and Kurz 2011). More precisely, ACM is a management approach aiming at providing the knowledge worker with the required information at the right time, and supports the knowledge worker to continuously re-plan, for example as a result of handling frequent exceptions which is common in knowledge intensive processes.

Situation-based selection of alternatives: The types of request that are handled affects if a WfM or an ACM approach is an appropriate choice. The difference here is a number of properties that affect how public organizations manage requests, including agents/personnel interaction and way of working, and system support needed. First, if it is common that a team of case handlers interacts to solve request instead of a single agent carrying out each task, ACM rather than WfM may be appropriate (White 2009; Koehler et al. 2012). Second, if case handlers are carrying out tasks on a case-to-case basis based on the understanding of the situational context of a request instead of carrying out a standardized set of actions, ACM is suitable. Third, if the role of the citizens is to be a co-creator of the final outcome from a case and not only as an initiator to the case, ACM may again be an appropriate approach.

7.5.5   Routing System

Description of IT system: A routing system can be used to route incoming requests so that a case can automatically be registered in the register system as well as automatically be started in the case handling systems when a citizen post a formal case request via a public web form or via email. Another function of the routing system is to send the request to the right case handler.

Problem or need to be addressed by the IT system: A common theme among Swedish public organizations is to create a common entry point for all requests. This theme manifest itself in that even large organization provide only one phone number, one email address and one address for regular mail. The general idea of this approach is to be able to centrally register all requests into a central register system, and then route the request to the appropriate case handler. The routing is based on expertise—the request need to reach an available case handler that has the right knowledge for the request. One issue here is to route the request to the correct case handler.

To summarize, from the public organizations' perspective the problem addressed by the routing system is to lower the amount of resources needed for managing formal cases.

Alterative IT/Technology solutions: Manu organization support routing by the use of registers of the personnel and their competencies, or by the use registers in form of a simple list of departments and contact persons at each department. These registers can be the base for two alternative routing solutions: *manual routing* and *automatic routing*. For example, the Swedish Transport Administration handles about 2,000 written request per month (Henkel et al. 2016). The agents' handling as well as the requests is divided into customer services and formal cases. The customer service handles request that can be quickly resolved, for example, requests regarding the current highway status and temporary routes. The case handling officers handle formal cases concerned with a number of sub-categories: railway, highways, ferries, transport logistics and large projects. One possible use of automatic case routing would be to first sift out the "small" cases that the customer service can handle promptly. The remaining cases could then be routed to a case handling officer. The category "large projects" are an example of a category that is changed often, and thus an automatic categorization must be updated to cover new projects as they are planned. An example of a project in the domain of the transport administration is the creation of a new turnpike. The creation of a new turnpike could cause a lot of questions from the citizens.

Situation-based selection of alternatives: The most common form of routing is manual routing. This works well if the public organization does not utilize a single entry point, but rather allows the citizens to contact separate departments directly. The reason for this is that the citizen to some extent does the routing themselves, that is, they are responsible for contacting the correct department. If the department is small enough, it is also very easy for the support personnel to know each case handler and their area of expertise. The other alternative, automatic routing relies on that the citizen can fill in the type of request, for example using a web form. Another approach is to use language technologies to detect the topic of the request and match that with a register of the case handlers.

7.5.6   Register System

Description of IT system: A register system is used to store a registry of formal cases. Both information about incoming requests and outgoing responses to the requests are stored. Since the system is a *registry* rather than a *repository*, the actual content of the request or response does not need to be stored—the content may be stored in other systems. Central to the register system is to assign each formal request and response a unique number—the register number. This number may be composite— for example it may consist of the year and a sequential number, such as "2016/123". Besides storing the identification for request and responses initially triggered by citizens, the register system is also used for storing information about formal documents that is created within a public organization. Examples of these kinds of documents are public protocols from meetings, or formal recommendations. Documents that are considered to be unfinished/work-in progress are generally not considered to be public documents and are thus not registered in the system.

   Problem or need to be addressed by the IT system: In order to be transparent, public organization should be able to upon request retrieve any formal document received or sent by the organization. If there is no IT support for this, there is a risk that each request for handing out a public document takes a lot of manual labor to resolve. In fact, handling the register is of such importance that many Swedish public organizations has assigned personnel and/or roles for this task.

   Alterative IT/Technology solutions: The function of the register system can be either implemented as a *standalone* system or as an *integrated* solution. The stand-alone solution implies that the system is separate, the users need to use the system to log register numbers for the documents that they create in other systems. Coupled with manual routines the standalone system may even require users to send an email to the person responsible for the register to get a document registered. However the work can be simplified if the register system functionality is integrated with other systems. For example, a case management system may request a unique number for each case request that is handled. The functionality may also be integrated with email systems.

   Situation-based selection of alternatives: An organization that to a large degree uses manual routines are more likely to have a standalone register system, since there is simply no other system to integrate the functionality into. If the organization has started to use for example case management systems, there is a potential gain in integrating it with a register system.

7.6   Overview of Alternatives

Table 7.1 summarizes the system types described in this chapter. Each system addresses a certain problem, and can be accompanied with a set of solution alternatives. The selection of an alternative is influenced by the situation or condition at hand in the public organization.

Table 7.1 Overview of the discussed system alternatives

System type	Problem	Alternative IT solutions	Situation influencing selection
Web info system	Citizens' need of planned and unplanned info 24/7, sometimes compiled from several sources. Lower the amount of resources for answering citizens' requests	• In-house provisioning (i.e. info from one organization) • Federated provisioning (i.e., compiled info from several organizations)	• Information needed is available in one organization • Information needed is a compilation of info from several organization and sources • Availability of open data
eMail system	Citizens' need of high quality as well as fast answers. Lower the amount of resources for answering high volume of citizens' requests	• Automatic answering systems • Answer templates	• Volumes of requests • Complexity of requests • Quality of answers needed
Web forms System	Citizens' need for interacting in an advanced and a user-friendly way. Lower the amount of resources for managing formal case requests	• Custom made • Form platform • Vendor portlets	• Availability of standard platforms • IT competence • Resources available for web form development • Cost of errors
Case handling system	Lower the amount of resources for managing cases. Enable several case handlers to collaborate	• Workflow management • Adaptive case management	• Amount of standardized cases • The number of different case managers that need to collaborate
Routing system	Lower the amount of resources for managing cases by sending request to the correct case handler	• Manual routing • Automatic routing	• Use of a single entry point for requests • Size of the organization
Register system	A need to be able to refer to documents belonging to a formal case. Lower the amount of resources for record keeping	• Standalone • Integrated	• Level of automation available

7.7 Conclusion

In this chapter, we have highlighted the possibility of using IT as a means to transform the interaction with citizens. We present a business and IT architecture model which provide an overview of the roles, information and IT systems commonly used in public organizations for citizens' interaction. We furthermore extend the model to show how different IT and technology alternatives could be used to enhance the interaction with citizens.

The business and IT architecture model and the provided IT and technology alternatives can be used by public organizations to:

- understand and reflect over which type of IT systems could be or need to be introduced and how they are related
- decide which alternative IT and technology solutions to use, based on the different properties of the alternatives and the situation at hand
- evaluate the existing use of IT and technology solutions in order to change solution in order to enhance the IT architecture

References

Batini, C. (2010). Chapter 9. Choice of projects. In: G. Viscusi, C. Batini & M. Mecella (Eds.), *Information Systems for eGovernment. A quality-ofservice perspective* (pp. 159–176). Springer

Cerratto-Pargman, T., Knutsson, O., Celikten, E., Sneiders, E., & Dalianis, E. (2011). User centered development of automatic e-mail answering for the public sector. In F. V. C. Ficarra, et al. (Eds.), *New horizons in creative open software, multimedia, human factors and software engineering*. Lecture Notes in Computer Science. Berlin, Germany: Springer. ISBN: 978-3-642-18347-8.

Cordella, A., & Iannacci, F. (2010). Information systems in the public sector: The e-government enactment framework. *The Journal of Strategic Information Systems, 19*(1), 52–66.

Coursey, D., & Norris, D. F. (2008) Models of e-government: Are they correct? An empirical assessment. *Public Administration Review, 68*(3), 523–536.

Dias, G. P., & Rafael, J. A. (2007) A simple model and a distributed architecture for realizing one-stop e-government. *Electronic Commerce Research and Applications, 6*(1), 81–90.

Ebrahim, Z., & Irani, Z. (2005). E-government adoption: Architecture and barriers. *Business Process Management Journal, 11*(5), 589–611. Emerald.

Fors, A. C. (2012). The ontology of the subject in digitalization. *Handbook of research on technoself: Identity in a technological society: Identity in a technological society* (Vol. 45).

Goldkuhl, G. (2009). Socio-instrumental service modelling: An inquiry on e-services for tax declarations. In A. Persson, & J. Stirna (Eds.), *PoEM 2009* (Vol. 39, pp. 207–221). LNBIP. Berlin: Springer.

Henkel, M., & Perjons, E. (2011). E-service requirements from a consumer-process perspective. In: D. Berry, X. Franch (Eds.), In *Proceeding of the 17th International Working Conference on Requirements Engineering: Foundation for Software Quality, (REFSQ 2011)* (Vol. 6606, pp. 121–135). LNCS. Essen, Germany: Springer.

Henkel, M., Perjons, E., & Drougge, U. (2016). Using open data to support case management, adaptiveCM. In *The IEEE Enterprise Computing Conference (EDOC'16)*. IEEE.

Henkel, M., Perjons, E., & Sneiders, E. (2016). Examining the potential of language technologies in public organizations by means of a business and IT architecture model. *International Journal of Information Management*. Elsevier.

Henkel, M., Perjons, E., & Sneiders, E. (2015). Supporting workflow and adaptive case management with language technologies. In *New contributions in information systems and technologies* (pp. 543–552). Springer International Publishing.

Henkel, M., Perjons, E., & Zdravkovic, J. (2007). Towards guidelines for the evolution of E-service environments. *International Journal of Public Information Systems, 3,* 183–200.

Herrmann, C., & Kurz, M. (2011). Adaptive case management: Supporting knowledge intensive processes with IT systems. In W. Schmidt (Ed.) *S-BPM one—learning by doing—doing by learning* (Vol. 213, pp. 80–97). Berlin: Springer.

Koehler, J., Hofstetter, J., & Woodtly, R. (2012). Capabilities and levels of maturity in IT-based case management. In A. Barros, A. Gal, & E. Kindler (Eds.), *Business process management* (Vol. 7481, pp. 49–64). Berlin: Springer.

Layne, K., & Lee, J. (2001). Developing fully functional e-government: A four stage model. *Government information quarterly, 18*(2), 122–136.

Mobilearn. (2016). Mobilearn website. Retrieved July 3, 2016, from https://se.mobilearn.com.

Pardo, T. A., Nam, T., & Burke, G. B. (2011). E-government interoperability: Interaction of policy, management, and technology dimensions. *Social Science Computer Review*. Sage Publisihing.

Riksrevisionen (2016) Den offentliga förvaltningens digitalisering —En enklare, öppnare och effektivare förvaltning? (RiR 2016:14) http://www.riksrevisionen.se/sv/rapporter/Rapporter/.

Salhofer, P., & Ferbas, D. (2007). A pragmatic approach to the introduction of e-government. In *Proceedings of the 8th annual international conference on digital government research: bridging disciplines and domains* (pp. 183–189). Digital Government Society of North America.

SAMMET. (2010). SAMMET project site. Retrieved July 3, 2016 from http://www.dsv.su.se/sammet.

The Swedish e-delegation (2015). Vidareutnyttjande av offentlig information (in Swedish). http://www.edelegationen.se/Documents/Vagledningar%20mm/V%C3%A4gledning-f%C3%B6r-vidareutnyttjande-av-offentlig-information.pdf (Accessed 2016-04-08).

Verksamt.se. (2016). verksamt.se website. Retrieved July 3, 2016, from https://www.verksamt.se/.

White, M. (2009). Case management: Combining knowledge with process, BPTrends.

Wirtz, B. W., & Birkmeyer, S. (2015). Open government: origin, development, and conceptual perspectives. *International Journal of Public Administration, 38*(5), 381–396.

Yildiz, M. (2007). E-government research: Reviewing the literature, limitations, and ways forward. *Government Information Quarterly, 24*(3), 646–665.

Author Biographies

Martin Henkel works as Senior Lecturer at the Department of Computer and Systems Sciences, Stockholm University. Martin's research areas are enterprise modelling and enterprise architecture. More specifically the research focus on how organizations can understand and design service oriented systems, service value networks and software services. Through research projects and consulting Martin has been involved in domains such as healthcare, IT systems for energy efficiency, and capability analysis and design. Martin has a PhD from the Royal institute of technology (KTH), Sweden.

Erik Perjons is a Senior Lecturer at Stockholm University, Department of Computer and Systems Sciences. Erik is engaged in research in enterprise modelling and supporting methods and tools. A special interest has been the use of modelling methods that support organizations to align their strategies and goals with performance indicators. Erik has practical experience from a number of research projects from the domains of telecom, health care and e-government. Erik has a PhD from Stockholm university.

Eriks Sneiders works as senior lecturer at the Department of Computer and Systems Sciences, Stockholm University. Eriks performs research on how language technologies can be applied to improve the quality and efficiency of public organizations. He has built, tested and deployed several novel tools based on language technologies for domains such as insurance, healthcare, and social care. Eriks has a PhD from the Royal institute of technology (KTH), Sweden.

Chapter 8
Problems of Enterprise Architecture Adoption in the Public Sector: Root Causes and Some Solutions

Dinh Duong Dang and Samuli Pekkola

Abstract Enterprise architecture (EA) is a comprehensive approach aimed at understanding and aligning an organization's business strategy and processes, information resources, and information technologies. However, implementing this approach in an organization is not an easy task as organizations have their preexisting siloes and fragmented procedures and departments. Comprehensive, inter-organizational practices, such as EA, usually break old procedures and habits, shift decision-making power, and challenge old values. This makes EA endeavors extremely difficult. In this paper, we conduct a qualitative multiple-case study. We use institutional theory to identify problems and their root causes in EA adoption in three cases. We also discuss possible solutions—by identifying eight root causes and several examples, both successful and not-so-successful—to mitigate or overcome these problems. We also argue that institutional theory and its three pillars provide a usable lens to analyze EA adoption.

8.1 Introduction

Enterprise architecture (EA) has gained increasing attention in recent years in both the private and public sectors (Dang and Pekkola 2017). EA aims to increase transparency and interoperability, help organizations reform their administrative procedures, and align business and IT perspectives. This broad goal has resulted in different interpretations. Some see EA as a strategic approach (Ross 2009) while others see it as a means to support individual projects (Janssen and Klievink 2012) or to model the organization (Löhe and Legner 2014). Our interpretation bridges all these interpretations: we see EA as an approach aimed at gaining understanding

D.D. Dang (✉) · S. Pekkola
Laboratory of Industrial and Information Management,
Tampere University of Technology, PO Box 541, 33101 Tampere, Finland
e-mail: duong.dang@tut.fi

S. Pekkola
e-mail: samuli.pekkola@tut.fi

© Springer International Publishing AG 2017
L. Rusu and G. Viscusi (eds.), *Information Technology Governance in Public Organizations*, Integrated Series in Information Systems 38,
DOI 10.1007/978-3-319-58978-7_8

about the organization so that it can achieve its strategic goals through the use of several models in IT projects.

EA has been enforced in many countries. For instance, it has been mandated by law in Finland since 2011 and in the US since 1996. Unfortunately, the results of EA programs show limited signs of success (Dang and Pekkola 2016b). Many scholars have studied EA challenges (Chuang and Loggerenberg 2013; Hauder et al. 2013; Kim and Everest 1994), including the lack of standard approaches to build the EA, lack of human resources, and poor understanding about the concept itself, among others. Dang and Pekkola (2016b) go further in their study of the root causes of EA problems during organizational adoption. They propose eight root causes: organization structure, legislation and regulation, politics and sponsors, EA team formation, the EA team's capabilities and skills, EA users' capabilities and skills, users' conflicting benefits, and EA fundamentals. They argue that identifying these root causes helps practitioners in reducing and avoiding risks in introducing EA to organizations. However, the literature has not yet examined how these root causes could be handled, which is the starting point of this study.

Institutional theory provides a lens through which to understand how different technologies and practices are introduced in an organization. It provides a view of practices (e.g., the internal view and local circumstances in organizations) and an external view in organizations such as cultural and societal factors (Orlikowski and Barley 2001). Despite the benefits, EA institutionalizations have not been extensively investigated. Rare examples include Iyamu (2009), who focuses on barriers to EA management, Weiss and colleagues' (2012, 2013) studies on architectural coordination, Hjort-Madsen's (2006, 2007) research on EA adoption, and Dang and Pekkola's (2016a) approach to the problems that different stakeholders face when institutionalizing EA. These studies do not focus, for example, on how organizations cope with the challenges of adopting EA. In this paper, we adapt institutional theory and its three institutional pillars, namely, norms, rules, and values (DiMaggio and Powell 1991) to explore these solutions.

Our research objective is: (a) to understand potential solutions to the root causes of problems in organizations' adoption of EA and (b) to identify a set of institutional conditions (e.g., norms, rules, and values) as potential solutions. Our findings are derived from three cases in different environmental settings. We therefore investigate the following research question: what are the root causes of problems in organizations' adoption of EA, and what are the potential solutions to these root causes?

An interpretive qualitative multiple-case study with semi-structure interviews, supplemented with secondary documents, was conducted. The findings show that eight generic root causes of problems and their potential solutions in certain institutional conditions are the first steps in helping scholars and practitioners in understanding problems in deploying EA programs, thus also seeking to avoid these problems. This would ultimately improve the success rate of EA projects.

The paper is organized as follows: first, the background is presented, followed by our research approach. The subsequent sections present our findings and analysis. The paper ends with a concluding section.

8.2   Background

8.2.1   Enterprise Architecture and Its Problems

First introduced in 1987 (Zachman 1987), EA provides a holistic view of the organization's strategy, processes, data, and information technology resources. It attempts to align and integrate business and information technology (Niemi and Pekkola 2017). EA is defined as:

> a strategic information asset base which defines the mission, the information necessary to perform the mission and the transitional processes for implementing new technologies in response to the changing mission needs. It helps to align resources to improve business performance and help agencies better execute their core missions. An enterprise architecture describes the current and future states of the agency and lays out a plan for transitioning from the current state to the desired future state (U.S. CIO 1999, C-5).

EA is, however, variously interpreted, with interpretations varying from IT implementation (Ross 2009) and strategic management (Simon et al. 2014) to IT-business alignment (Winter 2010) and IT consolidation (Magoulas et al. 2012). There are also several frameworks and approaches, such as Zachman, Federal Enterprise Architecture (FEA) and The Open Group Architecture Framework (TOGAF), aimed at facilitating EA development. EA stakeholders are defined as persons producing, using, or facilitating EA artefacts (Dang and Pekkola 2016b). They range from senior managers to project team members and users.

In the public sector context, EA has been used in more than 20 countries (Ramos and Júnior 2015). Unfortunately, EA adoption is not without difficulty. The literature indicates various challenges faced by organizations when adopting EA, for example, problems relating to governance structures and insufficient resources (Seppänen et al. 2009), limitations in modeling tools (Kaisler et al. 2005), lack of implementation ability and EA governance structures (Isomaki and Liimatainen 2008), and the legacy of rigid bureaucracy and coordination of different information systems (Weerakkody et al. 2007). Moreover, Lucke and colleagues (2010) and Kim and Everest (1994) have identified problems relating to unclearly defined roles and responsibilities. Kim and Everest (1994) also allude to the lack of interest among departments and short-lived commitments from top managers. There are also problems relating to organizational politics, organizational complexity, outdated results, understanding of benefits, inappropriate level of detail, and conflicting stakeholder needs (Löhe and Legner 2014; Hauder et al. 2013; Chuang and Loggerenberg 2013).

These challenges are extensive and important to diagnose. We thus attempt an understanding of their root causes and potential solutions.

8.2.2 Institutional Theory in EA Research

According to Scott (1995, 235), there is no single and universally agreed definition of an "institution" in institutional theory. Scott (1995, 33) maintains that "Institutions consist of cognitive, normative, and regulative structures and activities that provide stability and meaning to social behavior. Institutions are transported by various carriers' cultures, structures, and routines and they operate at multiple levels of jurisdiction." Institutional theory provides a lens through which to explain how and why EA is adopted in organizations (Weiß 2015). Organizations initiate EA differently according to their interpretations and applications. Thus norms, rules, and values drive and may explain the root causes of problems and their solution.

The institutionalization literature remains limited regarding EA studies (Dang and Pekkola 2016a). A few examples include Weiss and colleagues (2012, 2013) on the coordination of EAM stakeholders (e.g., IT, project, and line managers). They identify seven institutional influences, namely: efficiency, social legitimacy, organization grounding, governance, trust, enforcement, and goal alignment in the effectiveness of institutionalization in terms of architectural coordination. Along these lines, Iyamu (2009) has shown six internal barriers to institutionalizing EA, including economic investment, organizational structure, administrative process, technical capability, organizational politics, and the business' interest and understanding of EA. Furthermore, Magnusson and Nilsson (2006) note that institutional theory could be used to infuse the EA framework while Hjort-Madsen and Gøtze (2004) study interoperability challenges at different levels. Scholars have also investigated the political motives driving EA development (Hjort-Madsen 2006, 2007), the influence of EAM adoption in government agencies (Hjort-Madsen and Pries-Heje 2009; Janssen and Hjort-Madsen 2007), and institutionalizing EA in relation to different EA project phases (Dang and Pekkola 2016a).

These studies simply examine some perspective of institutions and institutionalization and do not, for example, focus on how institutions react when they face challenges as well as the seriousness of these challenges under different conditions. We will thus focus on these perspectives.

Depending on the institutional conditions (e.g., norms, rules, and values in organizations), EA projects may experience various challenges. We will identify the root causes of these challenges and potential solutions addressing these root causes in different EA projects. We find institutional theory to be a suitable approach because the challenges in EA projects are usually societal in nature (Dang and Pekkola 2016a), especially in relation to cooperating with different stakeholders in practice (Dang and Pekkola 2016a).

8.2.3 Theoretical Framework

Organizations legitimize their activities by conforming to institutional factors, such as beliefs, symbols, norms, and rules (DiMaggio and Powell 1983, 1991; Scott 1995). Institutional theory focuses on these factors (e.g., norms, rules, and values) and can thus be used in explanations of organizational practices. Each set of norms, rules, and values (the three pillars) corresponds with each isomorphic mechanism, namely: normative, coercive, and mimetic (DiMaggio and Powell 1983, 1991; Scott 1995). These mechanisms lead to shaping and influencing the extent to which institutional practices are diffused in an institutional environment. Institutions thus comply with sets of norms, rules, and values in certain environmental settings in order to become more legitimate (Mignerat and Rivard 2009). This research investigates the nature of each isomorphism in order to gain insights into the root causes of challenges and their potential solutions in EA adoption in the public sector. It does so by identifying the different assumptions, indicators, and mechanisms underlying those pillars (Scott 2005).

The first element consists of norms—normative pressures (DiMaggio and Powell 1983) or the normative pillar (Scott 1995). These are mostly formed by the organization's professionalization, such as training and networking that allow stakeholders to adopt mimetic behaviors from industry and others (DiMaggio and Powell 1983). Thus, norms illustrate appropriate approaches aimed at achieving objectives and goals or show how things should be done in certain social environments (e.g., organization). These norms can be formed through institutional policies or standard procedures for empowering or imposing professional activities. For example, Dang and Pekkola (2016a) argue that in different phases of EA institutionalization, EA has different effects on the normative pillar. In our context, we anticipate that different business associations and EA project phases will influence different solutions and root causes. Hjort-Madsen (2007) finds that norms could impact the internal resistance of change in administrative arrangements or IS planning.

The second institutional pillar consists of rules—coercive pressures (DiMaggio and Powell 1983)—or the regulative pillar (Scott 1995). It corresponds with coercive isomorphism to indicate how institutions regulate and constrain stakeholder behavior (Mignerat and Rivard 2009). Rules can be formed formally and informally though the power of enforcements or by imposing sanctions and other penalties from superior organizations, such as EA outcomes and objectives being affected by local government (Dang and Pekkola 2016a). Different institutions are likely to have different rules and policies that might affect the different solutions for root causes of challenges in EA adoption.

Values, or the cultural-cognitive pillar (Scott 1995), indicate the cultural-cognitive perspective of the institutional environment. This means that the institution's activities need to comply with the values rooted in those environments. Values are characterized by imitation whereby institutions tend to copy others that they consider to be leaders or models (Scott 1995). This is because by doing so, one could easily pursue support and commitment from stakeholders. The difference between norms and values is that norms tend to focus on social obligation, such as standards or policies, while values focus more on common social frameworks such as social routines or culture. In the context of our study, we anticipate that differences in culture will explain some of the root causes of problems and their solutions in EA adoption.

We argue that in the context of our study, norms, rules, and values can influence stakeholder groups in organizations when they adopt EA in their work. As a result, our research sheds light on understanding how organizations solve problems encountered in EA projects.

8.3 Research Approach

8.3.1 Methodology

We used a qualitative research approach to gain an in-depth understanding of the phenomenon (Myers 2009). We adopted a multiple-case study approach to understand how organizations adopt EA (Stake 2005). Three cases were investigated as they have different backgrounds and experiences with EA projects, different level of readiness and maturity, and are geographically dispersed so that the mimicking of next-door-neighbors did not pertain to them. We used face-to-face semi-structured interviews for the data collection from June 2015 to September 2015. Our respondents consisted of people playing key roles in EA projects. They were employed at multiple organizational levels and occupied various positions. They included senior management (senior managers, CIOs), EA team members (project managers, EA workers, enterprise architects) and EA users (IT specialists, civil servants). We invited new interviewees until theoretical saturation was reached. In total, 22 participants were interviewed using identical questions and topics to ensure consistency and validity (Walsham 2009).

Each interview was approximately 45–60 min. They were conducted in Vietnamese by the first author, who is familiar with the culture, language, and context of the cases. All interviews were audio-recorded and transcribed. We also used secondary sources such as project documents, newspaper articles, and power-point presentations to supplement our interview data.

8.3.2 Case Descriptions

The first case (Case A), a province, is one of the political and economic centers of the country. It has about seven million inhabitants. The province has deployed EA projects under a loan from the World Bank (Nguyen 2006; WorldBank 2005). In 2013, it was ranked second out of 63 provinces in terms of e-government ranking

(MIC 2014). The province has about nine years of EA experience. We interviewed eight people, including the senior manager, the CIO, the project manager, the enterprise architect, an EA worker, and an IT specialist. The primary objective of the EA program was to reform administrative procedures and improve interoperability within and between organizations. Four state agency levels were affected by the EA program, namely, central administration offices, departments, sub-departments, and local offices (communes).

The second province (Case B) has about 1.3 million inhabitants. Its EA program was established in 2010, and it has had an average e-government ranking over the past five years (MIC 2014). It has also had five years of EA experience. We interviewed six stakeholders: the CIO, the project manager, an EA worker, the enterprise architect, an IT specialist, and a civil servant. The main objective was to reduce complex and incomprehensible public services. Three state agency levels were affected by the EA projects.

The third case (Case C) is a province of about 2 million inhabitants. It has much less experience in e-government, just three years, as its EA program was established in 2012. Eight people were interviewed, including the CIO, the project manager, the enterprise architect, an EA worker, an IT specialist, and a civil servant. The main objectives of the EA project were to reform public services and increase information system interoperability. Three state agency levels were affected by the EA program.

These cases were chosen because multiple cases provide a better understanding of the insights as the researcher can compare the various findings (Myers 2009). Moreover, all cases had just completed their EA projects, so they had appropriate data available.

8.3.3 Data Analysis

We employed the coding technique of Strauss and Corbin (1998) and the ATLAS. TI software to analyze our data. To code the transcripts, we used the coding approach that defines a coding unit as a text piece no bigger than a paragraph and no smaller than a sentence. Single text pieces could have been assigned with multiple codes. The data was analyzed in Vietnamese; only illustrative quotations were translated into English by the first author. Tables 8.1 and 8.2 illustrate examples of how the quotations were coded.

We analyzed the data in three stages: first we identified the problems; second, we identified the root causes of those problems; and third, we sought to understand solutions to these root causes through the lens of institutional theory.

Stage one: *Identifying the problems*. First, all incidents or anecdotes that emerged and were considered as EA problems were coded. They included problems relating to pressure from sponsors or politicians. Second, the problems were grouped in sub-categories and appropriately labeled. Third, broader categories were

Table 8.1 Stage one: Identifying problems via ATLAS.TI

Example of quotations	Primary coded (step 1)	Sub-category (step 2)	Broader-category (step 3)
In some cases, we needed a year or longer to persuade the leader and staff to change their attitude due to conflicting benefits. (Enterprise architect, Case C)	Willingness	Conflicting benefits and willingness to use EA	User-related problems
I think that our leaders and staff are afraid that when EA is deployed, their roles and benefits will be reduced. (Enterprise architect, Case C)	Benefit		
The majority of the inhabitants in our province live in rural areas and have low computer literacy levels. It is difficult to change their behavior when we are deploying public services. We spend time training users. (IT specialist, Case B)	Capabilities	User's capabilities and skills	

Table 8.2 Root causes of problems

Category	Concept	Example quotations
Norms and normative isomorphism	It is the organization's professionalization, such as training, networking activities in the institution	Through professional forums, we were able to easily find a solution that we never had before. (Enterprise architect, Case C)
Rules and coercive isomorphism	It is about rules, policies, or regulations	The guidance from the central government is inappropriate in our agencies when it comes to practical issues. (IT specialist, Case A)
Values and mimetic isomorphism	It is about cognitive culture within the case environment setting	TOGAF seems to be too large and needs a business focus, and the FEA's approach requires high EA skills and capabilities in each sub-unit. These are impossible in our organization, even in the whole country. Thus, we will choose our own approach. (EA worker, Case B)

formed from the sub-categories, for instance, users' problems or organizational problems. All non-EA project relevant problems were excluded (Table 8.1).

Stage two: Identifying the root causes. We identified 16 problems within four categories from stage one. We then identified their root causes by using the cause–effect graph. The workings of the method are presented in detail in Sect. 4.2.

Stage three: Understanding solutions to root causes. The results of stage two included eight root causes. We then adopted institutional theory as a lens and examined how the stakeholders in each case dealt with these root causes, utilizing three pillars, namely, norms, rules, and values (Table 8.2).

8.4   Findings and Analysis

8.4.1   Identifying the Problems

We identified four groups of problems. They were related to the organization, EA project teams, EA users, and the EA itself. The problems are summarized in Table 8.3. We will describe these findings in detail in the following section.

8.4.1.1   Organization-Related Problems

Organization structure. Empirical evidence suggests that the structure of the organization could lead to complex business services such as numerous owners and multiple levels of services. Unfortunately, all cases (A, B, and C) encountered these problems. As a result, the organizations faced challenges when proposing

Table 8.3 Problems identified in EA programs in the public sector

Identified problems	Groups
Organization structure	**Organization**
Legislation and regulation	*Problems relating to the organization and its adoption of EA in its business*
EA objective	
Politic and sponsor	
Agencies cooperation	
Inactive implementation	
EA team formation	**EA Team**
EA team capability and skill	*Problems relating to the EA project team, which is responsible for building the EA*
Emphasized on IT	
EA product	
EA planning	
User capability and skill	**EA User**
Conflicting benefit	*Problems relating to users, those using EA products*
Willingness to use EA	
EA Fundamental	**EA itself**
Shared EA understanding	*Problems relating to the EA itself*

appropriate EA planning, approaches, and EA products. An EA worker in Case B said: "we have a multi-level organization and multiple-owner business services, each with different permissions and capabilities. Thus, we cannot choose FEA, TOGAF, or any other approach. The only notable way to solve the problem is to use our own approach."

Legislation and regulation. Although many countries have used EA in the public sector, only a few (e.g., Finland and the U.S. government) have legally enforced it. In the analyzed cases, there was no legal enforcement to utilize EA. The central government does have guidance and instructions relating to EA, but these are unclear and overly abstract, thus leading to misunderstanding about EA. An IT specialist in Case A maintained that "The guidance from the central government is inappropriate in our agencies when it comes to practical issues." Additionally, the central government allows the organizations to interpret EA in dissimilar ways, each depending on political stance, the person's background, and individual interests. As a result, many factors related to the EA project have changed. For instance, the objectives changed from business reform in IT alignment to an IT perspective (Case A) or simply to an IT perspective (Case B). A project manager in Case A stated that "We do not have a law or policy on EA programs, but it is just an option among a variety of approaches. This causes problems when working with other agencies. We decided to focus on IT perspectives rather than business perspectives."

EA objectives. Unclear EA objectives and objectives not containing quantitative metrics were evident. This may result in a negative impact on EA projects. It is even worse when objectives are built under pressure by politicians or sponsors. In these circumstances, the stakeholders could not understand why the organization had chosen a specific EA approach and its product. As voiced by the EA architect in Case B, "[Our] objectives for doing the EA and using EA products are unclear in the sense that the agencies cannot or are limited to using certain products in their business."

Politicians and sponsors. Our findings show that politicians and sponsors clearly negatively influenced EA projects. For example, they affected EA planning in Case A and changed the EA objectives in Case C. A project manager in Case C declared: "They [senior management] said that we must deploy an EA program in our agency. If we [agency] don't do it, we might lose financial support from the central government. There are political issues in the requirements documentation."

Inactive implementation. The influence of politicians, sponsors, or others has led organizations to the implementation of EA in an inactive way. Some organizations have simply jumped on the EA bandwagon and have chosen EA because others have done so. This has led them to act in a mindless way in many activities. One EA worker in Case A revealed that "The person who does not understand EA at all proposed EA!"

Agency cooperation. EA affects many agencies within organizations. This emphasizes cooperation as a project success factor. However, our findings show that the organizations faced problems as the agencies had a tendency to choose services that impacted only on their own business or had the least interference. This results from different backgrounds, experiences, points of focus, and EA models, as an IT specialist in Case B stated: "When implementing EA, our agency chose services that would only affect our business; we did not choose services related to other agencies because it would increase our risks".

8.4.1.2 Team-Related Problems

EA team formation. Some organizations formed inappropriate project teams. For example, in Case A, international consultants were recruited as project team members. However, they adapted approaches from their previous projects conducted in another country and applied them to this case. Unsurprisingly, the results were poor because of different environmental settings. An EA worker (Case A) noted that "Based on their experiences from previous EA projects in [country X], our EA teams proposed five key projects. However, it turned out that three of the five projects were not feasible in our social-technical environment." In a similar vein, if the responsibility was on the IT department or other agencies without appropriate credibility, efficient results would later be evident.

EA capability and skill. EA is a new approach; therefore, the lack of expertise was evident. In our cases, the project team members were mainly from the IT department. This emphasized the outcome being focused on IT issues. Moreover, the EA team had experience from IT projects but not from an EA project that incorporated both business and IT disciplines. When project team members could not handle the problems within the EA project, severe delays were evident. A senior manager in Case C said, "Nobody in our team had any experience in EA. All of us have a background in IT. We do not understand what EA is, whether a human resource issue, a financial issue, what the policies are, and so on. We are just spending a lot of time discussing the topic."

Emphasized on IT. An overemphasized IT perspective caused the organizations to focus on the purchase of software and hardware. This may have helped the project and may have been easy to implement, but it did not guarantee the objectives of the business perspective. This also led the organizations to divide the EA project into many sub-projects, causing delays in implementation and resulting in the projects being fragmented. An IT specialist in Case C said, "Our EA program is divided into several sub-projects. Some of them were not approved at all or were approved later than planned. In contrast, they [the managers] approved another project with the same objectives as it was seen as beneficial for themselves because of social relationships. This breaks down the whole unity of EA programs."

EA product. EA products were not explicit. The organizations found it difficult to apply them in practice or in relation to existing information systems. Moreover, this caused concerns about the role of EA in the organization—for example, which factors should be considered if the organization selects EA as a strategy, which model and approach should be used for EA planning. Unfortunately, there was no suitable solution for these questions. A CIO in Case B said, "We are planning EA independently of other programs. We learned this from other agencies, and we chose an international consultant to plan the EA because many agencies do the same."

EA planning. Planning the EA was another source of problems as all provinces changed their plans and planning practices, frequently affecting the results. This was because EA projects affect both within and in-between the organizations. Each organization had its own services, resources, and businesses. As a result, this caused conflict, variance in the quality of products, and budget overruns. An IT specialist in Case C said, "Our over 28 agencies and their over 28 IT units do their planning with unequal resources, different understandings about the benefits, and with their own backgrounds. This makes it difficult to plan because we have to constantly negotiate with other agencies."

8.4.1.3   User-Related Problems

User capability and skill. Users are persons who use and are affected by EA products. User-related issues include extra costs, visiting tours, and job training. These issues, or the lack thereof, result in varied user skills. An IT specialist in Case B pointed out that "The majority of the inhabitants in our province live in rural areas with low computer literacy levels. It is difficult to change their behavior when we are deploying public services. We spend a lot of time training users. However, the proportion of users who actually use the services is normally very low."

Conflicting benefit. EA is about cooperation and sharing information among agencies. This principle could propel leaders into anxiety about losing their "lucrative benefits," which come with their position in society and the organization. An enterprise architect in Case C observed that "In some cases, we needed a year or longer to persuade the leader and staff to change their attitude due to conflicting benefits."

Willingness to use EA. Some users were often unwilling to use EA products because it would necessitate changes in their behavior and practices. They simply preferred the traditional ones. Moreover, if they switched to EA products, which might help them to improve transparency and services, it would then reduce the "benefits" to users. An enterprise architect in Case C noted, "I think that our leaders and staff are afraid that when EA is deployed, their roles and benefits will be reduced."

8.4.1.4   EA Itself as a Problem

EA fundamental. Our data revealed that no common tool, approach, framework, or commercial product ensured efficient results. For example, one EA architect in Case A observed that "In that time, we did not have a clear definition, scope, scale, level of detail, method, or output of the EA program. In our EA planning, we did not focus properly on cooperation between agencies." Case B was faced with similar issues, as articulated by an EA worker: "TOGAF seems to be too large and needs a business focus, and the FEA approach requires high EA skills and capabilities in each sub-unit. These are impossible in our organization, even in the whole country. We thus chose our own approach."

Shared EA understanding. All cases faced problems finding a common understanding of EA among stakeholders and agencies. This finding is common to various examples: practices used in planning in the US (Hjort-Madsen 2007), strategy in Singapore (Saha 2009), and as a means of achieving interoperability, standardization, and reuse within agency boundaries in South Korea (Lee et al. 2013). One EA architect in Case A noted, "We did not have a clear definition, scope, scale, level of detail, method, and output of the EA program. In our EA plan, we did not focus properly on cooperation between agencies."

8.4.2 Root Causes of Problems with EA Programs in the Public Sector

From these 16 problems, we can identify their root causes by using a cause–effect graph that maps the causes to their consequences (effects):

Step 1: Identifying relationships among problems.
　　　　The relationships among the problems were analyzed by going through the transcripts and supplemented data to identify "causes" and "effects" related to the aforementioned problems. For example, an interview transcript of an architect in Case A illustrates: "one agency with multiple levels and owners for each service does not help in choosing an appropriate product," resulting in a relationship between "organization structure" and "EA product."

Step 2: Building a cause–effect graph.
　　　　From Step 1, if X leads to Y, a direction from X to Y was formed (an arrow from X to Y was drawn). For instance, if "politic and sponsor" leads to "inactive implementation," an arrow from the vertex "politic and sponsor" to the vertex "inactive implementation" was drawn (Fig. 8.1). We repeated this until all the "cause–effect" relations were exhausted. We also eliminated loops if they emerged. The final graph is shown in Fig. 8.1. Sixteen problems with 21 cause–effects were identified.

Step 3: Identifying root causes.
　　　　From Step 2, the root causes were identified as follows: X is a root cause if there are no problems (out of 16) leading to X. For example, "politic and sponsor" was a root cause because no other problem led to this. In contrast, "politic and sponsor" lead to three consequences, namely, "inactive implementation," "EA objective," and "EA planning." As a result, they were not the root causes. This method was repeated. Table 8.4 presents the list of the root causes.

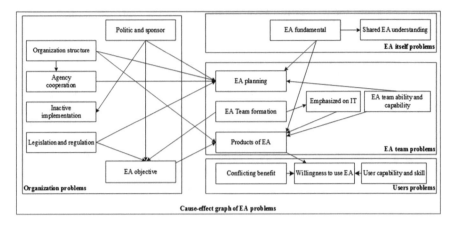

Fig. 8.1 Cause–effect graph of EA programs in the public sector (adapted from Dang and Pekkola 2016b, Fig. 8.1)

Table 8.4 Root causes of EA programs in the public sector (adapted from Dang and Pekkola 2016b, Table 8.4)

Group	#	Root causes	Consequences
Organization	1	Organization structure	EA product; EA planning; agency cooperation
	2	Legislation and regulation	EA objective; EA planning
	3	Politic and sponsor	EA planning; EA objectives; inactive implementation
EA team	4	EA team formation	Emphasized on IT; EA objective
	5	EA capability and skill	EA planning; EA product
EA user	6	User capability and skill	Willingness to use EA
	7	Conflicting benefit	Willingness to use EA
EA itself	8	EA fundamental	Shared EA understanding; EA planning; EA product

Our eight root causes for adopting EA include the organization group (e.g., organization structure, legislation and regulation, politic and sponsor), the EA team (e.g., EA team formation, EA capability and skill), EA users (user capability and skill, and conflicting benefit), and the EA itself (EA fundamental). We anticipated that if we could deal with these root causes, we would be able to control the problems faced by the organization to reduce risks and improve the success rate of EA projects.

8.4.3   Potential Solutions to the Root Causes

8.4.3.1   Institutional Perspective on Solutions

We used institutional theory as a lens through which to examine eight root causes to understand how they can be overcome. We summarized our findings in Table 8.5. The numbers in brackets in Table 8.5 refer to root causes from Sect. 4.2. We then analyzed how certain norms, rules, and values would help organizations cope with different root causes.

In relation to the *norms pillar*, the findings reveal several practices. Norms focus on social obligations, such as standards and policies. Our data shows that in order to deal with the root causes, organizations have used institutional norms approaches in implementing EA. For example, the root cause of "EA fundamental" (root cause #8) is rooted in the lack of a common EA definition and approach, leading organizations to interpret EA in their own way. As a result, the organizations found it difficult to identify appropriate approaches, models, frameworks, and relevant factors for their practices. Both Case A and Case B used certain high reputation professional fora to increase EA awareness and to identify a common base in relation to EA fundamentals (Table 8.5); Case C resolved this problem by using several practitioner workshops with experts from successful cases and industries. After those activities, the organizations seemed to find appropriate approaches to

Table 8.5 Summary of institutional settings affecting the root causes, assisting project member to overcome inter- and intra-organizational challenges

	Case A	Case B	Case C
Norms	Participants' professional training (5) Establishing EA chapter through ICT committees (8)	Organize seminar for on-job training (5) conferences and seminar (6) CIO forum as professional association to discuss EA (8)	Establishing contrast training center for user (6) Workshop with experts in successful case and industry for sharing experiences (8)
Rules	Regulation for loosely coupling from regular government regarding electronic local government model (2) Procedure for hiring experts as project members to help overcome difficult challenges (3)	Regulation for loosely coupling from regular government regarding electronic local government model (2)	Regulation for loosely coupling from regular government regarding electronic local government model (2) Policies for raising the power of the EA project management unit (3)
Values	Promote EA team-work under top manager (1) Use EA as planning (4) Allow more time for users to recognize benefits (7)	Extensive application of EA work as organizational procedure (7)	Senior manager serving as project manager for the pro-jects (1) EA as part of IT pro-jects (4)

steer the project. An enterprise architect in Case C articulated that "Through professional forums, we were able to easily find a solution that we never had before."

Additionally, the root cause relating to the EA team and their skills ("EA capability and skill," root cause #5) was variously tackled. Case A sent its team to participate in a professional training course to pursue international certificates (e.g., TOGAF) to help build their EA standard and to exchange experiences with other experts; Case B established an on-job training seminar in order to mimic successful models in similar cases in terms of structure and circumstance.

Moreover, the root cause "user capability and skill" (root cause #6) could lead organizations to face low management and adaptation skills and even computer illiteracy. This is more severe in EA as it bridges IT and business perspectives (Janssen and Klievink 2012). This requires users to change their behavior and work practices. Consequently, EA projects will be at risk if the organization is unable to cope with the problem. Case B organized several seminars and conferences for stakeholders and published guidelines, instructions, and reports. Case C established a training center for users. They designed courses and organized a "trainer training" class where experts trained the key users from each agency, who further trained key users in their departments.

In relation to the *rules pillar*, our findings reveal that the organizations used institutional rules approaches to deal with two root causes; "legislation and regulation" (root cause #2) and "politic and sponsor" (root cause #3). For example, Case A and Case C used more supervisory pressure in comparison to Case B. The root cause "legislation and regulation" (root cause #2) could affect both instances of EA implementation. Central government and its guidance to local governance formed a foundation for EA adoption. The drawback was that as the instructions and guidance were not explicit and were overly general, it was impossible to follow them in practice. The local governments thus had to use their own policies and legislation. This means that the organizations used "loosely coupling" approaches (Boxenbaum and Jonnson 2008) to deal with different institutional logics between central government and local governments. "Loosely coupling" indicates both coupled and decoupled alternative approaches when implementing EA. Local government, on one hand, should follow the legislation from central government to comply with their guidance (coupled). On the other hand, they used their own de facto approaches, such as their own policies and regulation, to comply with their own conditions, resources, and characters (decoupled). For instance, Case A used its own EA approach while Case A's project manager mentioned "… we decided to focus on IT perspectives rather than business perspectives." This was because "the guidance from central government was inappropriate in our agencies when it came to practical issues" (Case A, an IT specialist). Case C established a "new office" where all services from different departments were gathered. This approach did not follow guidance from central government. At the same time, Case C also established a taskforce to review and revise all service procedures. The team was formed from senior members in the departments. By so doing, they improved cooperation and interoperability and ultimately sped up the projects; they were also minimally affected by the central government's policies.

Similarly, "sponsor and politic" (root cause #3) seemed to affect other factors in the EA projects, such as "EA planning" and "EA objectives." This may have positive or negative effects. For example, a sponsor and politic may help cases to quickly adopt EA (Case A and Case C). However, it also had a negative influence by reducing trust among different stakeholders, such as between business and IT units. Each case employed a different strategy to deal with negative impacts. Case A revised the agreement between the organization and its sponsor while, in Case C, a decision was made that the EA project manager had similar decision-making power as senior managers to balance the power struggle between the politicians on the EA workers, such as identifying objectives and tasks and standardizing business procedures in and between the agencies. According to Case C's project manager, "our project unit operated under the senior management unit so that power was balanced and that it was easier to communicate with other agencies."

The *values pillar* focused on the cognitive-cultural compliance in the cases. Our findings indicate that the values pillar was used to deal with three root causes, namely, organization structure, EA team formation, and conflicting benefits (root causes #1, #4, and #7, respectively). For example, root cause #1, "organization structure," such as having multiple-level services with numerous owners and distributed resources and services, affected EA projects through inappropriate planning and problematic governance in EA implementation. To deal with this challenge, a senior manager in Case C served as the EA project manager while Case A promoted an EA team under senior managers. Moreover, root cause #4, "EA team formation" affected other problems like "EA objectives" or "emphasizing IT." These consequently influenced the EA results. This was evident as the organization had a technically-oriented team from their IT department; they faced challenges in terms of unfeasible schedules and objectives and experienced cooperation problems with other agencies. To deal with this root cause, Case A used EA for planning while Case C used EA in its IT projects. By doing so, they sought to balance IT with business perspectives.

Similarity, root cause #7 "conflicting benefit" originated from the users playing an important role for the success of EA projects. This is because EA can help organizations increase transparency. This can, in turn, reduce the "benefits" to users when they switch from traditional modus operandi to EA. In Case A, more time was consequently allowed for users to become familiar with EA and to be aware of EA benefits. Case B applied EA as an organizational procedure.

Three perspectives illustrate how different cases overcome the root causes in adopting EA. Our findings reveal that Case A and Case C had a strong presence of institutional pillars in supporting the agencies to deal with the challenges. For example, they had intense pressure from sponsors and politicians and a close network of professionals involved in resolving challenges. They also had a supporting culture in handling different problems. In contrast, Case B experienced fewer encounters with regulatory forces and had fewer professionals to solve problems. As a result, Case A and Case C seemed to be successful in comparison to Case B.

8.4.3.2   Potential Solutions to Root Causes in EA Adoption

Our analysis illustrates that organizations can apply institutional pillars in solving their EA deployment challenges. Analyzing institutionalization and legitimacy through norms, rules, and values provided a basis for our findings.

First, the normative factor, which is about education and social networks in the organization, show that using an official forum (e.g., CIO forum, ICT committee), establishing conferences and workshops with professional experts, and participating in professional training helped different stakeholders to improve their awareness of EA and helped organizations in building an EA reputation. They were then be able to deal with challenges relating to EA team members and EA users. For example, our findings show that practitioners could use institutional norms for coping with three root causes, namely, EA capability and skill (#5), user capability and skills (#6), and EA fundamental (#8).

Second, the rules factor is about regulations and policies with formal and informal power enforcements to impose sanctions and other penalties from superior organizations. Our findings indicate that local regulation could affect project results in positive and negative ways. Regulation is also used in overcoming challenges with sponsors or pressure from politicians by establishing influential taskforces to bridge inter- and intra-organizational boundaries. For example, institutional rules were used to address the root causes of legislation and regulation (#2) and politic and sponsor (#3).

Finally, the values factor, the cognitive-culture in the organizational environment, illustrates that by imitating successful cases, organizations may become familiar with different challenges, after which they can be overcome by adopting successful methods from others. For instance, institutional values were used for coping with organization structure (#1), EA team formation (#4), and conflicting benefits (#7). However, as values do not change easily, their analysis may provide a basis for understanding factors relating to failure rather than copying them as success factors.

8.5   Conclusion

In this paper, we have studied EA adoption problems, their root causes, and some solutions in three cases through the lens of institutional theory. This issue is scarcely studied in the literature. For example, we did not find any studies on the solutions to root causes, which may be very important for both practitioners and researchers. As a result, we contribute to the literature by illustrating how different institutional settings, namely norms, rules, and values, affect organizations' strategies and practices in responding to challenges. Future research is definitely needed. It may focus on different settings between and among countries or industry for a better understanding of the solutions. Research could thus provide a better generalizability and ultimately generate generic solutions to root causes.

Moreover, eight root causes were identified, leading to several consequences. Thus, we argued that organizations should focus on the root causes instead of their consequences. This would enable the formation of long-lasting solutions in EA adoptions and prevent the problems from re-emerging. This would thus help in the deployment of EA projects.

We also explained how organizations can resolve these root causes. Our findings are summarized in Table 8.5, which provides practitioners with different examples of how to resolve challenges. This may also assist researchers in gaining a better and deeper understanding of the complex phenomenon of EA adoption. This also opens new research avenues. For instance, how organizational activities evolve under different institutional conditions and how stakeholders affect organizational activities under which institutional conditions.

Technology plays an important role in successful IS projects, although it may also influence and create problems in organizations' activities (Ash et al. 2004; Dewett and Jones 2001; Markus and Robey 1988). Our data did not reveal any problems relating to technology. This can be explained by the fact that EA is about strategy, planning, and aligning business and IT. Under the circumstances, technology is not a priority. Another possible reason is that the scope did not emphasize the area, which has existed in the form of complex IT infrastructure and IT systems. Technology could cause problems as databases and consolidated systems are not on the list. Future research in the area is therefore a matter of urgency.

The paper has some limitations. Only three provinces in a single country were studied. Thus, the findings should be interpreted in the context of its case specificity. This research therefore calls for future studies, particularly on different countries, phases of EA projects, and different industries. Moreover, each root cause may have some institutional conditions for dealing with norms, rules, and values. In this paper, we focused only on single institutional conditions for each root cause.

Acknowledgements This study was partly funded by the Academy of Finland, grant #306000.

References

Aier, S., & Weiss, S. (2012). An institutional framework for analyzing organizational responses to the establishment of architectural transformation. In *The 20th European Conference on Information Systems (ECIS 2012), Barcelona: Paper 228*.

Ash, J. S., Marc, B., & Enrico, C. (2004). Some unintended consequences of information technology in health care: The nature of patient care information system-related errors. *Journal of the American Medical Informatics Association, 11*, 104–112. doi: 10.1197/jamia.M1471.

Boxenbaum, E., & Jonsson, S. (2008). Isomorphism, diffusion and decoupling. In R. Greenwood et al. (Eds.), *Handbook of organizational institutionalism* (pp. 78–98). London: Sage Publications.

Chuang, C.-H., & van Loggerenberg, J. (2013). Challenges facing enterprise architects: A South African Perspective. In T*he 43rd Hawaii International Conference on System Sciences*. Kauai, HI.

Dang, D. D., & Pekkola, J. S. (2017). Systematic literature review on enterprise architecture in the public sector. *Electronic Journal of e-Government, 15*(2), 130–154.

Dang, D. D., & Pekkola, S. (2016a). Institutionalising enterprise architecture in the public sector in vietnam. In *The 2016 European Conference on Information Systems, ECIS 2016*. İstanbul, Turkey.

Dang, D. D., & Pekkola, S. (2016b). Root causes of enterprise architecture problems in the public sector. In *PACIS 2016 Proceedings. Paper 287*.

DiMaggio, P. J., & Powell, W. W. (1983). The iron cage revisited: Institutional isomorphism and collective rationality in organizational fields. *American Sociological Review, 48*(2), 147–160.

DiMaggio, P. J., & Powell, W. W. (1991). *The new institutionalism in organizational analysis*. Chicago: The University of Chicago Press.

Dewett, T., & Jones, G. R. (2001). The role of information technology in the organization: A review, model, and assessment. *Journal of Management, 27*(3), 313–346.

Hauder, M., Roth, S., Matthes, F., & Schulz, C. (2013). An examination of organizational factors influencing enterprise architecture management challenges. In *The 21st European Conference on Information Systems*. Utrecht, The Netherlands.

Hjort-Madsen, K. (2006). Enterprise architecture implementation and management: A case study on interoperability. In *Proceedings of the 39th Hawaii International Conference on System Sciences (HICSS-39)*. Kauai: Computer Societry Press.

Hjort-Madsen, K. (2007). Institutional patterns of enterprise architecture adoption in government. *Transforming Government: People, Process and Policy, 1*(4), 333–349.

Hjort-Madsen, K., & Gøtze, J. (2004). Enterprise architecture in government—towards a multi-level framework for managing it in government. In *The Proceedings of ECEG04*. Dublin, Ireland.

Hjort-Madsen, K., & Pries-Heje, J. (2009). Enterprise architecture in government: Fad or future? In *The 42nd Hawaii International Conference on System Sciences (HICSS-42)*. Waikoloa, Big Island, Hawaii.

Isomaki, H., & Liimatainen, K. (2008). Challenges of government enterprise architecture work—stakeholders' views. In *Electronic Government: Proceedings of the 7th [IFIP WG 8.5] International Conference, EGOV 2008* (pp. 364-374). Turin, Italy.

Iyamu, T. (2009). The factors affecting institutionalisation of enterprise architecture in the organisation. In *The IEEE Conference on Commerce and Enterprise Computing (CEC'09)* (pp. 221–225).

Janssen, M., & Hjort-Madsen, K. (2007). Analyzing enterprise architecture in national governments: The cases of Denmark and the Netherlands. In *The 40th Hawaii International Conference on System Sciences* (p. 218a).

Janssen, M., & Klievink, B. (2012). Can enterprise architectures reduce failure in development projects? *Transforming Government: People, Process and Policy, 6*(1), 27–40.

Kaisler, S. H., Armour, F., & Valivullah, M. (2005). Enterprise architecting: Critical problems. In *The 38th Hawaii International Conference on System Sciences*.

Kim, Y.-G., & Everest, G. C. (1994). Building an is architecture: Collective wisdom from the field. *Information & Management, 26*(1), 1–11.

Lee, Y.-J., Kwon, Y.-I., Shin, S., & Kim, E.-J. (2013). Advancing government-wide Enterprise Architecture—A meta-model approach. In *The Advanced Communication Technology (ICACT)*.

Löhe, J., & Legner, C. (2014). Overcoming implementation challenges in enterprise architecture management: a design theory for architecture-driven IT management (ADRIMA). *Information Systems and e-Business Management, 12*(1), 101–137.

Lucke, C., Krell, S., & Lechner, U. (2010). Critical issues in enterprise architecting—a literature review. In *The 16th Americas Conference on Information Systems* (p. 305). Lima, Peru

Magnusson, J., & Nilsson, A. (2006). Infusing an architectural framework with neo-institutional theory: reports from recent change management initiatives within the Swedish public administration. In *The 39th Annual Hawaii International Conference on System Sciences*.

Magoulas, T., Hadzic, A., Saarikko, T., & Pessi, K. (2012). Alignment in enterprise architecture: A comparative analysis of four architectural approaches. *Electronic Journal Information Systems Evaluation, 15*(1), 88–101.

Markus, M. L., & Robey, D. (1988). Information technology and organizational change: Causal structure in theory and research. *Management Science, 34*(5), 583–598.

MIC. (2014). Information and data on information and communication technology Vietnam 2014. In *National Commission on Application of Information Technology*. Hanoi.

Mignerat, M., & Rivard, S. (2009). Positioning the institutional perspective in information systems research. *Journal of Information Technology & Politics, 24*(4), 369–391.

Myers, M. D. (2009). *Qualitative research in business and management*. London, UK: SAGA.

Nguyen, H.-C. (2006). Credit agreement C4116-VN conformed. Retrieved August 8, 2015, from http://documents.worldbank.org/curated/en/2006/06/6920738/credit-agreement-c4116-vn-conformed.

Niemi, E., & Pekkola, S. (2017). Using enterprise architecture artefacts in an organisation. *Enterprise Information Systems, 11*(3), 313–338.

Orlikowski, W. J., & Barley, S. (2001). Technology and institutions: What can research on information technology and research on organizations learn from each other. *MIS Quarterly, 25*(2), 145–165.

Ramos, K. H. C., & Júnior, R. T. D. S. (2015). Bibliometric analysis of enterprise architecture in the public administration. *International Journal on Information, 18*(2), 501–519.

Ross, J. W. (2009). Information technology strategy-creating a strategic it architecture competency: Learning in stages. In R. D. Galliers & D. E. Leidner (Eds.), *Strategic information management: Challenges and strategies in managing information systems* (p. 584). Routledge.

Saha, P. (2009). Architecting the connected government: Practices and innovations in Singapore. In *The 3rd International Conference on Theory and Practice of Electronic Governance*.

Scott, W. R. (1995). *Institutions and organizations foundations for organizational science*. London: Sage.

Scott, W. R. (2005). Institutional theory. In *encyclopedia of social theory* (pp. 408–414). Thousand Oaks, CA: Sage.

Seppänen, V., Heikkilä, J., & Liimatainen, K. (2009). Key issues in EA-implementation: Case study of two Finnish government agencies. In *The 11th IEEE Conference on Commerce and Enterprise Computing* (pp. 114–120).

Simon, D., Fischbach, K., & Schoder, D. (2014). Enterprise architecture management and its role in corporate strategic management. *Information Systems and E-Business Management, 12*(5), 5–42.

Stake, R. E. (2005). Qualitative case studies. In N. K. Denzin & Y. S. Lincoln (Eds.), *The sage handbook of qualitative research 3rd edition* (pp. 443–466). London: Saga.

Strauss, A., & Corbin, J. (1998). *Basics of qualitative research* (2nd ed.). Thousand Oaks: Saga.

U.S. CIO. (1999). Federal enterprise architecture framework (Version 1.1).

Walsham, G. (2009). Interpreting information systems in organizations: Creative commons Attribution 3.0 License.

Weerakkody, V., Janssen, M., & Hjort-Madsen, K. (2007). Integration and enterprise architecture challenges in e-government: A European perspective. *International Journal of Cases on Electronic Commerce*.

Weiß, K. S. (2015). *Institutionalizing architectural coordination in organizations*. Switzerland: University of St. Gallen.

Weiss, S., Aier, S., & Winter, R. (2013). Institutionalization and the effectiveness of enterprise architecture management. In *The Thirty Fourth International Conference on Information Systems*. Milan.

Winter, K., Sabine, B., Matthes, F., & Schweda, C. M. (2010). Investigating the state-of-the-art in enterprise architecture management methods in literature and practice. In *The Proceedings of the MCIS. Paper 90*.

WorldBank. (2005). Project information document. Retrieved August 8, 2015, from http://documents.worldbank.org/curated/en/2005/04/5796181/vietnam-ict-development-project.

Zachman, J. (1987). A framework for information systems architecture. *IBM Systems Journal, (26)* 3, 276–292.

Author Biographies

Dinh Duong Dang M.Sc. is a PhD candidate at the Laboratory of Industrial and Information Management, Tampere University of Technology, Tampere, Finland. His doctoral thesis is focused on business and technology management, particularly on enterprise architecture and its impact on organizations. Apart from enterprise architecture, his research is focused on e-Government, social data analysis, and information systems. His research articles have appeared in peer-reviewed out lets, such as, Electronic Journal of e-Government, International Series in Operations Research & Management Science of Springer, European Conference on Information Systems, and Pacific Asia Conference on Information Systems.

Samuli Pekkola PhD, is Professor of Information Systems at Tampere University of Technology and Adjunct Professor at University of Oulu. He has worked as visiting associate professor in University of Agder, and held several positions in University of Jyväskylä. His research focuses on users in different manifestations of information systems, IS management and acquisition, and enterprise architectures. His research articles have appeared in journals such as Information Systems Journal, Scandinavian Journal of Information Systems, Enterprise Information Systems, Enterprise Information Management, Decision Support Systems, Communications of the AIS, and The DATA BASE. He is Associate Editor in Business Information Systems and Engineering, and a member of advisory board and past Editor-in-Chief of Scandinavian Journal of Information Systems.

Part III
Cases

Chapter 9
IT Governance in E-Government Implementations in the Caribbean: Key Characteristics and Mechanisms

Arlene Bailey, Indianna Minto-Coy and Dhanaraj Thakur

Abstract There have been sustained calls related to the need for countries to improve public service delivery as well as the methods by which governments interface with citizens. E-government strategies have been proposed and developed with the aim of transforming the operations and effectiveness of public bodies. As a grouping of small island states, the Caribbean region is faced with unique institutional and structural challenges to the adoption and implementation of these measures. The results of various e-government strategies have been varied across the board. It is recognized that a key component in the implementation and further development of e-government initiatives entails the supporting IT governance framework. This paper offers a critical assessment of e-government strategies across the Caribbean focusing on the challenges, success factors and opportunities for implementation. The study explores the challenges and opportunities for advancing in and beyond e-government to c-government and more generally, in utilising emerging technologies and innovations, facilitated by IT governance mechanisms, towards improved public governance.

9.1 Introduction

Globally, there have been sustained calls for countries to modernise public administration and governance mechanisms. Specific attention has been placed on the need to improve public service delivery as well as the ways in which governments interface

A. Bailey (✉)
Sir Arthur Lewis Institute of Social and Economic Studies (SALISES),
The University of the West Indies, Mona, Jamaica
e-mail: arlene.bailey@uwimona.edu.jm

I. Minto-Coy
Mona School of Business and Management, The University of the West Indies,
Mona, Jamaica
e-mail: indianna.mintocoy@uwimona.edu.jm

D. Thakur
Alliance for Affordable Internet, The Web Foundation, Washington DC, USA
e-mail: dhanaraj.thakur@webfoundation.org

© Springer International Publishing AG 2017
L. Rusu and G. Viscusi (eds.), *Information Technology Governance in Public
Organizations*, Integrated Series in Information Systems 38,
DOI 10.1007/978-3-319-58978-7_9

with citizens. Aligned to these areas is the sustained search for means of increased transparency and accountability, through improved governance and e-government services (Belt 2005; Nielsen 2016; Scholl et al. 2016). These demands are increasingly being framed in terms of the role of emerging technologies and more specifically, information technology, e-government and connected government (c-government) to transform the operations and effectiveness of governments (Ramírez-Alujas and Dassen 2014; Imran and Gregor 2007). As a result of the increased reliance on information technologies to facilitate public service delivery through e-government mechanisms, IT governance is viewed as a critical component in implementing effective projects (Nfuka and Rusu 2013). As a grouping of small island developing states (SIDS), the region is faced with unique institutional and structural challenges to the adoption and implementation of these measures (The Commonwealth 2016; Bissessar 2010). These specific features of Caribbean small states also carry certain implications as it relates to the options, success factors and barriers to the adoption of ICT innovations in the public sector. Additionally, the results of various e-government strategies have been varied across the board (Durrant 2007; Rose and Grant 2010).

This chapter offers a critical assessment of e-government strategies across the Caribbean focusing on the challenges, success factors and opportunities for the implementation of e-government and other innovations such as cloud government across the region. In guiding the development and implementation of e-government initiatives, overall governance mechanisms need to be considered in the key areas of e-governance and related IT governance, as they inter-relate and support each component (Basu 2004). E-governance has been defined as "the public sector's use of information and communication technologies with the aim of improving information and service delivery, encouraging citizen participation in the decision-making process and making government more accountable, transparent and effective" (UNESCO 2011). There have been a number of definitions of IT governance (also sometimes referred to as ICT governance), many of which have common elements. The definition adopted in this paper is that "IT governance represents the framework for decision rights and accountabilities to encourage desirable behavior in the use of IT" (Weill 2004, p. 3). The chapter is also guided by what has been observed as a need for further research on the interactions between IT governance and e-government success (Aleem and Al-Qirim 2012; Scholl et al. 2016).

Hu et al. (2009) have highlighted the range of definitions and ongoing discussions on key elements of e-government. For this paper, we adopt the European Commission's (1999) definition which states that "Electronic government (e-government) can be defined as an ever increasing and pervasive use of information and communication technologies in the context of the Information Society, . . . to improve the functioning of public services concerned and to extend their interaction with the outside world". The paper responds to calls for further research in the Caribbean context, as Thakur (2012) notes that there is limited research on e-government in the Caribbean, particularly with regard to the efficacy of national e-government strategies.

The chapter proceeds as follows. The next section presents a brief review of the literature on e-government and characteristics related to the SIDS context. This is followed by an overview of the study's methodology, and then a discussion on e-government development in Barbados, Jamaica, member countries of the Organization of Eastern Caribbean States (OECS) and Trinidad and Tobago. A comparative assessment is then presented which is followed by the conclusion with implications for research and practice.

9.2   Related Literature

A major starting point in this review is to note the link that has been established between e-government and improved public sector performance (e.g. United Nations 2014; World Bank 2004). Other benefits relate to improved transparency and accountability, reduced costs, improved revenues and reduced transaction costs for customers. It has been highlighted that the perceived success of e-government initiatives is influenced both by the implementing and supporting mechanisms, as well as the value ascribed to the use of such services by the citizens (Scott et al. 2015; Viscusi 2010). This point has been underscored by Rose and Grant (2010) who in noting the importance of strategies and planning related to e-government initiatives also noted the challenges to formulating such strategies, which in turn influences the outcomes (Rose and Grant 2010; Viscusi 2010).

Small countries such as those in the Caribbean note the successes but also face a number of challenges in implementing e-government strategies. As noted by Dada (2006) many such strategies tend to fail in developing countries. To this end, the UN's 2014 e-government report considers the conditions of Small Island Developing States (SIDS) as a special category in the consideration of e-government (2014). Namely, SIDS are constrained by a number of vulnerabilities. These include, natural disasters (Awan 2013; Granvorka et al. 2016; Minto-Coy and Rao-Graham 2016), economic crises, the cost and other challenges around providing goods and services and infrastructure such as telecommunications, as well as small markets, population and influence (see e.g. UN 2014: 37; Briguglio 1995; Turvey 2007), resource (including human) constraints (Wint 2003). The suggestion is not that other states do not face these challenges. Rather, the specific combination of vulnerabilities and their very scale can be heightened in small states with what can be considered a sectoral or micro impact in a large country easily equating to a national disaster for a SIDS (Minto-Coy and Berman 2016). Indeed, Cullen and Hassall (2013) have also noted these challenges which have prevented some of the Pacific Islands from realising benefits, in spite of significant investments. Nonetheless, small size also suggests the possibility for easier organisation and management from the centre (though not always the case). Thus, in determining the best model for e-government implementation (i.e. central vs departmental) it has been observed that it may be easier to opt for the former in smaller countries (Cullen and Hassall 2013). This central body would coordinate the activities of the different bodies in the governance system.

More generally, the literature does suggest that certain conditions lend to more effective e-government programmes than others. It has been noted that there is some relationship between a country's ability to invest in the infrastructure and supporting policy areas for e-government development on the one hand and the level of economic development on the other. The indication too is that investments in e-government/ICTs must be accompanied by supporting investments, for example education (Ngwenyama, Andoh-Baidoo et al. 2006). Other enablers or indicators of readiness for the adoption of e-government include, wide access to the Internet, the existence of civil servants willing to re-conceptualise citizens as customers and share information. It has also been highlighted that e-participation and engagement among citizens is an important aspect of e-government implementation and success (Bailey and Ngwenyama 2011; United Nations 2015). Political support (e.g. champions) is also to be underscored in determining the extent of support and priority that an e-government agenda will receive (World Bank 2004). The matter of a champion(s) is important too in light of Joseph and Jeffers observation on the role of leadership, political influence and managerial outlook on the success of e-government in the Caribbean (2009). It has also been noted that e-government strategies are most effective when envisioned as part of a wider public sector performance enhancement programme (Ibid: 1; Heeks 1999). In this context, the area of IT governance is an essential factor to consider in relation to its influence on the impact and success of e-government implementations (Klischewski 2014; Wang et al. 2011). With increasing reliance on ICTs to support and enhance e-government service delivery, IT governance is an important consideration (Adaba and Rusu 2014). Further, e-governance is a key area which contributes to the overall management and fulfillment of objectives of e-government initiatives, and particular focus on e-governance is important in developing countries (Bissessar 2010; Basu 2004). As efforts continue to infuse ICTs in supporting government processes and public service delivery, e-governance mechanisms continue to evolve, with additional focus needed in assessing its impact on the transformation of administrative services (Dawes 2008). The need to further explore the process through which governments transition from traditional forms of governance to e-government modalities is key (Davison et al. 2005).

9.3 Methodology

This study uses a qualitative approach, comprising a review and content analysis of the e-government strategies, national ICT policies (indicative of the state of policy formulation, implementation, key players and institutions) and national development documents as it relates to e-government in select Caribbean States. A qualitative approach is particularly useful, in light of the dearth of information on e-government in the region, requiring the more focused attention to identifying the state of the sector. The specific countries selected are Barbados, Jamaica, and Trinidad and Tobago, and members of the Organization of Eastern Caribbean States

(OECS)—Antigua and Barbuda, Dominica, Grenada, St. Kitts and Nevis, St. Lucia, and St. Vincent and the Grenadines. The qualitative case studies were also constructed based upon material from national e-government websites which provided useful information on the development of the initiatives and the transition process (Davison et al. 2005). The countries are somewhat representative of the wider English-speaking Caribbean in terms of size, capacity and resources, as well as general culture and features of the administrative system. For instance in a 2009 study, Joseph and Jeffers conducted a cluster analysis using data based on a range of measures of e-government development among countries in the Caribbean and found these countries (along with St. Lucia) formed a unique cluster. They suggest that this group of countries provide a view of government efforts toward promoting and developing e-government initiatives across the region and as such, the rate of adoption, attitudes and specific issues faced by these states would be a good indicator of where the rest of the region exists in terms of likelihood for adopting new technologies. An overview of the study context is presented in Tables 9.1 and 9.2 below.

Table 9.2 below presents an overview of member countries of the Organization of Eastern Caribbean States participating in e-government implementation initiatives.

Table 9.1 Selected indicators for Barbados, Jamaica and Trinidad and Tobago

	Barbados	Jamaica	Trinidad and Tobago
Population	284,644	2,715,000	1,341,151
GDP per capita (PPP at current international $)	15,574 (for 2012)	8,892	30,446
Percentage of individuals using the Internet	75%	37.8%	63.8%
Fixed (wired)-broadband subscriptions per 100 person	23.82	5.06	14.56
Mobile cellular subscribers per 100 persons	108.1	102.24	144.94
Mobile-broadband subscriptions per 100 inhabitants	41.5	28.3	18.9
United Nations E-Government Development Index (2014)	0.5933	0.4388	0.4932
United Nations E-Government Development Index Global Rank (2014)	59	109	91
United Nations E-Government Development Index (2016)	0.6310	0.4534	0.5780
United Nations E-Government Development Index Global Rank (2016)	54	112	70
E-government and related indicators for Barbados, Jamaica, and Trinidad and Tobago (all data refer to 2013 unless otherwise stated)			

Sources ITU (2014), World Bank (2014), United Nations (2014)

Table 9.2 Selected indicators for member countries of the OECS

	Antigua and Barbuda	Dominica	Grenada	St. Kitts and Nevis	St. Lucia	St. Vincent and the Grenadines
Population	86,295	72,660	110,000	51,300	173,765	120,000
GDP per capita (PPP at current international $)	20,977	13,102	11,498	20,929	10,560	10,663
Percentage of individuals using the Internet	59%	55.18%	42.09%	79.35%	48.63%	47.52%
Fixed (wired)-broadband subscriptions per 100 person	5.73	11.86	13.69	27.25	13.59	12.45
Mobile cellular subscribers per 100 persons	201.83	152.47	121.35	156.76	125.50	123.87
Mobile-broadband subscriptions per 100 inhabitants	20.21	0.0	0.0	0.0	0.0	0.0
United Nations E-Government Development Index (2014)	0.5927	0.4338	0.5220	0.4980	0.4525	0.4158
United Nations E-Government Development Index Global Rank (2014)	60	110	78	90	104	113
United Nations E-Government Development Index (2016)	0.4892	0.4577	0.5168	0.5034	0.4531	0.4494
United Nations E-Government Development Index Global Rank (2016)	100	109	88	94	114	115
E-government and related indicators for members of the Organization of Eastern Caribbean States (OECS) - Antigua and Barbuda, Dominica, Grenada, St. Kitts and Nevis, St. Lucia, and St. Vincent and the Grenadines (all data refer to 2013 unless otherwise stated)						

Sources ITU (2014), World Bank (2014), United Nations (2014)

9.4   Overview of Selected Cases

In the following sections, a historical overview and analysis of the current implementation of e-government initiatives is discussed.

9.4.1   E-Government Development in Barbados

As one of the most economically developed countries in the Caribbean, Barbados often ranks the highest by most measures of ICT adoption and use (see Table 9.1). Indeed, the E-Government Development Index score for Barbados (from the United Nations E-Government Survey 2014) is the third highest in the Caribbean, and also highest among the three countries examined here (United Nations 2014).

However, such comparisons should not obfuscate the challenges that relate to the formulation and implementation of e-government and c-government policies in Barbados. In some ways these challenges are similar to Trinidad and Tobago and Jamaica, and include limited technical expertise, infrastructure, and inadequate alignment with public sector reform strategies.

Public sector reform is of course an ongoing feature of the public governance context in Barbados. The government's 2002 White Paper on Public Sector Reform highlighted the need for reform in a context of changing local and global socio-economic conditions. It envisioned a public sector that was proactive rather than reactive to these changing conditions (Government of Barbados 2002). However, it only considered the relationship between information and communication technologies (ICTs) and reform in specific cases such as a need for better management information systems in different sectors. The subsequent Public Service Act of 2007 also made limited references to information technologies for example, by specifying how public employees may or may not use them for work (Government of Barbados 2007).

Recent reviews of reform have taken a more expansive view of the role of ICTs where the government has sought to use e-government to improve the way it interacts with citizens as part of overall efforts at public sector modernization (Commonwealth Secretariat 2008). Much of the efforts of reform are monitored by the Office of Public Sector Reform. These include e-government projects on education infrastructure and pedagogy, customs and excise, court administration, and accessing government information (Best-Winfield 2006; Office of Public Sector Reform 2004). More recent projects include online payment of land taxes (Barbados Government Information Service 2012) or the Legislative Information Management System (Caribbean Journal 2012) which essentially makes the drafting of legislation more efficient and allows for online public access of legislation.

Crucially, e-government is explicitly viewed by the government as a part of its public sector reform efforts. While several e-government projects are underway in different sectors, the organization with shared responsibility for monitoring e-government efforts is the Ministry of Public Service (formerly the Ministry of Civil Service) (Office of Public Sector Reform 2013). This is somewhat different from other countries which often have a central information technology agency with this responsibility.

A draft e-Government strategy for Barbados was developed in 2006 by the Ministry of Civil Service which actually recommends (among other things) the creation of a central information management agency with overall responsibility for implementation of the government's e-government strategy and related programs. This strategy focuses on many of the infrastructure and technical requirements for achieving the broad goals of improving service delivery, transparency, and efficiency within the public sector. More importantly it correctly attempts to connect organizational reform with the incorporation of ICTs by emphasizing the need to first refine existing business processes (Ministry of Civil Service 2006). It is difficult to determine the extent to which an alignment of e-government initiatives and organizational reform is actually pursued by government agencies. There is as yet no central agency responsible for monitoring and implementing the e-Government strategy. As a result, competing ICT policies and standards exist among different government agencies (Ministry of Civil Service 2013).

In addition to the e-Government strategy there is also the National Information and Communication Technologies Strategic Plan of Barbados (2010–2015). As is consistent with similar plans internationally, it outlines the ways in which ICTs can help the country achieve its national goals in sectors such as business, the environment, and culture. More importantly, the plan also recommends that the government become a model user of ICTs in order to promote greater adoption and use within the population (Ministry Of Economic Affairs, Empowerment, Innovation, Trade, Industry and Commerce, and Government of Barbados 2010). However, some observers have found limited evidence that the government is a major user of ICT related services (Molla et al. 2006).

The draft e-Government strategy (2006) was scheduled to be updated by 2014 ostensibly to respond to new technologies and evolving public sector reform. However, this process is not yet complete. As a result, there is no unified strategy that government agencies can use in assessing how to employ innovations such as cloud based technologies, social networking platforms, or mobile applications in their work. Furthermore, new challenges continue to emerge. For example, across the world as access to ICTs increase there is a need for more public and private investment to protect cyber-security interests. In this regard, the government recently launched the Computer Incident Response Team although there remains the need for an overall cyber-security strategy.

The strategy of linking e-government initiatives to national public sector reform is both intelligent and pragmatic. In many ways this sets Barbados' e-government strategy apart from other countries. However, there has been little substantial follow-up since the initial draft strategy was developed in 2006. Recently, it has been announced that a new e-government master plan is being developed (Austin 2016). In the interim, it has meant that individual government agencies have limited direction when responding to new and emerging ICTs and practices. There are institutional reasons for this, such as the lack of a key responsible agency for managing the e-government program. As indicated by Ministry of Civil Service (2013), three agencies share the overall responsibility for IT governance. A centralized agency could also allow us to better understand how well the country has been able to actually pursue its goal of aligning e-government with public sector reform.

9.4.2   E-Government Development in Jamaica

The Government of Jamaica has framed efforts to introduce e-government in the context of a desire to improve the delivery of services to the public and modernize government. For instance, a 2005 e-government project document notes, "(t)he strategic objective of the project is to simplify e-governance for all stakeholders, resulting in a truly modernized public sector, and enhanced service delivery for the citizenry" (CITO 2005: Abstract). It has also been observed, that at least 25% of the PSR Modernization Unit's *Public Sector Modernisation Vision and Strategy 2002–2012* relates to e-government (CITO 2005; See Cabinet Office 2003). Furthermore, the national ICT Policy which deals extensively with e-government also extends these considerations to increased transparency and government accountability. The stated objectives of that policy are "To create a transformational state bureaucracy; on demand 'government through integrated end to end' processes across the Government service and with stakeholders; effective communication; stimulation of public involvement; empowerment of citizens; minimization of social exclusion, and realization of the knowledge based society" (Office of the Prime Minister 2011: 31). The link between IT and ICTs and development more generally has been observed in Jamaica's national development plan, Vision 2030 which notes the importance of ICTs in making the country a place to live and work.

Initiatives have been introduced across some of the critical areas of the public sector (see Table 9.3 below). These are also some of the more important revenue generating and business facilitation segments, suggesting a view of e-government not only as an efficiency-raising but also accountability and transparency tool (See Belt 2005). Many of these early initiatives (e.g. Inland Revenue and Customs) were undertaken with the support of the Inter-American Development Bank during 2003–4.

Many of the initiatives are aimed at facilitating online payments for taxes, tracking goods and services, online searches, access to government forms, registration and furnishing information. Thanks to these initiatives achievements have been noted, for instance in reduced transaction time and general improvement in the interface between government and citizens/clients (also see Table 9.2). Benefits have accrued not only to government in terms of increased income but also to Jamaicans at home and in the Diaspora who are able to access government much easier.

Table 9.3 Overview of e-government services in Jamaica

Agency	Initiative	Achievements
Jamaica Customs	Jamaica Customs e-Payment system	Reduced processing time for import-related transactions, in some cases from seven/eight days to two hours; increase tax compliance; increased revenues
Inland Revenue	Inland Revenue Tax Payment Portal	Increase ease in paying taxes
Office of the Registrar of Companies	Online fee payments, company registration and database search for subscribers	Reduced time in response to clients
National Land Agency (NLA)	e-Land Jamaica allows access to the NLA database, including certificates of title and online payments	Smoother process in registering land and formalizing ownership, etc.
Registrar General's Department (RGD)	RGD Online application for certificates, e.g. birth and marriage certificates	Reduced transactions costs for public and greater access to services
Management Institute for National Development	e-Learning Initiative	More flexibility in the delivery of educational programmers
Jamaica Trade Board (JTB)	JTB Information System facilitates online registrations and applications for licenses and fee payments	Increased ease in licensing and certification of products for import and export
E-Gov Jamaica	One Stop Company/Business Registration Form (Super Form) National Security Interest in Personal Property (NSIPP) Collateral Registry National Identification System (NIDS) Fiscal Administration Modernization Programme (FAMP)	Development and support of e-government initiatives; building increased linkages across sectors
E-Learning Jamaica	Tasked with infusing ICTs across secondary schools and increased access to educational resources via the Internet and cable television	Increased support to parents, teachers and students

In spite of these accomplishments, the issue remains one of integrating the various initiatives across individual units to achieve seamless e-government. Thus in 2005, the GoJ moved to revise and improve the role of ICTs in government. Reforms were aimed at moving towards more seamless governance and connectivity and by extension to achieve a coordinated national agenda which extended to the private sector. A major project was undertaken with the aid of the Government of Canada in 2005. The result was the transition of Fiscal Services (formerly responsible for government's digital revenue functions) into E-Gov Jamaica and its designation as the central coordinating body, offering ICT support to other government agencies (Jamaica Information Service 2013). This is one of the most important developments in the Jamaican context, as they work towards seamless coordination across government agencies.

The institutional landscape supporting e-government in Jamaica has, therefore, evolved over the years. This is also seen in the introduction of a number of facilitative legislations and regulations (e.g. the Electronic Transaction Act, 2007) and the introduction and demise of a number of organizations. Included here are Fiscal Services and the Central Information Technology Office (CITO), originally created to coordinate the introduction of ICTs in government but which transitioned to a policy unit in the line ministry in 2013 and also merging with E-Gov Jamaica. These transitions represent a core component of the overall IT governance mechanisms. In the 2014 Sectoral Debate, the then State Minister in the Ministry of Science, Technology, Energy and Mining (MSTEM) noted that the ICT Governance Framework is an integral part of the ICT enabled Public Modernization Programme.

Actions have been constrained by the size of the economy and the constraints which these place on action. Thus, along with the developments noted above has been the recruitment of a Chief Information Officer (CIO) by MSTEM to guide the overarching vision, supported by a National Advisory Committee (Robinson 2014). However, the actual engagement of a CIO was not completed until March 2015 after a failure to identify requisite skills locally as well as the Government's inability to offer a sufficiently attractive compensation package to international recruits.

There has also been some challenge in deriving an effective governance framework for IT and e-government. IT investments over the years, have also included improvement to facilitate e-procurement and improved tax payment, management and administration and to widen automation. Included here are Financial Management Information Systems. However, the failure to adopt an ecosystems or governance approach has meant that insufficient utilisation of such technology, with a view that their implementation (in and of itself) is sufficient to ensure successful results. Instead, significant government data continues to be housed in paper files, amidst a slow move to automation and some lingering preference for filing. Many of these practices have been recorded by Browne whose coverage relates not only to Jamaica but the wider Caribbean (2016).

The prospects for the adoption of new technologies such as cloud computing (i.e. c-government) as a means of achieving a more seamless integration of services and end user satisfaction is an area that has gained some interest. Indeed, E-Gov Jamaica has done some work towards introducing cloud technology in the public sector and research has been done to assess its potential (Jamaica Information Service 2011). E-Gov has moved towards acquiring infrastructure to facilitate the introduction of cloud/c-government services, including cloud telephony, cloud hosting and the back up and support of critical IT infrastructure to government entities but full implementation has yet to be realised. While e-government strategies have focused on the Internet and to a lesser extent, cable television (e.g. e-learning), there is a clear absence of the mobile phone in e-government particularly, given the over 100% penetration rate of mobile telephony vis-a-vis the number of Internet users.

Relatedly, given the size and capacity of the public sector and as noted in Barbados, the Government has the potential of being a leader in the adoption and use technology. However, movement remains slow, with some of the problems here being reminiscent of wider issues facing the society. For instance, the country generally remains at least a good 10 years behind in the adoption of new innovations including practices, laws and regulations as illustrated for instance in the timing of regulatory reform in the telecommunications industry in the late 1990s to early 2000. The pace of obtaining reform and culture change in the public sector has also been slow and also mirrors the experience of other Caribbean small states, while indicating the less than enthusiastic embrace of ICTs and new technologies across the public sector. The wider culture is also one where the Internet, mobile phones and other devices have been seen largely as instruments for social communication and entertainment, with the informational value still being underplayed (Horst and Miller 2005).

Relatedly, the 'C' in ICTs continues to be a central focus in Jamaica and indeed, across Caribbean societies (Minto-Coy 2016). As such, there is need for greater interactivity and power for citizen/clients to access and manipulate information as opposed to government websites largely being a repository for information to be communicated to citizens.

More recently (largely in 2014 to early 2016) the e-government discourse has begun its evolution to a greater focus on the role of open government and open data (see Gascó-Hernández 2014 for definitions). The aims of e-government remain the same but here the emphasis is also on increasing transparency, accountability and unlocking the potential of data for entrepreneurship and innovation. The emphasis has been on the need for government to make more of its data open (i.e. data that can be freely used and reused, as well as redistributed (Open Knowledge International (n.d.)). It remains to be seen, the extent to which the relics of secrecy and withholding information (even from other government departments and ministries) will be overcome.

The adoption of ICTs in government also remains uneven with some government agencies being more advanced than others. As such, there is need for more organization and consolidation of standards across the public sector (CITO 2005). Ironically, this mirrors the larger PSR programme in Jamaica where the creation of executive agencies ("agencification") have can to the creation of a two-tiered system characterised by a more advanced segment co-existing alongside a more traditionally bureaucratic and inefficient public sector (Minto-Coy 2011). Interestingly, this result is also to be expected, given that some of the agencies in which e-government was first introduced are some of the institutions created during agencification. These have been keen on adopting e-government as part of their drive for efficiency, improved service delivery and engagement with its customers.

As government moves to the adoption of new technologies and more availability of information and services online, the focus also naturally broadened to include issues such as cyber security, privacy and data protection. These are increasingly important as the government seeks to negotiate between the rights to individual security and privacy and the need to facilitate smoother, more personalized services. The case of the National Security Interest in Personal Property Registry which saw personal and private information, including addresses, tax payer registration numbers and other personal details being made publicly available by a government body (see Luton 2015), raises both the negative and positive implications of more extended e-government and increased openness.

Ultimately though, the introduction of these initiatives have not necessarily registered internationally, with the country facing successive declines in international rankings, including the Global Information Technology Report (from 45 in 2007/8 to 86 in 2013). This has been due to underperformance vis-a-vis the rest of the world in areas such as Internet penetration.

9.4.3 E-Government Development in Trinidad and Tobago

In 2000, Trinidad and Tobago's National Electronic Commerce Policy Committee recommended the establishment of an E-Government Unit. This unit was formed within the Ministry of Communications and Information Technology in 2001 (E-Government Unit 2002). Over the years responsibilities for e-government have moved between different ministries as they have evolved including the Ministry of Public Administration and Technology and the Ministry of Science and Technology (Ramsajan 2012).

The vision stated by the E-Government Unit was "Transforming the Public Service into an Electronic Government Organisation and providing online interactive and quality government services on a sustained "always on" basis, to all citizens of T&T and the wider community, regardless of time, distance and location" (E-Government Unit 2002). This was supported by a number of objectives identified as:

- "To facilitate, co-ordinate and encourage an increasing number of government services online as an alternative to traditional service delivery.
- To use Web Technologies for "linking" all Ministries, Statutory Boards and Departments within the Public Service.
- To act as a support centre to assist and guide Ministries in making increasingly better use of Information Systems and the Internet/World Wide Web.
- To provide the guiding framework for designing and implementing E-Government solutions.
- To maximize the effectiveness of e-governance.

- To develop, adopt, ensure and encourage the use of best practices in e-government.
- To promote learning and facilitate the transfer of knowledge of Information and Communications Technologies (ICTs), which drive E-Government initiatives throughout the Public Service." (E-Government Unit 2002).

The role of e-government development in influencing government efficiency and e-business is discussed in a study by Srivastava and Teo (2007). This study included data from some countries in the Caribbean region, including Trinidad and Tobago. Choudrie et al. (2009) examined the usability of e-government sites in developing countries, and found that Trinidad and Tobago was performing well in some aspects. In a study of website usability of Trinidad and Tobago's government ministry websites, Roach and Cayer (2010) highlighted dimensions which influenced users' ability to locate information and utilize services.

The Minister of Public Administration for Trinidad and Tobago indicated that the vision for e-government centred around "Our dream and our evidence that we have a truly transformed public service is the day when a citizen in any part of the country can use a cell phone to access any government service and provide inputs into public policy, ask to see the up-to-date expenditure on any project, or to perform that most fundamental of democratic functions—to vote" (Bridglal 2012). She also indicated that e-Payments legislation would be taken to the Parliament of Trinidad and Tobago during 2012.

As plans progressed, it was reported that the Minister of Science, Technology and Tertiary Education had indicated that the portal ttconnect had added 18 additional forms to facilitate citizens' access to government services online (Neaves 2012). It was also mentioned that a toll free number was available to support queries and assistance to citizens, and that over 70 e-services were planned for implementation over the ensuing three-year period (Neaves 2012).

Consultations on the national ICT plan were launched, and also involved the online input of citizens.

A draft national ICT plan for 2014–2018 was developed in 2013, building on previous plans and emerging ideas for national development. A key theme of this plan is e-government. This theme "focuses on working as an integrated Government and seeks to improve the Government's operational efficiency and customer service delivery" (Government of Trinidad and Tobago (GoTT) 2013, p. 11). The national ICT plan identified key imperatives associated with this theme as "Migrating to Transactional e-services and Collaborating to Implement Shared ICT Systems and Processes" (GoTT 2013, p. 11).

In developing the 2014 to 2018 plan, a review was conducted of their 2003 National ICT Plan, and among the goals achieved, the GoTT identified the promotion of effective government through "(1) Delivery of the award winning ttconnect, the vehicle for multi-channel Government services delivery and (2) A more connected government to enable inter- and intra-ministerial communications and information sharing" (GoTT 2013, p. 15).

The United Nations E-Government Survey 2014 indicates a dip in country ranking for Trinidad and Tobago from 67 in 2012 to 91 in 2014. The E-Government Development Index (see Table 9.1) is based on three key dimensions—Availability of Online Services, Telecommunication infrastructure and Human capacity (United Nations 2014). The report highlights initiatives by the GoTT in relation to facilitating interaction between business and government, including for example, the fisheries industry with a mobile application mFisheries connecting customers and fishers and enhancing safety. A number of partnerships among government ministries are included on the TTBizLink website which links to e-government applications related to imports and exports, company registration, port and maritime services, taxpayer registration and work permits. Recently, the Minister with responsibility for e-government services has announced a renewed focus on e-governance as part of the emphasis on the reform of the public sector. In terms of governance mechanisms, when asked about centralization and decentralization, he referred to the availability of government services online as a decentralization mechanism (Dowrich-Phillips 2016). These are considerations in overall IT governance decisions (Brown and Grant 2005).

9.4.4 E-Government Development in the Organization of Eastern Caribbean States (OECS)

The Organization of Eastern Caribbean States (OECS) consists of 7 member countries and 3 associated island states in the Eastern Caribbean. This regional organization represents the Eastern Caribbean region in several areas related to government policies, regional policies, and administrative and technological areas.

The OECS E-Government for Regional Integration Project (E-GRIP) is a project developed by the OECS in collaboration with the World Bank to facilitate a regional approach to the development of e-government services. Some of the elements considered in designing the initiative included the size of the countries, and economies of scale. Two of the OECS member states—Antigua and Barbuda and St. Kitts and Nevis, did not qualify for funding loans from the World Bank, due to their high per capita income status, and they were able to obtain funding through the Caribbean Development Bank to support their participation. A Regional E-Government Unit (REGU) was established within the OECS Secretariat in 2009 to facilitate project implementation across the participating Eastern Caribbean States. This represented a regional approach to governance of the initiative. Within each member state, further arrangements were developed to assist with the implementation at the country level.

In Antigua and Barbuda, the Ministry of Information, Broadcasting, Telecommunications, Science and Technology, established an E-GRIP Committee for the pilot of the project (United Nations 2013). In addition, a Country-Based Specialist was appointed who would "work with the Government to identify those key sectors that we think in the short term, we can improve the delivery platform" (Antigua Observer 2012). The project was framed as a collaboration between government and citizens in responding to citizens' needs for transparency and efficiency in the provision of quality services. The initial area of focus was public financial management, including tax and customs systems. It was also highlighted that there was collaboration in adopting a system for customs management from Jamaica (United Nations 2013).

In a recent report, it is noted that the Government of Antigua and Barbuda is now focusing on the development of a citizen e-portal and supporting infrastructural components, along with an e-government strategy (Nixon 2016).

Prior to the launch of the E-GRIP project, Dominica had formed an Information, Communication and Technology (ICT) Unit within the Ministry of Information, Telecommunications and Constituency Empowerment (GIS Dominica 2012). This governance mechanism was seen to have contributed to Dominica showing the highest jump in the world e-government rankings from position 105 in 2010 to 73 in 2012 (GIS Dominica 2012), and to have created an enabling platform to further build on for the E-GRIP initiatives (Dominica News Online 2012).

Recent reports indicate that there is national collaboration on projects within the regional E-GRIP initiative. Dominica has recently launched two new electronic database systems related to drivers and automobiles, and financial transaction investigation and tracking (GIS Dominica 2016). These were launched by the ICT Unit and the Ministry of National Security.

In addition to providing governance arrangements and guidance at the regional level, the OECS REGU Secretariat was also involved in implementing systems, funded from pooled resources which governments had borrowed through the EGRIP programme. One example of this is the tendering systems for procurement, starting with pharmaceuticals, with planned expansion related to procurement of resources for education, such as books (News.DM 2012).

The Government of Grenada indicated close alignment of its ICT and E-government strategies, highlighting the key role of e-government in articulating its vision, and the establishment of a Central Information Management Agency to enhance governance and support of the implementation (Government of Grenada 2009). They continued to pursue initiatives through the E-GRIP programme, and in consultation with other Caribbean countries. In a recent budget presentation, it was announced that they have signed an agreement with a US-based company to develop an e-governance portal and platform (Government of Grenada 2015).

St. Kitts and Nevis has recently launched an ICT Governance Board and an e-Government Initiative simultaneously (SKNIS 2016). St. Lucia established an ICT and e-Government Unit in 2006, and has embarked on a series of national initiatives to enhance the delivery of e-Government services. This has been combined with assistance with review and implementation, and recommendations of the appropriate governance mechanisms and structures to facilitate these initiatives. (St Lucia National ICT Office 2009). Horizontal (across the OECS region) and vertical (national) interventions were highlighted. Horizontal e-government interventions included initiatives related to policy, strategy, legal and institutional frameworks, and vertical interventions included specific systems implementations. As part of the EGRIP Project, St. Vincent and the Grenadines participated in a number of initiatives, including the implementation of health-related information systems.

The EGRIP project concluded in 2014, and OECS member states have continued to utilize some of the facilities that were provided, while embarking on new initiatives.

9.5 Successes, Challenges and the Adoption of New Technologies: A Critical Assessment of E-Government in the Caribbean

The chapter has reviewed the attempt to adopt e-government in a number of Caribbean States. Collectively, there is some desire to integrate ICTs and new technology in improving government. Indeed, all the cases presented have interpreted e-government in the context of the push for improved public services and the modernisation of government. However, slow movement, weak coordination and support for implementation of e-government policies and initiatives have been detrimental for the region, as indicated in the main, by its global standing. Several of the rankings have fallen from the 2012 to 2014 UN E-Government report. The results of the 2016 report will be of interest to identify progress made.

One of the key areas to consider in governance mechanisms related to information and communication technology and e-government initiatives is the role of regional cooperation. Williams and Marius (2016) note that there is debate in this area among experts in the Caribbean region. Some of the successful regional or sub-regional initiatives have depended on pre-existing cooperation, which have then been successful translated to e-government arrangements. In a review of the implementation progress and lessons learned in the E-GRIP initiative, it was indicated that "Governance arrangements can significantly contribute to successful implementation: Finding the appropriate institution to champion a reform or a new system can be critical to its rapid success." (World Bank, 2014). Further it was highlighted that there is a "Need for implementation of the national ICT policies in order to support E-Government for Regional Integration Project." (World Bank, 2014).

The CARICOM Region, which includes many Caribbean countries, has also developed a CARICOM eGovernment Strategy, which recognizes existing initiatives and collaborating bodies, and emphasizes the need to build on these for seamless integration. Its implementation depends on the perceived benefits and political will, and indicates that it requires a "structure and coordinated approach that is underpinned by cohesive and collaborative action" (CARICAD, 2010, p. 6). In essence, exploring lessons learned, and coordinating and integrating governance mechanisms across the Caribbean region, is a challenging but potentially useful approach in achieving successful e-government implementation (Williams and Marius 2016).

Each country will need to review its policy and legislative documents, whether for individual or regional governance mechanisms and implementations in the public sector. For instance, some of the relevant policy and legislative documents require clarification, updating as well as implementation. Greater coordination and management is needed to support the suggestion that small size could offer more ease for centralisation.

E-government services are shown to include the provision of online forms, applications, registration and payments. To this end, successes have been registered in areas such as improved compliance, greater transparency as it relates to government processes and forms, as well as increased revenues and greater ease in conducting business. This is also reflected in earlier reviews of progress toward implementing e-government strategies (CARICAD 2009). Additionally, the developments in areas such as cyber-security and open data in countries such as Jamaica do suggest that the Region is not far-behind in terms of the evolution in e-government discourse and practice.

The policy, legislative and regulatory landscape in support of e-government has also advanced. However, there is a far way to go in the adoption of new technology. For instance, the countries discussed here are among the Caribbean countries who are working on their e-government implementations, however it should be noted that the region as a whole have some way to go in activating the benefits of e-government and ICTs, more generally, for improving government.

More specifically, in comparing the e-government experiences of Barbados, Jamaica, and Trinidad and Tobago and reflecting on the literature, a number of points arise. Among these is the importance for governments generally to strategically align e-government strategies with public sector reform. The three cases demonstrate that there are differences in the extent to which this occurs. In Barbados, the government did make this incorporation an explicit part of its e-gov strategy, however there is as yet no major action that appears to follow such a strategy. In the case of Jamaica, it is observed that previous public sector reform has led to a two-tiered system within the public administration (Minto-Coy 2011). Partly as a result of this, executive agencies that were created during this process were also more likely to introduce e-gov initiatives. Finally, in the case of Trinidad there is some evidence of an alignment of public sector reform and e-government. The policy implication here is that simply articulating strategies that align e-government and public sector reform is not sufficient. Indeed, without such an alignment there is the potential of undermining e-government initiatives or worse exacerbating the differences between public sector agencies in their ability to leverage the benefits of ICTs to achieve their goals.

Another observation concerns how responsibility for implementing e-government strategy is distributed among public sector agencies. As observed in global best practice, what is important is that organizational responsibility and leadership for an e-government strategy is clearly assigned to a public agency or group of agencies, along with the requisite resources (the central vs departmental point raised earlier). For example, in Barbados, a review of the e-Government programme status indicates that three entities have shared responsibilities for provision of ICT services in support of government initiatives—e-Government Unit and Data Processing Department (Ministry of the Civil Service) and the Ministry of Commerce and Trade (e-Commerce and ICT Strategy) (Ministry of the Civil Service 2013). Noting the key implications for IT governance and the success of e-government deployment, the Barbados e-Government sub-committee had proposed a central management agency in 2006. Based on the above discussion, e-governance has been an evolving process in all three countries, as shown in Table 9.4. Indeed, other researchers have pointed to fragmentation in initiatives as well as gaps in the literacy, resource level and management capability of developing countries in the area of IT governance (Nfuka et al. 2009). The findings here suggest that the same issues linger in ICTs, more generally and also apply to the SIDS context. The larger challenge is the sustained inability to derive a governance framework for ICTs and IT, which continues to affect the Caribbean's ability to

Table 9.4 Organizations responsible for e-governance and IT governance

	Barbados	Jamaica	Trinidad and Tobago
Organization with responsibility for monitoring e-government initiatives	Ministry of the Civil Service, National Steering Committee	Central Information Technology Office Fiscal Services E-Gov Jamaica	E-Government Unit (Ministry of Communications and Information Technology) Then Ministry of Public Administration and Technology and the Ministry of Science and Technology Ministry of Public Administration and Communications
Organization with responsibility for IT governance	Ministry of Economic Affairs, Empowerment, Innovation, Trade, Industry and Commerce	Ministry of Science, Technology, Energy and Mining	Ministry of Public Administration and Communications
Related Areas of Alignment with Public Service Reform Agenda	Opportunities for participation and collaboration with systems of government	Accountability and transparency through citizen participation	Information and Communication and implementation of supporting technologies
Initiatives to Support Alignment	National Committee	Chief Information Officer	Open Government Partnership Independent Reporting Mechanism; Evaluation of e-Government and Knowledge Brokering Programme

realise the goals of e-government and other e-reforms. In recognition of this shortcoming, another Caribbean country, St. Kitts and Nevis has recently launched an ICT Governance Board and an e-Government Initiative simultaneously (SKNIS 2016).

The current higher e-government indices reflected for Barbados and Trinidad and Tobago vis-à-vis Jamaica lends some support to the observation about the relationship between economic development and gains in e-government (see Table 9.1). As such, Jamaica and other countries in the region that have not done as well economically are also those that are lower in international rankings related to e-government. It is also not coincidental that Jamaica has relied heavily on international support in the development and implementation of its e-government agenda, given its lower economic standing among its neighbours.

Notwithstanding, many Caribbean territories are also listed among the middle and high income groups. As such, making improvements in e-government is not only about levels of economic development but also about political will and vision in determining the level of resources and support which will be allocated to an e-government strategy (Awan 2013). As Joseph and Jeffers (2009) note, e-government development in the Caribbean may require more than new agencies and "may in fact represent a subtle interplay of intangible variables such as leadership, managerial outlook, and political influence" (pg. 67). Indeed, the failure to align these factors may account for some of the findings highlighted in the cases.

Another point worth noting is that successful e-government is not simply about rolling out the infrastructure but also the need for a governance approach that also considers policies, actors and processes and the way these interact to deliver the best results. To this end, it is also about making improvements in related policy areas such as education, towards more effective and informed utilisation of ICT technologies. This point also finds resonance in the UN's observation that SIDS (including those investigated here) need to address challenges related to infrastructure, low access to broadband, literacy levels and increased online presence by government in order to benefit fully from e-government (2014: 25 and 37).

9.5.1 Resulting Policy Recommendations

Based on the above case studies and analyses, we make a number of general policy recommendations. Among these is the importance of champions who are knowledgeable, interested and willing to be advocates and support e-government initiatives. UN (2016) highlights the importance of a national coordinating body for e-government development, through CIO or institutions with overarching authority for implementations. These champions are needed at the helm of governments, but also within individual ministries and within the private sector and voluntary organizations. These can also be organisational but must be adequately resourced and networked.

The most recent UN E-Government Survey 2016 (United Nations 2016) reflects a decline in the E-government index and global ranks for most of the countries in the region. This may be a reflection of the end of earlier project cycles related to the development of e-governance initiatives. In this regard, IT governance within public organizations plays an important role in sustainability of initiatives. Support for the roll-out of e-government across the region has come from international organizations. Internally, there is recognised need for such advancements but there has also been a tendency for reforms initiated from outside the region to result in a lack of ownership and support at the local level. Thus, while this dependence on international funding for local reforms is understandable in the context of small and developing states, the reality too is that this can affect the level of support and rate of implementation on the ground. This is heightened where implementation may be the responsibility of civil servants already undergoing reform fatigue and in cultures where the 'I' in ICTs (see Minto-Coy 2016) has yet to be embraced fully.

Relatedly, and in line with Cullen and Hassall's (2013) comments on the role of culture in SIDS and the impact on e-government success, the cases suggest a need to develop strategies that are mindful of national and public sector cultures. This involves the extent to which citizens tend to be engaged (or are willing to engage with the state) as well as the norms which govern the nation and way in which the public sector operates.

Innovations such as m-government and c-government have not yet emerged meaningfully within governments, even where the current context (i.e. high mobile penetration rates) may suggest a natural appetite for such services. There remains a need to consider more proactively the role of mobile phones in realising the objectives of e-government agendas across the region.

More public education and awareness is also necessary across the region. This is as it relates to increasing knowledge of the role and uses of ICTs and new technology, e-government, and correspondingly measures for guarding against abuse and threats related to the use of these new technologies. Awareness raising will also relate to the legislative mechanisms in support of e-government and the implications which they have for individuals and organizations. Government is also shown as needing to increase its stewardship and use of citizen data, and facilitate interactive access. Countries that have shown an improvement in the UN E-Government Development Index Global Rank include Barbados and Trinidad and Tobago. Trinidad and Tobago, which has shown a marked increase in the ranking, for example, is one of the countries in the region that has been involved with the Open Government Partnership since 2012, which provides progress assessments of initiatives related to governance and e-government (Drayton 2015). This mechanism may be a useful approach to support governance structures of IT resources.

9.6 Conclusion

This chapter has explored the implementation of e-government strategies and examined reasons for the present scenario. It argues that certain factors influence the region's ability to make further advances, such as challenges related to its size and public administration culture, including, resources, activating the 'I' in ICTs and varying commitment and acceptance within government and among public servants of the value of such advances, particularly in improving public administration. Furthermore, some of the challenges which have been underscored in earlier discussions around government adoption of ICTs also surface in this discussion on emerging technologies. These include, demand side challenges which exist in the way of access and use of ICTs. A focus is also needed on alignment between public sector reform efforts and e-government strategies across the region. Lessons learned from sub-regional and regional cooperation on some aspects of e-governance strategy and implementations, highlights the relevance of further exploring IT governance and e-governance arrangements at the national and regional levels within the Caribbean. Ultimately, this assessment should have resonance for small and developing states as it relates to the challenges and opportunities for advancing in the areas of e-government to c-government and open government, supported by overall IT governance mechanisms, in utilising emerging technologies and innovations towards improved public governance.

References

Adaba, G. B., & Rusu, L. (2014). IT Governance practices in a public organization in Ghana. *International Journal of Innovation in the Digital Economy (IJIDE), 5*(2), 14–23.

Aleem, S., & Al-Qirim, N. (2012, January). IT governance framework for. In *ACIS 2012: Location, location, location: Proceedings of the 23rd Australasian Conference on Information Systems 2012* (pp. 1–9). ACIS.

Antigua Observer. (2012, April 17) Antigua & Barbuda Implements E-grip Project, The Antigua Daily Observer. Retrieved from http://antiguaobserver.com/antigua-barbuda-implements-e-grip-project/.

Austin, S. (2016, January 7). New plan being developed by, *Caribbean News Now!* Retrieved from http://www.caribbeannewsnow.com/topstory-New-e-government-plan-being-developed-by-Barbados-28878.html.

Awan, O. (2013). E-Governance in small states. In A. Ming, O. Awan & N. Somani (Eds.), *E-Governance in small states*. London: Commonwealth Secretariat.

Bailey, A., & Ngwenyama, O. (2011). The challenge of e-participation in the digital city: Exploring generational influences among community telecentre users. *Telematics and Informatics, 28*(3), 204–214.

Basu, S. (2004). E-government and developing countries: an overview. *International Review of Law, Computers & Technology, 18*(1), 109–132.

Belt, J. (2005). E-Government as a Tool to Promote Public Sector Efficiency, Effectiveness and Transparency. Presentation: IV Global Forum on Fighting Corruption, Brasilia, June 8 2005. Retrieved May 13, 2016, from http://pdf.usaid.gov/pdf_docs/Pnadm954.pdf. Accessed: May 13, 2016.

Best-Winfield, G. (2006). *Case Study—public sector reform. The experience*. St. Michael, Barbados: The Caribbean Centre for Development Administration (CARICAD).

Bissessar, A. M. (2010). The challenges of e-governance in a small, developing society: the case of. In C. Reddick (Ed.), *Comparative E-government. Integrated Series in Information Systems* (pp. 313–329). New York: Springer.

Bridglal. (2012, October 30). Carolyn wants an e-friendly govt set-up, Trinidad Express Newspaper, Trinidad. Retrieved from 1488622883 http://www.trinidadexpress.com/business/Carolyn_wants_an_e-friendly_Govt_set-up-176520851.html.

Briguglio, Lino. (1995). Small island developing states and their economic vulnerabilities. *World Development, 23*(9), 1615–1632.

Brown, A. E., & Grant, G. G. (2005). Framing the frameworks: A review of IT governance research. *Communications of the Association for Information Systems, 15*(1), 38.

Cabinet Office. (2003). *Government at your Service: Public Sector Modernisation Vision and Strategy 2002– 2012/Ministry paper No. 56*. Retrieved May 13, 2016, from http://unpan1.un.org/intradoc/groups/public/documents/caricad/unpan012825.pdf.

Caribbean Journal. (2012). Eyes Digital Legislation. Retrieved from http://www.caribjournal.com/2012/05/10/barbados-eyes-digital-legislation/.

CARICAD. (2009). Report from the 1st Caribbean 2009–2012 eGovernment Strategic Planning workshop held in January 28th & 29th 2009, Caribbean Centre for Development Administration.

Commonwealth Secretariat. (2008). *Electronic Government in and the Cayman Islands*. London: Commonwealth Secretariat.

Choudrie, J., Wisal, J., & Ghinea, G. (2009). Evaluating the usability of developing countries' sites: a user perspective. *Electronic Government, An International Journal, 6*(3), 265–281.

Cullen, R., & Hassall, G. (2013). An information ecology approach to sustainable E-government of small island developing states in the Pacific. In *2013 46th Hawaii International Conference on System Sciences (HICSS)* (pp. 1922–1931). *IEEE*.

Dada, D. (2006). The failure of in developing countries: A literature review. *The Electronic Journal of Information Systems in Developing Countries, 26*.

Dawes, S. S. (2008). The evolution and continuing challenges of e-governance. *Public Administration Review, 68*(s1), S86–S102.

Davison, R. M., Wagner, C., & Ma, L. C. (2005). From government to: a transition model. *Information Technology & People, 18*(3), 280–299.

Dominica News Online. (2012, December 6). Dominica improves E government ranking. Retrieved from http://dominicanewsonline.com/news/homepage/news/technology/-ranking/.

Dowrich-Phillips, L. (2016, April 6). Online Services part of Cuffie's Public Service Reform Plan. http://www.looptt.com/content/online-services-part-cuffies-public-service-reform-plan.

Drayton, J. (2015). Independent Reporting Mechanism (IRM): Progress Report, 2014–2015. Open Government Partnership.

Durrant, F. (2007). *Caribbean E-Government portals or gateway websites: implications for libraries and librarians* (pp. 125–142). In Best Practices in Government Information: A Global Perspective.

European Commission. (1999). Public sector information: a key resource for Europe. Green paper on public sector information in the information society.

E-Government Unit. (2002). The E-Government Unit, Government of. Retrieved from http://unpan1.un.org/intradoc/groups/public/documents/caricad/unpan008482.pdf.

Gascó-Hernández, M. (2014). *Open government: Opportunities and challenges for public governance*. New York: Springer.

GIS Dominica. (2012). *Dominica 73 in United Nations E-Government Ranking*. Retrieved from http://news.gov.dm/index.php/news/-ranking.

GIS Dominica. (2016). *Government Launches Databases for Drivers and the Financial Intelligence Unit*. Retrieved from http://news.gov.dm/index.php/news/3509-government-launches-databases-for-drivers-and-the-financial-intelligence-unit

Government Information Service. (2012). *Online payment system introduced*. Retrieved from http://gisbarbados.gov.bb/index.php?categoryid=9&p2_articleid=8709.

Government of Barbados. (2002). *White Paper on Public Sector Reform* (p. 130). Bridgetown, Barbados: Government of Barbados.

Government of Barbados. (2007). *Public Service Act 2007*. Bridgetown, Barbados: Government of Barbados.

Government of Grenada. (2015). 2016 Budget Statement. Retrieved from http://www.gov.gd/egov/docs/budget_speech/Budget-2016.pdf.

Government of Grenada. (2009). e-Government and ICT Status Report. Retrieved from http://unpan1.un.org/intradoc/groups/public/documents/un/unpan040214.pdf.

Government. (2013). smarTT National ICT Plan 2014–2018. Retrieved from http://www.scitech.gov.tt/downloads/smarTT%20Draft%202014-05-07.pdf.

Heeks, R. (Ed.). (1999). *Reinventing government in the information age: International practice in IT-enabled public sector reform*. London; New York: Routledge.

Horst, H., & Miller, D. (2005). From Kinship to link-up: Cell phones and social networking in 1. *Current Anthropology, 46*(5), 755–778.

Hu, G., Pan, W., Lu, M., & Wang, J. (2009). The widely shared definition of e-government: An exploratory study. *The Electronic Library, 27*(6), 968–985.

Imran, A., & Gregor, S. (2007). A comparative analysis of strategies for egovernment in developing countries. *Journal of Business Systems, Governance and Ethics, 2*(3), 89–99.

ITU. (2014). *World Telecommunication/ICT Indicators Database 2014*. Geneva: International Telecommunications Union. Retrieved from http://www.itu.int/ITU-D/icteye/Indicators/Indicators.aspx.

Joseph, R. C., & Jeffers, P. I. (2009). E-Government in Nations. *Journal of Global Information Technology Management, 12*(1), 52–70.

Klischewski, R. (2014). From strategy to services: challenges of inter-organizational IT governance in Egypt. In *Proceedings of the 8th International Conference on Theory and Practice of Electronic Governance* (pp. 190–199). ACM.

Luton, D. (2015). Privacy Alarm—Concerns raised over public disclosure of personal info on credit registry. *Gleaner*. Retrieved from http://mobile.jamaica-gleaner.com/gleaner/20150213/lead/lead1.php.

Ministry of Civil Service. (2006). *Draft E-Government strategy*. Bridgetown: Government of Barbados.

Ministry of Civil Service. (2013). *e-Government programme status update*. Bridgetown, Barbados: Government of Barbados.

Ministry of Economic Affairs, Empowerment, Innovation, Trade, Industry and Commerce, & Government of. (2010). *National information and communication technologies strategic plan of Barbados 2010–2015*. Bridgetown, Barbados: Government of Barbados.

Minto-Coy, I. D. (2011). Towards public sector reform. In: What can local and international experiences tell us about successful public sector reform, *Caribbean Policy Research Institute Policy Paper*, Kingston, Jamaica.

Minto-Coy, I. (2016). Policy and regulation of communications industry. In I.D. Minto-Coy & E. Berman (Eds.), *Public administration and policy in the Caribbean*. Boca Raton, London, New York: CRC Press.

Minto-Coy, I. D., & Berman, E. M. (2016). Public administration and policy. In I.D. Minto-Coy & E. Berman (Eds.), *Public administration and policy in the Caribbean* (pp. 1–32). Boca Raton, London, New York: CRC Press.

Minto-Coy, I. D. & Rao-Graham, L. (2016). *Mainstreaming disaster risk management in management education*. White Paper presented at the Florida International University Workshop on Disaster Risk Management and Management Education, Shulich Business School, York University in Toronto Canada, March 23–24, 2016.

Molla, A., Taylor, R., & Licker, P. S. (2006). E-Commerce diffusion in small island countries: the influence of institutions. In *The Electronic Journal of Information Systems in Developing Countries, 28*(2), 1–15.

Neaves, J. (2012, March 23). Govt puts more services online, *Trinidad Express Newspapers*. Retrieved from http://www.trinidadexpress.com/news/Govt_puts_more_services_online-144058576.html.

News.DM. (2012, November 6). OECS E-Government to Launch Partial Electronic Tendering System, Retrieved from http://www.news.dm/-to-launch-partial-electronic-tendering-system/.

Nfuka, E. N., & Rusu, L. (2013). Critical success framework for implementing effective IT governance in Tanzanian public sector organizations. *Journal of Global Information Technology Management, 16*(3), 53–77.

Nfuka, E. N., Rusu. L., Johannesson, P., & Mutagahywa, B. (2009). The State of IT governance in organizations from the public sector in a developing country. In *Proceedings of the 42nd Hawaii International Conference on System Sciences*. Retrieved from http://ieeexplore.ieee.org/stamp/stamp.jsp?tp=&arnumber=4755742.

Nielsen, M. M. (2016, January). The role of governance, cooperation, and eservice use in current Egovernment stage models. In *2016 49th Hawaii International Conference on System Sciences (HICSS)* (pp. 2850–2860). IEEE.

Ngwenyama, O., Andoh-Baidoo, F. K., Bollou, F., & Morawczynski, O. (2006). Is there a relationship between ICT, health, education and development? An empirical analysis of five West African Countries from 1997–2003. *The Electronic Journal of Information Systems in Developing Countries, 23*.

Nixon, P. (2016, April 14) SPOTLIGHT: Antigua & Barbuda's quantum leap to, BN Americas. Retrieved from http://www.bnamericas.com/en/news/technology/spotlight-antigua-barbudas-quantum-leap-to-e-government.

Office of Public Sector Reform. (2004). *Public Sector Reform (PSR) Initiatives*. Bridgetown,: Government of Barbados.

Office of Public Sector Reform. (2013). *Select Public Sector Reform Initiatives within the Public Sector*. Bridgetown, Barbados: Government of Barbados. Retrieved from http://reform.gov.bb/website/images/majorselect.pdf.

Office of the Prime Minister. (2011). *Government of information and communications technology Policy*. Retrieved from http://www.japarliament.gov.jm/attachments/596_Information%20and%20Communications%20Technology%20%28ICT%29%20Policy.pdf.

Open Knowledge International. (n.d.). *Open data handbook*. Retrieved from http://opendatahandbook.org/guide/en/what-is-open-data/.

Ramírez-Alujas, Á., & Dassen, N. (2014). Winds of change: the progress of open government policymaking in Latin America and, Inter-American Development Bank Technical Paper.

Ramsajan, D. (2012, October 17). Govt's ICT One Stop Shop…24/7 or open only 7 to 11? *Guardian*. Retrieved from http://www.guardian.co.tt/business-guardian/2012-10-17/govts-ict-one-stop-shop%E2%80%A6-247-or-open-only-7-11.

Roach, C. M., & Cayer, N. J. (2010). Bridging the other divide: An assessment of the usability of government ministry websites. In C. Reddick (Eds.), *Comparative E-government* (pp. 483–504). New York: Springer.

Robinson, J. (2014) Information and communication technologies as enablers for growth and development, GoJ MSTEM Sectoral Debate Presentation, Government of

Rose, W. R., & Grant, G. G. (2010). Critical issues pertaining to the planning and implementation of E-Government initiatives. *Government Information Quarterly, 27*(1), 26–33.

Scholl, H. J., Glassey, O., Janssen, M., Klievink, B., Lindgren, I., Parycek, P. & Soares, D. S. (Eds.). (2016). *Electronic Government: 15th IFIP WG 8.5 International Conference, EGOV 2016, Guimarães, Portugal, September 5–8, 2016, Proceedings* (Vol. 9820). Springer.

Scott, M., DeLone, W., & Golden, W. (2015). Measuring eGovernment success: a public value approach. *European Journal of Information Systems*.

SKNIS (2016) A Modern Government Launches E-Government Portal that promises Cost-Effectiveness and Time Efficiency, http://timescaribbeanonline.com/-portal-that-promises-cost-effectiveness-and-time-efficiency/.

Srivastava, S. C., & Teo, T. S. (2007). E-government payoffs: Evidence from cross-country data. *Journal of Global Information Management (JGIM), 15*(4), 20–40.

St Lucia National ICT Office. (2009). Electronic/Mobil government: Building capacity in knowledge management through partnerships. Retrieved from http://unpan1.un.org/intradoc/groups/public/documents/un/unpan036953.pdf.

Thakur, D. (2012). Leveraging information and communication technologies for development (ICTD). *Geography Compass, 6*(1), 1–18.

The Commonwealth. (2016). Key principles of public sector reforms: Case studies and frameworks. Retrieved from http://thecommonwealth.org/sites/default/files/news-items/documents/P14763_PSG_PGSU.pdf.

Turvey, R. (2007). Vulnerability assessment of developing countries: the case of small-island developing states. *Development Policy Review, 25*(2), 243–264.

UNESCO. (2011). E-Governance. Retrieved from http://portal.unesco.org/ci/en/ev.php-URL_ID=3038&URL_DO=DO_TOPIC&URL_SECTION=201.html.

United Nations (2015) Expert Group Meeting. United Nations E-Government Survey 2016: E-government for sustainable development. UNDESA. Retrieved from http://workspace.unpan.org/sites/Internet/Documents/UNPAN94330.pdf.

United Nations. (2016). United Nations E-Government Survey 2016, United Nations Department of Social and Economic Affairs. Retrieved fromhttp://workspace.unpan.org/sites/Internet/Documents/UNPAN96407.pdf.

United Nations. (2014). United Nations E-Government Survey 2014, United Nations Department of Social and Economic Affairs. Retrieved from http://unpan3.un.org/egovkb/Portals/egovkb/Documents/un/2014-Survey/E-Gov_Complete_Survey-2014.pdf.

United Nations. (2013). *Compendium of Innovative E-government Practices*. UNDESA: United Nations Department of Social and Economic Affairs.

Viscusi, G. (2010). The different facets of egovernment initiatives: paradigms and approaches. In G. Viscusi, C. Batini, & Mecella, M. (Eds.), *Information systems for eGovernment: A quality-of-service perspective*. Springer.

Wang, T., Sun, B., & Yan, Z. (2011). IT Governance: The key factor of e-government implementation in China. In *E-Life: Web-Enabled Convergence of Commerce, Work, and Social Life* (pp. 274–285). Berlin, Heidelberg: Springer.

Weill, P. (2004) Don't Just Lead Govern: How Top-Performing Firms Govern IT. *MIS Quarterly Executive* (3)1, 1–17.

Williams, R., & Marius, M. (2016). Regional approaches to initiatives in, Studies and Perspectives Series—The Caribbean, No. 47, ECLAC. Retrieved from http://repositorio.cepal.org/bitstream/handle/11362/39858/S1501269_en.pdf;jsessionid=B8E434EC068858CC5D2AC46F34D88AE8?sequence=1.

Wint, A. (2003). *Competitiveness in Small Developing Economies*. Kingston.: UWI Press.

World Bank. (2004). Building blocks of E-government: Lessons from developing countries. Poverty Reduction and Economic Management Notes, 91 (August).

Author Biographies

Dr. Arlene Bailey is currently a Lecturer/Research Fellow, and Associate Dean, Research and Innovation in the Faculty of Social Sciences, University of the West Indies, Mona. Her Ph.D. in Information Systems is from the University of the West Indies. Arlene's research areas include information and communication technologies (ICTs) for development, virtual communities and communities of practice. Her work adopts a critical focus on the design of ICT interventions for social and economic development.

Dr. Indianna D. Minto-Coy is Senior Research Fellow, Mona School of Business and Management (UWI), Research Affiliate—International Migration Research Centre (Wilfrid Laurier University) and a Caribbean Open Institute Researcher. She has held appointments at the Skoll Centre for Social Entrepreneurship (University of Oxford), University of Waterloo, Centre for International Governance Innovation and Shridath Ramphal Centre for Trade Policy, Law and Services. Dr Minto-Coy's research, publications and consultancies span diasporas and migration, entrepreneurship, public policy, ICTs and their intersection. Indianna's publications appear in internationally rated journals and books including her 2016 book on Public Administration and Policy in the Caribbean (with Evan Berman), and Diaspora Networks in International Business: Perspectives for Understanding and Managing Diaspora Business and Resources (with Maria Elo, Springer, 2017). She holds a PhD from the London School of Economics.

Dr. Dhanaraj Thakur currently leads research at the Alliance for Affordable Internet. His work focuses on telecommunications policy and regulation, technology and political participation, and gender and ICTs in low and middle income countries. Dhanaraj previously held faculty positions in public administration at Tennessee State University (Nashville, USA) and political science at the University of the West Indies (Mona, Jamaica). A former Fulbright scholar, he holds a PhD in Public Policy from the Georgia Institute of Technology (USA), and is a graduate of the London School of Economics and the University of West Indies (Mona, Jamaica).

Chapter 10
IT Organizational Structure Relationship with IT Governance Performance: Case of a Public Organization

Parisa Aasi, Lazar Rusu and Dorothy Leidner

Abstract Information Technology (IT) is widely used in organizations and managers continue to struggle with how to govern IT. IT governance concerns the decision rights and division of responsibilities to achieve value from IT investments. Any IT governance approach is incorporated into a given organizational structure. However in the particular context of public organizations, there is little research on IT organizational structure relationship with IT governance performance. In this research, a case study is done in a public organization to find out how suitable is the organizational structure of the IT department is in relation with the IT governance performance. The results reveal that the IT department organizational structure needs to suit the IT governance performance desired outcomes. In this case, operating as a public organization has actuated the organization to focus on IT governance outcome of effective use of IT for growth. This together with the IT governance archetypes of this public organization for different IT decisions led the IT department leaders to adopt a matrix organizational structure.

10.1 Introduction

Information Technology (IT) has a critical role in organizations. How an organization governs its IT can play an important part in determining how much value the organization achieves through its IT investments (Hardy 2006; ITGI 2011; Couto et al. 2015; De Haes and Van Grembergen 2015; Sesay and Ramirez 2016). IT

P. Aasi (✉) · L. Rusu
Department of Computer and Systems Sciences, Stockholm University,
Kista, Stockholm, Sweden
e-mail: parisa@dsv.su.se

L. Rusu
e-mail: lrusu@dsv.su.se

D. Leidner
Department of Management Information Systems, Baylor University, Waco, USA
e-mail: dorothy_leidner@baylor.edu

© Springer International Publishing AG 2017
L. Rusu and G. Viscusi (eds.), *Information Technology Governance in Public Organizations*, Integrated Series in Information Systems 38,
DOI 10.1007/978-3-319-58978-7_10

229

governance (ITG) concerns the IT decision rights and responsibilities necessary to achieve the best value from IT investments based on business objectives (2004). IT governance has a significant influence on how well and organization is able to achieve business objectives (Sohal and Fitzpatrick 2002; Trites 2004; Bowen et al. 2007; Bernroider 2008; Nfuka and Rusu 2013). The Sarbanes Oxley act of the U.S. brought attention to governance in organizations and consequently to the concept of IT governance. How well organizations implement and sustain IT governance has become an area of increased attention (Van Grembergen and De Haes 2005; De Haes and Van Grembergen 2009). A very important issue in IT governance is providing the correct information to the correct users and people with correct decision rights at the right time (Kappelman et al. 2014). Bergeron et al. (2017) suggests that IT governance practices in congruence with the organization structure can provide a competitive advantage based on IT value to the business. According to Janahi et al. (2015) organizational structure defines the arrangements for authorities, communications, decision rights and tasks among staff of a specific unit Chan (2002) has also noticed that if organizational structure is adapted properly, it can improve IS performance. Schwarz and Hirschheim (2003, p.2) also state that "historically IT governance has been strongly associated with the structure or configuration of the IT function, thus reflecting the locus of responsibility for making IT management decisions". Furthermore, Janahi et al. (2015) count organizational structure together with IT decision making authority, processes and relational mechanisms as factors that are related to IT governance. Moreover, Janahi et al. (2015) propose a conceptual IT governance model in which they emphasize the role of organizational structure as a linkage between the objectives of the organization and the IT governance processes and activities. Many studies have noted that organizational structure plays a significant role in IT governance and should be coordinated with it (Van Grembergen 2004; Grant et al. 2007; Ko and Fink 2010; Nicolian et al. 2015). However, what we know about IT governance is largely drawn from studies of large private organizations even though IT governance in general varies widely between public and private organizations (Denford et al. 2015). It is also important to study IT governance performance in public organizations. In many countries, governmental or public organizations constitute more than a third of the total economy (2004). Many issues regarding services, structure, budgeting and transparency are specific to public organizations (2004; Tonelli et al. 2015). In spite of what is often a tight budget, public organizations that are funded by the government are significant users of IT (2004; Janahi et al. 2015). According to a study done by Othman and Chan (2013) in a public organization, an "unsuitable organizational structure" is a barrier for IT governance implementation. In general though, there are very few studies on issues about IT governance implementation in public organizations (Nfuka and Rusu 2013; Winkler 2013). In a literature review done by Wiedmann and Weeger (2016) it is stated that organizational factors such as structure and governance should be in unison with the social aspects as the key characteristics of IT functions. Therefore it is very important for the IT departments to have a suitable organizational structure in relation with their

IT governance. Where, a suitable organizational structure for the IT department is defined as one that improves the desired IT governance performance outcomes.

Over the last few years, both industry and academia have emphasized the importance of IT governance and organizational structure. However there is a lack of research on how an IT department organizational structure is suitable in relation with the IT governance performance. Therefore, this research aims to explore the relation between organizational structures in IT governance performance in public organizations. Accordingly the specific research question through which this research is conducted is *"How suitable is the IT organizational structure in relation with IT governance performance in a public organization?"*

The remainder of this paper is organized through the following sections: research background, research methodology, analysis of the results, discussion, and conclusions and future research.

10.2   Research Background

This section includes the definitions and concepts from research literature used in this study.

10.2.1   IT Governance

IT governance is an issue that has received increasing attention in research and practice since the mid-nineties (Simonsson and Johnson 2006). IT governance is a part of corporate governance, which is the "system through which the organization is controlled, monitored and organized" (Van Grembergen and De Haes 2009, p.4). Since it is very rare in today's world to find organizations with little dependency on information systems, it is not surprising that corporate governance is strongly related to IT governance (Van Grembergen and De Haes 2009). Different researchers and practitioners have presented various definitions for IT governance. According to IT Governance Institute (ITGI 2003, p.10) "IT Governance is the responsibility of the board of directors and executive management. It is an integral part of enterprise governance and consists of the leadership and organisational structures and processes that ensure that the organisation's IT sustains and extends the organisation's strategies and objectives". Another definition of IT governance is proposed by Simonsson and Johnson (2006) that have conducted a research literature review and according to them "IT governance is basically about IT decision-making: The preparation for, making and implementation of decisions regarding goals, processes, people and technology on a tactical and strategic level" (Simonsson and Johnson 2006, p.14). Furthermore in authors' opinion in order to assess the effectiveness of IT governance, the above factors from their definition need to be considered. But in this study the appropriate definition for answering our research question is given by (2004). According to them "IT governance is defined as specifying the frameworks for decision rights and accountabilities to encourage desirable behavior in the use of IT" (2004, p. 2).

10.2.1.1 IT Governance in Public Organizations Context

Public organizations have specific characteristics that differentiate them different from private organizations. IT governance consequently may be different in some important ways in public and private organizations. Because public organizations are financially supported by the government and their users are citizens and tax-payers, it is important to consider the main objectives of each public organization and the IT governance that is needed to achieve those objectives (Juiz et al. 2014). In contrast to the private organization mission of generating value for shareholders, public organizations serve the community and have public values (Moore 2004). Public value is the value created for society by the governmental organization (Kelly et al. 2002) and it is not only through the outcomes but also through processes that bring trust and equality to the citizens that public value is created (O'Flynn 2007). Measuring and advancing the public value in public organizations is more complex than measuring and improving the benefits in private organizations (Al-Raisi and Al-Khouri 2010).

10.2.1.2 IT Governance Performance

According to ITGI (2003), IT governance performance tracks and monitors the implementation of strategies and projects and should be done regularly. IT governance performance can be measured through four objectives weighted by their importance to the enterprise (Weill and Ross 2004) and these are: "(1) Cost-effective use of IT, (2) Effective use of IT for asset utilization, (3) Effective use of IT for growth and (4) Effective use of IT for business flexibility" (p. 121). These objectives define by Weill and Ross (2004) is shortly described below:

1. Cost—effective use of IT is mostly engaged with how beneficial IT has been for the business.
2. Effective use of IT for growth concerns how effective IT has been in learning, being innovative, gain competitive advantage and making improving changes.
3. Effective use of IT for asset utilization concerns how successful IT has been in using the knowledge based assets in an organization.
4. Effective use of IT for business flexibility concerns how successful IT has been in responding to the internal and external changes of the business.

In order to use the above objectives in an organization, senior managers must first identify the importance of each of four objectives. The weight of importance is indicated on a 1–5 scale (1 for not important and 5 for very important). By using this scale the senior managers could rate the success in each of four objectives of ITG through a 1–5 scale (1 for not successful and 5 for very successful). After the senior managers have done this rating they could calculate the overall ITG performance score to with a maximum of 100 by using the following weighted average formula proposed by Weill and Ross (2004):

$$\frac{\sum n = 1 \text{ to } 4(\text{importance of outcome}) * \text{influence of IT governance} * 100}{\sum n = 1 \text{ to } 4 \, (5 * (\text{importance of outcome}))}$$

According to this formula, first the importance of each ITG performance outcome is rated (scale of 1–5) that as we noticed may be different in different companies. Next the degree to which the company is successful in reaching each of those outcomes is scored (scale of 1–5) and then the overall ITG performance of the company is calculated.

In their study Weill and Ross (2004) has calculated the ITG performance in 256 companies from 23 countries by using the formula proposed above. The average score of ITG performance in these 256 companies was 69 out of 100, with minimum score of 20. The authors have noticed that only one third of the companies have scored over 74 and that only seven percent have scored over 90.

10.2.1.3   The Importance of IT Governance Archetypes

The importance of ITG archetypes has been mentioned by Weill and Ross (2004) that have defined six archetypes for IT governance in organizations. According to Weill and Ross (2004) these archetypes are explaining how each of the five key IT decisions is made. Furthermore the authors have defined five key IT decisions that are including: (1) IT principles, (2) IT architecture, (3) IT infrastructure strategies, (4) Business application needs, and (5) IT investments. According to Weill and Ross (2004) we have also six archetypes that are the followings: (1) Business monarchy, (2) IT monarchy, (3) Feudal, (4) Federal, (5) IT duopoly, and (6) Anarchy. A short description of each of the IT governance archetypes proposed by Weill and Ross (2004) are summarized as is following:

(1) Business monarchy: In business monarchy archetype the input or decision rights come from a group of business executives or individual business managers (the CIO may be or may not be involved) but the IT executives are not involved in decisions.
(2) IT monarchy: In IT monarchy archetype the input or decision rights are made by IT individuals or group executives.
(3) Feudal: In feudal archetype the input or decision rights originate from the business unit leaders or the key process owners.
(4) Federal: In federal archetype the managers involved in making input or decision rights are the business groups and IT executives for different units and processes.

(5) IT duopoly: In IT duopoly archetype the input or decisions rights originate from the IT executives and one other group that can be business or process units.

(6) Anarchy: In anarchy archetype the input or decision rights come from each individual user.

In the study done by Weill and Ross (2004) on 256 both private and public enterprises, they have found that the IT governance in public enterprises is more a federal archetype for inputs to all key IT decisions. Therefore, when we should decide on different IT governance aspects, an organization needs to know which governance archetypes would work. The IT governance archetypes are not completely under the control of the IT side and as we noticed the business side also affects the chosen archetype. In opinion of Weill (2004) the top performing enterprises govern their IT in various ways and they have different IT governance archetypes for each of the five key IT decisions. In summary, the IT governance archetypes play an important role in how the key decisions regarding IT governance are made in an organization and who provides an input to these decisions. We therefore consider as very important to identify the IT governance archetypes in this research while studying how suitable is organizational structure in relation with IT governance performance.

10.2.2 *Organizational Structure in Public Organizations*

According to Dow (1988), organizational structure defines patterns for actions and interactions between different roles and positions in an organization. Organizational structure can be defined for the general organization or can be defined for each department and unit of an organization separately, in order to specify the way of how employees are performing their tasks. Furthermore organization structure needs to be purposeful and should support the organizations' objectives. In fact organizational structure is defined by the managers with the purpose of directing the activities and relationships among the organization members towards achieving the organization goals. A well-suited organizational structure can have a positive influence on organization performance (Janićijević 2013). Information systems and IT governance should be reflected in the design of the organization's (IT department's) physical structure. According to Pearlson and Saunders (2013, p. 79) "in an ideal situation, the organizational structure should be adapted in order to expedite the communication and work processes required for achieving the organizations' objectives". Therefore, organizations can choose different types of organizational structures based on their business objectives. Jones (2007) has stated that for an organization, the suitable structure is the one that makes the organization capable of effectively responding to the problems and changes of the environment, technology, market or human resources.

In the public sector organizations as well in the private ones we can found different organizational structure types. These can be vertical, horizontal or divided structures. They can also be formal or informal organizational structures (Ostroff 1999). On the other hand organizational structure can be viewed in terms of the degree of centralization/decentralization. In case of IT departments, the centralized organization structure brings more control over IT standards and is helpful in achieving economy of scale whereas the decentralized organizational structure is more effective in achieving customization and higher speed in responding to special business unit needs (Olson and Chervany 1980). In fact the public organization may have one structure and the IT department, another one. In other words the IT department can have its own specific organizational structure or the same structure as the general organization. According to Pearlson and Saunders (2013) the organizational structure of IT departments should be designed in such a way as to support business and IT strategies. In authors opinion organizational structures could be hierarchical, flat, matrix or networked and such structures are commonly studied by IT governance researchers (Dameri 2013; Winkler 2013; de Souza Bermejo et al. 2014). A briefly description of the four forms of IT organizational structures proposed by Pearlson and Saunders (2013) are included below.

Hierarchical Organizational Structure

The hierarchical organizational structure is based on the division of control, labor, expertise and unity of demand. Decisions are usually made top down and centralized. The process of work starts by ordering from the top level and the middle managers have the role of primary information processing.

Flat Organizational Structure

This type of structure entails less top-down decision making and command chain. Usually there is no specific organization chart; rather, the relationships, job definitions and reporting systems are fluid. In the flat organizational structure, everyone does whatever needed to complete a business task and is also eligible to make needed decisions about it. Decision-making is usually decentralized in flat organizations but when the department grows and more individuals are added to the groups, some hierarchy will be necessary.

Matrix Organizational Structure

The matrix organizational structure is the third popular organizational structure (Pearlson and Saunders 2013) and in this matrix organizational structures, the workers are assigned to two or more supervisors. Each supervisor is specialized in one issue and directs a different aspect of the business. In this way, the organization makes sure it uses its human resources in the most appropriate projects. In this type of organization, the team members should report to both of their supervisors. It is the team managers who make needed decisions. The matrix organizational structure is appropriate for organizations with complicated decision making processes and unstable environments. There are also some drawbacks with matrix organizations such as confusion for employees regarding their task definitions and reporting to two managers.

Networked Organizational Structure

This type of organizational structure is only possible through advanced IT systems. The decision rights are highly decentralized in these organizations. The controls are based on information systems sharing and communication systems. The networked structures simultaneously aim to enable high creativity and flexibility using information systems and to maintain control on operational processes. Decision-making can be performed very fast since the needed data for decision-making is shared, stored and analyzed instantly.

10.2.3 The Importance of Organizational Structure in IT Governance

A study done by Pereira and da Silva (2012) has looked to find the determinant factors that influence IT governance implementation. The authors have extracted nine factors from the research literature among which is included organizational structure. Pereira and da Silva (2012) have also indicated that among those nine factors, we have also culture, structure, industry and maturity of the organization as the most relevant factors in IT governance implementation. The authors' opinion is that these nine factors are not present in any IT governance framework and therefore the managers should consider them. Furthermore, organizational issues that are including the structure can influence people and organizations, and can play a role in sharing information, communication and also in sharing the experience to preventing repeat mistakes (Leidner and Kayworth 2006; Vieru and Rivard, 2014).

Janićijević (2013) have stated that organizational structure is among those concepts that have very important explanatory and influencing role in understanding the causes of many different issues in organizations. However, there is a lack of research on understanding the relationship between organizational structure and IT governance.

Wilkin and Chenhall (2002) have also noticed that organizational structure formed around IT project management and IT governance will vary depending on the particularities of the organization and its internal and external circumstances. The research in the field of IT governance performance and its relation with organizational structure has not advanced significantly and there are scarce theories addressing this issue (De Haes and Van Grembergen 2008). Therefore it is important to identify the relationship between organization structure and IT governance and the way organizational structure should be adapted in accordance with the IT governance performance and IT governance archetypes. The conceptual framework on which this research has based one is shown in Fig. 10.1.

As is shown in Fig. 10.1, this research investigates the relation between IT organizational structure with IT governance performance outcomes. Apart from IT governance performance outcomes we have also considered to identify the IT governance archetypes that play an important role on how hey IT decisions in IT governance. The research has looked to investigate how suitable is the organizational structure of an IT department in relation with IT governance performance outcomes.

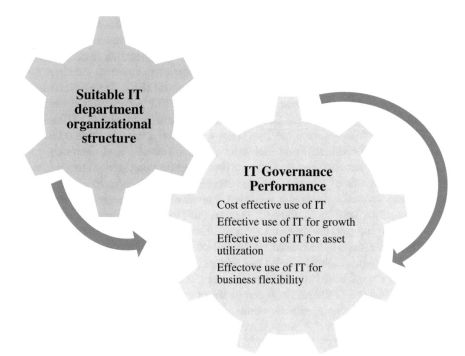

Fig. 10.1 Research conceptual framework

10.3   Research Methodology

The research method used in this paper is case study research. According to Yin (2013), case study is suitable in situations when the research has questions about "how" or "why" and when researchers have no control over the studied situation. Case study research is an appropriate choice in an organizational context where the authors' creativity should be used to interpret the existing environmental issues to understand complex processes and events (Benbasat et al. 1987; Myers 2009). The research question in this study is "*How suitable is the IT organizational structure in relation with IT governance performance in a public organization?*"

The case study focuses on the IT department of a public research and education organization in a developing country. This research aims to uncover the opinions and perceptions of participants with respect to the way their IT department organizational structure is designed to improve their IT governance performance. A qualitative approach is taken in this research because it is more likely to obtain more information during the data collection process than the quantitative approach (Myers 2009). This is manly useful when having "how" research questions and data collectors can make changes in their questions according to the data they have gained in each phase of data collection.

The data was collected through in-depth semi-structured interviews with focus group in the case organization. A focus group is selected for this research since this is an appropriate method for performing an unstructured explorative research (Fisher 2007). Apart from the focus group, we also participated in informal meetings with the managers of the public organization (hereafter named IHC). The data collection from the focus group took place during March 2016. The participants of the focus group in this study included the CIO, head of network and security, the IT architect and the heads of the research faculty. There were three semi-structured interviews (two hours each) conducted with the focus group members. In all interviews, the CIO, the head of network and security, and the IT architect participated together with different research faculty heads who also served as the project leaders.

The data collected from the recorded interviews were transcribed and then analyzed qualitatively by looking for themes, clusters and patterns. As Braun and Clarke (2006) suggest, the thematic analysis of the data can be done in six iterative steps. These six steps include reading the collected data or listening to the recorded interviews, determining some codes and grouping the codes into the themes that are desired to be used based on the research perspective, reviewing the themes and writing the analysis of the results based on those extracted themes. In this research, some of the codes that specifically emerged in the interviews included "IT deci-sions", "projects budgets", "competitive advantage", "IT projects", "IT role", "cost savings", "IT resources", "strategic objectives", "structure", "IT teams" and "per-formance". The broader themes derived from the research question itself included "IT governance in public organization", "the most important component of IT governance performance", "IT organizational structure and IT governance arche-types" and "IT organizational structure type and IT governance performance". Appendix A includes a table presenting the codes extracted from the collected data and the themes they are related to. The relations between these themes and patterns were also found. Additionally the used data included the organization's internal documents and the informal discussions with managers at IHS.

In such cases when different types of data are available, triangulation is sug-gested to enhance the validity and reliability of the research (Myers 2009; Runeson et al. 2012). Therefore to achieve the data triangulation we have used multiple sources of evidences like the data collected from the focus group interviews, and the data collected from the organization's internal documents and from the informal discussions with respondents.

10.4 Results and Discussion

In this section, first the IHS organization and IT department case description is presented, second the ITG performance for IT department of IHS is assessed, third the IT governance archetypes for IT decisions are determined and finally the IT organizational structure adapted with IT governance performance and IT gover-nance archetypes is explored.

10.4.1   Case Description

The case used in this research is a public organization in a developing country that is doing research and education in the humanities area. This organization is anonymously called IHS and has around 500 employees with an IT department of 16 employees. IHS is funded by the government and have both research and education activities in humanities and cultural studies for over 30 years. This organization is part of an old university located in a developing country. During the last 10–12 years, the organization has placed a considerable effort into modernizing its IT. Now IHS consists of seven departments (faculties) with masters and PhD programs and about 1184 graduates. The organizational chart of HIS and its IT department is shown in Fig. 10.2.

As we see from Fig. 10.2, the IT Department of HIS is directly placed under the supervision of the IHS head. The reason for this subordination is that this organization has a specific focus on IT in its recent plans. The IT Department consists of 16 employees that are under the management of a Chief Information Officer (CIO). The IT department as well as the human resources (HR) unit, financial office and the other faculties are also under the supervision of the head of IHS.

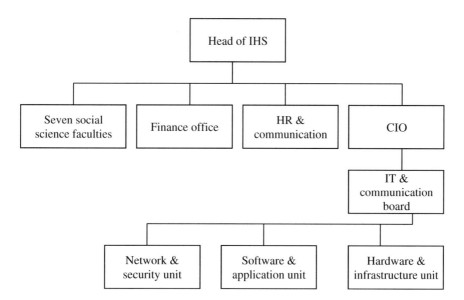

Fig. 10.2 Organizational chart of IHS and its IT Department

10.4.2   IT Governance Archetypes of the IT Department at IHS

The importance of IT Governance archetypes for this research study has been explained in the other sections and is mainly concerning on those who makes decisions regarding the information systems and where the inputs for those decisions come from (Weill and Ross 2004). As we see IT governance archetypes is an important factor in IT governance therefore the IT governance archetypes in IHS need to be identified. In fact IT governance archetypes are in relation with IT governance performance and therefore their relation with the IT organizational structure in the IT Department of IHS cannot be ignored. In IT Department of IHS, the inputs for most of the decisions are involving the business side represented by the IHS general managers and this is reflected in the federal archetype of the IT governance that we have found in three key IT decisions. In the study done of Weill and Ross (2004) 74 public organizations have been found to have federal arrangements for all IT decisions. The findings coming out from our case study in IHS and concerning IT governance archetypes of the IT Department at IHS are presented in Table 10.1.

As is shown in Table 10.1, the business monarchy archetype is used for inputs and decisions on IT investments. This is explained by the fact that at IHS as a public organization every investment decision should be finalized by the general finance department of IHS. Furthermore, we can notice that the IT monarchy archetype is used only for IT architecture decisions. However if these decisions need great investments, they need to be made together with the general finance office of IHS. Finally, the duopoly archetype is the one used for input into the business application needs since most of these needs are coming from the faculty and research staff that define the new projects and consult the IT Department regarding them.

10.4.3   IT Governance Performance of the IT Department at IHS

The IT governance performance measurement formula suggested by Weill and Ross (2004) was used to score the IT governance performance of the IT department at IHS.

The CIO and mangers at IT Department of IHS provided scores for four components of IT governance performance including: (1) cost effective use of IT, (2) effective use of IT for growth, (3) effective use of IT for asset utilization, and 4) effective use of IT for business flexibility. The total score of IT governance performance for IHS is 55.91 out of 100. Weill and Ross (2004) in their study of 74 public organizations found an average IT governance performance score of 70 out of 100. Considering this average score, the IT governance performance score of

Table 10.1 IT governance archetypes for IT decisions of the IT Department at HIS (adapted from Weill and Ross 2004)

Archetypes	Decision									
	IT Principles		IT Architecture		IT Infrastructure Strategy		Business Application Needs		IT Investments	
	Input	Decision	Input	Decision	Input	Decision	Input	Decision	Input	Decision
Business Monarchy									BU yearly IT budget	BUGM
IT Monarchy			IT Helpdesk	Head of IT network and security						
Feudal										
Federal	BU heads + CIO	IT board + BUGM			BU unit heads + CIO	Head of IT network and security + BUGM		IT board + BUGM		
Duopoly							CIO + BU unit heads			

BU heads—Business heads that is IHS heads in this case
BUGM—Business General Managers that is IHS units' managers in this case

Fig. 10.3 IT governance performance scores of IT Department at IHS

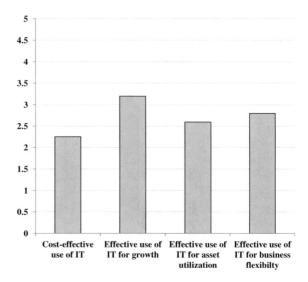

IHS (55.91) is lower. According to the CIO "In a developing country, using IT in different organizations has started later than the developed countries and that is why they are not very matured in their IT governance performance and still need to deal with many basic issues but they also need to move fast to be competitive". The internal documents of IHS also stated that "IHS is under major transition and IT has a significant role in this transition". Based upon the data collected we have obtained different scores for each of ITG performance outcomes as is shown in Fig. 10.3.

As represented in Fig. 10.3, cost effective use of IT has the lowest score (2.25 out of 5) and effective use of IT for growth has the highest score (3.2 out of 5).

The sections bellow explain how each of the scores in Fig. 10.3 are received and what they demonstrate according to the interviews.

Cost Effective use of IT

According to the IT managers "IHS does not care so much about how much IT can save costs for them" and that is why cost effective use of IT did not achieve a high score. Decreasing the costs of IHS by IT is one issue and doing IT projects with the lowest possible costs is another. "For IHS the latter is the one that matters". The CIO mentions "we calculated how much some processes-for instance a book a publication- costs and how much we have saved by using a new IT system, but IHS heads are not interested in that".

This can be also related to IHS's budgeting plan as a public organization. As the IT networks and security manager states, "IHS does not have functional budget, it has cash budget instead which means total budget for IHS and IT Department comes yearly from the government".

Effective use of IT for Growth

Effective use of IT for growth received the highest score at IT Department of IHS and this component has the highest rate of importance for IHS too. This has come from the need of using IT for growth to such a degree that IHS has even defined in its vision as: "Advancing research and education in all humanities fields and higher up the rank of IHS as a research institute and university." Therefore improving the effective use of IT for growth can reflect this vision most visibly. There are also many potential improvements that if will be accomplished at the right time they can provide a great competitive advantage for IHS. The CIO counts some examples of IT projects that have brought competitive advantage for IHS such as: "The portal of humanities" which includes all publications in humanities and provides different categorizations. Another one is the IHS website which was ranked number one in the country for university websites, and the first "local language database" designed by the faculty of linguistics head.

In effective use of IT for asset utilization and business flexibility, IHS has received a lower score. The reason for this goes back to the characteristics of this public organization and the fact that the IT Department does not have its own HR or financial office. According to the IT architect and head of network and security, "in many projects there are minimum IT assets and they cannot perform with an acceptable standard".

10.4.4 IT Department Organizational Structure at IHS Relationship with ITG Performance

As we have noticed the IT Department of IHS has a matrix organizational structure. In this organizational structure, each employee can be involved in different projects at the same time. According to the CIO, this is mainly attributable to the many new projects and the "need to use the most from the resources". Most of the experts employed at the IT Department are familiar with the needed skills of all projects and if not they will be trained. Figure 10.4 explains how these projects are spread throw the matrix organizational structure.

In Fig. 10.4, the row on the top shows how the IT Department functioning groups are vertically operating in different projects. The column on the left includes some examples of the projects running by IT Department. The selection of matrix organizational structure is related to the IT governance performance and IT governance archetypes.

Moreover, the industry and region are among the important factors that influence ITG. IHS is a public organization operating a developing country. Together with specific characteristics of his, these factors influence IT governance performance and the IT organizational structure chosen to complement the IT governance.

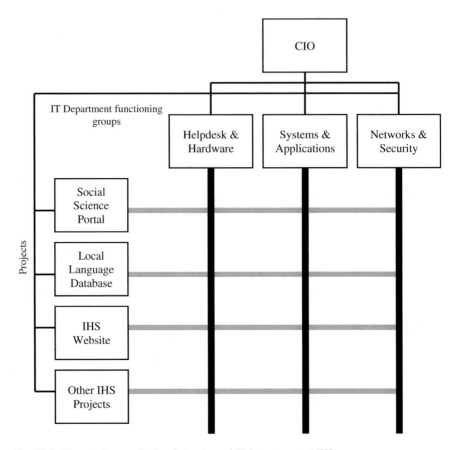

Fig. 10.4 The matrix organizational structure of IT Department at IHS

10.4.5 Organizational Structure of IT Department at HIS Relationship with Cost Effective Use of IT

Being a public organization in a developing country that has a lot of income from the oil industry makes the budgeting issue different in IHS than other organizations in other countries. The budget for the IT Department comes yearly as cash. Therefore, the cost effective use of IT does not have a significant importance and does not have a high score in ITG performance measurement. Moreover, the IT governance archetype for the IT Department is a business monarchy archetype for IT investment decisions. The IT Department HR and finance are the same as IHS general HR and finance office. The IT Department has a federal archetype for three other types of IT decisions, which means that business units (IHS general managers) have roles in making those IT decisions too. This limits the IT Department recruitment of new expert staff and management of resources, leading to the use of pre-existing resources from other projects. According to the CIO, this is why he chose a matrix structure for the IT Department.

10.4.6   Organizational Structure of IT Department at HIS Relationship with Effective Use of IT for Growth

Effective use of IT for growth has the highest score and also is the most important component of IT governance for the IT Department. In accordance with this, IHS is aiming for new competitive advantages that rely on IT. The head of IHS and heads of faculty suggest new projects such as an improved web page and a portal for humanities research. This results in the IT Department running many projects at the same time and pushing the CIO to choose a matrix organizational structure. The CIO is planning for some improvements by having more formal and common meetings with IHS managers and involving them in IT projects. "The IHS managers should get informed more regularly and in details on how the IT projects can improve their research projects and this way they will support more". The faculty heads also claim that "we are interested to get aligned with the IT and know more about how our IT department can help us in our projects but at the moment most of the times we only ask them to support us in a project which is already defined by some faculty group." The faculty heads then state that "it happens so often that when a complete pre-defined project by them is introduced to IT, there is a lot of issues brought by the IT managers that sometimes even makes the project impractical or make it delayed for a long time". The CIO believes that if the IT group is involved in the projects led by the faculty members from the beginning, then they can be a lot more helpful. The IT managers find the solution in "planning regular meetings with faculty members and more communication with different projects' leaders and IHS head". The relationship between different components of IT governance performance and IT governance archetypes and the IT Department organizational structure at IHS are summarized in Fig. 10.5.

As shown in Fig. 10.5, the matrix organizational structure is recognized as the suitable IT organizational structure for the IT Department in relation with the IT governance performance and the IT governance archetypes. In Fig. 10.5 in the left side are presented the IHS characteristics and in the right side the IT governance performance outcomes and IT governance archetypes and their relationship with organizational structure of IT Department at IHS.

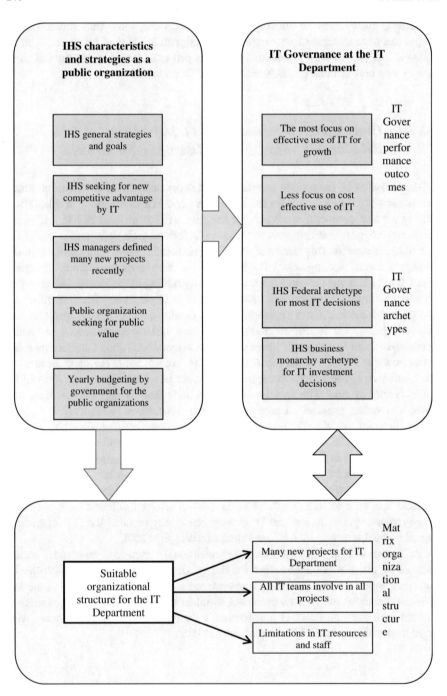

Fig. 10.5 Organizational structure of IT Department at HIS relationship with IT governance performance and IT governance archetypes

10.4.7 Discussion

In IHS as a public organization, there are many factors influencing the strategic IT decisions. The studied public organization in this case is located in a developing country in which IT is playing a critical role for most organizations. This developing country has a lot of income from selling oil and public organizations receive large budgets for their IT projects. Different organizations compete with each other for implementing new IT platforms and the organizations that are faster in adapting IT infrastructure and use IT as a strategic partner are more successful in this completion. In the case of IHS, the heads of the organization seek to improve the ranking of IHS as a research and educational university and they seek to do so through the use of IT in a strategic way. The IT Department of IHS is also looking for ways to improve IT governance by adapting the most suitable organizational structure. The results of this case study revealed that the matrix organizational structure for the IT department works best according to the general IHS and IT department objectives. There are different advantages of adapting a matrix organizational structure for IT Department. The first advantage is that the matrix organizational structure enables the IT Department to work on several IT projects that are supervised by both the IT Department managers and the IHS research faculty who are the designers of many projects. The other advantage is that the IT Department is using its resources in an optimized way. In this public organization, the IT Department does not have its own financial and human resource management and it is very difficult for them to employ new experts. Therefore, the matrix structure allows them to use different IT employees in different projects and also train them for different tasks. There are some drawbacks for the matrix organizational structure of this IT Department too. First, there is not strong communication between the matrix project teams and each team supervisors. Even the CIO bemoans the lack of communication between the IT Department and IHS heads. Another drawback is that the prioritization of the projects is not clearly defined. In some cases the changes in IHS faculties management may cause a change on the IT project led by them and team members working on those projects may not be able to perform on all their projects as expected from the beginning. These issues together affect the performance of the matrix structure and accordingly, the IT governance performance. According to the CIO of the IT Department, improving the communication between the IT Department and IHS faculty heads and projects managers can increase the IT Department performance. More regular meetings during the whole lifetime of a project clarifies the priorities, objectives, requirements and achievements of each project and can improve the IT governance performance too. Therefore the IT Department at HIS has adopted a matrix organizational structure since it is believed to be the most suitable one for them in relation with IT governance performance.

10.5 Conclusions and Future Research

This research contributes to the existing knowledge on the relationship between organizational structure and IT governance by highlighting the importance of having a suitable organizational structure for improvement of IT governance performance in a public organization. The coordination between the organizational structure of the IT department, IT governance objectives and IT governance archetypes is very crucial when IT managers are seeking to improve the IT governance performance in a public organization. The results of this case study in a public organization have revealed that the suitable IT organizational structure for the IT Department is the matrix organizational structure. In this public organization the effective use of IT for growth component of IT governance receives the most attention. This is because this organization is aiming to improve its rank as an education and research institute. To improve its rank, one of the main objectives defined by the heads of this public organization is to use IT in all new projects. It has already started some projects and is seeking to start more research projects that are perceived as competitive advantage. IT is the enabler in all of these projects. Additionally, in accordance with the business monarchy archetype for IT investment decisions, the IT Department does not have much freedom in IT investments. This leads the CIO to rely as much as possible on existing resources and to choose a matrix organizational structure as the suitable IT organizational structure for the IT Department. The matrix organizational structure involves all IT staff in many projects at the same time. The matrix organizational structure also allows the IT Department to focus on different projects using different IT resources that are supervised by both the IT managers and the heads of each project at the same time. This matrix organizational structure also works best with the existing business monarchy archetype for most of the IT investment decisions in this public organization. This research is affected by some limitations too. The first limitation is that most of the participants of the focus group that have interviewed are heads of the IT department and faculties and the head of IHS was not among them. However the CIO of IT department has mentioned that he is in direct contact with the head of IHS and has provided some insights from him too. Another limitation is that the research was conducted in a specific developing country and that the country situation affects many issues even the IT decisions in this case. Therefore in order to generalize the findings of this research it is suggested to perform multiple case studies in other public organizations of this country to explore the relationship between IT organizational structure and IT governance performance and IT governance archetypes.

Appendix A

The codes extracted from the interviews conducted at IHS and the themes they are assigned to.

Themes	Codes from the interviews
Organizational structure	• Structure the IT department according to the needs • Set up teams based on each new defined project • Teams set ups are with the current employees • Matrix structure including all IT Department staff • Each project is leaded by both research faculty and IT managers • With matrix organizational structure, IT department uses and trains staff for different tasks
IT governance performance in cost effective use IT	• It is important to perform IT projects with lowest costs • It is not high priority for IT Department to reduce IHS cost by using IT in different parts
IT governance performance in effective use of IT for growth	• The most important metric for assessing IHS performance is the research projects • Other IHS metrics are the number students and graduates, publications, professors and promotions • IHS has a specific focus on using IT for the research projects • IHS first priority is higher up the rank of their university • Large number of new projects have been defined in the recent years at IHS all involving IT
IT governance performance in effective use of IT for asset utilization	• There is not enough assets to perform IT projects with an acceptable standard • IT is not used to integrate knowledge assets in IHS
IT governance performance in effective use of IT for business flexibility	• IHS strategic plan focuses on using IT to respond to the IT evolution in this developing country
IT governance archetypes	• It is not easy to ask the IHS to employ new team members for IT Department • The general budget discussions are between the CIO and IHS financial heads • The projects are defined by the research faculty heads • The budget for each project is allocated by the IHS finance department • There is no IT-business board regular meetings yet • Small IT project decisions are made inside IT Department • Medium and large IT project decisions are made by IHS heads

References

Al-Raisi, A. N., & Al-Khouri, A. M. (2010). Public value and ROI in the Government sector. *Advances in Management, 3,* 1–5.

Benbasat, I., Goldstein, D. K., & Mead, M. (1987). The case research strategy in studies of information systems. *MIS Quarterly,* 369–386.

Bergeron, F., Croteau, A. M., Uwizeyemungu, S., & Raymond, L. (2017). A framework for research on information technology governance in SMEs. In *Strategic IT Governance and alignment in business settings, 53.*

Bernroider, E. W. (2008). IT Governance for enterprise resource planning supported by DeLone–McLean model of information systems success. *Information & Management, 45*(5), 257–269.

Bowen, P. L., Cheung, M. Y. D., & Rohde, F. H. (2007). Enhancing IT Governance practices: A model and case study of an Organization's efforts. *International Journal of Accounting Information Systems, 8*(3), 191–221.

Braun, V., & Clarke, V. (2006). Using thematic analysis in psychology. *Qualitative Research in Psychology, 3*(2), 77–101.

Chan, Y. E. (2002). Why haven't we mastered alignment? The importance of informal organization structure. *MIS Quarterly Executive, 1*(2), 97–112.

Couto, E. S., Lopes, M. F. C., & Sousa, R. D. (2015). Can IS/IT Governance contribute for business agility? *Procedia Computer Science, 64,* 1099–1106.

Dameri, R. P. (2013). From IT Governance to IT service delivery. implementing a comprehensive framework at ansaldo STS. *Organizational Change and Information Systems, 2,* 33–40.

De Haes, S., & Van Grembergen, W. (2008). An exploratory study into the design of an IT Governance minimum baseline through Delphi research. *The Communications of the Association for Information Systems, 22,* 443–458.

De Haes, S., & Van Grembergen, W. (2009). An exploratory study into IT Governance implementations and its impact on business/IT alignment. *Information Systems Management, 26*(2), 123–137.

De Haes, S., & Van Grembergen, W. (2015). *Enterprise Governance of IT: Achieving alignment and value* (2nd ed.). Springer.

Denford, J. S., Dawson, G. S., & Desouza, K. C. (2015). An argument for centralization of IT Governance in the public sector. In *Proceedings of 48th Hawaii international conference on system sciences (HICSS)* (pp. 4493–4501). IEEE.

de Souza Bermejo, P. H., Tonelli, A. O., & Zambalde, A. L. (2014). Developing IT Governance in Brazilian Public Organizations. *International Business Research, 7*(3), 101.

Dow, G. K. (1988). Configurational and coactivational views of organizational structure. *Academy of Management Review, 13*(1), 53–64.

Fisher, C. (2007). *Researching and writing a dissertation: a guidebook for business students.* Essex, England: Pearson Education.

Grant, G., McKnight, S., Uruthirapathy, A., & Brown, A. (2007). Designing Governance for shared services organizations in public service. *Government Information Quarterly, 24*(3), 522–538.

Hardy, G. (2006). Using IT governance and COBIT to deliver value with IT and respond to legal, regulatory and compliance challenges. *Information Security Technical Report, 11*(1), 55–61.

ITGI (2003). Board briefing on IT Governance (2nd ed.). Retrieved May 5, 2016 from www.itgi. org.

ITGI. (2011). *Global status report on the governance of enterprise IT (GEIT).* IL: Rolling Meadows.

Janahi, L., Griffiths, M., & Al-Ammal, H. (2015). A conceptual model for IT Governance in public sectors. In *Proceeding of forth international conference on future generation communication technology (FGCT)* (pp. 1–9). IEEE.

Janićijević, N. (2013). The mutual impact of organizational culture and structure. *Economic Annals, 58*(198), 35–60.

Jones, G. R. (2007). *Organizational theory, design, and change* (5th ed.). NJ: Pearson Prentice Hall.

Juiz, C., Guerrero, C., & Lera, I. (2014). Implementing good governance principles for the public sector in information technology governance frameworks. *Open Journal of Accounting, 3*(1).

Kappelman, L. A., Mclean, E., Johnson, V., & Gerhart, N. (2014). The 2014 SIM IT key issues and trends study. *MIS Quarterly Executive, 13*(4), 237–263.

Kelly, G., Mulgan, G., & Muers, S. (2002). Creating public value: An analytical framework for public service reform. Discussion paper prepared by the cabinet office strategy unit, United Kingdom.

Ko, D., & Fink, D. (2010). Information technology Governance: An evaluation of the theory-practice gap. *Corporate Governance, Emerald Group, 10*(5), 662–674.

Leidner, D. E., & Kayworth, T. (2006). Review: A review of culture in information systems research: toward a theory of information technology culture conflict. *MIS Quarterly, 30*(2), 357–399.

Moore, M., & Khagram, S. (2004). On creating public value: what business might learn from Government about strategic management. Corporate Social Responsibility Initiative Working Paper, 3.

Myers, M. (2009). *Qualitative research in business and management*. London: SAGE.

Nicolian, N., Welch, C., Read, M., & Roberts, M. (2015). Critical organizational challenges in delivering business value from IT. In search of hybrid IT value models. *The Electronic Journal Information Systems Evaluation, 18*(2), 129–145.

Nfuka, E. N., & Rusu, L. (2013). Critical success framework for implementing effective IT Governance in Tanzanian public sector organizations. *Journal of Global Information Technology Management, 16*(3), 53–77.

O'Flynn, J. (2007). From new public management to public value: Paradigmatic change and managerial implications. *Australian Journal of Public Administration, 66*(3), 353–366.

Olson, M. H., & Chervany, N. L. (1980). The Relationship between organizational characteristics and the structure of the information services function. *MIS Quarterly, 4*(2), 57–69.

Ostroff, F. (1999). *The horizontal organization: What the organization of the future looks like and how it delivers value to customers*. Oxford University Press on Demand.

Othman, M. F. I., & Chan, T. (2013). Barriers to formal IT Governance practice–Insights from a qualitative study. In *Proceedings of 46th Hawaii international conference on system sciences (HICSS)* (pp. 4415–4424). IEEE.

Pearlson, K. E., & Saunders, C. S. (2013). *Strategic management of information systems* (5th ed.). NJ: Wiley.

Pereira, R., & da Silva, M.M. (2012). IT Governance implementation: The determinant factors. communications of the IBIMA (pp. 1–16).

Runeson, P., Höst, M., Rainer, A., & Regnell, B. (2012). *Case study research in software engineering: Guidelines and examples,* (1st ed.). NJ: Wiley.

Sesay, A., & Ramirez, R. (2016). Theorizing the IT Governance role in IT sourcing research. In *Proceedings of 22nd Americas conference in information systems*.

Schwarz, A., & Hirschheim, R. (2003). An extended platform logic perspective of IT Governance: Managing perceptions and activities of IT. *The Journal of Strategic Information Systems, 12* (2), 129–166.

Simonsson, M., & Johnson, P. (2006). Defining IT Governance- a Consolidation of Literature. In Proceedings of 18th Conference on Advanced Information Systems Engineering.

Sohal, A. S., & Fitzpatrick, P. (2002). IT Governance and management in large Australian organisations. *International Journal of Production Economics, 75*(1–2), 97–112.

Tonelli, A. O., de Souza Bermejo, P. H., dos Santos, P. A., Zuppo, L., & Zambalde, A. L. (2015). IT Governance in public sector: A conceptual model. *Information Systems Frontiers*, 1–18.

Trites, G. (2004). Director responsibility for IT Governance. *International Journal of Accounting Information Systems, 5*(2), 89–99.

Van Grembergen, W. (2004). Strategies for information technology Governance. IGI Global.

Van Grembergen, W., & De Haes, S. (2005). Measuring and improving IT Governance through the balanced scorecard. *Information Systems Control Journal, 2*(1), 35–42.

Van Grembergen, W., & De Haes, S. (2009). *Enterprise Governance of information technology: Achieving strategic alignment and value.* NY: Springer Science & Business Media.

Vieru, D., & Rivard, S. (2014). Organizational identity challenges in a post-merger context: A case study of an information system implementation project. *International Journal of Information Management, 34*(3), 381–386.

Weill, P. (2004). Don't just lead, govern: How top-performing firms govern IT. *MIS Quarterly Executive, 3*(1), 1–17.

Weill, P., & Ross, J. W. (2004). *IT Governance: How top performers manage IT decision rights for superior results.* MA: Harvard Business School Press.

Wilkin, C. L., & Chenhall, R. H. (2002). A review of IT Governance: a taxonomy to inform accounting information systems. *Journal of Information Systems, 24*(2), 107–146.

Wiedemann, A., & Weeger, A. (2016). How to design an IT Department? A review and synthesis of key characteristics. In *Proceedings of 22nd Americas conference on information systems (AMCIS).*

Winkler, Till J. (2013). IT Governance mechanisms and administration/IT alignment in the public sector: A conceptual model and case validation. In *Wirtschaftsinformatik Proceedings 2013.* Paper 53.

Yin, R. K. (2013). *Case study research: design and methods* (5th ed.). CA: Sage.

Author Biographies

Parisa Aasi is a PhD candidate at Stockholm University, Sweden. She received her MSc in Engineering and Management of Information Systems at Royal Institute of Technology (KTH), Sweden. Her PhD topic is organizational culture and structure influence on IT governance and her research areas of interest are in IT governance, organizational culture, organizational structure, IT governance performance, organizational culture change and IT outsourcing. Parisa Aasi has published papers in the International Journal of Business/IT Alignment and Governance and conferences such as HICSS and AMCIS. She is also a teacher assistant in IT management courses at Stockholm University.

Lazar Rusu PhD is Professor at Department of Computer and Systems Sciences, Stockholm University, Sweden. He isinvolved in teaching and research in IT management and has a professional experience of over 30 years both industrial and academic in information systems area. His research interest is mainly in IT governance, business-IT alignment and IT outsourcing. The results of his research have been published in proceedings of top international conferences like ECIS, HICSS, AMCIS, PACIS, ISD and journals like Computers in Human Behavior, Industrial Management & Data Systems, Information Systems Management, Journal of Global Information Technology Management, Journal of Information Technology Theory and Applications,among others. He is associate editor of International Journal of IT/Business Alignment and Governance.

Dorothy E. Leidner PhD is the Ferguson Professor of Information Systems at Baylor University and a visiting professor at the University of Lund, Sweden. She has over 50 refereed publications in such journals as MIS Quarterly, Information Systems Research, Organization Science, and the Journal of Management Information Systems, among others. Dorothy serves as Editor-in-Chief of MIS Quarterly Executive and Senior Editor for Information Systems Research and for the Journal of the Association of Information Systems. Previously, she served as co-Editor-in-Chief of Data Base for Advances in IS, associate editor and senior editor for MIS Quarterly, associate editor for Decision Sciences Journal, and senior editor for the Journal of Strategic Information Systems.

Chapter 11
Ambidextrous IT Governance in the Public Sector: A Revelatory Case Study of the Swedish Tax Authorities

Johan Magnusson, Jacob Torell, Lidija Polutnik and Urban Ask

Abstract Contemporary organizations are increasingly turning their attention towards utilizing information technology not solely for achieving efficiency gains but also for attaining innovation. The literature suggests that the trade-off between efficiency and innovation may be avoided through adopting what is referred to as organizational ambidexterity. Using a revelatory case study of the Swedish tax authorities informed by organizational ambidexterity, we develop an understanding of how the strive for ambidexterity is effectuated through IT Governance. Our research shows that despite the best intentions of the organization in stipulating ambidextrous IT Governance, the implementation of said governance invariantly becomes laden with trade-offs. In addition to providing insights about the relatively novel phenomenon of Ambidextrous IT Governance, the study contributes to the literature on organizational ambidexterity with an empirical investigation into the difficulties associated with achieving ambidexterity within the public sector.

11.1 Introduction

The burgeoning literature on the performance related impacts of information technology (IT) spend (Saunders and Brynjolfsson 2016; Schmitz et al. 2016) has recently acknowledged positive effects of utilizing IT for a combination of cost reduction and revenue generation (Mithas and Rust 2016). In other words, the

J. Magnusson (✉) · J. Torell · U. Ask
University of Gothenburg, Gothenburg, Sweden
e-mail: johan.magnusson@gu.se

J. Magnusson · U. Ask
Westerdal Oslo School of Arts, Communication and Technology, Oslo, Norway

L. Polutnik
School of Business, Economics and Law, University of Gothenburg, Gothenburg, Sweden

L. Polutnik
Babson College, Wellesley, USA

© Springer International Publishing AG 2017
L. Rusu and G. Viscusi (eds.), *Information Technology Governance in Public Organizations*, Integrated Series in Information Systems 38,
DOI 10.1007/978-3-319-58978-7_11

organization using IT for the full scope of what the technology has to offer out-performs its competitors using IT solely for the limited scope.

These contemporary findings shed light on not only the dual purposes of IT but on the means through which we govern IT. In Schmitz et al. (2016), a survey informed by structuration theory is used to explore how certain behavior related to malleable IT use moderates the performance related impacts of IT. According to their findings, behavior defined as either explorative or exploitative (March 1991; Raisch and Birkinshaw 2008) positively contributes to performance. Perhaps more interestingly, the explorative behavior (i.e. use geared towards innovation) is found to have a higher positive impact on performance than exploitative (i.e. use geared towards efficiency).

There is a long tradition of seeing innovation and efficiency as subject to sub-stantial trade-offs (Stigler 1939; Merton 1958; Stettner and Lavie 2014). The underlying idea is that an organization striving for innovation will have to sacrifice efficiency (and vice versa). Despite being continually questioned by researchers such as MacDuffie et al. (1997) and Suarez et al. (1996), the trade-off constitutes a tenet of management studies (Adler and Borys 1996).

More recent contributions have incorporated the notion of organizational ambidexterity into the IT Governance field (Gregory et al. 2015; Roberts et al. 2016). Through seeing the trade-off as avoidable, researchers such as Xue et al. (2012) push the idea that IT Governance should be configured to achieve both efficiency and innovation. In concrete terms, this involves supporting not only the efficient use of IT in the organization (making the IT department function in the factory-mode) but also the proactive involvement as an innovation partner to the business (Banker et al. 2011). These different modes have previously been regarded as discriminatory by researchers such as Guillemette and Paré (2012), but are now increasingly more seen as complements. In this study we posit that innovation and efficiency exist as modes of IT Governance in all organizations, i.e. all organiza-tions are ambidextrous to *some* degree. That being said, we acknowledge that the distribution of activities between these modes may not be optimal, and that the role of IT Governance in formulating and implementing ambidextrous IT Governance poses a particular challenge.

IT Governance has predominantly been studied within large firms in the private sector (Pang 2014). As noted by Tonelli et al. (2015) in their literature review on IT Governance, only a small fraction of all cases conducted within IT Governance are focused on the public sector (Ali and Green 2007; Pang 2014; Nfuka and Rusu 2011). In their study of contextual differences between public and private sector IT Governance, Campbell et al. (2010) argue that there are substantial differences between the two sectors. Despite these apparent differences, we posit that the role of IT Governance and the necessity for ambidextrous IT Governance is not only a highly relevant area of study within the public sector, but findings from the public sector are transferrable into the private sector and IT Governance in general.

The objective of this study is to explore the in situ adoption of ambidextrous IT Governance. This is achieved through a revelatory case study of the Swedish Tax Authorities, guided by the following research question:

How is ambidexterity formulated and implemented in IT Governance practice within the public sector?

The remainder of the paper is organized accordingly. After a brief review of previous findings on the trade-offs of efficiency and innovation and the construct of ambidexterity, the method of the study is presented. This is followed by the results in the form of the case, and a concluding discussion where the research question is answered and the findings assessed in terms of implications for both theory and practice. The paper ends with some notes on future studies of ambidextrous IT Governance within the public sector.

11.2   Precursory Findings and Theoretical Background

11.2.1   On the Notion of Trade-Offs Between Efficiency and Innovation

The notion of trade-offs between efficiency and innovation constitute a tenet within management studies (Adler and Borys 1996). From earlier works within economics such as Stigler (1939) identifying a direct link between flexibility and higher average cost of production, on to sociologists like Merton (1958) identifying a link between goal displacement and rigidity and Hannan and Freeman (1977) pushing the notions of excess capacity versus specialization, trade-offs have been a natural stomping ground for students of organizations.

Albeit central to the field, there has been substantial work miss-crediting the inevitability of trade-offs. In studies such as that of MacDuffie (1997) and Suarez et al. (1996), the research did not identify any impact of variety on productivity or of product mix flexibility on cost or quality. From this perspective, the very notion of there being a naturally occurring and necessary trade-off within management is questioned. This is further substantiated by Adler et al. (1999, 2009), who found that the trade-off per se was contingent upon the general performance of the firms in question.

Within Information Systems research, several researchers have touched upon the notion of a trade-off between efficiency and innovation. In Xue et al. (2012), the link between market dynamism and IT investment strategy is investigated with the conclusion that in highly dynamic markets, IT investments that focus on innovation lead to increased performance. In markets with low dynamics, strategies that are focused on investments for efficiency are positively associated with increased performance.

These findings are contrasted in Mithas and Rust (2016), where the findings show that firms that avoid the trade-off of innovation and efficiency through following what is referred to as a "dual strategy" for IT investments outperform single strategy firms in terms of higher positive impacts on both market value and financial performance.

The majority of previous research has been focused on the strategic dimension of managing the trade-off between innovation and efficiency (Wu et al. 2015; Banker et al. 2011). In contrast, several recent studies have devoted attention to the perspective of use and the implications on innovation. Roberts et al. (2016) investigation of the role of innovative versus routine IS revealed that innovative use drives idea volume and diversity, two pre-requisites for successful innovation. This is complemented in Schmitz et al. (2016) that demonstrates that the positive impact of explorative use impacts performance more that the exploitative use.

11.2.2 Ambidextrous IT Governance

IT Governance (here defined in line with DeHaes and Van Grembergen 2009 as the structures, processes and relational mechanisms for attaining efficiency and effectiveness from IT) has become tightly associated with the aforementioned trade-offs. IT Governance should simultaneously act to support digitalization and innovation as well as drive efficiency. This has been acknowledged as a paradox (Gregory et al. 2015) within the IT Governance literature, where notions of parallel logics need to be pursued in the day-to-day work. In conjunction with this, recent studies such as that of Mithas and Rust (2016) have found significant positive impacts of what they refer to as a "dual focus" of IT, i.e. strategies that involve using IT for both cost-cutting and revenue generation.

Turning our attention to a potential avoidance of trade-offs, research within what is commonly referred to as "organizational ambidexterity" aim to solve this issue of paradoxal management (Smith et al. 2016). Stemming from research conducted by Jim March on organizational learning, organizational ambidexterity (Duncan 1976; March 1991; Raisch and Birkinshaw 2008) refers to the ability of being "aligned and efficient in their management of todays business demands while simultaneously adaptive to changes in the environment" (Raisch and Birkinshaw 2008). In this respect, notions such as contextual and structural (Raisch and Birkinshaw 2008) ambidexterity are pushed as solutions for how this may be practically implemented.

Stettner and Lavie (2014) offer a critique towards the very notion of ambidexterity on the premise that it undermines firm performance through conflicting routines, negative transfer and limited specialization. At the same time, researchers such as O'Reilly and Tushman (2013) and Magnusson et al. (2015) criticize studies of organizational ambidexterity for severe shortcomings in construct validity.

11.3 Method

11.3.1 Empirical Selection

In the spring of 2016, the research team was contacted by leading representatives from the Swedish Tax Authority (STA). The STA representatives signaled being worried that the current level of innovation in the agency was sub-optimal, and that they were loosing out on the potential benefits of continued digital transformation. In response to this, they wanted to invite the research team to help them shed some light on what was currently going on and what the potential shortcomings could be.

After three initial workshops, the research group presented a project proposal that was accepted by STA. The main objective was to investigate the current practice in terms of IT Governance within the agency. This involved a particular focus on the underlying assumptions in the existing governance, and the balancing of innovation and efficiency in both governance and operations.

The research team designed a revelatory case study (Yin 2013). The rationale for the case being revelatory is two-fold. First, STA is internationally acknowledged for having contributed to Sweden having a best-in-class taxation system, with a high level of acceptance for paying tax from the population. Second, STA has been instrumental in the digital transformation of government in Sweden. With a high degree of independence from state oversight and coordination signifying the Swedish system, issues related to technological standards have not been pushed through a centralized perspective. Instead, the agencies have been granted substantial autonomy, which historically has led to a highly fragmented and sub-optimal adoption of e-Government practice. In this environment, STA has taken a different stance and pushed for national standards with them being both the developer and primary adopter of said standards. This has resulted in e-Government becoming less fragmented as other agencies gradually followed suite. STA has roughly 10 000 employees, and, an IT department comprised of 800 employees with a budget of €300 Million.

11.3.2 Data Collection

The data collection involved a series of workshops, secondary material in the form of IT Governance steering documents, consultancy reports, financial reports and project charters, and continuous e-mail based communications between the research group and a representative from STA. These data sources are described in more detail in Table 11.1.

Table 11.1 Overview of data collection

Focus	Data source	Description	Amount
Problem	Workshops	Workshops (1 h each) with key representatives from STA and the research team focused on discussing and defining the research agenda	4 workshops
	Correspondence	Emails between the research team and representatives from STA pertaining to the focus of the study	150 emails
Formulation	ITG Steering documents	Formal documents detailing the current configuration of IT Governance at STA	21 documents
	Consultancy reports	Reports created by external parties to STA with recommendations for how to improve IT Governance	9 documents
Implementation	Financial reports	Accumulated yearly (2016) figures with total spend, budgets et cetera for each project	4 documents
	Project charters	Formal documents focused on describing and defining development and maintenance projects' scope, stakeholders, team and objectives	103 documents

11.3.3   Method of Analysis

In the spirit of design science and collaborative practice research we strived for including practitioners in the identification of underlying problems to be addressed in the study. This was not restricted to designing the general outline of the research project, but also to the different venues of analysis that would be of particular interest. Among the issues pushed by the practitioners in the workshops was the potential miss-alignment of the current framework for maintenance with notions of innovation, the mechanisms used for balancing efficiency and innovation and how the agency could improve its digital capabilities.

Innovation and efficiency are defined in conjunction with Xue et al. (2012) and inspiration from the literature concerning ambidexterity (Raisch and Birkinshaw 2008). Innovation refers to activities that are explorative in nature, seeking new opportunities. Efficiency refers to activities that are explorative in nature, focusing on eliciting advantages from the existing resource base. Through utilizing these definitions, issues related to e.g. continuous improvements would be categorized as efficiency rather than innovation. The rationale for using these definitions rather than traditional innovation and efficiency definitions lies in the ambition to contribute to the burgeoning literature surrounding ambidexterity.

In terms of studying the formulation of ambidextrous IT governance at STA the research team conducted content analysis of the formal steering documents associated with IT Governance. This included going through the material in several iterations looking for specific wordings and phrases associated with innovation and efficiency. This was done in order to ascertain the distribution of ambidextrous focus of the documents, i.e. how much innovation versus efficiency was being pushed. In order to assess this balance, word count analysis was performed utilizing keywords and signifiers for efficiency and innovation. In regard to efficiency, terms such as "cost efficiency", "efficient" et cetera were utilized, and in regard to innovation, terms such as "dynamic", "innovation", "innovative", "new development" et cetera were used. On the basis of this word count, a balance between innovation and efficiency was calculated. All documents were treated as equally important, with the rationale of these being selected as core steering documents by the informants.

With the formulation being dependent upon external consultancy reports as an input to the process, the research team conducted a similar analysis of said reports in order to gain an understanding of what distribution was present among these documents.

In terms of studying the implementation of ambidextrous IT governance at STA the research team used the financial budgets for 2016 and project charters of all major projects that together constitute roughly two thirds of the total IT budget of the organization. Based on the project charters, the research team coded the objectives of each project into discriminating categories of efficiency or innovation. Based on this, the distribution of objectives was re-interpreted through financial data from the budgets to arrive at a cost distribution for each project in terms of efficiency versus innovation. In other words, each objective as specified in the project charter was seen as either innovation or efficiency, and the total balance in monetary terms was calculated through taking the total budget for the project, and indiscriminately dividing it with the number of objectives.

11.4   Results: The Case of Ambidextrous Governance at STA

This section is organized through two underlying sections covering the formulation and implementation of ambidextrous IT Governance at STA.

11.4.1   The Formulation of Ambidextrous IT Governance

The process of formulating IT Governance at STA is owned by the office of the CIO and is continuous, with regular iterations of the steering documents resulting in changes in governance. The input for said formulation consists primarily of reports from both internal and external parties. In terms of the external parties, these consist of highly renowned global industrial analyst and consulting firms.

Through a content analysis mapping the ambidextrous balance between efficiency and innovation in the external reports, we found that the balance was tilted towards efficiency. 83.47% of the statements in the documents were focused on driving efficiency, whereas only 16.53% were focused on driving innovation. Given the outset of this study with STA being worried about under-performing in terms of innovation, this signaled a cause for concern.

Continuing the analysis of the external reports we focused on conducting an analysis inspired by narrative structures (Silverman 2005). We analyzed the documents for assumptions and recommendations, and on the basis of this we analyzed which type of mode (in terms of efficiency versus innovation) the recommendations would support. The results of this analysis are found in Table 11.2.

As seen, several of the underlying assumptions could be criticized for not amply taking into account recent findings and notions of ambidexterity. As an example of this, the equation of governance to formalism and centralization signals a particular stance on driving economies of scale rather than economies of scope, and the perception of pluralism as a source of inefficiency goes in direct conflict with findings from e.g. Smithet et al. (2016) and Schmitz et al. (2016).

Looking at the recommendations, we see a bias where the organization (provided it follows the recommendations out-of-the-box) will run the risk of only focusing on driving efficiency at the expense of innovation, i.e. manifesting a direct trade-off between the two. The consequence of this would hence be the optimization of IT at STA for a situation with a low degree of external change and dynamism and large, capital investment focused projects. In line with this, the resulting governance would be seen as sub-optimized for an environment with a higher degree of dynamism and change, and smaller less capital intensive projects. Given the strategic intent of STA and the increasing level of dynamism as a result of digitalization (McAffe and Brynjolfsson 2008), the bias in the assumptions and recommendations constitute a cause for concern.

Table 11.2 Assumptions and Recommendations

Assumptions	Recommendations
Portfolio management = Efficiency IT cost/unit should be minimized	Strive for repetitive, standardized, person-independent predictable results
Governance = Cost transparency = Efficient use	Reduce complexity, take control for cost efficiency and productivity
Governance = Centralization + Formalization = Control	Centralize, assign control to Finance
Formalization = Maturity = Efficiency Pluralism = Inefficiency	Increase formalization, decrease room for interpretation, directly allocate costs

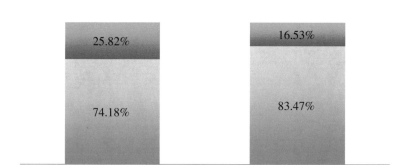

Fig. 11.1 Overview of the formulation of IT governance

In terms of the formulation of governance as analyzed through the formal steering documents, this displayed a predominant focus directed towards efficiency (74.18%) as opposed to innovation (25.82%) (Fig. 11.1).

Through follow up discussions with STA, this balance was expressed as "probably close to the balance that we are aiming for" (Strategy Executive, Workshop 3), with the motivation that provided the role and function of IT for an organization such as STA (with it being critical to operations, and with there being substantial economies of scale in play through massive transaction volumes and low acceptance for down-time), there needs to be a predominant focus on efficiency as opposed to innovation. At the same time, the representatives expressed concerns that they believed that albeit in the formal governance, they believed that the factual level of innovation was actually lower than what the steering documents prescribed.

11.4.2 The Implementation of Ambidextrous IT Governance

The process of implementing IT Governance at STA was primarily studied through the two different portfolios constituting the vast majority (>98%) of the IT budget of the organization. The two portfolios were directed towards Maintenance and Development, where the first of these was the largest constituting roughly two thirds of the total IT budget.

Looking into how the plans for each project[1] were operationalized through objectives, the total balance was found to be 97.53% efficiency and 2.47%

---

[1]We use the notion of "Project" for entities in both portfolios, despite the original terminology used in Sweden makes a distinction between Projects and Maintenance Objects.

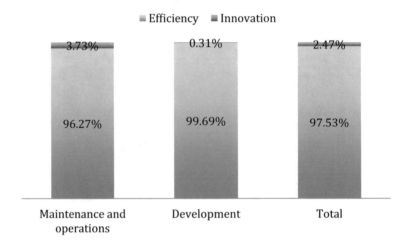

Fig. 11.2 Overview of the implementation of IT governance

innovation. Upon presenting this to the STA in a first workshop, they responded with "We are not surprised, but must admit that it is a tad off-putting".

Through further breaking this down into the two portfolios, we found that the level of innovation was greater in the maintenance portfolio (96.27/3.73%) than in the development portfolio (99.69/0.31%). This was counter-intuitive, since previous findings seem to indicate that the development activities are the primary drivers of innovation within IT (Xue et al. 2012) (Fig. 11.2).

The rationale for development being so highly tilted towards efficiency rather than innovation was found to rest partly on the operationalization of the general purposes of each project into underlying objectives. As described previously, our analysis consisted of coding each underlying objective in the development projects, i.e. we paid no attention to the overarching purpose and aim of the projects themselves. The rationale for this type of coding was that we saw that the formulation of overarching project aims display a higher degree of ambiguity than the objectives (i.e. making them harder to code and lacking in reliability) and that the objectives of each project constitute an operationalization of the aim.

11.5   Discussion

In the introduction for this chapter we posited that all organization display ambidextrous capabilities in their IT Governance. Through this assumption, this study has focused on investigating how the ambidextrous balance is both formulated and implemented in and through IT Governance. As the results show, the organization displayed a bias in implementing the balance as formulated in IT Governance. The balance as ascertained through the IT Governance steering documents showed a roughly three-fourths focus on efficiency and one fourth on innovation. As expressed by the case organization, this was seen as a feasible balance in order to achieve its objectives associated with being a leading actor in e-Government. Through studying the balance as present in the project portfolios, the bias towards an almost unanimous focus on efficiency rather than innovation was deemed to illustrate a miss-alignment and miss-execution of the intended focus of IT Governance.

The findings show that the formulation and implementation of ambidexterity as part of IT Governance practice is highly complex. Perceiving Ambidextrous IT Governance as a top-down process (in light of previously dominating perspectives Wu et al. 2015), leads to a conclusion that ambidexterity becomes lost in translation as it is effectuated in practice. This would assume that there is a general tendency of the IT organization to downplay innovation as opposed to efficiency, a finding that is controversial and counter-intuitive provided previous findings such as Weill and Ross (2004).

With the lower degree of innovation found in the development (as opposed to the maintenance) portfolio, it would be easy to assume that the maintenance portfolio has better pre-requisites for innovation than the development portfolio. This conclusion is, however problematic since we are dealing with two severely tilted distributions. Both portfolios display significant biases, and hence need to be analyzed separately.

In discussions with senior representatives from STA during the workshops the bias found in the development portfolio was elaborated upon as partly dependent upon the development projects being large and necessary due to changes in regulation and hence compliance driven. This raises the question of how to view compliance motives for investments within IT. As noted by Salge (2015), regulative motives for investments in IT are dominant particularly in environments where legitimacy is deemed of utmost importance. This implies that to avoid said bias would be problematic for STA due to its strong institutional environment.

As for the maintenance portfolio, the underlying framework for portfolio management (Nordström 2005) can be criticized for overly emphasizing efficiency at the expense of innovation. Core to this particular model is the compartmentalization of systems into objects, and the assignment of control and accountability to a dyad consisting of individuals from the IT department and Business). Hence, it amalgamates the separation of business and IT and manifests this into a governance framework. In addition to this, the model suffers from several of the faulty assumptions as found in the external reports, and hence is biased towards ascertaining efficiency in maintenance management, which is clearly visible in the PhD thesis that proposed the model originally (Nordström 2005).

This study has three primary contributions to research. First, it offers an account of how ambidextrous IT Governance is formulated and implemented in a large public-sector organization. With this being the first example of a study directed towards this, the revelatory nature of the case should provide a basis for future studies. Since we refrain from theorizing in this first part of our study, there is ample rom for theory building. Second, the finding that innovation was present to a larger extent in maintenance than in development contrasts previous findings and assumptions of information systems organizational studies (Wu et al. 2015). From this perspective, students of IT driven innovation should not shun away from also empirically incorporating the maintenance portfolio in future studies of innovation. This would require an increased granularity and sensitivity into the very notion of maintenance within IT departments in the public sector. Third, the inherent lack of innovation in the development portfolio calls for additional studies into why and how. In this, we add empirical evidence to what has recently been highlighted by Salge et al. (2015) within healthcare.

In terms of contributions to practice, this study adds through offering a method for auditing the ambidextrous balance within IT Governance. Despite Campbell's (2010) arguments concerning the innate differences between the public and private sector, we see the issue of balance to be universal (not saying the inherent levels of balance should/would be similar). In addition to this, the patterns that we have shown in this study, i.e. the bias between formulation and implementation are, despite not being generalizable a cause for concern. If IT Governance is to function as a means through which the organization secures the efficient and effective use of IT (De Haes and Van Grembergen 2009), then instrumentality needs to be assured. In other words, the potential imbalance could be used as an indicator of sub-par IT Governance (either in formulation or implementation). Since the public sector (much like the private sector) is highly dependent upon IT in order to fulfill its mission, this continuous balancing of efficiency and innovation and the avoidance of trade-offs becomes a core capability for future success.

The study three main limitations, both related to the selected methods. First, the method of utilizing content analysis to ascertain the ambidextrous balance in steering documents and reports suffers from traditional limitations associated with finding the right keywords signifying the theoretical categories. Second, the method of discriminating coding of project objectives into theoretical categories could be criticized for over-simplification. Since most of the projects are substantial in terms of workload and associated costs, the limited list of concise objectives would inherently show internal balances between innovation and efficiency. With this research being the first empirical attempt at capturing the balance of IT portfolios, we justify this simplification through practical feasibility, where the amount of work necessary for a more "balanced" approach would too costly. Third, the even break-down of project budget into objectives could also be criticized for being an over simplification. With the different objectives being different in terms of cost-intensity, a more nuanced break-down based on interviews with the project managers would have increased the reliability. In line with the justification for the second limitation presented above, the rationale for the selected method was based on feasibility and will be re-assessed in future analysis of our material.

This research will now continue to pursue additional avenues of analysis of the collected material as well as additional material currently under collection. The direct next step will consist of a survey directed towards the 55 senior staffers at

STA who are owners or project managers for the contents of the two portfolios. This survey is inspired by Activity Based Costing and designed to measure the in situ implementation of ambidextrous IT Governance at STA. This will offer additional insights into how ambidexterity is implemented on the operational level in the organization. In addition to this, we will pursue theory development with the aim of providing concrete theoretical support for how ambidextrous IT Governance may function as a means for more efficient and effective IT Governance.

11.6 Conclusion

With IT Governance being an understudied phenomenon within the context of the public sector (Pang 2014), this study adds to what we hope will be a burgeoning field. The study showed that there are clear aspects of ambidexterity present within the formulation of IT Governance, yet this ambidexterity was not present in the following implementation. From having an expressed balance between exploration and exploitation (i.e. innovation and efficiency) of 24 versus 76% in the formulation, the implementation consisted of an entirely different balance (2 versus 98%). This can be seen as a sign of a substantial misalignment of the tactical governance in relation to the strategic. The result of said imbalance (i.e. the bias towards efficiency rather than innovation) is translated into problems with achieving innovation for the organization in question, primarily through having an over-emphasis on efficiency in the tactical governance. In addition to this, the study found the same time of bias in the external reports utilized as input for formulating governance. This pattern can be seen as one potential source for said bias in the implementation.

Acknowledgements The authors would like to express their sincere thanks to the Marianne and Marcus Wallenberg foundation for the monetary support necessary for conducting this research. In addition to this, we wish to extend our sincere thanks to the informants at the Swedish Tax Authorities, in particular Karolin Wallström.

References

Adler, P. S., & Borys, B. (1996). Two types of bureaucracy: Enabling and coercive. *Administrative Science Quarterly*, 61–89.

Adler, P. S., Goldoftas, B., & Levine, D. I. (1999). Flexibility versus efficiency? A case study of model changeovers in the Toyota production system. *Organization Science, 10*(1), 43–68.

Adler, P. S., Benner, M., Brunner, D. J., MacDuffie, J. P., Osono, E., Staats, B. R., & Winter, S. G. (2009). Perspectives on the productivity dilemma. *Journal of Operations Management, 27*(2), 99–113.

Ali, S., & Green, P. (2007). IT governance mechanisms in public sector organisations: An Australian context. *Journal of Global Information Management, 15*(4), 41–63.

Banker, R. D., Hu, N., Pavlou, P. A., & Luftman, J. (2011). CIO reporting structure, strategic positioning, and firm performance. *MIS Quarterly, 35*(2), 487–504.

Campbell, J., McDonald, C., & Sethibe, T. (2010). Public and private sector IT governance: Identifying contextual differences. *Australasian Journal of Information Systems, 16*(2).

De Haes, S., & Van Grembergen, W. (2009). An exploratory study into IT governance implementations and its impact on business/IT alignment. *Information Systems Management, 26*(2), 123–137.

Duncan, R. B. (1976). The ambidextrous organization: Designing dual structures for innovation. *The Management of Organization, 1,* 167–188.

Gregory, R. W., Keil, M., Muntermann, J., & Mähring, M. (2015). Paradoxes and the nature of ambidexterity in IT transformation programs. *Information Systems Research, 26*(1), 57–80.

Guillemette, M. G., & Paré, G. (2012). Toward a new theory of the contribution of the IT function in organizations. *MIS Quarterly, 36*(2), 529–551.

Hannan, M. T., & Freeman, J. (1977). The population ecology of organizations. *American Journal of Sociology,* 929–964.

Magnusson, J., Ask, U., & Nilsson, A. (2015). Ambidexterity and Paradexterity: A typology of IT governance contradictions. In *AMCIS Conference Proceedings.*

March, J. G. (1991). Exploration and exploitation in organizational learning. *Organization Science, 2*(1), 71–87.

MacDuffie, J. P. (1997). The road to root cause: shop-floor problem-solving at three auto assembly plants. *Management Science, 43*(4), 479–502.

McAfee, A., & Brynjolfsson, E. (2008). Investing in the IT that makes a competitive difference. *Harvard Business Review, 86*(7/8), 98.

Merton, R. K. (1958). The functions of the professional association. *The American Journal of Nursing,* 50–54.

Mithas, S., & Rust, R. T. (2016). How information technology strategy and investments influence firm performance: conjectures and empirical evidence. *MIS Quarterly, 40*(1), 223–245.

Nfuka, E. N., & Rusu, L. (2011). Critical success factors framework for implementing effective IT governance in public sector organizations in a developing country. In *AMCIS* Conference Proceedings.

Nordström, M. (2005). *Styrbar systemförvaltning: att organisera systemförvaltningsverksamhet med hjälp av effektiva förvaltningsobjekt.* Linköpings universitet. (In Swedish).

O'Reilly, C. A., & Tushman, M. L. (2013). Organizational ambidexterity: Past, present, and future. *The Academy of Management Perspectives, 27*(4), 324–338.

Pang, M. S. (2014). IT governance and business value in the public sector organizations—The role of elected representatives in IT governance and its impact on IT value in US state governments. *Decision Support Systems, 59,* 274–285.

Raisch, S., & Birkinshaw, J. (2008). Organizational ambidexterity: Antecedents, outcomes, and moderators. *Journal of management.*

Roberts, N., Campbell, D. E., & Vijayasarathy, L. R. (2016). Using information systems to sense opportunities for innovation: integrating postadoptive use behaviors with the dynamic managerial capability perspective. *Journal of Management Information Systems, 33*(1), 45–69.

Saunders, A., & Brynjolfsson, E. (2016). Valuing information technology related intangible assets. *MIS Quarterly, 40*(1), 83–110.

Schmitz, K. W., Teng, J. T., & Webb, K. J. (2016). Capturing the complexity of malleable IT use: Adaptive structuration theory for individuals. *MIS Quarterly, 40*(3), 663–686.

Silverman, D. (2005). Doing qualitative research. *Sage.*

Smith, W.K., Lewis, M.W. & Tushman, M.L. (2016). "Both/And" leadership. Harvard Business Review, May.

Stettner, U., & Lavie, D. (2014). Ambidexterity under scrutiny: Exploration and exploitation via internal organization, alliances, and acquisitions. *Strategic Management Journal, 35*(13), 1903–1929.

Stigler, G. (1939). Production and distribution in the short run. *The Journal of Political Economy,* 305–327.

Suarez, F. F., Cusumano, M. A., & Fine, C. H. (1996). An empirical study of manufacturing flexibility in printed circuit board assembly. *Operations research, 44*(1), 223–240.

Tonelli, A. O., Bermejo, P. H. S., dos Santos, P. A., Zuppo, L., & Zambalde, A. L. (2015). It governance in the public sector: A conceptual model. *Information Systems Frontiers*, 1–18.

Weill, P., & Ross, J. W. (2004). *IT governance: How top performers manage IT decision rights for superior results*. Harvard Business Press.

Wu, S. P. J., Straub, D. W., & Liang, T. P. (2015). How information technology governance mechanisms and strategic alignment influence organizational performance: Insights from a matched survey of business and IT managers. *MIS Quarterly, 39*(2), 497–518.

Xue, L., Ray, G., & Sambamurthy, V. (2012). Efficiency or innovation: how do industry environments moderate the effects of firms' IT asset portfolios? *MIS Quarterly, 36*(2), 509–528.

Yin, R. K. (2013). *Case study research: Design and methods*. Sage Publications.

Author Biographies

Dr. Johan Magnusson is Associate Professor at the University of Gothenburg and Westerdal Oslo School of Art, Communication and Technology. He is associated with the Swedish Center for Digital Innovation, and his research is focused on IT Governance and the role of the CIO. He is active as advisor to both government and industry.

Jacob Torell is a research assistant in Digital Leadership at University of Gothenburg and Chalmers University of Technology. His research interests include the role of the CIO and IT Governance.

Dr. Lidija Polutnik is a Professor of Economics and Chair of the Economics Division at Babson College, in Boston, MA. Dr. Polutnik is also a Visiting Professor at the School of Business, Economics and Law at the University of Gothenburg, Sweden. Dr. Polutnik has done research and consulted in the area of pricing, revenue management and strategic cost management.

Dr. Urban Ask is Associate Professor at the Department of Applied IT, University of Gothenburg and an associate member of the Swedish Center for Digital Innovation. His research is focused on Business Intelligence and Analytics, Big Data and Management Control.

Chapter 12
Conflicting Institutional Logics in Healthcare Organisations: Implications for IT Governance

Jenny Lagsten and Malin Nordström

Abstract IT governance is a challenging area in healthcare organisations. Healthcare organisations are under pressure to transform and make use of new information technologies in order to be more effective and serve a growing number of patients. Healthcare IT implementation projects typically involve multiple stakeholders whose ideas and images of processes and results can differ severely. In this case study, at a large Swedish hospital, we investigate how different institutional logics conflict and interplay in a Health IT project and what this implies for IT governance. Our research questions are (i) How do institutional logics influence IT project activities and interactions? (ii) What implications have an institutional logics perspective for IT governance in healthcare organisations? Institutionalised views of different stakeholders may enable or slow down IT development and implementation. We have identified four logics affecting actions and interactions in the studied project which are; medical logic, management logic, IT function logic and vendor logic. The institutional logics perspective contributes to important understanding on complexities in Health IT projects and guidance on how to overcome complications providing important implications for IT governance.

12.1 Introduction

IT governance is concerned with the alignment between business and IT in organisations. IT governance generally consists of structures, processes, and relational mechanisms to enhance business/IT alignment which is perceived to be of fundamental importance for organisational effectiveness and performance

J. Lagsten (✉)
CERIS, Department of Informatics, Örebro University, Örebro, Sweden
e-mail: jenny.lagsten@oru.se

M. Nordström
Information Systems, Department of Management and Engineering,
Linköping University, Linköping, Sweden
e-mail: malin.nordstrom@ki.se

© Springer International Publishing AG 2017   269
L. Rusu and G. Viscusi (eds.), *Information Technology Governance in Public Organizations*, Integrated Series in Information Systems 38,
DOI 10.1007/978-3-319-58978-7_12

(Chan 2002; De Haes and Van Grembergen 2009; Wu et al. 2015). The rapid pace of digitalisation within organisations brings challenges for IT governance. The loci of IT production has become significantly dispersed in recent years, and the view that the IT function is primary delivery agent to operational management has become outdated (Debreceny 2013). Decisions concerning IT require collaboration between stakeholders, integrated goals and shared responsibilities for IT directions and outcomes. Empirical knowledge is needed to understand how stakeholders involved in IT decision making, development and operations, enacts IT governance structures, processes and mechanisms in this changing technological environment.

IT governance is a challenging area in healthcare. Healthcare organisations are under pressure to transform and make use of the new information technology in order to be more effective and serve a growing number of patients (EC 2012). The pace of health information technology development is furious and digital innovation in healthcare is high on the political agenda. Additionally, the installed base of information systems in healthcare is diverse making the sharing of medical information between different actors of health both demanding and challenging (Hanseth and Bygstad 2015). In order to handle the transformation healthcare organisations are in need of relevant underpinning IT Governance (Whitehouse et al. 2011; Rosenmöller 2012). Considering the diverse information system landscape, and that IT governance in healthcare is still in its infancy (Beratarbide and Kelsey 2012) in combination with the pressure to use IT in the transformation of healthcare, this is an urgent area for IT governance research.

Healthcare IT development and implementation projects typically involves multiple stakeholders whose ideas and images of processes and results differ (Jensen et al. 2009; Melin and Axelsson 2014; Offenbeek and Vos 2015). Previous research has shown that an institutional logics perspective is a powerful theoretical lens for understanding and explaining different stakeholders actions and interactions due to cultural dimensions (Thornton et al. 2012). As for example, managerialism and medical professionalism has been identified as two dominant logics in healthcare organisations influencing actions and communication concerning IT implementation. Such knowledge is important for understanding and strengthening IT governance in practice. In this study we contribute to deeper understanding of stakeholder's different rationales in a health IT project by using an institutional logics perspective, revealing important implications for IT governance.

The aim of the study is to understand and explain difficulties and challenges in health IT projects by using the institutional logics perspective. We are interested in exploring what knowledge that could be gained by using the institutional logics perspective as an analytical lens, and how this new understanding can be used for advancing IT governance in healthcare organisations. The research questions elaborated is consequently: (i) How do institutional logics influence IT project activities and interactions? (ii) What implications have an institutional logics perspective for IT governance in healthcare organisations?

In the next section we provide an introduction of the institutional logics perspective and in Sect. 3 we present our research approach. Thereafter, in Sect. 4, we present our case which is a story describing an IT project aiming to design and implement an information system supporting the management of catheters in care processes. In Sect. 5 we analyse the case using the frame of institutional logics shedding light on conflicting logics and implications for IT governance. Section 6 provides a discussion of the analysis and Sect. 7 provides our conclusions.

12.2   The Institutional Logics Perspective

The institutional logics perspective is a framework, on a metatheoretical level, for analysing relationships among institutions, individuals, and organisations in social systems (Thornton et al. 2012). Institutional logics is defined as "the socially constructed, historical patterns of cultural symbols and material practices, including assumptions, values, and beliefs, by which individuals and organizations provide meaning to their daily activity, organize time and space, and reproduce their lives and experiences (Thornton et al. 2012; Martin et al. 2015). The perspective gives support to researchers who are interested in how individuals and organisational actors are influenced by their situation in interinstitutional systems. Institutional logics perspective represent frames of reference that condition actors' choices for sense-making, the vocabulary they use to motivate action, and their sense of self and identity (Thornton et al. 2012). An institutional logics perspective has been used by scholars to understand and explain social behaviour and change in healthcare organisations as for example the transformation of the medical profession in response to government programs, purchasers of health care, and consumer activism (see for example (Jensen et al. 2009; Reay and Hinings 2009; Nigam and Ocasio 2010; Timmermans and Oh 2010; Choi et al. 2011; O'Reilly and Reed 2011; Martin et al. 2015)).

Organisational actors' motives and actions can be understood by their professional occupation. Professions are essentially the knowledge based category of occupations which follows from a period of education, training and experience (Evetts 2003). Professional practice is a form of organisation to be understood partly as the relations that an individual practitioner has with individual clients, and partly as a way of organising work that could not exist without being embedded in a system of professional institutions that protect and sustains it (Friedson 1989). Professional work are linked to a class of professionally treatable problems and inter-professional rivalry and competition can rise when different professional groups claim jurisdictional control over the classification of a problem and take action (Samuel et al. 2005).

The institutional logics perspective offers a useful conceptual starting point for understanding professionalism in health care (Martin et al. 2015). The analysis of tensions, conflicts and interplay between medical professionalism and managerialism in healthcare settings can be studied by using accounts of "ideal types". Ideal types are a tools to interpret cultural meanings into their logically pure components (Thornton et al. 2012). In Table 12.1 we use the accounts provided by Thornton

Table 12.1 Interinstitutional system ideal types (examples of profession and corporation) (Thornton et al. 2012, p. 56)

Category	Profession (professionalism)	Corporation (managerialism)
Root metaphor	Relational network	Hierarchy
Source of legitimacy	Personal expertise	Market position of firm
Source of authority	Professional association	Top management
Source of identity	Quality of craft, personal reputation	Bureaucratic roles
Basis of norms	Associational membership	Firm employment
Basis of attention	Status in profession	Status in hierarchy
Basis of strategy	Increase personal reputation	Increase size of firm
Informal control mechanisms	Celebrity professionals	Organization culture
Economic system	Personal capitalism	Managerial capitalism

et al. (2012) to give an example of how accounts of ideal types of professionalism and managerialism can be defined.

In our study we use "ideal types" as a way to comprehend the underlying logic that guides different stakeholders thinking and acting in the organisational setting. The logic is taken for granted and has a tacit knowledge function in organisational stakeholder groups due to that the logic has been nurtured and cultivated by individuals through education, training and experience.

More recently scholars have started to explore how collaborative institutional contexts shapes interactions between actors from different stakeholder groups in business/IT alignment processes and IT governance. The concept of organisational culture has been suggested in order to better understand how goals, values, beliefs, norms, customs etc. affects implementation of IT governance mechanisms and business/IT alignment (El-Mekawy and Rusu 2011; Rowlands et al. 2014). Also interpretive and stakeholder based approaches has been advocated to better take into account implications of interacting actors in public sector alignment processes (Vander Elst and De Rynck 2014). Offenbeek et al. (2013), in line with Jensen et al. (2009), mean that IT governance is not pre-determined by institutional forces but rather a result from enactments of these logics in stakeholders' shared sense making efforts. According to Offenbeek et al. (2013) the institutional logics approach highlights how cultural dimensions of institutions both enable and constrain social action. And this is the main reason for why we have chosen this perspective in our study. We use institutional logics as analytical base in order to better understand the actions, and interactions, of different stakeholders' in our case, and explore how the belonging to a logic can explain why and how actions are taken, actions that can be perceived as enabling or constraining. We think that the understanding of project actions, through an institutional logics lens, can make explicit different rationales due to stakeholder background and knowledge. We also think that the unravelling of different logics can create understanding between different stakeholders and that this understanding give potential for wider interplay amongst logics that can improve both IT implementation and governance in multi-stakeholder settings.

12.3 Research Approach

The study has been conducted in the context of an IT project management office, the eHealth Lab, at a large Swedish university hospital. The eHealth Lab was established in late 2013 with the mission to support and facilitate IT initiatives in the healthcare organisation. The overall research approach in the Lab has been ongoing evaluation (Svensson et al. 2009) where we have been involved in nearly 30 IT projects in various health and technology areas. The studied IT initiatives have primarily originated from clinicians in the health care organisation. The authors have had different roles in the projects as on-going evaluators, coordinators and advisers which have provided rich access and insights into what has been happening in the health IT projects.

In this case study we have analysed one of the studied projects in depth, the Catheter project. The Catheter project aimed to design and implement an information system supporting the management of catheters in care processes at the hospital. We have chosen this project as a case for this study because the data is rich and the case involves four central stakeholders adhering to different logics typically involved in health IT initiatives. The case is also representative for patterns that we have observed in other projects in the eHealth Lab which makes us believe that the findings are of a more general character.

The research has an interpretive case study design (Walsham 2002) and the analysis has been performed in two steps. The first step was to reconstruct the project process. The second step was to analyse the project process using the analytical framework of institutional logics elaborated to focus on core values and beliefs related to IT governance (as presented below).

The reconstruction of the project process was done by iteratively interviewing the project manager about the process, the activities and interactions that had occurred. From the first interview we created a story that described in temporal order what had happened, who was involved, and the results of these activities. The project manager then read the descriptions in several follow up interviews to refine the storyline, details on activities and interactions in the project. The process of creating the story lasted during one week where the written story document were sent back and forth by mail and discussed both in meetings and by telephone. To our help in the reconstruction of the project we accessed an extensive amount of project documentation stored in the project management system. The documents analysed included minutes from project meetings (11 documents), the project plan in different versions (5 documents), system requirement specifications (12 documents), background study of catheter use at the hospital, presentations of project progress, also mail conversations (about 15 emails) were consulted. In addition we had also participated, as specialists and coordinators, in meetings with project members (about 10) on different occasions and had our own notes and memos. In chapter four the resulting story of The Catheter Project is reproduced in a shortened version.

The second step was to analyse the uncovered project storyline with the analytical frame of the institutional logics perspective. Our framework for analysis is designed by using the accounts of *management logic*, *medical professional logic* and *technical professional logic* in the context of IT governance presented by Offenbeek et al. (2013).

After the first analytical round we divided the account of *technical professional logic* into two separate accounts, namely *IT function logic*, referring to the IT professionals employed by the IT department internally in the healthcare organisation, and *vendor logic*, referring to the IT professionals working as consultants in the healthcare organisation employed by an external IT vendor. This because we, in our analysis, discovered that we were dealing with two different technical logics guided by different overall goals and values. Even though the IT professionals at the internal IT function and those employed by the IT vendor had similar education and competences concerning IT development and operations, their guiding logic parted in notable ways. We believe that the differences is due to the overall market paradigm guiding the IT vendor and the IT function belonging to a public sector organisation in the realm of bureaucracy. In our analysis we have used the following accounts for analysing actions and interactions in our case in the light of different institutional logics relating to IT governance:

Medical Logic—Medical professionalism core values and beliefs related to ITG: patient-centred, IT support is for professionals, clinical diversity and professional autonomy.

Management logic—Managerialism core values and beliefs related to ITG: integration, common standards, controllability, cost effectiveness, patient satisfaction.

IT function logic—Internal technical professionalism core values and beliefs related to ITG: compatible and maintainable, standardisation, centralisation, systems need to be reliable, control.

Vendor logic—External technical professionalism core values and beliefs related to ITG: technology push, state of the art technology, reputation in market, solution orientation.

12.4 Case Description—The Catheter Project

In 2011 a catheter vendor contacts the department of urology and present a new catheter that they claim reduces the risk for urinary infection. The clinicians meant that the advantages of this new catheter could not be demonstrated due to the lack of studies and systematic evidence concerning catheters and catheter use and the relation to infections in the clinical processes at the hospital. In order to find evidence the clinicians performed a survey of the practices and knowledge of urinary catheters and found that there were major gaps concerning knowledge and management of urinary catheters at the hospital, and that this gap probably was representative for healthcare in general. Further they concluded that better knowledge and management of catheters would give potential to reduce illness and suffering and that measures must be taken to reduce healthcare associated infections due to use of catheters. One promising measure suggested was to develop and implement an information system supporting a structured process for catheterisation to be used cross clinical borders at the hospital. The information system would also provide a tool for standardised documentation and information on catheters and catheter use in treatments making informed medical decisions and evaluations possible.

The clinicians contacted the eHealth Lab, in late 2013 to get support for carrying out a project with the aim to develop and implement the Catheter IT system. The eHealth Lab appointed a project manager and connected the clinic with a suitable vendor who, in collaboration with the clinic, analysed the present IT based documentation concerning catheters used at the hospital. Documentation related to catheterisation was found to be done in five different information systems using different terminology.

A pilot information system was then being planned, based on the vendor IT platform. System requirements was worked out in collaboration between vendor and clinicians including information and documentation needs, terminology, use cases, processes and user interface.

At this time the responsible medical director (MD) at the hospital level (one of four) joined the project due to its possible positive medical implications to reduce healthcare associated infections. Until now the medical professionals had been working together with the external IT vendor. It was now time for populating the pilot database with data in order to conduct a proof of concept.

This required cooperation with the IT function at the hospital which was responsible for the operations and maintenance of the five IT systems that kept track of catheter information in different treatment processes. The project manager and the MD set up a meeting with the IT function. The IT function was represented by the IT manager for the electronic health record (EHR) system, one of the systems that captured and stored central data needed for the Catheter system.

At the meeting the IT manager explained that the IT department could not see the use of developing a new information system, based on data from several systems, for handling the catheter process. Further, the IT manager believed that the entire process could be handled through the EHR system.

After considerations amongst project participants (vendor, clinicians, project manager, MD) they decided to continue according to the plan to develop a new information system. The MD were requested from the IT department to fill out the form "Requests for new or further development of IT-services" for requesting the necessary data to the pilot from the five involved systems. The MD had difficulties in understanding the complex form (4 pages) requesting problem specification and change needs in a technical manner using different dimensions and terminology than the already made analysis in the project.

The MD handed over the form to the project manager who elaborated the project needs, filled the form, and posted the request. The answer came some time later that the request was rejected, that the IT function did not have time available to assist in the development.

Both the project manager and the MD were now confused about how to collaborate with the internal IT function, and what roles that should be involved and who that had decision rights concerning the project issues. The project manager stated "*we did not know what decision paths we were supposed to take, who or which that had the mandate to make decisions regarding the involved IT systems in the project*".

Several meetings were held on a management level to resolve how to move on, but that did not change the outcome that the IT function renounced involvement due to lack of time. Soon the project started to lose momentum, the IT vendor had invested a considerably large amount of time and resources into the project, with the long term goal to develop a commercial product. When the hospital did not respond with the corresponding arrangements the IT vendor withdrew their commitments in setting up the pilot. Soon thereafter, in September 2014 the project was put on indefinite hold.

12.5   Analysis—Conflicting Institutional Logics and Implications for IT Governance

In the following analysis, we interpret what happened in the Catheter project, which actions and interactions the came into conflict and interplay, by using institutional logics as the basis for understanding. We started with identifying the conflicts which we grouped into four IT governance areas: "Roles and decision rights", "Development and innovation versus IT operations", "Competencies, procedures and language for collaboration" and "Gap between internal and external technical professionals". In the following sections we analyse the identified concerns using the involved logics, and further the implications for IT governance.

12.5.1   Roles and Decision Rights

After the meeting with the internal IT function the project took a new turn. Both the project manager and the MD stated that they did not understand who, and how, to approach the IT function. It became evident that, in practice, the MD did not have decision rights above the IT manager. The MD, representing the clinical needs on a hospital level, was surprised that the IT manager had contradicting ideas concerning how to solve an informational need in the medical practice. The roles where conflicting and not clarified in practice and much time was spent in different meetings trying to sort out who was responsible in order to proceed. Clearly the medical logic was in conflict with the IT function logic. The IT manager referred to lack of time and resources due to budget constraints. Budget issues belong to a management logic. The IT function did not have resources for new IT development, all resources were tied up in ready-laid plans and the IT function did not have the right to decide on changes in the budget and reprioritise allocated resources during the fiscal year. The management logic then overruled both IT function logic and medical logic.

The implications for IT governance is that there is a need for a role that can make decisions and prioritise resources from a medical information perspective. The role of a Chief Medical Information Officer (CMIO) could be a solution for this (Kannry. et al. 2016). Also the economic model, concerning resources for development and IT operations, highly affects or restricts what IT decisions that can be made. Effective IT governance must be in alignment with a relevant economic model. Clearly, the different roles and decisions rights also need to be clarified and communicated to be effective in practice. Clarification and communication of roles can also help role holders to act according to their role.

12.5.2 Development and Innovation Versus IT Operations

The project had a steering group consisting of managers representing the medical practice and representatives from the vendor. Decisions on how to proceed in the project and the division of labour between the IT vendor and the medical professionals were uncomplicated. In this respect the medical logic and vendor logic were interplaying, they shared common goals and matched with additionally competences in order to get the work done. But the steering group lacked authority to make organisational decisions, they only had decision rights concerning their own organisational territory, on medical issues, which did not include IT issues as systems development and creation of a data warehouse from different operating information systems. In practice the steering group became more of an interest group. If the IT function had decided to include the project into the planned IT operations agenda maybe the needed authorisations could have been made. There was nevertheless no invitation to queue the "Request for new or further development of IT-services" into the following year's plan which implicates that the mechanism for supporting clinical IT development requirements into operations is halting.

It is obvious that the IT function and the medical professionals are working according to different logics that are in conflict. We think that a key reason for the lack of capability to accommodate the request for development can be found in the IT strategy. In the current IT strategy it is to be read "*In need of a new IT solution, the first choice is to use existing IT systems within the region, the second choice is choosing a standard solution on the market, the third choice is to order or develop a solution in collaboration with other regions, the fourth choice is to wait for a suitable system to be available on the market, and as a last alternative develop its own system*". In practice the consequence of this strategy is that it is almost impossible for medical professionals to engage in development of new and promising health IT and digital innovation. This is a strong example showing that the medical logic and the IT function logic do not align. Digital innovations are most often developed on top of the existing installed base of systems by recombining parts that can be detached from their original context (Lusch and Nambisan 2015), thus requiring collaboration in repackaging. Considering the pressure on healthcare organisations to transform using the possibilities of new information technologies, this IT strategy is a major obstacle.

Implications for IT governance is that the IT governance framework needs to cater for structures, processes and mechanisms for new IT development and digital innovation, accompanied with a relevant model for resource allocation. The current IT strategy do not seem to be up to date with the medical professional logic and the pressure to transform. Medical professionals need to have support for acting on promising IT initiatives important for treating patients and preventing suffering. In parallel, the installed base of systems needs to be operated. Balancing resources between old and new information systems is a major IT governance challenge.

12.5.3   Competencies, Procedures and Language for Collaboration

The MD and the project manager didn't understand how to properly fill out the request form and needed assistance in expressing the needs and requirements. The IT function expected the medical professionals to place an order. The order form was technically complex and followed other dimensions than the analyses, terminology and specifications they had worked out in collaboration with the IT vendor. Evidently there was a gap between the medical logic and IT function logic resulting in communication difficulties due to different languages and starting points. There were no official role or procedure in place that could support with translation between organisational change needs and specifications concerning functional and non-functional requirements. The project manager then took this role but had to considerably revise analyses made in the project to map the form dimensions.

This indicates that there is a need for a translator role in healthcare IT governance. Medical professionals do not have, and must not have, the language and grammar for the modelling of ideas into usable IT specifications. In our case the medical people had done this in collaboration with a third part, the IT vendor. IT governance thus needs to cater for procedures and roles of a medical business analyst or a health informatics specialist, as translator between medical and IT logic and language.

12.5.4 Gap Between Internal and External Technical Professionals

The last area we highlight in our analysis is the relation between internal and external IT professionals. In the Catheter project the clinic had teamed up with the IT vendor. The vendor had a high ambition, investing several amount of time and resources in analysis and prototyping, aiming to build and test a pilot for commercial purposes. The IT vendor presupposed, as did the clinic that the next step would be to expand the cooperation involving the relevant competencies, as for example IT architects, from the internal IT function. This was a relevant step in order to populate the prototype with data by making the integration of data sets from the five identified information systems. The healthcare organisation could not match the IT vendor with competences and resources needed for advancing the prototype into a pilot. In order to launch the pilot and make necessary tests and evaluations the hospital needed to have contributed with resources as a requirements analyst, a business architect and an IT architect or equivalent roles. This did not happen. The IT vendor logic was in conflict with the IT function logic as they had different expectations of each other.

Relations between external an internal IT specialists should be a concern for IT governance. A large part of hospital IT production is performed by external IT specialists situated at IT vendors, and this causes a need for governing the collaboration between internal and external technical professionals. It is not unusual either that more than one external IT partner is involved in hospital IT development projects. Another implication following this is the question of what relevant competences are needed for collaboration between internal and external IT specialists.

12.6 Discussion

Before we started using the institutional logics perspective we struggled to make sense of why things happened in the projects, why suddenly projects started to lose momentum or what made them flow. We agree with Offenbeek et al. (2013) that institutionalised views may enable or slow down IT development. Using an institutional logics perspective contributes to important understanding on encountered difficulties in Health IT projects but also on how to overcome complications due to mismatching logics. IT project management and systems development in health care is recognised for being difficult and the literature has shown that project stakeholder management is critical for project success (Offenbeek and Vos 2015). Difficulties, events and actions in project processes can be understood by recognising the involved stakeholders' different logics. From the perspective of one stakeholder their behaviour and decisions are rational according to their logic while other stakeholders have difficulties understanding what is happening and why positions are taken. IT governance in healthcare would benefit from recognising the different institutional logics that comes into play in IT initiatives in order to manage multiple logics and avoid that conflicting logics prevent progress.

Roles are needed that can serve as translators between logics and their accompanying languages. We have suggested the role, or profession, of an *health informatics specialist* (Duquenoy et al. 2012) that can improve the communication between medical operations and IT operations (Beratarbide and Kelsey 2012). The medical profession is highly specialised and rely on expertise directly related to different diagnoses that requires a corresponding specialised language end exact terminology. The health informatics role should translate clinical needs into information systems requirements as well as clarifying IT related preconditions and consequences for clinicians. One example of a translator role in this case is that the IT vendor had employed physicians, with proper IT skills, to be the ones that carried out the cooperation with the clinicians at the hospital. This seems to be a successful strategy that we also have observed in other Health IT companies. Another logic interface to advance is that between the IT function logic and the medical logic at the hospital level where the role of a *Chief Medical Information Officer (CMIO)* has been suggested (Rosenmöller 2012, Kannry. et al. 2016) matching the Chief Information Officer (CIO) at the level of CEO. A CMIO has the corresponding role to a CIO but can prioritise, balance and coordinate healthcare related IT needs and initiatives from the overall medical perspective.

Research on IT governance and business/IT alignment can benefit from a comprehensive theory of the organisation and we have found that the institutional logics perspective brings understanding on the "business side" of the alignment. The likelihood of successfully aligning IT to business could be strengthen by taking into account the multi-stakeholder organisational behaviour and conditions that constitute the business practice. Healthcare organisations are guided by strong medical professionalism. One might maybe compare healthcare organisations with university organisations where the autonomy of departments and research groups is strong. Professional researchers, as well as clinicians have strong associations with their field of knowledge, and measures are taken in care processes in order to keep up with the best knowledge in the field. In such culture cooperation between scholars at other universities or hospitals in the same field can be more relevant than in-between institutions and departments at the own organisation. Both universities and hospitals are built on strong professional logic guiding operations, and management logic has probably a weaker influence in comparison with private sector companies.

Another interesting dimension is that the boundaries of healthcare IT are elastic. Healthcare IT is dependent on cooperation and partnership with a wide range of IT vendors maintaining, supporting and upgrading the installed base of information systems inside the health organisation. Traditionally development is done outside the organisation, information systems have mainly been regarded as products on a market, where the IT vendor is responsible for product accuracy through CE marking and similar standards. This perspective might have been inherited from the use of health technologies and devices as ultrasound products, x-ray machines or pace makers. For reasons of digital innovation and healthcare transformation, integration and interoperability are important capabilities requiring these IT vendors and IT specialists to cooperate both inside and outside health organisation boundaries. In line with Debreceny (2013) we have found that the loci of IT production in healthcare is significantly dispersed and do not well map IT governance literature that typically sees the IT function as being the primary delivery agent responding to demands from operational management. Business/IT alignment is not unidirectional but requires integration and shared responsibilities between the medical function and the IT function, and in addition external IT specialists also have a role affecting governance structures and practices.

12.7 Conclusions

Our aim in this study was to understand and explain difficulties and challenges in health IT projects by using the institutional logics perspective. We were interested in exploring what knowledge that could be gained by using the institutional logics perspective as an analytical lens. And further what implications this knowledge has for IT governance in healthcare organisations.

The analysis showed that institutionalised views may slow down or enable IT development and implementation. We have identified four different logics affecting actions and interactions in a health IT project which are; medical logic, management logic, IT function logic and vendor logic. The use of the institutional logics perspective contributed to important understanding on complexities in health IT projects and guidance on how to overcome complications providing important implications for IT governance.

A first implication for IT governance in healthcare that we found was that additional roles are needed. We suggest the role of a Chief Medical Information Officer (CMIO) matching the Chief Information Officer (CIO) at the level of CEO in order to balance IT decisions and decision rights between the medical logic and the IT function logic. Also a health informatics role is needed having the function of translating clinical needs into information systems requirements as well as clarifying IT related preconditions and consequences for clinicians.

Secondly, the appropriate distribution of capabilities between development and operations and maintenance of implemented systems is a key issue. The IT strategy and the intensions with the IT governance structures, processes and mechanisms should be reflected in the overall economic model, where the economic model relates to management logic. If not there is risk that managerial structures, unintentionally, overrides IT governance practices.

Finally, we also found that internal and external IT specialists followed different logics which we have named IT function logic and vendor logic. In our case these logics where not interplaying which led to difficulties. As it is common with external IT specialists working in health IT projects this indicates that cooperation between internal and external IT specialists is an issue for IT Governance.

Our findings build on an in-depth analysis of one IT project in one hospital setting. But because we have seen similar patterns in other health IT projects we have reasons to think that our findings have a fair degree of transferability to comparable settings. Since we found the institutional logics perspective to be a useful analytical frame, we will continue to develop the analytical framework that we used in this study in more detail, and thereafter analyse further health IT projects. Future research will then provide the opportunity to and make comparisons between cases. Research on IT governance in healthcare is in its beginning. The perspective of shared responsibility for IT direction and outcomes, where different institutional logics come into play, is challenging having important implications for IT governance research and practice.

References

Beratarbide, E., & Kelsey, T. (2012). *eHealth Governace in Scotland: A cross-sectoral and cross national comparison eHealth: Legal, ethical and governance challenges* (pp. 329–348). Berlin: Springer.

Chan, Y. (2002). Why haven't we mastered alignment? The importance of the informal organization structure. *MIS Quarterly Executive, 1*(2), 97–112.

Choi, S., Holmberg, I., et al. (2011). Executive management in radical change The case of the Karolinska University Hospital merger. *Scandinavian Journal of Management, 27*(1), 11–23.

De Haes, S., & Van Grembergen, W. (2009). An exploratory study into IT governance implementations and its impact on business/IT alignment. *Information Systems Management, 26*(2), 123–137.

Debreceny, R. S. (2013). Research on IT governance, risk, and value: Challenges and opportunities. *Journal of Information Systems, 27*(1), 129–135.

Duquenoy, P., Nermen, M., et al. (2012). *Patients, trust and ethics in information privacy in eHealth. eHealth: Legal, ethical and governance challenges* (pp. 329–348). Berlin: Springer.

EC. (2012). eHealth Action Plan 2012–2020: Innovative healthcare for the 21st century. Retrieved December 12, 2016, from https://ec.europa.eu/digital-single-market/en/news/ehealth-action-plan-2012-2020-innovative-healthcare-21st-century.

El-Mekawy, M., & Rusu, L. (2011). Organizational culture impact on business-IT alignment: A case study of a multinational organisation. In *Proceedings of the 44th Hawaii International Conference on Systems Sciences*. IEEE Computer Society.

Evetts, J. (2003). The sociological analysis of professionalism: Occupational change in the modern world. *International Sociology, 18*(2), 395–415.

Friedson, E. (1989). Theory and the professions. *Indiana Law Journal, 64*(3).

Hanseth, O., & Bygstad, B. (2015). Flexible generification: ICT standardization strategies and service innovation in health care. *European Journal of Information Systems, 24*(6), 645–663.

Jensen, T., Kjærgaard, A., et al. (2009). Using institutional theory with sensemaking theory: A case study of information system implementation in healthcare. *Journal of Information Technology*, 243–353.

Kannry, J., et al. (2016). The Chief Clinical Informatics Officer (CCIO). *Applied Clinical Informatics, 7*(1), 143–176.

Lusch, R. F., & Nambisan, S. (2015). Service innovation: A service-dominant logic perspective. *MIS Quarterly, 39*(1), 155–175/March 2015.

Martin, G., Armstrong, N., et al. (2015). Professionalism redundant, reshaped, or reinvigorated? Realizing the "Third Logic" in contemporary health care. *Journal of Health and Social Behavior, 56*(3), 378–397.

Melin, U., & Axelsson, K. (2014). Implementing healthcare information systems—Mirroring a wide spectrum of images of an IT Project. *Health Policy and Technology, 3*(26–35).

Nigam, A., & Ocasio, W. (2010). Event attention, environmental sensemaking, and change in institutional logics: An inductive analysis of the effects of public attention to clinton's health care reform initiative. *Organization Science, 21*(4), 823–841.

O'Reilly, D., & Reed, M. (2011). The Grit in the Oyster: Professionalism, managerialism and leaderism as discourses of UK public services modernization. *Organization Studies, 32*(8), 1079–1101.

Offenbeek, M., Boonstra, A., et al. (2013). The dynamic interplay among institutional logics influencing hospital IT governance. ECIS 2013 Completed Research. Paper 82. 21st European Conference on Information Systems, 5–8 June 2013, Utrecht, The Netherlands, AIS Electronic Library (AISeL).

Offenbeek, M. & Vos, J. (2015). An integrative framework for managing project issues accross stakeholder groups. *International Journal of Project Management*, Article in Press.

Reay, T., & Hinings, B. (2009). Managing the rivalry of competing institutional logics. *Organization Studies, 30*(06), 629–652.

Rosenmöller, M. (2012). *IT governance in healthcare institutions. eHealth: Legal, ethical and governance challenges* (pp. 329–348). Berlin: Springer.

Rowlands, B., De Haes, S., et al. (2014). Exploring and developing an IT governance culture framework. In *Thirty Fifth International Conference on Information Systems, Auckland 2014*.

Samuel, S., Dirsmith, M., & McElroy, B. (2005). Monetized medicine: From the physical to the Fiscal. *Accounting, Organizations and Society, 30*, 249–278.

Svensson, L., et al. (2009). *Learning through ongoing evaluation*. Sverige: Studentlitteratur Lund.

Thornton, P., Ocaasio, M., et al. (2012). *The institutional logics perspective; A new approach to culture, structure, and process*. Oxford University Press.

Timmermans, S., & Oh, H. (2010). The continued social transformation of the medical profession. *Journal of Health and Social Behaviour, 51*(S), 94–106.

Walsham, G. (2002). Interpretive case studies in IS research: nature and method. In M. D. Myers & D. Avison (Eds.), *Qualitative research in information systems*. London: SAGE.

Vander Elst, S., & De Rynck, F. (2014). Alignment processes in public organizations: An interpretive approach. *Information Polity, 19*, 195–206.

Whitehouse, D., George, C., et al. (2011). *eHealth: Legal, ethical and governance challenges: An overview*. Med-e-Tel 2011, Luxembourg, 6–8 April 2011. Middlesex University's Research Repository at http://eprints.mdx.ac.uk/7728/.

Wu, S., Straub, D., et al. (2015). How information technology governance mechanisms and strategic alignment influence organizational performance: Insights from a matched survey of business and it managers. *MIS Quarterly, 39*(2), 497–518.

Author Biographies

Jenny Lagsten is a Senior Lecturer in Information Systems at Örebro University School of business, Sweden. She has 20 years of experience teaching and researching information systems in organisations. Her fields of expertise are method development, information systems evaluation, and public sector innovation. Jenny has extensive experience from action research projects in public sector organisations (social welfare services, healthcare organizations and other public agencies) where the research focus has been on organisational development through IT in parallel with developing theoretical results.

Malin Nordström has been teaching and researching information systems for 20 years. Malin holds a PhD in Information Systems Development from Linköping University, Sweden. She has developed the Swedish industry standard pm3 for IT governance. Malin has in recent year's commercialised research within the concept of Triple Helix with crossing over boundaries between business and academy. Her fields of expertise are IT Governance, Information Systems and IT Service Management.

Index

© Springer International Publishing AG 2017
L. Rusu and G. Viscusi (eds.), *Information Technology Governance in Public Organizations*, Integrated Series in Information Systems 38,
DOI 10.1007/978-3-319-58978-7

Printed in the United States
By Bookmasters